Charles Carrington

**Poetry of the Anti-Jacobin**

Political and Satirical Poems

Charles Carrington

**Poetry of the Anti-Jacobin**
*Political and Satirical Poems*

ISBN/EAN: 9783744705233

Printed in Europe, USA, Canada, Australia, Japan

Cover: Foto ©Thomas Meinert / pixelio.de

More available books at **www.hansebooks.com**

# POETRY OF THE ANTI-JACOBIN.

*Large paper edition of this work, limited to* 250 *copies, each of which is numbered and signed by the Author, containing an ADDITIONAL FOLIO PLATE, entitled NEW MORALITY, or, The Promised Installment of the High Priest of the Theophilanthropists ; containing numerous portraits and a numbered explanatory key plate.*

Crown 4to, price 21/-, same publishers.

# POETRY

OF

# THE ANTI-JACOBIN:

COMPRISING THE CELEBRATED

## POLITICAL AND SATIRICAL POEMS,

OF

THE RT. HONS. G. CANNING, JOHN HOOKHAM FRERE, W. PITT,
THE MARQUIS WELLESLEY, G. ELLIS, W. GIFFORD,
THE EARL OF CARLISLE, AND OTHERS.

EDITED, WITH EXPLANATORY NOTES, ETC.

BY

## CHARLES EDMONDS,

EDITOR OF "THE PYTCHLEY HUNT, PAST AND PRESENT," ETC., ETC.

*THIRD EDITION, CONSIDERABLY ENLARGED, WITH SIX ILLUSTRATIONS
BY JAMES GILLRAY.*

LONDON:
SAMPSON LOW, MARSTON, SEARLE, & RIVINGTON,
*Limited,*
St. Dunstan's House,
FETTER LANE, FLEET STREET, E.C.
1890.

# EDITOR'S PREFACE.

THE fate which usually attends political and satirical writings that owe their origin to passing events, has in no way affected the POETRY OF THE ANTI-JACOBIN, which, after a lapse of more than ninety years, still continues to interest and amuse. Public opinion never fails, sooner or later, to arrive at a just conclusion as to the merits both of individuals and actions; and though it may often neglect to preserve a meritorious work, never perpetuates a worthless one. Poetry which lashed with so remorseless a hand the patriotic proceedings, and held up to ridicule the persons and habits, of the most distinguished Whig leaders, must have possessed no common merit to have won the encomiums of such liberal politicians and such critics as MACKINTOSH and JEFFREY, MOORE and BYRON.

MOORE, in his *Life of Sheridan*, observes: "*The Rolliad* and *The Anti-Jacobin* may, on their respective sides of the question, be considered as models of that style of political satire whose lightness and vivacity give it the appearance of proceeding rather from the wantonness of wit than of ill-nature, and whose very malice, from the fancy with which it is mixed up, like certain kinds of fire-works, explodes in sparkles". This criticism might be applied to some of his own political squibs.

As the poems refer to occurrences long since past, a rapid glance at the state of events at that time (1797-8) may render them more intelligible to the generality of readers.

The affairs of England were then in a critical position. The ministry of PITT was carrying on a fierce war with republican France, the necessity for which had split the public into two great parties. The liberal party alleged, that "the whole misfortunes of Europe and all the crimes of France had arisen from the iniquitous coalition of kings to overturn its infant freedom;—that, if its government had been left alone, it would neither have stained its hands with innocent blood at home nor pursued plans of aggrandizement abroad; and that the Republic, relieved from the pressure of external danger, and no longer roused by the call of patriotic duty, would have quietly turned its swords into pruning-hooks, and, renouncing the allurements of foreign conquests, thought only of promoting the internal felicity of its citizens ".

These sentiments, though supported by the extra-ordinary eloquence of Fox, SHERIDAN, ERSKINE, and others, had but little weight with the minister or the great body of the public. It was impossible to deny that the power of the French Republic was daily increasing, and threatened the subjugation of the greater part of Europe. BUONAPARTE had overrun Italy, and broken the power of Austria, which, by the treaty of Leoben, was compelled to cede the Netherlands to France, allow the free navigation of the Rhine, and recognise the independence of the newly-erected Italian republics.

Spain, also, had declared war against Britain, which was thus left to contend singly against the power of France ; for the Directory had refused the basis of peace proposed by LORD MALMESBURY, that of a mutual restitution of conquests. To add to these embarrassments, during the year 1797 credit became affected, and the Bank of England suspended cash payments ; mutinies broke out in the fleets at Spithead and the Nore ; and Ireland was on the verge of rebellion. But the talents of PITT were equal to the occasion, and his power rose higher than ever, when his prognostications were shortly after (in December, 1797) confirmed by the unprovoked attack upon Switzerland by the French. The impolicy of this proceeding was equal to its infamy ; for nothing ever done by the revolutionary government contributed so powerfully to cool the ardour of its partisans in Europe, and to open the eyes of the intelligent and respectable classes in every other country to its ultimate designs. Its effect on the friends of freedom in England may be judged of from the indignant protest of SIR JAMES MACKINTOSH, himself once a warm admirer of the French Revolution, who, in his defence of JEAN PELTIER, in 1803, for a libel on BUONAPARTE, declared, " the invasion and destruction of Switzerland an act, in comparison with which all the deeds of rapine and blood perpetrated in the world are innocence itself ". Even before this, the true character of the revolution had been detected by the democratic COLERIDGE, who gave public utterance to his feelings of horror and disgust in that noble *Ode to France* written in February, 1797. In a word, to say

nothing of her other conquests, France, at the beginning
of 1798, had three affiliated republics at her side, the
Batavian, Cisalpine, and the Ligurian ; before its close
she had organized three more, the Helvetic, the Roman,
and the Parthenopeian.

PITT's influence was further increased by the threatened
invasion of Great Britain by the French, a proceeding
which, as it affected every class in the country, raised
the national enthusiasm to the highest pitch, inflamed
as it already was by the recent glorious victories off Cape
St. Vincent and Camperdown.    That they were likely
to be in earnest had been already shown by their expeditions to Bantry Bay and Pembrokeshire, and BUONA-
PARTE's boast at Geneva, that " he would democratize
England in three months," proved how much he relied
upon the support of the malcontents both in Great
Britain and Ireland.    The estimates and preparations for
defence were enormous ; taxes, to an extent utterly unknown before, were laid on ; the Volunteer Bill was
passed (SHERIDAN assisting), by which, in addition to the
regular army, a hundred and fifty thousand volunteers
were, in a few weeks, in arms ; THE KING was authorized
by another bill, in the event of an invasion, to call out the
levy, *en masse*, of the population ; the Alien Bill was re-
enacted ; and the suspension of the Habeas Corpus Act
continued for another year.

But the genius of one man, however great, can effect
but little, unless suitably supported by others.    The sagacious mind of PITT had long seen that his party in
Parliament were, with very few exceptions, no match for

his numerous opponents, powerful both in talent and
social position ; among whom were Fox, Sheridan,
Erskine, Horne Tooke, Whitbread, Nicholls, Courtenay, Fitzpatrick, the Dukes of Norfolk and Bedford,
Lord Stanhope, the Duchess of Devonshire, and others.
He was always anxious, therefore, to secure whatever
available talent presented itself, and immediately on their
appearance enlisted under his banners Canning, Jenkinson, Huskisson, and Castlereagh, all men of the same
standing, for the first three were born in 1770, and the
last in 1769.

The important assistance of Canning was immediately
felt, for he was, in the words of Byron, "a genius—
almost a universal one ; an orator, a wit, a poet, a statesman ". Though he entered Parliament at the early age
of 23 (in 1793), and attained the post of Under-Secretary
of State for the Foreign Department two years after, he
was by no means inexperienced either as a writer or as an
orator ; for while a student at Eton he had won distinction by his contributions to *The Microcosm*, a weekly paper
published by the more advanced Etonians, and also in
the discussions of their Debating Society, which were
conducted with strict regard to parliamentary usages.
And afterwards, while studying for the law, he took an
active part in the proceedings of the debating societies of
the metropolis, in which he achieved so much reputation
as to lead to his introduction to Pitt, whose party he
unhesitatingly joined.

Canning early saw the necessity of the Government's
possessing some literary engine, which, like the Whig

*Rolliad*, published some years before, should carry confusion into the ranks of its enemies. In a lucky hour he
conceived the idea of *The Anti-Jacobin*, a weekly newspaper, interspersed with poetry, the avowed object of
which was to expose the vicious doctrines of the French
Revolution, and to turn into ridicule and contempt the
advocates of that event, and the sticklers for peace and
parliamentary reform. The editor was WILLIAM GIFFORD,
whose vigorous and unscrupulous pen had been already
shown in his *Baviad* and *Mæviad* ; and among the regular
writers were : JOHN HOOKHAM FRERE, JENKINSON (afterwards EARL OF LIVERPOOL), GEORGE ELLIS (who had
previously contributed to the Whig *Rolliad*), LORD CLARE,
LORD MORNINGTON (afterwards MARQUIS WELLESLEY),
LORD MORPETH (afterwards EARL OF CARLISLE), BARON
MACDONALD, and others. These gentlemen entered upon
their task with no common spirit. Their purpose was
to blacken their adversaries, and they spared no means,
fair or foul, in the attempt. Their most distinguished
countrymen, whose only fault was their being opposed to
government, were treated with no more respect than their
foreign adversaries, and were held up to public execration
as traitors, blasphemers, and debauchees. So alarmed,
however, became WILBERFORCE and others of the more
moderate supporters of ministers at the boldness of the
language employed, that PITT was induced to interfere,
and, after an existence of eight months, *The Anti-Jacobin*
(in its original form) ceased to exist.

*The Poetry of the Anti-Jacobin* is not exclusively political.
*The Loves of the Triangles*, a parody on DR. DARWIN's *Loves*

*of the Plants*, is, in the opinion of a celebrated critic (Lord Jeffrey) of the highest degree of merit; as is also *The Progress of Man*, a parody on PAYNE KNIGHT's *Progress of Civil Society ;* and *The Rovers,* a burlesque on the German dramas then in vogue, the extraordinary plots of which, as well as their language, alternately ultrasentimental and domestically bathotic, well marked them out for ridicule, is distinguished by sharp wit and broad humour of the happiest kind. CANNING and his coadjutors in this piece did a real service to literature, and assisted in a purification which GIFFORD, by his demolition of the Della Cruscan school of poetry, had so well begun. Of *The Friend of Humanity and the Knife-grinder* it is unnecessary to speak ; perhaps no lines in the English language have been more effective, or oftener quoted.

But CANNING's greatest power is shown in *New Morality*, which, being the last of the series, seems to have been reserved as a concentrating medium for his pent-up scorn and contempt of the Whigs and their adherents. So that their blows fall thick (for he was powerfully seconded by Frere, Gifford, and Ellis), they care little who suffer from them, and the modern reader is surprised to find CHARLES LAMB and other non-intruders into politics, figuring as congenial conspirators with TOM PAINE !

It is somewhat difficult to regard PITT in the character of a Wit and a Poet, as from the narrative of most of his biographers, he might be considered as uniformly cold, stiff, and unbending ; but his intimate friend WILBER-FORCE, in his *Memoirs*, thus describes him : " PITT, when free from shyness, and amongst his intimate companions, was the very soul of merriment and conversation. He was the wittiest man I ever knew, and what was quite peculiar to himself, had at all times his wit under entire controul. Others appeared struck by the unwonted association of brilliant images ; but every possible combination of ideas seemed always present to his mind, and he could at once produce whatever he desired. I was one of those who met to spend an evening in memory of Shakespeare, at the Boar's Head, Eastcheap. Many professed wits were present, but PITT was the most amusing of the party, the readiest and most apt in the required allusions." It is not, therefore, at all unlikely, that he now and then contributed witty verses to *The Anti-Jacobin*, in addition to those which the Editor has, on probable grounds, ascribed to him in the present volume.

" Critical commentary," says a critic of the previous edition, " on the merits of *The Anti-Jacobin*, would be superfluous. Its satire is distinguished for the terse language of its poignant personality, which was often excessively stinging, but seldom offensively coarse. Its best contributors, CANNING and FRERE, were not mere pamphleteers in verse, like the writers for *The Rolliad*. They had poetical inspiration and a sprightly joyousness springing from a genial play of the mental faculties. They were ' Conservatives ' not only in their politics but in their loyal adherence to the ordinances and traditions of classical English literature. False sentiment, tumid diction, mawkish cant, were chastised by them with exemplary efficacy. On the fourth edition of the complete work (1799, 2 Vols. 8vo, containing both prose and poetry), they placed the epigraph, *Spursosque recolligit ignes;* and in the very last paper (No. 36), the motto on discontinuance was exquisitely happy :—

> " ' We shall miss thee ;
> But yet thou shalt have freedom.
> So to the elements
> Be free ; and fare thou well ! '

"And these lines, taken from *The Tempest* (probably by CANNING), have been prophetic of the popularity of their witty verse, still quoted and admired by all lovers of the genius that is airily elegant and strong."

CHARLES EDMONDS.

WATER ORTON, BIRMINGHAM.

# ADDITIONS TO THE PRESENT EDITION.

Numerous new Biographical and other Notes.

Additions and Corrections to the List of presumed AUTHORS of "THE POETRY".

Selections from the PROSE portion of the work, written by the RT. HON. G. CANNING and his coadjutors.

Account of the various EDITIONS of *The Anti-Jacobin*, and its successors.

Enlarged articles on the opposition NEWSPAPERS abused by *The Anti-Jacobin* writers.

The curious ABUSIVE AND SATIRICAL INDEX to *The Anti-Jacobin*; and specimens of a similar Index to *The Anti-Jacobin Review and Magazine*.

Selections from *The Anti-Jacobin Review and Magazine*—the successor to *The Anti-Jacobin*—showing that though written by a different body of Authors, both works were animated by the same spirit.

# EDITIONS OF THE ANTI-JACOBIN;

## AND ITS SUCCESSORS.

THE ANTI-JACOBIN, or WEEKLY EXAMINER. Sparsosque recolligit ignes. From Nov. 20, 1797, to July 9, 1798. 4to. London.
——— Nos. 1 to 36; with a Prospectus (complete).
——— The Same. Second and third editions, in 4to.
——— The Same. Fourth edition, revised and corrected. 2 vols. 8vo. London, 1799.
Every Number contained Poetry, the presumed Names of the Authors of which will be found in the Table of Contents of the present volume.

---

THE POETRY OF THE ANTI-JACOBIN. 4to. London, 1801.
This volume includes the whole of the POETRY contained in the original *Anti-Jacobin*, with a few verbal corrections. Previous to its publication, it was announced that it would be illustrated by 40 plates expressly designed by GILLRAY; but they never appeared. Numerous editions in 12mo subsequently appeared, but without any additions, till those mentioned below.

---

THE POETRY OF THE ANTI-JACOBIN. A New Edition, with Explanatory Notes by CHARLES EDMONDS. 12mo. London, 1852.
——— The Same. Second edition, by CHARLES EDMONDS; with additional Notes, the original Prospectus (by the Rt. Hon. G. CANNING), and a complete List of the Authors. Illustrated by six etchings after the designs of JAS. GILLRAY. 12mo. London, 1854.

---

THE ANTI-JACOBIN REVIEW AND MAGAZINE; or Monthly Political and Literary Censor. From the commencement in July, 1798, to its close in 1821. (*The first few vols. contain engravings by Gillray and others, and much POETRY is scattered through the volumes.*) 61 vols. 8vo. London, 1798-1821.
For reasons stated on a previous page, CANNING and other political friends of PITT thought it prudent to withdraw themselves from the original *Anti-Jacobin*, but by a preconcerted arrangement it was determined that the spirit which had pervaded that work, and which had had so powerful an effect on the popular mind, and thereby, in connection with Gillray's caricatures, so undoubtedly strengthened the hands of the Ministry, should not die, if it could be kept alive by other and congenial writers. In the words of MR. FOX BOURNE (in his valuable work on *English Newspapers*, 1887): "Though *The Anti-Jacobin* made its last appearance on July 9, 1798, there was started a few days before a monthly *Anti-Jacobin Review and Magazine* of the same politics, but much less brilliant, and more ponderous. Strange to say, it also was edited by a GIFFORD, or one who so called himself. JOHN RICHARDS GREEN was a bold and versatile adventurer, who, having to fly from his creditors in 1782, returned from France in 1788, as JOHN GIFFORD, and was connected with several newspapers [including the establishment of *The British Critic*], besides editing *The Anti-Jacobin Review*. [He also wrote a *History of France*, and other works.] Befriended in

*b*

many ways by PITT, he wrote a four-volume pamphlet [3 vols. 4to, and also
6 vols. 8vo, both dated 1809], styled the *Life of William Pitt*, after his patron's
death. JAMES MILL, the friend and associate of JEREMY BENTHAM, was glad
to earn money in his struggling days by writing non-political articles for *The
Anti-Jacobin Review*. WILLIAM GIFFORD, it is hardly necessary to state, besides
editing Ben Jonson's Works, and other useful occupations, was the first editor
of *The Quarterly Review* in 1809."

In the British Museum are two copies of *The Anti-Jacobin Review and
Magazine*. In one of them the first six vols. contain the Names of the Authors
of most of the articles, among whom are the REV. JOHN WHITAKER, author of
*The History of Manchester*, the REV. SAM. HENSHALL, author of works on Domes-
day Book, the REV. C. E. STEWART, a copious poetaster, etc., and many other
clergymen.

---

THE NEW ANTI-JACOBIN REVIEW.    Delenda est Carthago.

Nos. 1 to 3 seem to be all that were published, and appeared May 6, June 9,
and June 23, 1827 ; price two shillings each.

No. 2 includes what is called a *Patriot Portrait Exhibition*, which is continued
in No. 3. In the latter No. is also an article entitled *Canningiana*. Published
by Saunders and Otley.

---

THE NEW ANTI-JACOBIN ; a Monthly Magazine of Politics, Commerce, Science,
    Literature, Art, Music, and the Drama.

Consists of only Nos. 1 and 2. Published by Smith, Elder, & Co., and
Carpenter & Son ; dated respectively April and May, 1833.

No. 2 contains *Horace in Parliament*, an Ode to William Cobbett ; being a
Parody on Horace—*In Barinen*, Ode 4, Lib. 2. It is accompanied by a full-
length portrait of Cobbett.

The above two works, in accordance with their titles, advocate high Tory
principles ; but though written with great spirit they had but a very short
existence. Copies of both will be found in the British Museum.

---

ENGLISH ACTORS IN THE FRENCH REVOLUTION, AND EYE-WITNESSES OF THE
    SAME.

The most complete details hitherto furnished on these interesting subjects
will be found in the Nos. for October, 1887, and July, 1888, of *The Edinburgh
Review*, the work of MR. JOHN G. ALGER, the Paris correspondent of *The Times*.
They have since been published in a volume. (*Englishmen in the French Revolution :* Low & Co., 1889.)

# CONTENTS OF THE POETRY OF THE ANTI-JACOBIN,

## WITH THE NAMES OF THE AUTHORS.

The following notices of the writers of the POETRY OF THE ANTI-JACOBIN are derived from the copies mentioned below, and each name is authenticated by the initials of the authority upon which each piece is ascribed to particular persons :—

C. .. CANNING'S own copy of the Poetry.
B. . LORD BURGHERSH'S copy.
W. .. WRIGHT the publisher's copy.
U. .. Information of W. UPCOTT, amanuensis.

[Although many of the pieces in the following list are attributed to wrong authors, it has been thought more convenient to reprint them as they stood in the previous edition, in order to insert any corrections, as far as FRERE is concerned. These are derived from the information of FRERE himself given to his nephews, who afterwards edited his works in 1872. They are therefore placed beneath the Title of the piece—between brackets.

The pieces, printed in *Italics*—between brackets—appear for the first time in an edition of *The Poetry*.—ED.]

"WRIGHT, the publisher of the *Anti-Jacobin*, lived at 169, Piccadilly, and his shop was the general morning resort of the friends of the ministry, as DEBRETT'S was of the oppositionists. About the time when the *Anti-Jacobin* was contemplated, OWEN, who had been the publisher of BURKE'S pamphlets, failed. The editors of the *Anti-Jacobin* took his house, paying the rent, taxes, &c., and gave it up to WRIGHT, reserving to themselves the first floor, to which a communication was opened through WRIGHT'S house. Being thus enabled to pass to their own rooms through WRIGHT'S shop, where their frequent visits did not excite any remarks, they contrived to escape particular observation."

"Their meetings were most regular on Sundays, but they not unfrequently met on other days of the week, and in their rooms were chiefly written the poetical portions of the work. What was written was generally left open upon the table, and as others of the party dropped in, hints or suggestions were made; sometimes whole passages were contributed by some of the parties present, and afterwards altered by others, so that it is almost impossible to ascertain the names of the authors. Where, in the above notes, a piece is ascribed to different authors, the conflicting statements may arise from incorrect information, but sometimes they arise from the whole authorship being assigned to one person, when, in fact, both may have contributed. If we look at the references, 167, 185, we shall see CANNING naming several authors, whereas LORD BURGHERSH assigns all to one author. CANNING'S authority is here more to be relied upon. *New Morality* CANNING assigns generally to the four contributors. WRIGHT has given some interesting particulars by appropriating to each his peculiar portion."

"GIFFORD was the working editor, and wrote most of the refutations and corrections of the *Lies, Mistakes,* and *Misrepresentations.*"

"The papers on finance were chiefly by PITT: the first column was frequently kept for what he might send; but his contributions were uncertain, and generally very late, so that the space reserved for him was sometimes filled up by other matter. He only once met the editors at WRIGHT'S."

"W. UPCOTT, who was at the time assistant in WRIGHT'S shop, was employed as amanuensis, to copy out for the printer the various contributions, that the author's handwriting might not be detected."—*E. Hawkins.*

## "THE RIGHT HON. GEORGE CANNING AS A MAN OF LETTERS."

[The following is part of a review, under the above title, of the present editor's previous edition of *The Poetry of the Anti-Jacobin*, and appeared in *The Edinburgh Review* of July, 1858. It is reprinted in the *Biographical and Critical Essays* of A. HAYWARD, Esq., Q.C., 2 vols., 8vo., 1873. It is introduced here as throwing some additional light on the *Writers of the various pieces*.]

". . . We can hardly say of CANNING'S satire what was said of SHERIDAN'S, that—

" ' His wit in the combat, as gentle as bright,
Never carried a heart-stain away on its blade '.

But its severity was redeemed by its buoyancy and geniality, whilst the subjects against which it was principally aimed gave it a healthy tone and a sound foundation. Its happiest effusions will be found in *The Anti-Jacobin*, set on foot to refute or ridicule the democratic rulers of revolutionary France and their admirers or apologists in England, who, it must be owned, were occasionally hurried into a culpable degree of extravagance and laxity by their enthusiasm. . ."

" We learn from MR. EDMONDS that almost all his authorities practically resolve themselves into one, the late MR. W. UPCOTT, and that he never saw either of the alleged copies on which his informant relied. As regards the principal one, CANNING'S own, after the fullest inquiries amongst his surviving relatives and friends, we cannot discover a trace of its existence at any period. LORD BURGHERSH (the late EARL OF WESTMORELAND) was under fourteen years of age during the publication of *The Anti-Jacobin*; and we very much doubt whether either the publisher or the amanuensis (be he who he may) was admitted to the complete confidence of the contributors, or whether either the prose or poetry was composed as stated. In a letter to the late MADAME DE GIRARDIN, à *propos* of her play, *L'École des Journalistes*, JULES JANIN happily exposes the assumption that good leading articles ever were, or ever could be, produced over punch and broiled bones, amidst intoxication and revelry. Equally untenable is the belief that poetical pieces, like the best of *The Anti-Jacobin*, were written in the common rooms of the confraternity, open to constant intrusion, and left upon the table to be corrected or completed by the first comer. The unity of design discernible in each, the glowing harmony of the thoughts and images, and the exquisite finish of the versification, tell of silent and solitary hours spent in brooding over, maturing, and polishing a cherished conception; and young authors, still unknown to fame, are least of all likely to sink their individuality in this fashion. We suspect that their main object in going to WRIGHT'S was to correct their proofs and see one another's articles in the more finished state. Their meetings, if for these purposes, would be most regular on Sundays, because the paper appeared every Monday morning. The extent to which they aided one another may be collected from a well-authenticated anecdote. When FRERE had completed the first part of *The Loves of the Triangles*, he exultingly read over the following lines to CANNING, and defied him to improve upon them :—

" ' Lo, where the chimney's sooty tube ascends,
The fair TROCHAIS from the corner bends !
Her coal-black eyes upturned, incessant mark
The eddying smoke, quick flame, and volant spark ;
Mark with quick ken, where flashing in between,
Her much-loved *Smoke-Jack* glimmers through the scene ;

> Mark, how his various parts together tend,
> Point to one purpose,—in one object end ;
> The spiral grooves in smooth meanders flow,
> Drags the long chain, the polished axles glow,
> While slowly circumvolves the piece of beef below : '

" CANNING took the pen and added—

> " ' The conscious fire with bickering radiance burns,
> Eyes the rich joint, and roasts it as it turns '.

"These two lines are now blended with the original text, and constitute, we are informed on the best authority, the only flaw in FRERE'S title to the sole authorship of the First Part. The Second and Third Parts were by CANNING.

"By the kindness of [the late] LORD HATHERTON, we have now before us a bound volume containing all the numbers of *The Anti-Jacobin* as they originally appeared, eight pages quarto, with double columns, price sixpence. On the fly-leaf is inscribed : ' This copy belonged to the Marquess Wellesley, and was purchased at the sale of his library after his death, January, 1842. H.' On the cover is pasted an engraved label of the arms and name of a former proprietor, CHARLES WILLIAM FLINT, with the pencilled addition of ' Confidential Amanuensis '. In this copy CANNING'S name is subscribed to (amongst others) the following pieces, which are also assigned to him (along with a large share in the most popular of the rest) by the most trustworthy rumours and traditions :—*Inscription for the Door of the Cell in Newgate where Mrs. Brownrigg, the Prenticide, was confined previous to her execution ; The Friend of Humanity and the Knife-Grinder ;* the lines addressed *To the Author of the Epistle to the Editors of The Anti-Jacobin ; The Progress of Man* (all three parts) ; and *New Morality.**

"With the single exception of *The Friend of Humanity and the Knife-Grinder,* no piece in the collection is more freshly remembered than the *Inscription for the Cell of Mrs. Brownrigg,* who

> " ' Whipp'd two female prentices to death,
> And hid them in the coal-hole '.

"The Answer to *The Author of the Epistle to the Editors of The Anti-Jacobin* is less known, and it derives a fresh interest from the fact, recently [c. 1854] made public, that *The Epistle* (which appeared in *The Morning Chronicle* of January 17, 1798) was the composition of WILLIAM LORD MELBOURNE. The beginning shows that the veil of incognito had been already penetrated.

> " ' Whoe'er ye are, all hail!—whether the skill
> Of youthful CANNING guides the ranc'rous quill ;
> With powers mechanic far above his age,
> Adapts the paragraph and fills the page ;
> Measures the column, mends whate'er's amiss,
> Rejects THAT letter, and accepts of THIS ;
> Or HAMMOND, leaving his official toil,
> O'er this great work consume the midnight oil—
> Bills, passports, letters, for the Muses quit,
> And change dull business for amusing wit.'

"After referring to ' the poetic sage, who sung of Gallia in a headlong rage,' *The Epistle* proceeds :—

> " ' I swear by all the youths that MALMESBURY chose,†
> By ELLIS' sapient prominence of nose—

---

* On the subject of the respective authorship of the contributions to *The Anti-Jacobin,* see *The Works of John Hookham Frere, in verse and prose, with Prefatory Memoir. Edited by his Nephews, H. and Sir Bartle Frere,* and *The Edinburgh Review* for April, 1872, p. 476.

† It will be remembered that these eminent persons were chosen by Lord Malmesbury to accompany him on his mission to Lille and were associated with him in the abortive negotiations for peace.

By MORPETH's gait, important, proud and big—
*By Leveson Gower's crop-imitating wig,*
That, could the pow'rs which in those numbers shine,
Could that warm spirit animate my line,
Your glorious deeds which humbly I rehearse—
Your deeds should live immortal as my verse ;
And, while they wonder'd whence I caught my flame,
Your sons should blush to read their fathers' shame '.

" Happily the eminent and accomplished sons of these fathers will smile,
rather than blush, at this allusion to their sires, and smile the more when they
remember from which side the attack proceeded. It is clear from the Answer,
that, whilst the band were not a little ruffled, they had not the remotest suspicion
that their assailant was a youth in his nineteenth year. Amongst other prefatory
remarks they say :—
" ' We assure the author of the epistle, that the answer which we have here
the honour to address to him, contains our genuine and undisguised sentiments
upon the merits of the poem.
" ' Our conjectures respecting the authors and abettors of this performance
may possibly be as vague and unfounded as theirs are with regard to the
EDITORS of *The Anti-Jacobin.* We are sorry that we cannot satisfy their
curiosity upon this subject—but we have little anxiety for the gratification of
our own.
" ' It is only necessary to add, what is most conscientiously the truth, that this
production, such as it is, is *by far the best* of all the attacks that the combined
wits of the cause have been able to muster against *The Anti-Jacobin.*'
" The Answer opens thus :—

" ' BARD of the borrow'd lyre ! to whom belong
The shreds and remnants of each hackney'd song ;
Whose verse thy friends in vain for wit explore,
And count but *one good line,* in eighty-four !
Whoe'er thou art, all hail ! Thy bitter smile
Gilds our dull page, and cheers our humble toil !'

" The ' one good line ' was ' By Leveson Gower's crop-imitating wig,' but the
Epistle contains many equally good and some better. The speculations as to
its authorship afforded no slight amusement to the writer and his friends. . . .
" *New Morality* is commonly regarded as the master-piece of *The Anti-Jacobin ;*
and, with the exception of a few lines, the whole of it is by CANNING. It appeared in the last number, and he is said to have concentrated all his energies
for a parting blow. The reader who comes fresh from DRYDEN or POPE, or even
CHURCHILL, will be disappointed on finding far less variety of images, sparkling
antithesis, or condensed brilliancy of expression. The author exhibits abundant
humour and eloquence, but comparatively little wit ; *i.e.,* if there be any truth
in SYDNEY SMITH's doctrine ' that the feeling of wit is occasioned by those
relations of ideas which excite surprise, and surprise *alone* '. We are commonly
prepared for what is coming, and our admiration is excited rather by the just-
ness of the observations, the elevation of the thoughts, and the vigour of the
style, than by a startling succession of flashes of fancy. If, as we believe, the
same might be said of JUVENAL, and the best of his English imitators, JOHNSON,
we leave ample scope for praise ; and *New Morality* contains passages which have
been preserved to our time and bid fair to reach posterity. How often are the
lines on *Candour* quoted in entire ignorance or forgetfulness of their author. . . .
" The drama of *The Rovers,* or *Double Arrangement,* was written to ridicule the
German Drama, then hardly known in this country, except through the medium
of bad translations of some of the least meritorious of SCHILLER'S, GOETHE'S,
and KOTZEBUE'S productions. The parody is now principally remembered by
Rogero's song, of which, Mr. Edmonds states, the first five stanzas were by
CANNING. " Having been accidentally seen, previously to its publication, by
PITT, he was so amused with it that he took a pen and composed the last stanza
on the spot. . . .

"CANNING'S reputed share in *The Rovers* excited the unreasoning indignation, and provoked the exaggerated censure, of a man who has obtained a world-wide reputation by his historical researches, most especially by his skill in separating the true from the fabulous, and in filling up chasms in national annals by a process near akin to that by which CUVIER inferred the entire form and structure of an extinct species from a bone. The following passage is taken from NIEBUHR'S *History of the Period of the Revolution* (published from his Lectures, in two volumes, in 1845) :—

"'CANNING was at that time (1807) at the head of foreign affairs in England. History will not form the same judgment of him as that formed by contemporaries. He had great talents, but was not a great Statesman ; he was one of those persons who distinguish themselves as the squires of political heroes. He was highly accomplished in the two classical languages, but without being a learned scholar. He was especially conversant with Greek writers. He had likewise poetical talent, but only for Satire. At first he had joined the leaders of opposition against PITT'S ministry : LORD GREY, who perceived his ambition, advised him, half in joke, to join the ministers, as he would make his fortune. He did so, and was employed to write articles for the newspapers and satirical verses, which were often directed against his former benefactors.

"'Through the influence of the ministers he came into Parliament. So long as the great eloquence of former times lasted, and the great men were alive, his talent was admired ; but older persons had no great pleasure in his petulant, epigrammatic eloquence and his jokes, which were often in bad taste. He joined the Society of the Anti-Jacobins, which defended everything connected with existing institutions. This society published a journal, in which the most honoured names of foreign countries were attacked in the most scandalous manner. German literature was at that time little known in England, and it was associated there with the ideas of Jacobinism and revolution. CANNING then published in *The Anti-Jacobin* the most shameful pasquinade which was ever written against Germany, under the title of *Matilda Pottingen*. Göttingen is described in it as the sink of all infamy ; professors and students as a gang of miscreants ; licentiousness, incest, and atheism as the character of the German people. Such was CANNING'S beginning : he was at all events useful, a sort of political Cossack' (*Geschichte des Zeitalters der Revolution*, vol. ii., p. 242).

"'Here am I,' exclaimed RALEIGH, after vainly trying to get at the rights of a squabble in the courtyard of the Tower, 'employed in writing a true history of the world, when I cannot ascertain the truth of what happens under my own window.' Here is the great restorer of Roman history—who, by the way, prided himself on his knowledge of England—hurried into the strangest misconception of contemporary events and personages, and giving vent to a series of depreciatory misstatements, without pausing to verify the assumed groundwork of his patriotic wrath. His description of 'the most shameful pasquinade,' and his ignorance of the very title, prove that he had never seen it If he had, he would also have known that the scene is laid at Weimar, not at Göttingen, and that the satire is almost exclusively directed against a portion of the dramatic literature of his country, which all rational admirers must admit to be indefensible. The scene in *The Rovers*, in which the rival heroines, meeting for the first time at an inn, swear eternal friendship and embrace, is positively a feeble reflection of a scene in GOETHE'S *Stella* ; and no anachronism can exceed that in SCHILLER'S *Cabal und Liebe*, when Lady Milford, after declaring herself the daughter of the Duke of Norfolk who rebelled against Queen Elizabeth, is horrified on finding that the jewels sent her by the Grand Duke have been purchased by the sale of 7000 of his subjects to be employed in the American war. *

---

* It is surprising that the satirist's attention was not attracted to the scene in *Stella*, in which one of the heroines describes the rapid growth of her passion to its object: "I know not if you observed that you had enchained my interest from the first moment of our first meeting. I at least soon became aware that your eyes sought mine. Ah, Fernando, then my uncle brought the music, you took your violin, and, as you played, my eyes rested upon you free from care. I studied every feature of your face ; and, during an unexpected pause, you fixed

" Amongst the prose contributions to *The Anti-Jacobin*, there is one in which, independently of direct evidence, the peculiar humour of CANNING is discernible, —the pretended report of the meeting of the Friends of Freedom at the Crown and Anchor Tavern.* The plan was evidently suggested by TICKELL's *Anticipation*, in which the debate on the Address at the opening of the Session was reported beforehand with such surprising foresight, that some of the speakers, who were thus forestalled, declined to deliver their meditated orations.

" At the meeting of the Friends of Freedom, ERSKINE, whose habitual egotism could hardly be caricatured, is made to perorate as follows, &c. . . . A long speech is given to MACKINTOSH, who, under the name of *Macfungus*, after a fervid sketch of the Temple of Freedom which he proposes to construct on the ruins of ancient establishments, proceeds with kindling animation, &c. . . .†

" The wit and fun of these imitations are undeniable, and their injustice is equally so. ERSKINE, with all his egotism, was, and remains, the greatest of English advocates. He stemmed and turned the tide which threatened to sweep away the most valued of our free institutions in 1794 ; and (we say with LORD BROUGHAM) ' Before such a precious service as this, well may the lustre of statesmen and orators grow pale '. MACKINTOSH was pre-eminently distinguished by the comprehensiveness and moderation of his views ; nor could any man be less disposed by temper, habits, or pursuits towards revolutionary courses. His lectures on *The Law of Nature and Nations* were especially directed against the new morality in general, and GODWIN'S *Political Justice* in particular.

" At a long subsequent period (1807) CANNING, when attacked in Parliament for his share in *The Anti-Jacobin*, declared that ' he felt no shame for its character or principles, nor any other sorrow for the share he had had in it than that which the imperfection of his pieces was calculated to inspire '. Still, it is one of the inevitable inconveniences of a connection with the Press that the best known writers should be made answerable for the errors of their associates ; and the license of *The Anti-Jacobin* gave serious and well-founded offence to many who shared its opinions and wished well to its professed object. In WILBERFORCE'S *Diary* for May 18, 1799, we find ' PITT, CANNING, and PEPPER ARDEN came in late to dinner. I attacked CANNING on indecency of *Anti-Jacobin*.' COLERIDGE, in his *Biographia Literaria*, complains bitterly of the calumnious accounts given by *The Anti-Jacobin* of his early life, and asks with reason, ' Is it surprising that many good men remained longer than perhaps they otherwise would have done adverse to a party which encouraged and . openly rewarded the authors of such atrocious calumnies ? '

" Mr. Edmonds says that PITT got frightened, and that the publication was discontinued at the suggestion of the Prime Minister. It is not unlikely that CANNING, now a member of the House of Commons and Under-Secretary of State for Foreign Affairs, found his connection with it embarrassing, as his hopes rose and his political prospects expanded. Indeed, it may be questioned whether a Parliamentary career can ever be united with that of the daily or weekly journalist without compromising one or both. At all events, the original *Anti-Jacobin* closed with the number containing *New Morality*, and CANNING had nothing to do with the *monthly review* started under the same name."

---

your eyes upon—upon me ! They met mine ! How I blushed, how I looked away ! You observed it, Fernando ; for from that moment I felt that you looked oftener over your music-book, often played out of tune, to the disturbance of my uncle. Every false note, Fernando, went to my heart. It was the sweetest confusion I ever felt in my life."

* The whole of this *jeu d'esprit* has been claimed for FRERE, but on unsatisfactory evidence. It is much more in CANNING'S way as a student of oratory, which FRERE was not.

[† See pages 32, 34.—ED.]

# THE *ANTI-JACOBIN* AS AN AID TO GOVERNMENT.

[Considering *The Anti-Jacobin* from a national as well as a literary point of view, we cannot do better than use a portion of an Essay on English Political Satires by the late JAS. HANNAY, in the *Quarterly Review*, April, 1857.]

". . . In the case of *The Anti-Jacobin*, what are we to say? A hundred opinions may be adopted respecting the French Revolution. Some hate it with unmitigated hatred. Some regret it, but accept its consequences as beneficial to mankind on the whole. Some cherish its memory as a new political revelation of which they hope to see still further results. But a candid man of any of these persuasions must remember that the aim of *The Anti-Jacobin* was to keep *Britain* from revolution during 1797-8 It was therefore necessary to fight as our soldiers afterwards did in Spain—to wage such a *literary* war as suited the agitated spirit of Europe. While we blame CANNING, therefore, for speaking as he did of MADAME ROLAND, we must not forget the indecorum of her Memoirs, or that it was from persons of her party that vile aspersions were cast upon the character of MARIE ANTOINETTE. There were men quite ready to begin the same work over here that had been done in France, and that in a spirit of vulgar imitation, and under quite different circumstances. They had to be shot down like mad dogs; for a cur, though contemptible in ordinary cases, becomes tragic when he has hydrophobia.

"For *The Anti-Jacobin* must be claimed an honour which can be claimed for scarce one of the works we have passed under review. Let us waive the question how much we may have owed it for helping to inspire that unity and stout insular self-confidence which carried us through the great war,—whole within and impervious without. Let us consider it only in a literary point of view, and we shall find it enjoying the rare distinction that its best Satires live in real popular remembrance. The *Knife-Grinder*, with his

"'*Story! God bless you, I have none to tell, sir,*'

is almost as widely known as our nursery rhymes.

"But if *The Anti-Jacobin* excels all similar works in popularity, and in the eminence of its contributors, it also excels them in another important particular. It contains on the whole a greater number of really good things than any one of them. The *Loves of the Triangles*, in which,

"'Th' obedient Pulley strong Mechanics ply,
And wanton Optics roll the melting eye!'

is an irresistible parody, and likely to keep the original of Darwin [*Loves of the Plants*] in remembrance. Gray's Odes have survived the burlesques of Colman ; and the *Country and City Mouse* of Prior and Montague is neglected by nine-tenths of those who read with admiration the *Hind and the Panther*. But Darwin's case is peculiar. Other poems live in spite of ridicule ; and his *Loves of the Plants* in consequence of it. The Attic salt of his enemies has *preserved* his reputation.

"There is always a purpose in *The Anti-Jacobin's* view something more important than the mere persiflage that teases individuals. Like the blade of Damascus, which has a verse of the Koran engraved on it, its fine wit glitters terribly in the cause of sacred tradition."

# DESCRIPTION OF THE PLATES.

THE GIANT FACTOTUM AMUSING HIMSELF. (FRONTISPIECE.)

PITT, with his right hand is playing at cup and ball; the latter being a globe to denote his influence over foreign countries as well as at home. His right foot is supported by DUNDAS and WILBERFORCE, and is extended to be submissively kissed by his ministerial followers, foremost of whom is CANNING. With his left foot he has crushed the Opposition. On the same side is a document labelled "Resources for supporting the War," with a collection of coin, evidently destined for foreign subsidies. On his right side are various official returns of volunteers, seamen, regulars, and militia. He is thus prepared to carry on the war abroad, and maintain tranquillity at home.

Scene, the Borough of Southwark, with a portrait of GEORGE TIERNEY, its able and radical representative. Published Dec. 4, 1797, as a graphic illustration of the Parody of Southey's poem, *The Widow*.

A characteristic portrait of the gallant and excellent EARL OF MOIRA, afterwards MARQUIS OF HASTINGS, and Governor-General of India. The engraving is in ridicule of his complaint, in the House of Lords, of the cruelties exercised by the Government troops on the Irish Rebels. In the distance is seen Moll Coggin, an Irish witch, mounted on a black Ram with a blue tail, and on the hill an Oak-boy, carrying an uprooted oak, on the branches of which are numerous swans—in allusion to the unfounded nature of his charges.

Representing the DUKE OF NORFOLK giving at a dinner at the Crown and Anchor Tavern in honour of the birth-day of FOX his famous toast, "Our Sovereign's Health—The Majesty of the People". On the left is JOHN NICHOLLS, Member for Tregony; next to him is the DUKE OF BEDFORD; on the other side of the table are SHERIDAN and FOX.

The statue of FOX was placed between those of Demosthenes and Cicero, by the EMPRESS CATHERINE OF RUSSIA, as a compliment to him for having successfully opposed the sending of the armament prepared by PITT, in conjunction with Prussia and Holland, to compel her to give up Ockzakow which she had seized. As this caricature, including the verses, was originally published in March, 1793, the latter in *The Anti-Jacobin* must have been suggested by them.

In allusion to the influence exercised by FOX over FRANCIS, fifth DUKE OF BEDFORD, who had become one of the most zealous of the popular party.

# PROSPECTUS

OF

# THE ANTI-JACOBIN;

OR,

## WEEKLY EXAMINER,

The FIRST NUMBER of which will be published on MONDAY, the 20th of NOVEMBER, 1797, to be continued every Monday during the sitting of Parliament.   Price 6d.

> ———*Possit quid vivida virtus*
> *Experiare, licet : nec longe scilicet hostes*
> *Quærendi.*

AT a moment, when whatever may be the habits of inquiry and the anxiety for information upon subjects of public concern diffused among all ranks of people, the vehicles of intelligence are already multiplied in a proportion nearly equal to this encreased demand, and to the encreased importance and variety of matter, some apology may perhaps be necessary for the obtrusion of a new Paper upon the World; and some account may reasonably be expected of the views and principles on which it founds its pretensions to notice, before it can hope to make its way through the crowd of competitors which have gotten the start of it in the race for public favour.

[As this *Prospectus* was written by MR. CANNING, and it has been prefixed only to the former edition of the *Poetry* by the present Editor, it is again considered an interesting addition to the present one.]

1

THE grounds upon which such pretensions have usually been rested by those who have engaged in undertakings of this kind, are accuracy, variety, and priority of Intelligence, connections at home, correspondence abroad, and, above all, a profession of impartial and unprejudiced attention to all opinions, and to all parties and descriptions of men.

⟶ ON none of these Topicks is it Our intention to enlarge.

OF Our means of information, and of the use which We make of them, our readers will, after a very short trial, be enabled to form their own opinion. And to that trial We confidently commit ourselves : professing, however, at the same time, that if the only advantage which We were desirous of holding out to our Readers, were that of having it in our power to apprize them an hour or a day sooner than those Journals, which are already in their hands, of any event however important —We should bring to the undertaking much less anxiety for success, and should state our claims on public attention with much less boldness, than We are disposed to do in the consciousness of higher purposes, and more beneficial views.

NOVELTY indeed We have to announce. For what so new in the present state of the daily and weekly PRESS (We speak generally, though there are undoubtedly exceptions which we may have occasion to point out hereafter) as THE TRUTH? To this object alone it is that Our labours are dedicated. It is the constant violation, the disguise, the perversion of the Truth, whether in narrative or in argument, that will form the principal subject of our WEEKLY EXAMINATION : and it is by a diligent and faithful discharge of this duty—by detecting

falsehood, and rectifying error, by correcting misrepresentation, and exposing and chastising malignity—that We
hope to deserve the reception which We solicit, and to
obtain not only the approbation of the Country to our
attempt, but its thanks for the motives which have given
birth to it.

THESE are strong words. But We are conscious of
intending in earnest what they profess. How far the
execution of our purpose may correspond with the design,
it is for others to determine. It is ours to state that
design fairly, and in the spirit in which we conceive it.

OF the utility of such a purpose, if even tolerably
executed, there can be little doubt, among those persons
(a very large part of the community) who must have
found themselves, during the course of the last few years,
perplexed by the multiplicity of contradictory accounts of
almost every material event that has occurred in that
eventful and tremendous period ; and who must anxiously
have wished for some public channel of information on
which they could confidently rely for forming their
opinion.

BUT before We can expect sufficient credit from persons
of this description, to enable us to supply such a defect,
and to assume an office so important, it is natural that
they should require some profession of our principles as
well as of our purposes ; in order that they may judge
not only of our ability to communicate the information
which We promise, but of our intention to inform them
aright.

To that freedom from *partiality* and *prejudice*, of which
We have spoken above, by the profession of which so
many of our Contemporaries recommend themselves, We

make little pretension—at least in the sense in which those terms appear now too often to be used.

WE have not arrived (to our shame perhaps we avow it) at that wild and unshackled freedom of thought, which rejects all habit, all wisdom of former times, all restraints of ancient usage, and of local attachment; and which judges upon each subject, whether of politicks or morals, as it arises, by lights entirely its own, without reference to recognized principle, or established practice.

WE confess, whatever disgrace may attend such a confession, that We have not so far gotten the better of the influence of long habits and early education, not so far imbibed that spirit of liberal indifference, of diffused and comprehensive philanthropy, which distinguishes the candid character of the present age, but that We have our feelings, our preferences, and our affections, attaching on particular places, manners, and institutions, and even on particular portions of the human race.

IT may be thought a narrow and illiberal distinction—but We avow ourselves to be *partial* to the COUNTRY *in which we live*, notwithstanding the daily panegyricks which we read and hear on the superior virtues and endowments of its rival and hostile neighbours. We are *prejudiced* in favour of *her* Establishments, civil and religious; though without claiming for either that ideal perfection, which modern philosophy professes to discover in the other more luminous systems which are arising on all sides of us.

THE safety and prosperity of *these kingdoms*, however unimportant they may seem in abstract contemplation when compared with the more extensive, more beautiful, and more productive parts of the world, do yet excite in

our minds a peculiar interest and anxiety; and will probably continue to occupy a share of our attention by no
means justified by the proportional consequence which
speculative reasoners may think proper to assign to them
in the scale of the universe.
We should be averse to hazarding the smallest part of
the practical happiness of *this Country;* though the
sacrifice should be recommended as necessary for accomplishing throughout the world an uniform and beautiful
system of theoretical liberty : and We should at all times
exert our best endeavours for upholding its constitution,
even with all the human imperfections which may belong
to it, though We were assured that on its ruins might be
erected the only pillar that is yet wanting to complete
the "*most glorious fabrick which the Integrity and Wisdom
of man have raised since the Creation*".
IF, as Philosopher MONGE* avers, in his eloquent and
instructive address to the Directory, "*The Government
of England and the French Republick cannot exist together,*"
We do not hesitate in our choice; though well aware
that in that choice we may be much liable, in the opinion
of many critics of the present day, to the imputation of a
want of candour or of discernment.

---

[* A very eminent Mathematician and Physicist, and the
inventor of descriptive geometry; born in 1746. In 1792 he
was appointed Minister of Marine; and afterwards took an
active part in the equipment of the Army. After founding the
*École Polytechnique,* he was sent into Italy to receive the
pictures and statues seized by Buonaparte. He then joined
the expedition to Egypt, and rendered great service both in the
war operations and in the labours of the *Egyptian Institute,*
the results of which were published by command of Napoleon
in that magnificent and extensive work the *Description de
l'Égypte.* He died in 1818.—ED.]

ADMIRERS of military heroism, and dazzled by military success in common with other men, We are yet even *here* conscious of some qualification and distinction in our feelings : We acknowledge ourselves apt to look with more complacency on bravery and skill, when displayed in the service of our Country, than when We see them directed against its interests or its safety ; and, however equal the claims to admiration in either case may be, We feel our hearts grow warmer at the recital of what has been atchieved by HOWE, by JERVIS, or by DUNCAN, than at the *" glorious victory of Jemappe,"* or *" the immortal battle of the bridge of Lodi "*.

IN MORALS We are equally old-fashioned. We have not yet learned the modern refinement of referring in all considerations upon human conduct, not to any settled and preconceived principles of right and wrong, not to any general and fundamental rules which experience, and wisdom, and justice, and the common consent of mankind have established, but to the internal admonitions of every man's judgment or conscience in his own particular instance.

WE do not dissemble,—that We reverence LAW,—We acknowledge USAGE,—We look even upon PRESCRIPTION without hatred or horror. And we do not think these, or any of them, less safe guides for the moral actions of men, than that new and liberal system of ETHICS, whose operation is not to bind but to loosen the bands of social order ; whose doctrine is formed not on a system of reciprocal duties, but on the supposition of individual, independent, and unconnected rights ; which teaches that all men are pretty equally honest, but that some have different notions of honesty from others, and that the most received notions are for the greater part the most faulty.

WE do not subscribe to the opinion, that a sincere conviction of the truth of no matter what principle, is a sufficient defence for no matter what action; and that the only business of moral enquiry with human conduct is to ascertain that in each case the principle and the action agree. We have not yet persuaded ourselves to think it a sound, or a safe doctrine, that every man who can divest himself of a moral sense in theory, has a right to be with impunity and without disguise a scoundrel in practice. It is not in our creed, that ATHEISM is as good a faith as CHRISTIANITY, provided it be professed with equal sincerity; nor could we admit it as an excuse for MURDER, that the murderer was in his own mind conscientiously persuaded that the murdered might for many good reasons be better out of the way.

OF all these and the like principles, in one word, of JACOBINISM in all its shapes, and in all its degrees, political and moral, public and private, whether as it openly threatens the subversion of States, or gradually saps the foundations of domestic happiness, We are the avowed, determined, and irreconcileable enemies. We have no desire to divest ourselves of these inveterate prejudices; but shall remain stubborn and incorrigible in resisting every attempt which may be made either by argument or (what is more in the charitable spirit of modern reformers) by force, to convert us to a different opinion.

IT remains only to speak of the details of our PLAN.

IT is our intention to publish Weekly, during the Session of Parliament, a Paper, containing,

FIRST, An Abstract of the important events of the week, both at home and abroad.

SECONDLY, Such Reflections as may naturally arise out of them : and,

THIRDLY, A contradiction and confutation of the falsehoods and misrepresentations concerning these events, their causes, and their consequences, which may be found in the Papers devoted to the cause of SEDITION and IRRELIGION, to the pay or principles of FRANCE.

THIS last, as it is by far the most important, will in all probability be the most copious of the three heads ; and is that to which, above all others, We wish to direct the attention of our Readers.

WE propose diligently to collect, as far as the range of our own daily reading will enable us, and we promise willingly to receive, from whatever quarter they may come, the several articles of this kind which require to be thus contradicted or confuted ; which will naturally divide themselves into different classes, according to their different degrees of stupidity or malignity.

THERE are, for instance (to begin with those of the highest order), the LIES of the Week ; the downright, direct, unblushing falsehoods, which have no colour or foundation whatever, and which must at the very moment of their being written, have been known to the writer to be wholly destitute of truth.

NEXT in rank come MISREPRESENTATIONS which, taking for their ground-work facts in substance true, do so colour and distort them in description, as to take away all semblance of their real nature and character.

LASTLY, The most venial, though by no means the least mischievous class, are. MISTAKES; under which description are included all those Hints, Conjectures, and Apprehensions, those Anticipations of Sorrow and Deprecations of Calamity, in which Writers who labour under too great an anxiety for the Public Welfare are apt to indulge; and which, when falsified by the event, they are generally too much occupied to find leisure to retract or disavow:—A trouble which We shall have great pleasure in taking off these Gentlemen's hands.

To each of these several articles We shall carefully affix the name and date of the Publication from which We may take the liberty of borrowing it.

WITH regard to the PROCEEDINGS IN PARLIAMENT, We shall not fail to mark to Our Readers the progress of the public business; though it does not enter into our Plan to give a regular detail of the Debates: nor would the limits of our Paper allow of it.

WE have a further reason for not occupying this province, which will equally account for our determination, not to receive Advertisements—our earnest desire not to lessen the circulation of any existing Public Print.

IT is obvious upon every ground of fairness and of policy, that We must entertain this desire very strongly with regard to the respectable Papers which are directed by principles and attachments like our own: an attachment (We have no wish to disguise it) to the cause of a GOVERNMENT, with whose support, whose popularity and consequent means of exertion, the circumstances of the present times have essentially connected the existence of THIS COUNTRY as an independent Nation.

As little should we wish to circumscribe the sale of those JOURNALS, upon whose errors or perverseness, upon whose false statements and pernicious doctrines We reckon for the main support, as they have been the principal cause of our undertaking. These We would entreat to proceed with fresh vigour and increased activity. It is our wish to be seen together, and to be compared with them. Every week of misrepresentation will be followed by its weekly comment; and with this corrective faithfully administered, the longest course of MORNING CHRONICLES or MORNING POSTS, of STARS or COURIERS, may become not only innocent but beneficial.

WITH these views then We commence our undertaking. Whatever may be the success or the merit of its execution in our hands, the want of something like it has so long been felt and deplored by all thinking and honest men, that We cannot doubt of the approbation and encouragement with which the attempt will be received.

WE claim the support, and We invite the assistance, of ALL, who think with US that the circumstances and character of the age in which We live require every exertion of every man, who loves his COUNTRY in the old way, in which till of late years the LOVE of one's COUNTRY was professed by most men, and by none disclaimed or reviled; of ALL who think that the PRESS has been long enough employed principally as an engine of destruction, and who wish to see the experiment fairly tried whether that engine, by which many of the States which surround us have been overthrown, and others shaken to their foundations, may not be turned into an instrument of defence for the ONE remaining COUNTRY which has ESTAB-LISHMENTS to protect, and a GOVERNMENT with the spirit, and the power, and the wisdom to protect them; of ALL who look with respect to public honour, and with attachment to the decencies of private life; of ALL who have so little deference for the arrogant intolerance of JACOBINISM as still to contemplate the OFFICE and the PERSON of a KING with veneration, and to speak reverently of RELIGION, without apologizing for the singularity of their opinions; of ALL who think the blessings which we enjoy valuable, and who think them in danger; and who, while they detest and despise the principles and the professors of that NEW FAITH by which the foundations of all those blessings are threatened to be undermined, lament the lukewarmness with which its propagation has hitherto been resisted, and are anxious, while there is yet time, to make every effort in the cause of their COUNTRY.

Published by J. WRIGHT, No. 169, opposite Old Bond Street, Piccadilly : by whom Orders for the Papers, and all Communications of Correspondents, addressed to the Editor of the ANTI-JACOBIN, or WEEKLY EXAMINER, will be received. Sold also by all the Booksellers and Newsmen in Town and Country.

# POETRY

OF

# THE ANTI-JACOBIN.

. ## No. I.

INTRODUCTION.

Nov. 20, 1797.

IN our anxiety to provide for the amusement as well as information of our readers, we have not omitted to make all the inquiries in our power for ascertaining the means of procuring poetical assistance. And it would give us no small satisfaction to be able to report that we had succeeded in this point precisely in the manner which would best have suited our own taste and feelings, as well as those which we wish to cultivate in our readers.

But whether it be that good Morals, and what we should call good Politics, are inconsistent with the spirit of true Poetry—whether "*the Muses still with freedom found*" have an aversion to *regular* governments, and require a frame and system of protection less complicated than king, lords, and commons :—

> "Whether primordial *nonsense* springs to life*
> In the wild war of *democratic* strife,"

and there only—or for whatever other reason it may be, whether physical, or moral, or philosophical (which last

---

[* Parodied from Payne Knight's poem, "*The Progress of Civil Society*," which is admirably ridiculed in No. XV. *post.*—ED.]

is understood to mean something more than the other two, though exactly *what*, it is difficult to say), we have not been able to find one good and true Poet, of sound principles and sober practice, upon whom we could rely for furnishing us with a handsome quantity of sufficient and approved verse—such verse as our readers might be expected to get by heart, and to sing; as the worthy philosopher MONGE describes the little children of Sparta and Athens singing the songs of Freedom, in expectation of the coming of *the Great Nation*.

In this difficulty we have had no choice but either to provide no poetry at all—a shabby expedient—or to go to the only market where it is to be had good and ready made, that of the *Jacobins*—an expedient full of danger, and not to be used but with the utmost caution and delicacy.

To this latter expedient, however, after mature deliberation, we have determined to have recourse; qualifying it at the same time with such precautions as may conduce at once to the safety of our readers' principles, and to the improvement of our own poetry.

For this double purpose, we shall select from time to time from among those effusions of the *Jacobin* Muse which happen to fall in our way, such pieces as may serve to illustrate some one of the principles on which the poetical as well as the political doctrine of the NEW SCHOOL is established—prefacing each of them, for our readers' sake, with a short disquisition on the particular tenet intended to be enforced or insinuated in the production before them—and accompanying it with an humble effort of our own, in imitation of the poem itself, and in further illustration of its principle.

By these means, though we cannot hope to catch "*the wood-notes wild*" of the Bards of Freedom, we may yet acquire, by dint of repeating after them, a more complete knowledge of the secret in which their greatness lies than we could by mere prosaic admiration ; and if we cannot become poets ourselves, we at least shall have collected the elements of a *Jacobin* Art of Poetry for the use of those whose genius may be more capable of turning them to advantage.

It might not be unamusing to trace the springs and principles of this species of poetry, which are to be found, some in the exaggeration, and others in the direct inversion of the sentiments and passions which have in all ages animated the breast of the favourite of the Muses, and distinguished him from the "vulgar throng".

The poet in all ages has despised riches and grandeur.

The *Jacobin* poet improves this sentiment into a hatred of the rich and the great.

The poet of other times has been an enthusiast in the love of his native soil.

The *Jacobin* poet rejects all restriction in his feelings. *His* love is enlarged and expanded so as to comprehend all human kind. The love of all human kind is without doubt a noble passion : it can hardly be necessary to mention that its operation extends to *freemen*, and them only, all over the world.

The old poet was a warrior, at least in imagination ; and sung the actions of the heroes of his country in strains which "made Ambition Virtue," and which overwhelmed the horrors of war in its glory.

The *Jacobin* poet would have no objection to sing battles too—but *he* would take a distinction. The prowess of Buonaparte, indeed, he might chant in his loftiest strain of exultation. *There* we should find nothing but trophies and triumphs and branches of laurel and olive, phalanxes of Republicans shouting victory, satellites of despotism biting the ground, and geniuses of Liberty planting standards on mountain-tops.

But let his own country triumph, or her allies obtain an advantage : straightway the " beauteous face of war " is changed; the " pride, pomp, and circumstance " of victory are kept carefully out of sight, and we are presented with nothing but contusions and amputations, plundered peasants, and deserted looms. Our poet points the thunder of his blank verse at the head of the recruiting serjeant, or roars in dithyrambics against the lieutenants of pressgangs.

But it would be endless to chase the coy Muse of *Jacobinism* through all her characters. *Mille habet ornatus.* The *Mille decenter habet* is perhaps more questionable. For in whatever disguise she appears, whether of mirth or of melancholy, of piety or of tenderness ; under all disguises, like *Sir John Brute* in woman's clothes, she is betrayed by her drunken swagger and ruffian tone.

In the poem which we have selected for the edification of our readers and our own imitation this day, the principles which are meant to be inculcated speak so plainly for themselves, that they need no previous introduction.

# INSCRIPTION*

*For the Apartment in Chepstow Castle, where Henry Marten, the Regicide, was imprisoned thirty years.*

FOR thirty years secluded from mankind
Here MARTEN lingered. Often have these walls
Echoed his footsteps, as with even tread
He paced around his prison : not to him
Did Nature's fair varieties exist;
He never saw the sun's delightful beams,
Save when through yon high bars he pour'd a sad
And broken splendour. Dost thou ask his crime?
He had REBELL'D AGAINST THE KING, AND SAT
IN JUDGMENT ON HIM ; for his ardent mind
Shaped goodliest plans of happiness on earth,
And peace and liberty. Wild dreams! but such
As Plato loved ; such as with holy zeal
Our Milton worshipp'd. Blessed hopes! awhile
From man withheld, even to the latter days
When Christ shall come, and all things be fulfill'd!

--------

IMITATION.

# INSCRIPTION

*For the Door of the Cell in Newgate, where Mrs. Brownrigg, the 'Prentice-cide, was confined previous to her Execution.*

FOR one long term, or e'er her trial came,
Here BROWNRIGG linger'd. Often have these cells
Echoed her blasphemies, as with shrill voice
She screamed for fresh Geneva. Not to her
Did the blithe fields of Tothill, or thy street,

[* By SOUTHEY.—ED.]

St. Giles, its fair varieties expand ;
Till at the last, in slow-drawn cart she went
To execution.   Dost thou ask her crime?
SHE WHIPP'D TWO FEMALE 'PRENTICES TO DEATH,
AND HID THEM IN THE COAL-HOLE.   For her mind
Shaped strictest plans of discipline.   Sage schemes!
Such as Lycurgus taught, when at the shrine
Of the Orthyan goddess he bade flog
The little Spartans ; such as erst chastised
Our Milton when at college.   For this act
Did Brownrigg swing.   Harsh laws!   But time shall
    come
When France shall reign, and laws be all repeal'd !

[Mrs. Elizabeth Brownrigg was executed at Tyburn on Monday, 14th Sept.,
1767, for murdering one of her apprentices, Mary Clifford.—ED.]

[HENRY MARTEN was one of the most interesting and remarkable of the
Regicides, not only from his abilities and consistent honesty, but from the
elegance of his manners, his wit, and the fascinating gaiety of his conversation ;
and, moreover, from his humane disposition and generosity to fallen foes.
His private life, however, was disgraced by the most reckless debauchery,
which might seem more appropriate in such libertines as Rochester and Sedley
than in a coadjutor of the strict Puritan party.   But from a note in Grey's
edition of *Hudibras*, pt. ii., ch. i., p. 313, it would appear that the general
opinion at that time was that profligacy of a pronounced character was indulged
in privately by more than a few of that sanctimonious sect.
    He was the son of Sir Henry Marten, LL.D., a loyal Judge of the
Admiralty.   After receiving a learned education at Oxford, he entered one of
the Inns of Court, and travelled in France.   Having a stake in Berkshire—for he
inherited a property of £3000 a year, besides several thousand pounds in money—
he was elected, 1640, one of the members for the county in the last two Parliaments of King Charles I.   His chief seat was at Becket, in the parish of Shriven-
ham.   He afterwards obtained a grant of £1000 a year to him and his heirs out
of the forfeited estates of the Duke of Buckingham.   His early marriage with a
rich widow, selected by his father, but not affected by himself, also benefited
his finances.
    From the commencement of the Civil Wars he was a violent Republican ;
and as early as 1643 openly expressed his opinion of the desirability of the
destruction of the King and his children, for which rather premature advice
he was expelled the House of Commons, and underwent a short imprisonment
in the Tower.   He was appointed by the House of Commons a Colonel of
Horse and Governor of Reading, but made less mark as a soldier than as a
rapacious spoiler of the adherents of the King, which earned him the opprobrious nickname of " Plunder-master General ".
    Being empowered to dispose of the Regalia and royal trappings, he once
invested GEORGE WITHER—who had been made one of Cromwell's Major-
Generals—with them, and so accoutred induced the old Poet to strut up and
down Westminster Abbey to the scandal of right-thinking people.

To him also were referred the alterations in the public arms, the Great
Seal, and the legends upon the money.  Upon the latter was a shield bearing
the cross of St. George, encircled by a palm and olive branch, and inscribed
*The Commonwealth of England*, and on the reverse, *God with us, 1648;* which
occasioned the remark "that God and the Commonwealth were not on the
same side".

Nothing apparently could damp the ill-timed jocosity too often prevalent in
those troublous times, for at MARTEN'S trial, 16th October, 1660, Ewer, who
had been his servant. swore that "at the signing of the warrant for the
King's execution he did see a pen in Mr. CROMWELL'S hand, and he marked
Mr. MARTEN in the face with it, and Mr. MARTEN did the like to him".  But
many of his excesses were condoned in the eyes of both his friends and enemies
by his generous and humane spirit.

D'ISRAELI, in his *Commentaries on the Life and Reign of Charles I.*, describes
the ingenious way in which MARTEN saved the life of DAVID JENKINS, a loyal
and obstinate Welsh judge, who, when brought to the bar of the House of
Commons to answer for imprisoning several persons for bearing arms against
the King, peremptorily disowned their jurisdiction, and defied them in the
following bold terms : "'But, Mr. Speaker, since you and this House have
renounced your allegiance to your Sovereign, and are become a den of thieves,
should I bow myself in this House of Rimmon the Lord would not pardon me'.
The whole House were electrified. . . . He was voted guilty of high treason
without any trial.  The day of execution was then debated.  HARRY MARTEN,
who had not yet spoken, rose, not to dissent from the vote of the House, he
observed, but he had something to say about the time of the execution.
'Mr. Speaker,' said he, 'everyone must believe that this old gentleman here
is fully possessed in his head resolved to die a martyr in his cause, for otherwise he would never have provoked the House by such biting expressions.  If
you execute him, you do precisely that which he hopes for, and his execution
will have a great influence over the people, since he is condemned without a
jury.  I therefore move that we should suspend the day of execution, and in
meantime force him to live in spite of his teeth.'  The drollery of the motion
put the House into better humour, and he was reprieved.  After being kept in
various prisons for eleven years, he was released by Cromwell, and died in 1663,
aged eighty-one."

Another instance may be given of MARTEN'S felicitous humour and humane
temper.  When the Commons had rid themselves of the Sovereign, *they voted
the Lords to be dangerous and useless.*  But MARTEN proposed an amendment in
their favour ; namely, that *they were useless, but not dangerous.*

His speeches in the House were represented to have been not long, "but
wondrous poynant, pertinent, and witty.  He was exceedingly apt in apt
instances ; he alone hath sometimes turned the whole House."

He wrote several tracts on parliamentary subjects, and *Verses on the Death
of his Nephew, Charles Edmonds, 7th July, 1661, æt. 30.*  But the most amusing of
the publications bearing his name is one entitled *Familiar Letters to his Lady of
Delight ; also her kinde Returnes : with his Rivall R. Pettingall's Heroicall Epistles.*
Printed by Edmundus de Speciosâ Villâ [*i.e.*, EDMUND GAYTON].  *Bellositi
Dobunorum* [Oxford], 1662 and 1663, 4to.  Another edition, with additions, appeared
in 1685.  "These epistles," says D'Israeli, "paint to the life the loose habits
and *espiègleries* of this witty profligate ; and I think they have been referred to
by some inconsiderate writers as a *genuine* correspondence."  They were probably altogether concocted by GAYTON.  He was severely attacked in various
scurrilous lampoons, some of which are printed among the *Rump Songs*, 1662.

On his trial he was found guilty and sentenced to death ; but the good
feeling created among many who had in his prosperous days enjoyed his
society and hospitality, and even among many of his former opponents by his
generous treatment of them when in danger, stood him in good stead, and it
was by a well-timed and humorous appeal to the Judges—such as he himself
might have used—that his life was saved.  Henry, fourth Viscount FALKLAND,
whose virtuous and heroic father fell at the first Battle of Newbury while
fighting for the King, said to the Judges : "Gentlemen, ye talk here of making
a *sacrifice :* it was old law that all sacrifices were to be without spot or blemish ;

and now you are going to make an old rotten rascal a sacrifice ". This piece of wit pleased his Judges, and his sentence was commuted to imprisonment for life. He was confined in Chepstow Castle, Monmouthshire, for twenty years, and died in September, 1680, aged seventy-eight.

He must have felt some contrition for his vicious life, for some time before his death he made this epitaph, by way of *acrostic*, on himself :

H ere, or elsewhere (all's one to you, to me),
E arth, air, or water gripes my ghostly dust,
N one knowing when brave fire shall set it free.
R eader, if you an oft tryed rule will trust,
Y ou'll gladly do and suffer what you must.
M y life was worn with serving you and you,
A nd now death's my pay, it seems, and welcome too.
R evenge destroying but itself, while I
T o birds of prey leave my old cage, and fly.
E xamples preach to the eye, care (then mine says)
N ot how you end, but how you spend your days.

" In Cromwell's time CHEPSTOW CASTLE served as a place of imprisonment for Jeremy Taylor ; and, after the Restoration, it received a less illustrious occupant in the person of HARRY MARTEN, the Regicide, whose imprisonment here has attracted more than its share of notice in consequence of the foolish lines written by SOUTHEY in his days of republicanism and pantisocracy, but which are as untrue in *fact* as they are mischievous in *sentiment*. As to the *fact*, it is notorious that MARTEN—at all events after the first few years of his imprisonment—was little more than a prisoner on parole ; allowed to visit the neighbouring gentry, and occupying at Chepstow Castle, with his family and servants, spacious and comfortable apartments in the tower which still bears his name. As to the *sentiment*, the lines received their best antidote in the clever parody of Canning and Frere in *The Anti-Jacobin."—Annals of Chepstow Castle*, by J. F. Marsh, 1883 ; 4to.

# No. II.

Nov. 27, 1797.

IN the specimen of JACOBIN POETRY which we gave in our last number was developed a principle, perhaps one of the most universally recognised in the Jacobin creed; namely, "that the animadversion of *human law* upon *human actions* is for the most part nothing but *gross oppression;* and that, in all cases of the administration of *criminal justice,* the truly benevolent mind will consider only the *severity of the punishment,* without any reference to the *malignity of the crime*". This principle has of late years been laboured with extraordinary industry, and brought forward in a variety of shapes, for the edification of the public. It has been inculcated in bulky quartos, and illustrated in popular novels. It remained only to fit it with a poetical dress, which had been attempted in the INSCRIPTION for CHEPSTOW CASTLE, and which (we flatter ourselves) was accomplished in that for MRS. BROWNRIGG'S CELL.

Another principle, no less devoutly entertained, and no less sedulously disseminated, is the *natural and eternal warfare of the* POOR *and the* RICH. In those orders and gradations of society, which are the natural result of the original difference of talents and of industry among mankind, the Jacobin sees nothing but a graduated scale of violence and cruelty. He considers every rich man as an oppressor, and every person in a lower situation as the victim of avarice, and the slave of aristocratical insolence and contempt. These truths he declares

loudly, not to excite compassion, or to soften the consciousness of superiority in the higher, but for the purpose of aggravating discontent in the inferior orders.

A human being, in the lowest state of penury and distress, is a treasure to the reasoner of this cast. He contemplates, he examines, he turns him in every possible
light, with a view of extracting from the variety of his
wretchedness new topics of invective against the pride of
property. He, indeed (if he is a true Jacobin), refrains
from *relieving* the object of his compassionate contemplation ; as well knowing that every diminution from the
general mass of human misery must proportionably
diminish the force of his argument.

This principle is treated at large by many authors. It
is versified in sonnets and elegies without end. We
trace it particularly in a poem by the same author
[SOUTHEY] from whom we borrowed our former illustration of the Jacobin doctrine of crimes and punishments.
In this poem, the pathos of the matter is not a little
relieved by the absurdity of the metre. We shall not
think it necessary to transcribe the whole of it, as our
imitation does not pretend to be so literal as in the last
instance, but merely aspires to convey some idea of the
manner and sentiment of the original. One stanza, however, we must give, lest we should be suspected of painting from fancy, and not from life.

The learned reader will perceive that the metre is
SAPPHIC, and affords a fine opportunity for his *scanning*
and *proving*, if he has not forgotten them.


Cōld wăs thē nīght wīnd; drĭftĭng fāst thĕ snōws fĕll ;
Wīde wĕre thē dōwns, ānd shĕltĕrlĕss ănd nākĕd :

Whĕn ă poōr wānd'rēr strŭgglĕd ōn hĕr joūrnĕy,
  Wēāry ănd wāy-sōre.*

---

[* The original poem, by Southey, is here subjoined :—

## THE WIDOW.

### SAPPHICS.

Cold was the night wind; drifting fast the snows fell;
Wide were the downs, and shelterless and naked;
When a poor wand'rer struggled on her journey,
    Weary and way-sore.

Drear were the downs, more dreary her reflections ;
Cold was the night wind, colder was her bosom :
She had no home, the world was all before her,
    She had no shelter.

Fast o'er the heath a chariot rattled by her :
" Pity me ! " feebly cried the poor night wanderer.
" Pity me, strangers ! lest with cold and hunger
    Here I should perish.

"Once I had friends—but they have all forsook me !
Once I had parents—they are now in heaven !
I had a home once—I had once a husband—
    Pity me, strangers !

"I had a home once—I had once a husband—
I am a widow, poor and broken-hearted ! "
Loud blew the wind, unheard was her complaining ;
    On drove the chariot.

Then on the snow she laid her down to rest her ;
She heard a horseman : " Pity me ! " she groaned out.
Loud was the wind, unheard was her complaining ;
    On went the horseman.

Worn out with anguish, toil, and cold and hunger,
Down sunk the wanderer ; sleep had seized her senses :
There did the traveller find her in the morning—
    God had released her.]
1796.

of HUMANITY and the KNIFE-GRINDER, — Scene.The Borough.
n Imitation of Mr Southey's Sapphics. — Vide Anti-Jacobin. p. 15.

der! whither are you going?
d. your Wheel is out of order.
last; — your Hat has got a hole in't,
   So have your Breeches!
nder! little think the proud ones,
oaches roll along the turnpike —
t work 'tis crying all day 'Knives and
   Scissars to grind O!'
grinder, how came you to grind knives?
om tyrannically use you?
uire? or Parson of the Parish?
   Or the Attorney?
uire for killing of his Game? or
on for his Tythes distraining?
zeyer made you lose your little
   All in a law-suit?
read the Rights of Man, by Tom Paine?
astrom tremble on my eye-lids,
as soon as you have told your
   Pitiful story"

Knife-grinder.. "Story!. God bless you! I have none to tell , Sir,
   Only last night a-drinking at the Chequers,
   This poor old Hat and Breeches, as you see, were
     Torn in a scuffle.
"Constables came up for to take me into
   Custody; they took me before the Justice;
   Justice Oldmixon put me in the Parish —
     -Stocks for a Vagrant,
'I should be glad to drink your Honour's health in
   A Pot of Beer if you would give me Sixpence;
   But for my part, I never love to meddle
     With Politics, Sir."
Friend of Hum? I give thee Sixpence! I will see thee damn'd first.
   Wretch! whom no sense of wrongs can rouse to ven
   Sordid unfeeling, reprobate, degraded,
     Spiritless outcast!
(Kicks the Knife-grinder, overturns his Wheel, and exit in
  a transport of republican enthusiasm and universal
- - - - - - - - - - - - - philanthropy.)

This is enough; unless the reader should wish to be informed how
Făst o'ĕr thē blēak hēăth răttlĭng drōve ă chārĭŏt;
Or how, not long after,
Loūd blĕw thē wīnd, ūnhēărd wăs hēr cŏmplāinĭng—
Ōn wĕnt thĕ hōrsemān.
We proceed to give our IMITATION, which is of the *Amœbœan* or *Collocutory* kind.

## SAPPHICS.

### THE FRIEND OF HUMANITY AND THE KNIFE-GRINDER.

FRIEND OF HUMANITY.*

"NEEDY Knife-grinder! whither are you going?
Rough is the road, your wheel is out of order—
Bleak blows the blast; your hat has got a hole in't,
So have your breeches!

"Weary Knife-grinder! little think the proud ones,
Who in their coaches roll along the turnpike-
-road, what hard work 'tis crying all day "Knives and
Scissars to grind O!"

"Tell me, Knife-grinder, how you came to grind knives?
Did some rich man tyrannically use you?

---

[*GEORGE TIERNEY, M.P. for Southwark, who in early times was among the more forward of the Reformers. "He was," says Lord Brougham, "an assiduous member of the *Society of Friends of the People*, and drew up the much and justly celebrated Petition in which that useful body laid before the House of Commons all the more striking particulars of its defective title to the office of representing the people, which that House then, as now, but with far less reason, assumed." Notwithstanding the above severe verses, Tierney served under Canning as Master of the Mint, during the latter's short administration in 1827.—ED.]

Was it the squire? or parson of the parish?
　　　　　　　Or the attorney?
" Was it the squire, for killing of his game? or
Covetous parson, for his tithes distraining?
Or roguish lawyer, made you lose your little
　　　　　　　All in a lawsuit?
" (Have you not read the Rights of Man, by Tom Paine?)
Drops of compassion tremble on my eyelids,
Ready to fall, as soon as you have told your
　　　　　　　Pitiful story."

KNIFE-GRINDER.

" Story! God bless you! I have none to tell, sir,
Only last night a-drinking at the Chequers,
This poor old hat and breeches, as you see, were
　　　　　　　Torn in a scuffle.

" Constables came up for to take me into
Custody; they took me before the justice;
Justice Oldmixon put me in the parish-
　　　　　　　-Stocks for a vagrant.

" I should be glad to drink your Honour's health in
A pot of beer, if you will give me sixpence;
But for my part, I never love to meddle
　　　　　　　With politics, sir."

FRIEND OF HUMANITY.

" *I* give thee sixpence! I will see thee damned first—
Wretch! whom no sense of wrongs can rouse to ven-
　　geance—
Sordid, unfeeling, reprobate, degraded,
　　　　　　　Spiritless outcast!"
[*Kicks the Knife-grinder, overturns his wheel, and exit in a transport
of Republican enthusiasm and universal philanthropy.*]

# No. III.

Nov. 30, 1797.

WE have received the following from a loyal correspondent, and we shall be very happy at any time to be
relieved, by communications of a similar tendency, from
the drudgery of Jacobinical imitations.

## THE INVASION; *

OR, THE BRITISH WAR SONG.

*To the Tune of* " Whilst happy in my native land ".

I.

WHILST happy in our native land,
   So great, so famed in story,
Let's join, my friends, with heart and hand
   To raise our country's glory :
When Britain calls, her valiant sons
   Will rush in crowds to aid her—
Snatch, snatch your muskets, prime your guns,
   And crush the fierce invader !
      Whilst every Briton's song shall be,
      " O give us Death—or Victory ! "

[* In Feb., 1797, about 1400 Frenchmen landed at Pembroke,
but surrendered without resistance to the country people, whom
Lord CAWDOR (who had been elevated to the Peerage in the
preceding year) had armed with scythes and pitchforks. He
was succeeded by his elder son, who was created Earl Cawdor
in 1827, and died 1860.—ED.]

II.

Long had this favour'd isle enjoy'd
  True comforts, past expressing,
When *France* her hellish arts employ'd
  To rob us of each blessing :
These from our hearths by force to tear
  (Which long we've learned to cherish)
Our frantic foes shall vainly dare ;
  We'll keep 'em or we'll perish—
    And every day our song shall be,
    "O give us Death—or Victory ! "

III.

Let France in savage accents sing
  Her bloody Revolution ;
We prize our country, love our king,
  Adore our constitution ;
For these we'll every danger face,
  And quit our rustic labours ;
Our ploughs to firelocks shall give place ;
  Our scythes be changed to sabres ;
    And clad in arms, our song shall be,
    " O give us Death—or Victory ! "

IV.

Soon shall the proud invaders learn,
  When bent on blood and plunder,
That British bosoms nobly burn
  To brave their cannon's thunder :
Low lie those heads, whose wily arts
  Have plann'd the world's undoing !

Our vengeful blades shall reach those hearts
Which seek our country's ruin;
And night and morn our song shall be,
" O give us Death—or Victory!"

v.

When, with French blood our fields manured,
The glorious struggle's ended,
We'll sing the dangers we've endured,
The blessings we've defended:
O'er the full bowl our feats we'll tell,
Each gallant deed reciting;
And weep o'er those who nobly fell
Their country's battle fighting—
And ever thence our song shall be,
" 'Tis VALOUR leads to VICTORY".

---

[The following Song which furnished the hints for the one
above was written by MILES PETER ANDREWS, M.P. for
Bewdley, and a dealer in gunpowder; but his Plays, Prologues,
Verses, &c., by no means resemble so active a composition.
He, with other members of the " Della Crusca," was savagely
attacked and extinguished by W. Gifford in " The Baviad".
His song was set to music by Sir HENRY BISHOP. He died in
1814.

I.

Whilst happy in my native land
I boast my country's charter,
I'll never basely lend my hand
Her liberties to barter.
The noble mind is not at all
By poverty degraded;
'Tis guilt alone can make us fall,
And well am I persuaded,
Each free-born Briton's song should be,
"Oh! give me Death or Liberty!"

## II.

Though small the pow'r which Fortune grants,
  And few the gifts she sends us,
The lordly hireling often wants
  That freedom which defends us.
By law secur'd from lawless strife,
  Our house is our *castellum ;*
Thus, blessed with all that's dear in life,
  For lucre shall we sell 'em ?
    No,—ev'ry Briton's song should be,
    "Oh! give me Death or Liberty!"

                                    ED.]

# No. IV.

Dec. 4, 1797.

WE have been favoured with the following specimen of Jacobin Poetry, which we give to the world without any comment or imitation. We are informed (we know not how truly) that it will be sung at the meeting of the Friends of Freedom; an account of which is anticipated in our present paper.*

## LA SAINTE GUILLOTINE.

A New Song.

ATTEMPTED FROM THE FRENCH.

*Tune*—"O'er the vine-covered hills and gay regions of France".

I.

FROM the blood-bedew'd valleys and mountains of France,
See the Genius of Gallic INVASION advance!
Old ocean shall waft her, unruffled by storm,
While our shores are all lined with the "*Friends of Re-form*".†
Confiscation and Murder attend in her train,
With meek-eyed Sedition, the daughter of PAINE; ‡
While her sportive *Poissardes* with light footsteps are seen
To dance in a ring round the gay *Guillotine*. §

---

[* This account will be found on p. 32, *et seq.*—ED.]
† See proclamation of the Directory.
‡ The "*too long calumniated* author of the *Rights of Man*". — See a Sir Something Burdett's speech at the Shakspeare, as referred to in the *Courier* of Nov. 30.
§ The Guillotine at Arras was, as is well known to every Jacobin, painted "*Couleur de Rose*".

II.

To *London*, "the rich, the defenceless"* she comes—
Hark! my boys, to the sound of the Jacobin drums!
See Corruption, Prescription, and Privilege fly,
Pierced through by the glance of her blood-darting eye.
While patriots, from prison and prejudice freed,
In soft accents shall lisp the Republican creed,
And with tri-colour'd fillets, and cravats of green,
Shall crowd round the altar of *Saint Guillotine*.

III.

See the level of Freedom sweeps over the land—
The vile Aristocracy's doom is at hand!
Not a seat shall be left in a House *that we know*,
But for *Earl* BUONAPARTE and *Baron* MOREAU.
But the rights of the Commons shall still be respected,
Buonaparte himself shall approve the elected;
And the Speaker shall march with majestical mien,
And make his three bows to the grave *Guillotine*.

IV.

Two heads, says the proverb, are better than one,
But the Jacobin choice is for Five Heads or none.
By Directories only can Liberty thrive;
Then down with the ONE, Boys! and up with the FIVE!
How our bishops and judges will stare with amazement,
When their heads are thrust out at the *National Casement!*†
When the *National Razor* † has shaved them quite clean,
What a handsome oblation to *Saint Guillotine!*

---

* See *Weekly Examiner*, No. 11.   Extract from the *Courier*.
† *La petite Fenétre*, and *la Razoire Nationale*, fondling expressions applied to the Guillotine by the Jacobins in France, and
their pupils here.

[The following *Lines* were written by an ardent reformer, W. Roscoe, the accomplished author of the "Life of Leo X.," and other works, to commemorate the taking of the Bastille (14th July, 1789), and the publication by the National Assembly (on 20th August following) of the famous "Declaration of Rights"— a manifesto which became the creed of the Revolution, and which promulgated, as the basis of social government, the specious but impracticable doctrines of *liberty, equality*, and *the sovereignty of the people* exercised by universal suffrage. How the hopes and anticipations of moderate reformers, as embodied in these lines, were falsified by the spoliations and massacres which rapidly followed are but too well known.

When, therefore, the *Anti-Jacobin* was established to combat the principles of the Revolution, these *Lines* were, for party purposes, maliciously referred to, and significantly recommended to be "recited on the anniversary of the 14th August". To make this allusion more clear, it must be remembered that on the 10th August, 1792, after frightful massacres, the Hotel de Ville was seized and the Tuileries stormed. On the 13th the king and family were imprisoned in the Temple. His deposition, the dismissal of the Ministers, and the formation of a National Convention, on more popular principles than the Legislative Assembly, were decreed by the victors. On the 14th Le Brun became Minister for Foreign Affairs, Danton for Justice, and Monge for Marine ; while the Girondist Ministers, Roland, Servan, and Clavière, resumed their former functions as Ministers of the Interior, War, and Finance respectively.

The Song, *La Sainte Guillotine*, was evidently written as a *Contrast*, and not as a *Parody*—a few lines at the beginning only excepted, which serve as an introduction to verses on another promised phase of the Revolution, the invasion of England.—ED.]

# LINES.

Written for the purpose of being recited on the Anniversary of the 14th of August. BY WILLIAM ROSCOE, Esq.

O'er the vine-covered hills and gay regions of France,
See the day-star of liberty rise ;
Through the clouds of detraction unsullied advance,
And hold its new course through the skies !
An effulgence so mild, with a lustre so bright,
All Europe with wonder surveys ;
And, from deserts of darkness and dungeons of night,
Contends for a share of the blaze.

Ah ! who 'midst the horrors of night would abide,
That can breathe the pure breezes of morn ?
Or who, that has drunk the pure crystalline tide,
To the feculent flood would return ?
When the bosom of Beauty the throbbing heart meets,
Ah, who can the transport decline ?
Or who, that has tasted of Liberty's sweets,
The prize but with life would resign ?

Let Burke like a bat from its splendour retire,
A splendour too strong for his eyes ;
Let pedants and fools his effusions admire,
Entrapt in his cobwebs like flies.
Shall insolent Sophistry hope to prevail
Where Reason opposes her weight,
When the welfare of millions is hung in the scale,
And the balance yet trembles with fate ?

But 'tis over—high Heaven the decision approves,
Oppression has struggled in vain,
To the hell she has form'd Superstition removes,
And Tyranny bites his own chain.
In the records of Time a new era unfolds,
All nature exults in its birth ;
His creation benign the Creator beholds,
And gives a new charter to earth.

Oh ! catch the high import, ye winds, as ye blow ;
Oh ! hear it, ye waves, as ye roll,
From regions that feel the sun's vertical glow,
To the farthest extremes of the Pole.
*Equal rights, equal laws,* to the nations around,
Peace and friendship its precepts impart,
And wherever the footsteps of man shall be found,
He shall bind the decree on his heart.

---

[The Account of what was "anticipated to take place at the *Meeting of the Friends of Freedom*—alluded to on page 29—duly appeared in *The Anti-Jacobin*, but has never hitherto formed a part of the collection of its *Poetry*. As it is marked by much ability, and has been often quoted, it appears to the editor desirable to introduce some portion of it into the present edition of the *Poetry*.

MEETING OF THE FRIENDS OF FREEDOM.

The *House of Russell* being given, LORD JOHN and LORD WILLIAM both rose at once.

LORD JOHN made a very neat, and LORD WLLIIAM a very appropriate speech.

ALDERMAN COOMBE made a very impressive speech.

MR. TIERNEY made a very pointed speech.

MR. GREY made a very fine speech. He described the ministers as "bold bad men"—their measures he repeatedly declared to be not only "weak, but wicked".

MR. BYNG said a few words.

GENERAL TARLETON and the *Electors of Liverpool* being given, the General, after an eulogium on Mr. Fox, begged to anticipate their favourite concluding toast, and to give "*The Cause of Freedom all over the World*". This toast unfortunately gave rise to an altercation which threatened to disturb the harmony of the evening. Olaudah Equiano, the African, and Henry Yorke, the mulatto, insisted upon being heard ; but as it appeared that they were entering upon a subject which would have entirely altered the complexion of the Meeting, they were, though not without some difficulty, withheld from proceeding further.

MR. ERSKINE rose, in consequence of some allusions which had been made to Trial by Jury. He professed himself to be highly flattered by the encomiums which had been lavished upon him ; at the same time he was conscious that he could not, without some degree of reserve, consent to arrogate to himself those qualities which the partiality of his friends had attributed to him. He had, on former occasions, declared himself to be clothed with the infirmities of man's nature ; and he now begged leave in all humility to reiterate that confession ; he should never cease to consider himself as a feeble, and with respect to the extent of his faculties in many respects, a finite being—he had ever borne in mind, and he hoped he should ever continue to bear in mind, those words of the inspired Penman, "Thou hast made him less than the angels, to crown him with glory and honour". These lines were indeed applicable to the state of man in general, but of no man more than himself ; they appeared to him pointed and personal, and little less than prophetic ; they were always present to his mind ; he could wish to wear them in his breast as a sort of amulet against the enchantment of public applause, and the witcheries of vanity and self-delusion ; yet if he were indeed possessed of those super-human powers—all pretensions to which he again begged leave most earnestly to disclaim—if he were endowed with the eloquence of an angel, and with all those other faculties which we attribute to angelic natures, it would be impossible for him to do justice to the eloquence with which the Honourable Gentleman who opened the meeting had defended the Cause of Freedom, identified as he conceived it to be with the persons and government of the DIRECTORY. In his present terrestrial state he could only address it as a prayer to God and as counsel to Man that the words which they had heard from that Honourable Gentleman might work inwardly in their hearts, and in due time, produce the fruit of Liberty and Revolution.

He had not the advantage of being personally acquainted with any of the Gentlemen of the DIRECTORY ; he understood, however, that one of them (MR. MERLIN) previous to the last change, had stood in a situation similar to his own —he was, in fact, nothing less than a leading Advocate and Barrister in the midst of a free, powerful and enlightened people.

The conduct of the DIRECTORY with regard to the exiled Deputies had been objected to by some persons on the score of a pretended rigour. For his part he should only say that having been, as he had been, both a Soldier and a Sailor, if it had been his fortune to have stood in either of those two relations to the DIRECTORY—as a Man and as a Major-General he should not have scrupled to direct his artillery against the National Representation :—as a Naval Officer he would undoubtedly have undertaken for the removal of the Exiled Deputies ; admitting the exigency,under all its relations, as it appeared to him to exist, and the then circumstances of the times, with all their bearings and dependencies, branching out into an infinity of collateral considerations, and involving in each a variety of objects political, physical, and moral ; and these again under their distinct and separate heads, ramifying into endless subdivisions which it was foreign to his purpose to consider.

Having thus disposed of this part of his subject, MR. ERSKINE passed in a strain of rapid and brilliant allusions over a variety of points characteristic of the conduct and disposition of the present Ministry ; Mr. Burke's metaphor of "the Swinish Multitude," Mr. Reeves' metaphor of the "Tree of Monarchy," "the Battle of Tranent," "the March to Paris," the phrase of "Acquitted Felons," and the exclamation of "Perish Commerce"—which last expression he declared he should never cease to attribute to Mr. Windham ; so long, at least, as it should please the Sovereign Dispenser to continue to him the power of utterance and the enjoyment of his present faculties. He condemned the expedition to Quiberon, he regretted the "Fate of Messrs. Muir and Palmer," he exulted in the "Acquittal of Citizens Tooke, Hardy, Thelwall, Holcroft and others," and he blessed that Providence to which (as it had been originally allotted to him (Mr. Erskine) the talents which had been exerted in their defence) the preservation of those Citizens might perhaps be indirectly attributed. He then descanted on the captivity of La Fayette, and the Dividend on the Imperial Loan.

After fully exhausting these subjects, MR. ERSKINE resumed a topic on which he had only slightly glanced before. In a most delicate and sportive vein of humour he contended, that if the people were a Swinish Multitude, those who represented them must necessarily be a Swinish Representation. It would be in vain to attempt to do justice to the polite and easy pleasantry which pervaded this part of MR. ERSKINE'S speech. Suffice it to say that the taste of the Audience showed itself in complete unison with the genius of the Orator, and the whole of this passage was crowned with loud and reiterated plaudits. After a speech of unexampled exertion, MR. ERSKINE now began to enter much at length into a recital of select passages from our most approved English authors, concluding with a copious extract from the several Publications of the late MR. BURKE; but such were the variety and richness of his quotations which he continued to an extent far exceeding the limits of this paper, that we found ourselves under the necessity, either of considerably abridging our original matter, or omitting them altogether, which latter alternative we adopted the more readily as the greater part of these brilliant citations have already past through the ordeal of a public and patriotic auditory; and as there is every probability that the circumstances of the times will again call them forth on some future emergency.

MR. ERSKINE concluded by recapitulating, in a strain of agonizing and impressive'eloquence, the several more prominent heads of his speech:—He had been a Soldier and a Sailor, and had a son at Winchester school—he had been called by Special Retainers, during the summer, into many different and distant parts of the country—travelling chiefly in Post-chaises—He felt himself called upon to declare that his poor faculties were at the service of his Country—of the free and enlightened part of it at least—He stood here as a Man—He stood in the Eye, indeed in the Hand of GOD—to whom (in the presence of the Company and Waiters) he solemnly appealed—He was of Noble, perhaps, Royal Blood —He had a house at Hampstead—was convinced of the necessity of a thorough and radical Reform—His Pamphlet had gone through Thirty Editions—skipping alternately the odd and even numbers—He loved the Constitution, to which he would cling and grapple—And he was clothed with the infirmities of man's nature—He would apply to the present French Rulers (particularly BARRAS and REUBEL) the words of the poet:—

" Be to their Faults a little blind;
" Be to their Virtues very kind,
" Let all their ways be unconfin'd,
" And clap the Padlock on their mind!"

And for these reasons, thanking the Gentlemen who had done him the honour to drink his Health, he should propose " MERLIN, *the late Minister of Justice, and Trial by Jury!*" MR. ERSKINE here concluded a speech which had occupied the attention and excited the applause of his Audience during a space of little less than three hours, allowing for about three quarters of an hour, which were occupied by successive fits of fainting, between the principal subdivisions of his discourse.—MR. ERSKINE descended from the Table, and was conveyed down stairs by the assistance of his friends. On arriving at the corner of the Piazzas, they were surprized by a very unexpected embarrassment. MR. ERSKINE'S horses had been taken from the carriage, and a number of able Chairmen engaged to supply their place; but these fellows having contrived to intoxicate themselves with the money which the Coachman had advanced to them on account, were become so restive and unruly, so exorbitant in their demands (positively refusing to abide by their former engagement) that MR. ERSKINE deemed it unsafe to trust himself in their hands, and determined to wait the return of his own more tractable and less chargeable animals. This unpleasant scene continued for above an hour.

MR. SHERIDAN'S health was now drunk in his absence and received with an appearance of general approbation; —when in the midst of the applause MR. FOX arose, in apparent agitation, and directed the attention of the Company to the rising, manly virtues of MR. MACFUNGUS.

MR. MACFUNGUS declared that to pretend he was not elated by the encomiums with which MR. FOX had honoured him was an affectation which he disdained ;—such encomiums would ever form the proudest recompense of his patriotic labours—he confessed they were cheering to him—he felt them warm at his heart—and while a single fibre of his frame preserved its vibration, it would throb in unison to the approbation of that Honourable Gentleman. The applause of the Company was no less flattering to him—he felt his faculties invigorated by it, and stimulated to the exertion of new energies in the race of mind. Every other sensation was obliterated and absorbed by it ; for the present, however, he would endeavour to suppress his feelings, and concentre his energies for the purpose of explaining to the Company why he assisted now for the first time at the celebration of the Fifth Revolution which had been effected in regenerated France. The various and extraordinary talents of the Right Hon. Gentleman —his vehement and overpowering perception, his vigorous and splendid intuition would for ever attract the admiration of all those who were in any degree endowed with those faculties themselves or capable of estimating them in others ; as such, he had ever been among the most ardent admirers, and on many occasions, among the most ardent supporters of the Right Hon. Gentleman—he agreed with him in many points—in his general love of Liberty and Revolution ; in his execration of the War ; in his detestation of Ministers ; but he entertained his doubts, and till those doubts were cleared up, he could not, consistently with his principles, attend at the celebration of any Revolution whatever.

These doubts, however, were now satisfactorily done away. A pledge had been entered into for accomplishing an effectual radical Revolution ; not for the mere overthrow of the present System, nor for the establishment of any other in its place ; but for the effecting such a series of Revolutions as might be sufficient for the establishment of a Free System.

MR. MACFUNGUS continued he was incapable of compromising with first principles, of acquiescing in short-sighted temporary palliative expedients : if such had been his temper he should assuredly have rested satisfied with the pledge which that Right Hon. Gentleman had entered into about six months ago on the subject of Parliamentary Reform, in which pledge he considered the promise of that previous and preliminary Revolution, to which he had before alluded, as essentially implicated.

" Whenever this Reform takes place," exclaimed MR. MACFUNGUS, " the present degraded and degrading system must fall into dissolution ; it must sink and perish with the corruptions which have supported it. The national energies will awake, and shaking off their lethargy as their fetters drop from them, they will follow the Angel of their Revolution, while the Genius of Freedom soaring aloft beneath the orb of Gallic Illumination will brush away as with the wing of an Eagle all the cobwebs of Aristocracy. But before the Temple of Freedom can be erected in their place, the surface which they have occupied must be smoothed and levelled—it must be cleared by repeated Revolutionary Explosions from all the lumber and rubbish with which Aristocracy and Fanaticism will endeavour to encumber it, and to impede the progress of the holy work.—The sacred level, the symbol of Fraternal Equality, must be passed over the whole.—The completion of the Edifice will indeed be the more tardy, but it will not be the less durable for having been longer delayed—Cemented with the blood of tyrants, and the tears of the Aristocracy, it will rise a monument for the astonishment and veneration of future ages. The remotest posterity, with our children yet unborn, and the most distant portions of the Globe, will crowd around its Gates and demand admission into its Sanctuary.—The Tree of Liberty will be planted in the midst of it, and its branches will extend to the ends of the Earth, while the Friends of Freedom meet and fraternize and amalgamate under its consolatory shade. There our Infants shall be taught to lisp in tender accents the Revolutionary Hymn— there with wreaths of myrtle, and oak, and poplar, and vine and olive and cypress and ivy ; with violets and roses and daffodils and dandelions in our hands we will swear respect to childhood and manhood and old age, and virginity and womanhood and widowhood ; but above all to the Supreme Being. —There we will decree and sanction the Immortality of the Soul.—There pillars and obelisks, and arches and pyramids, will awaken the love of Glory and of our Country.—There Painters and Statuaries, with their chisels and colours, and Engravers with their engraving tools will perpetuate the interesting features of our Revolutionary Heroes ; while our Poets and Musicians, with an honourable emulation, strive to immortalize their memory. Their bones will be entombed in the Vault below, while their sacred Shades continue hovering over our Heads—those venerated Manes which from time to time will require to be appeased by the blood of the remaining Aristocrats.—Then Peace and Freedom, and Fraternity and Equality will pervade the whole Earth—while the Vows of Republicanism, the Altar of Patriotism, and the Revolutionary Pontiff, with the thrilling volcanic Sympathies, whether of Holy Fury or of ardent Fraternal Civism, uniting and identifying, produce as it were an electric Energy."

MR. MACFUNGUS here paused for a few moments, seemingly overpowered by the excess of Sensibility, and the force of the ideas which he was labouring to convey.—The whole Company appeared to sympathize with his unaffected emotions. After a short interval, he recovered himself from a very impressive silence, and continued as follows:

"These prospects, Fellow-Citizens, may possibly be deferred. The Machiavelism of Governments may for the time prevail, and this unnatural and execrable contest may yet be prolonged; but the hour is not far distant ; Persecution will only serve to accelerate it, and the blood of Patriotism streaming from the severing axe will call down vengeance on our oppressors in a voice of Thunder. I expect the contest, and I am prepared for it.—I hope I shall never shrink nor swerve nor start aside wherever duty and inclination may place me. My services, my life itself, are at your disposal—Whether to act or to suffer, I am yours—With HAMPDEN in the field, or with SIDNEY on the scaffold. My example may be more useful to you than my talents: and this head may perhaps serve your cause more effectually, if placed on a pole on Temple Bar, than if it was occupied in organizing your Committees, in preparing your Revolutionary Explosions, and conducting your Correspondence."

MR. MACFUNGUS said he should give, as an unequivocal test of his sentiments, "BUONAPARTE AND A RADICAL REFORM".

The conclusion of Mr. MACFUNGUS'S speech was followed by a simultaneous burst of rapturous approbation from every part of the room. The applause continued for several minutes, during which MR. MACFUNGUS repeatedly rose to express his feelings.

The conversation now became more mixed and animated ; several excellent Songs were sung, and Toasts drank, while the progressive and patriotic festivity of the evening was heightened by the vocal powers of several of the most popular Singers. A new Song written by Captain MORRIS received its sanction in the warmest expression of applause. The whole company joined with enthusiasm in their old favourite Chorus of Bow ! Wow !! Wow !!!

[MACFUNGUS stands for SIR JAMES MACKINTOSH, who, after studying medicine in Edinburgh, settled in London, and wrote for the opposition newspapers, particularly the *Morning Post*, Daniel Stuart, the proprietor, being his father-in-law. The first work that brought him into notice was his *Vindiciæ Gallicæ* (1791), in reply to Burke's *Reflections* on the French Revolution, which splendid philippic it greatly surpassed in philosophic thought, sound feeling, and common sense. It was enthusiastically received by the Liberal party, whose leaders eagerly sought his acquaintance and co-operation ; and when the *Association of the Friends of the People* was formed, he was appointed Secretary. His subsequent successful career as an Advocate. Indian Judge, Member of Parliament, Minister under Lord Grey, and as an English historian, bore out the promise of his youth. He was born in 1765 and died in 1832.—ED.]

## No. V.

Dec. 11, 1797.

WE have already hinted at the principle by which the followers of the Jacobinical sect are restrained from the exercise of their own favourite virtue of charity. The force of this prohibition, and the strictness with which it is observed, are strongly exemplified in the following poem. It is the production of the same author [SOUTHEY] whose happy effort in English Sapphics we presumed to imitate ; the present effusion is in Dactylics, and equally subject to the laws of Latin Prosody.

### THE SOLDIER'S WIFE.

Wēarȳ wăy-wāndĕrĕr, lānguĭd ănd sĭck ăt hĕart,
Trāvĕllĭng pāinfŭllȳ ōvĕr thĕ rūggĕd roăd ;
Wĭld vĭsăg'd wāndĕrĕr—āh fŏr thȳ hĕavȳ chănce.

We think that we see him fumbling in the pocket of his blue pantaloons ; that the splendid shilling is about to make its appearance, and to glitter in the eyes, and glad the heart of the poor sufferer. But no such thing —the bard very calmly contemplates her situation, which he describes in a pair of very pathetical stanzas ; and after the following well-imagined topic of consolation, concludes by leaving her to Providence.

Thy husband will never return from the war again ;
Cold is thy hopeless heart, *even as charity* ;
Cold are thy famished babes—*God help thee*, widow'd
    one !

We conceived that it would be necessary to follow up this general rule with the particular exception, and to point out one of those cases in which the embargo upon Jacobin bounty is sometimes suspended ; * with this view we have subjoined the poem of

## THE SOLDIER'S FRIEND.

### DACTYLICS.

COME, little Drummer Boy, lay down your knapsack here :
I am the soldier's friend—here are some books for you ;
Nice clever books by TOM PAINE, the philanthropist.†

---

* [The original poem is here subjoined : —

### THE SOLDIER'S WIFE.

### DACTYLICS.

Weary way-wanderer, languid and sick at heart,
Travelling painfully over the rugged road ;
Wild-visaged wanderer ! Ah ! for thy heavy chance.

Sorely thy little ones drag by thee barefooted,
Cold is the baby that hangs at thy bending back—
Meagre and livid, and screaming its wretchedness.

Woe-begone mother, half anger, half agony,
As over thy shoulder thou lookest to hush the babe,
Bleakly the blinding snow beats in thy haggard face.

Thy husband will never return from the war again ;
Cold is thy hopeless heart, even as charity—
Cold are thy famished babes—God help thee, widowed one !]
1795.

† [" Walked to the Old Bailey to see DAVID ISAAC EATON in the pillory. The mob was decidedly friendly to him. His having published PAINE's *Age of Reason* was not an intelligible offence to them."—*Crabb Robinson's Diary*, i. 386.

The Proclamation against *Seditious Writings*, however, was supported by some influential Whigs. " PITT had previously sent copies of it to several members of the Opposition in both Houses, requesting their advice," says Lord Malmesbury. Whether PITT desired it or not, no measure could have been more effectual for dividing the Whig party.—ED.]

Here's half-a-crown for you—here are some handbills
too—
Go to the barracks, and give all the soldiers some.
Tell them the sailors are all in a mutiny.

> *Exit Drummer Boy, with handbills and half-a-*
> *crown.—Manet Soldier's Friend.*

Liberty's friends thus all learn to amalgamate,
Freedom's volcanic explosion prepares itself,
Despots shall bow to the fasces of liberty.
　Reason, philosophy, " fiddledum diddledum,"
Peace and fraternity, higgledy, piggledy,
Higgledy, piggledy, " fiddledum diddledum ".

> *Et cetera, et cetera, et cetera.*

---

## SONNET.—TO LIBERTY.

Just Guardian of man's social bliss ! for thee
　The paths of danger gladly would I tread :
　For thee ! contented, join the glorious dead,
Who nobly scorn'd a life that was not free !

But worse than death it pains my soul to see
　The Lord of Ruin, by wild Uproar led,
　Hell's first-born, Anarchy, exalt his head,
And seize thy throne, and bid us bow the knee !

What though his iron sceptre, blood-imbrued,
　Crush half the nations with resistless might ;
Never shall this firm spirit be subdued :
　In chains, in exile, still the chanted rite,
O Liberty ! to thee shall be renew'd :
　O still be sea-girt Albion thy delight !　　D.

# No. VI.

Dec. 18, 1797.

WE cannot enough congratulate ourselves on having been so fortunate as to fall upon the curious specimens of classical metre and correct sentiment which we have made the subject of our late Jacobinical imitations.

The fashion of admiring and imitating these productions has spread in a surprising degree. Even those who sympathise with the principles of the writer selected as our model, seem to have been struck with the ridicule of his poetry.

There appeared in the *Morning Chronicle* of Monday a *Sapphic Ode*, apparently written by a friend and associate of our author, in which he is however travestied most unmercifully. And to make the joke the more pointed, the learned and judicious editor contrived to print the ode *en masse*, without any order of lines, or division of stanza ; so that it was not discovered to be *verse* till the next day, when it was explained in a hobbling *erratum*.

We hardly know which to consider as the greater object of compassion in this case—the original *Odist*, thus parodied by his friend, or the mortified *Parodist* thus mutilated by his printer. " *Et tu, Brute !*" has probably been echoed from each of these worthies to his murderer, in a tone that might melt the hardest heart to pity.

We cordially wish them joy of each other, and we resign the modern *Lesbian lyre* into their hands without envy or repining.

Our author's DACTYLICS have produced a second

imitation (conveyed to us from an unknown hand), with which we take our leave of this species of poetry also.

## THE SOLDIER'S WIFE.*
### DACTYLICS.
" Wēarȳ wăy-wāndĕrĕr," &c. &c.

IMITATION.

DACTYLICS.

*Being the quintessence of all the Dactylics that ever were, or ever will be written.*

HUMBLY ADDRESSED TO THE AUTHOR OF THE ABOVE.

WEARISOME Sonnetteer, feeble and querulous,
Painfully dragging out thy demo-cratic lays—
Moon-stricken Sonnetteer, "ah ! for thy heavy chance ! "

Sorely thy Dactylics lag on uneven feet :
Slow is the syllable which thou wouldst urge to speed,
Lame and o'erburthen'd, and " screaming its wretched-
ness ! "

. . . . . . . .†

Ne'er talk of ears again ! look at thy spelling-book ;
*Dilworth* and *Dyche* ‡ are both mad at thy quantities—
DACTYLICS, call'st thou 'em—God help thee, silly one ! "

---

[* See p. 38.—ED.]

† My worthy friend the bellman had promised to supply an additional stanza; but the business of assisting the lamp-lighter, chimney-sweeper, &c., with complimentary verses for their worthy masters and mistresses, pressing on him at this season, he was obliged to decline it.    [A quiz at the third stanza, which was contributed by COLERIDGE.—ED.]

[‡ Thomas Dyche was a clergyman, and kept a school at Stratford-le-Bow.  He was the author of an English dictionary, a spelling-book, a Latin vocabulary, &c.  He died about 1750. Thomas Dilworth, whose educational works were long popular, was for some time his assistant, and then set up a school for himself at Wapping.  He died in 1781.—ED.]

[The following is the *Sapphic Ode* alluded to above, which was intended by the poet of the *Morning Chronicle* as a "retort courteous" to the *Friend of Humanity*. The printer of that paper, unfortunately, being new to "such branches of learning," and not dreaming it could be intended for *poetry*, printed it as below. The mistake seems to have been immediately discovered, for it re-appeared next day (Dec. 12) in the guise of verse.—ED.]

## THE COLLECTOR AND THE HOUSEHOLDER.

*The Hint taken from the Anti-Jacobin, "Needy Knife-Grinders".*

*H.* Greedy Collector, whither are you going, thus with your inkhorn in your button-hole, and ledger so snugly underneath your coat? Say, greedy Collector.

*C.* Much I rejoice that I have met you here, friend: turn back, I pri'thee, 'tis with you I want to speak; I am come on business of importance—gentle Householder.

*H.* Greedy Collector, well I know your business, 'tis for my taxes you are come to dun me; well! 'tis the last time you will have a right to ask me for money. Buggy, no longer do I drive a smart one; smash went my gig, as long [ago] as Easter; down Highgate hill we tumbled al-together, horse, wife, and I, Sir. One broke his knees, and* another broke his collar-bone; there's an end of pleasuring on Sundays. Take my last payment; there is your two pounds twelve shillings and nine-pence.

*C.* Gentle householder, much are you mistaken; Order, Religion,          Constitution, Laws, and rational freedom, all demand from you a—triple assessment.

*H.* Triple Assessment! What beside the old tax?

*C.* Certainly: come, deposit, I'm a waiting.

*H.* Wait      and      be      damned. What is it you are after?

*C.* Ten pounds eleven.

*H.* Ten pounds eleven! have I not informed thee gig I have none? I've sent it to the hammer; Pay for a gig and not [to] have it!

*C.* But you had one at Easter!

*H.* Easter is past and gone. I'll never pay thee.

*C.* Gentle Householder, then I must proceed to shew thee a little bit of parchment, called a writ of distringer [for *distringas*].

[*Exit* Collector to take posses-sion of the Householder's bed and furniture.

[* *and* should have been omitted.—ED.]

The verses which we here present to the public were written immediately after the Revolution of the 4th of September. We should be much obliged to any of our classical and loyal correspondents for an English translation of them.

## LATIN VERSES

*Written immediately after the Revolution of the 4th of September.*

IPSA mali Hortatrix scelerumque uberrima Mater
In se prima suos vertit lymphata furores,
Luctaturque diù secum, et conatibus ægris
Fessa cadit, proprioque jacet labefacta veneno.

Mox tamen ipsius rursúm violentia morbi
Erigit ardentem furiis, ultróque minantem
Spargere bella procul, vastæque incendia cladis,
Civilesque agitare faces, totumque per orbem
Sceptra super Regum et Populorum subdita colla
Ferre pedem, et sanctas Regnorum evertere sedes.

Aspicis! Ipsa sui bacchatur sanguine Regis,
Barbaraque ostentans feralis signa triumphi,
Mole giganteâ campis prorumpit apertis,
Successu scelerum, atque insanis viribus audax.

At quà Pestis atrox rapido se turbine vertit,
Cernis ibi, priscâ morum compage solutâ,
Procubuisse solo civilis fœdera vitæ,
Et quodcunque Fides, quodcunque habet alma verendi
Religio, Pietasque et Legum fræna sacrarum.

Nec spes Pacis adhuc—necdum exsaturata rapinis
Effera Bellatrix, fusove expleta cruore.
Crescit inextinctus Furor, atque exæstuat ingens

Ambitio, immanisque irâ Vindicta renatâ
Reliquias Soliorum et adhuc restantia Regna
Flagitat excidio, prædæque incumbit opimæ.

Una etenim in mediis Gens intemerata ruinis
Libertate probâ, et justo libramine rerum,
Securum faustis degit sub legibus ævum;
Antiquosque colit mores, et jura Parentum
Ordine firma suo, sanoque intacta vigore,
Servat adhuc, hominumque fidem, curamque Deorum.
Eheu! quanta odiis avidoque alimenta furori!
Quanta profanatas inter spoliabitur aras
Victima! si quando versis Victoria fatis
Annuerit scelus extremum, terrâque subactâ
Impius Oceani sceptrum fædaverit Hostis!

# No. VII.

Dec. 25, 1797.

WE have been favoured with a translation of the Latin verses inserted in our last Number. We have little doubt that our readers will agree with us, in hoping that this may not be the last contribution which we shall receive from the same hand.*

PARENT of countless crimes, in headlong rage,
War with herself see frantic *Gallia* wage,
Till worn and wasted by intestine strife,
She falls—her languid pulse scarce quick with life.
But soon she feels through every trembling vein,
New strength collected from convulsive pain :
Onward she moves, and sounds the dire alarm,
And bids insulted nations haste to arm ;
Spreads wide the waste of war, and hurls the brand
Of civil discord o'er each troubled land,
While desolation marks her furious course,
And thrones subverted bow beneath her force.

Behold ! she pours her Monarch's guiltless blood,
And quaffs with savage joy the crimson flood ;
Then, proud the deadly trophies to display

[* The Latin Verses, much admired at the time, were written by the Marquis WELLESLEY at Walmer Castle, in 1797, at the desire of PITT, and were published after the author's departure for India, in the *Anti-Jacobin*. The beautiful translation of them was by Lord MORPETH, afterwards sixth Earl of CARLISLE, whose mother was the daughter of GRANVILLE LEVESON GOWER, first Marquis of STAFFORD. He died in 1848.]

Of her foul crimes, resistless bursts away,
Unaw'd by justice, unappall'd by fear,
And runs with giant strength her mad career.

Where'er her banners float in barbarous pride,
Where'er her conquest rolls its sanguine tide,
There, the fair fabric of establish'd law,
There social order, and religious awe,
Sink in the general wreck; indignant there
Honour and Virtue fly the tainted air;
Fly the mild duties of domestic life
That cheer the parent, that endear the wife,
The lingering pangs of kindred grief assuage,
Or soothe the sorrows of declining age.

Nor yet can Hope presage th' auspicious hour,
When Peace shall check the rage of lawless Power;
Nor yet th' insatiate thirst of blood is o'er,
Nor yet has Rapine ravaged every shore.
Exhaustless Passion feeds th' augmented flame,
And wild Ambition mocks the voice of Shame;
Revenge, with haggard look and scowling eyes,
Surveys with horrid joy th' expected prize;
Broods o'er each remnant of monarchic sway,
And dooms to certain death his fancied prey.

For midst the ruins of each falling state,
ONE FAVOUR'D NATION braves the general fate—
One favour'd nation, whose impartial laws
Of sober Freedom vindicate the cause;
Her simple manners, midst surrounding crimes,
Proclaim the genuine worth of ancient times;

True to herself, unconquerably bold,
The rights her valour gain'd she dares uphold ;
Still with pure faith her promise dares fulfil,
Still bows submission to th' Almighty will.

Just Heav'n ! how Envy kindles at the sight !
How mad Ambition plans the desperate fight !
With what new fury Vengeance hastes to pour
Her tribes of rapine from yon crowded shore !
Just Heav'n ! how fair a victim at the shrine
Of injured Freedom shall her life resign,
If e'er, propitious to the vows of hate,
Unsteady Conquest stamp our mournful fate,
If e'er proud France usurp our ancient reign,
And ride triumphant o'er th' insulted main !

     *     *     *     *     *     *

Far hence th' unmanly thought—the voice of Fame
Wafts o'er th' applauding deep her DUNCAN's name.
What though the Conqueror of th' Italian plains
Deem nothing gain'd, while this fair isle remains ;
Though his young breast with rash presumption glow,
He braves the vengeance of no vulgar foe :
Conqueror no more, full soon his laurel'd pride
Shall perish—whelm'd in Ocean's angry tide ;
His broken bands shall rue the fatal day,
And scatter'd fleets proclaim BRITANNIA's sway.

# No. VIII.

Jan. 1, 1798.

A CORRESPONDENT has adapted the beautiful poem of the BATTLE OF SABLA, in "Carlyle's Specimens of Arabian Poetry," to the circumstances of the present moment. We shall always be happy to see the poetry of other times and nations so successfully engaged in the service of our country, and of the present order of society.

## THE CHOICE.

(FROM THE BATTLE OF SABLA, BY JAAFER BEN ALBA.)

I.

Hast thou not seen th' insulting foe
   In fancied triumphs crown'd?
And heard their frantic rulers throw
   These empty threats around?
"Make now YOUR CHOICE! The terms we give,
   Desponding Britons, hear!
These fetters on your hands receive,
   Or in your hearts the spear."

Can we forget our old renown;
   Resign the empire of the sea;
And yield at once our sovereign's crown,
   Our ancient laws and liberty?

Shall thus the fierce destroyer's hand
Pass unresisted o'er our native land?
Our country sink, to barb'rous force a prey,
And ransom'd.ENGLAND bow to *Gallic* sway?

II.

"Is then the contest o'er?" we cried,
    "And lie we at your feet?
And dare you vauntingly decide
    The fortune we shall meet?
A brighter day we soon shall see;
    No more the prospect lours;
And Conquest, Peace, and Liberty
    Shall gild our future hours."

Yes! we will guard our old renown;
    Assert our empire o'er the sea;
And keep untouch'd our sovereign's crown,
    Our ancient laws and liberty.

Not thus the fierce destroyer's hand
Shall scatter ruin o'er this smiling land;
No barb'rous force shall here divide its prey;
Nor *ransom'd* ENGLAND bow to *Gallic* sway.

III.

The foe advance. In firm array
    We'll rush o'er Albion's sands—
Till the red sabre marks our way
    Amid their yielding bands!
Then as they lie in death's cold grasp,
    We'll cry, "OUR CHOICE IS MADE!
These hands the sabre's hilt shall clasp,
    Your hearts shall feel the blade".

Thus Britons guard their ancient fame,
    Assert their empire o'er the sea,
And to the envying world proclaim,
    One nation still is brave and free—
4

Resolv'd to conquer or to die,
True to their KING, their LAWS, their LIBERTY :
No barb'rous foe finds here an easy prey—
*Un-ransom'd* ENGLAND spurns all foreign sway.*

* The original poem as translated, or rather paraphrased, by Prof. J. D. Carlyle, is here subjoined :—

## THE CHOICE.

Sabla ! thou saw'st th' exulting foe
    In fancied triumphs crown'd :
Thou heard'st their frantic females throw
    These galling taunts around :

" Make now YOUR CHOICE—the terms we give,
    Desponding victims, hear !
These fetters on your *hands* receive,
    Or in your *hearts* the spear."

" And is the conflict o'er," we cried,
    And lie we at your feet,
" And dare you vauntingly decide
    The fortune we must meet ?

" A brighter day we soon shall see,
    Tho' now the prospect lowers,
And Conquest, Peace, and Liberty
    Shall gild our future hours."

The foe advanc'd—in firm array
    We rush'd o'er SABLA'S sands,
And the red sabre mark'd our way
    Amidst their yielding bands.

Then as they writh'd in death's cold grasp,
    We cried, " OUR CHOICE is made !
These *hands* the sabre's hilt shall clasp,
    Your *hearts* shall have the blade ! "

As Carlyle's version is although a spirited not a faithful one, the Editor is induced to present a literal translation, from *Translations of Ancient Arabian Poetry, by C. J. Lyall,* 1885, 8vo., p. 10. The contest was not a battle but one of the frequent skirmishes between neighbouring clans. *Sabla* is Carlyle's rendering of *Sahbal a Wady,* in Arabia, overlooked by twin peaks.

THE FOLLOWING POEM has been transmitted to us, without preface or introduction, by a gentleman of the name of IRELAND.* We apprehend from the peculiarities of the style, that it must be the production of a remote period. We are likewise inclined to imagine, that it may contain allusions to some former event in English history. What that event may have been, we must submit to the better judgment and superior information of our readers, from whom we impatiently expect a solution of this interesting question. The editor has been influenced solely by a sense of its poetical merit.

JA'FAR SON OF 'ULBAH, OF THE BANU-L-HÂRITH.

The Poet, with two companions, went forth to plunder the herds of 'Ukail, a neighbour-tribe, and was beset on his way back by detached parties of that tribe in the valley of Sahbal, whom he overcame and reached home safely.

That even when under Sahbal's twin peaks upon us drave
  the horsemen troop after troop, and the foemen pressed
  us sore—
They said to us—"Two things lie before you: now must ye
  choose—
  the points of the spears couched at you, or, if ye will not,
  chains".
We answered them—"Yea, this thing may fall to you after
  fight,
  when men shall be left on ground, and none shall arise
  again ;
But we know not, if we quail before the assault of Death,
  how much may be left of life: the goal is too dim to see".
We strode to the strait of battle: there cleared us a space
  around
  the white swords in our right hands which the smiths had
  furbished fair.
To them fell the edge of my blade on that day of Sahbal dale,
  and mine was the share thereof whereover my fingers closed.
                                                          ED.

[* W. H. Ireland, the Shakespeare forger.—ED.]

# THE DUKE AND THE TAXING-MAN.*

WHILOME there liv'd in fair Englonde
A Duke of peerless wealth,
And mickle care he took of her
Old Constitution's health.
Full fifty thousand pounds and more
To him his vassals paid,
But ne to King, ne Countree, he
Would yield th' assessment made.
The taxing-man, with grim visåge
Came pricking on the way ;
The taxing-man, with wrothful words,
Thus to the Duke did say :
" Lord Duke, Lord Duke, thou'st hid from me,
As sure as I'm alive,
Of goodly palfreys *seventeen*,
Of varlets *twenty-five* ".
Then out he drew his gray goose quill,
Ydipp'd in ink so black,
And sorely to SURCHARGE the Duke,
I trowe, he was ne slack.
Then 'gan the Duke to looken pale,
And stared as one astound,
Twaie coneynge Clerks† eftsoons he spies
Sitting their board around.

[* The above ballad refers to an attempt by FRANCIS, fifth
DUKE OF BEDFORD, to escape the payment of the Assessed
Taxes upon twenty-five of his servants, on the plea that as
the Helpers did not wear a Livery, and were engaged by the
week, they were not liable to the duty. This defence was,
however, unsuccessful.—ED.]

† *Twaie coneynge Clerks.*—*Coneynge* is the participle of the verb
to *ken* or *know*. It by no means imports what we now denomi-
nate a *knowing one:* on the contrary, *twaie coneynge clerks* means
*two intelligent and disinterested clergymen.*

" O woe is me," then cried the Duke,
  " Ne mortal wight but errs !
I'll hie to yon twaie coneynge Clerks,
  Yclept Commissioners."
The Duke he hied him to the board,
  And straight 'gan for to say,
" A seely * wight I am, God wot,
  Ne ken I the right way.
" These varlets twenty-five were ne'er
  *Liveried in white and red ;*
Withouten this, what signifie
  Wages, and board, and bed?
" And by St. George, that stout horseman,
  My palfreys *seventeen,*
For two years, or perchance for three,
  I had forgotten clean."
" Naie," quoth the Clerk, " both horse and foot
  To hide was thine intent,
Ne seely wight be ye, but didst
  With good advisament.†
" Surcharge, surcharge, good Taxing-man,
  Anon our seals we fix,
Of sterling pounds, Lord Duke, you pay
  Three hundred thirty-six."‡

---

* *Seely* is evidently the original of the modern word *silly.* A
*seely wight,* however, by no means imports what is now called a
*silly fellow,* but means a man of simplicity of character, devoid
of all *vanity,* and of any strange, ill-conducted ambition, which,
if successful, would immediately be fatal to the man who indulged it.

† *Good advisament* means—*cool consideration.*

[‡ FRANCIS, fifth DUKE OF BEDFORD, died after a severe sur-
gical operation, March 2, 1802, at the early age of thirty-six.
" The Duke of Bedford's energetic and capacious mind," says

# EPIGRAM ON THE PARIS LOAN,*

CALLED

## THE LOAN UPON ENGLAND.

THE Paris cits, a patriotic band,
Advance their cash on British freehold land.
But let the speculating rogues beware—
They've bought the *skin*, but who's to kill *the bear?*

---

Lord Ossory, "his enlarged way of thinking, and elevated sentiments, together with the habits and pursuits of his life, peculiarly
qualified him for his high station and princely fortune. He was
superior to bad education and disadvantages for forming his
character, and turned out certainly a first-rate man, though not
free from imperfections. His uprightness and truth were un-
equalled; his magnanimity, fortitude and consideration, in his
last moments, taken so unprepared as he was, were astonishing."
On the 16th March, C. J. Fox, in moving for a new writ for
the borough of Tavistock, vacated by Lord John Russell, who
had succeeded to the titles and estates of his deceased brother,
took occasion to pronounce a beautiful and glowing eulogium
on his departed friend and firm supporter.—ED.]

[* The *Anti-Jacobin* (in No. 8) thus speaks of the threatened
invasion of this country, for which "they have publicly formed,
and (as they term it) *organized* their ARMY OF ENGLAND. Its
Advanced Guard is to be formed from a chosen Corps of Ban-
ditti, the most distinguished for Massacre and Plunder. It is
to be preceded, as it naturally ought, by *the Genius of French
Revolutionary Liberty,* and it will be *welcomed,* as they tell us,
'on the *ensanguined* shores of Britain, by the generous friends
of Parliamentary Reform'. In the interval, however, till these
golden dreams are realized, it is necessary that this '*Army of
England,*' while it yet remains in France, should be fed, paid,
and clothed. For this purpose a new and separate fund is
provided (in the same spirit with the rest of their measures),
and is to be termed 'THE LOAN OF ENGLAND,' to be raised by
anticipation on the security and mortgage of all the Lands and
Property of this Country. This *gasconade,* which sounds too
extravagant for reality, is nevertheless seriously announced by
a message from the Executive Directory; and we are told that
the Merchants of Paris are eagerly offering to advance, on such
a security, the money which is to defray the expenses of the
Expedition against this country."—ED.]

# No. IX.

Jan. 8, 1798.

## ODE TO ANARCHY.

### BY A JACOBIN.

(BEING AN IMITATION OF HORACE, ODE XXXV. BOOK I.)

*O Diva, gratum quæ regis Antium !*

GODDESS, whose dire terrific power
Spreads from thy much-loved Gallia's plains
Where'er her blood-stain'd ensigns lower,
Where'er fell Rapine stalks, or barb'rous Discord reigns !

Thou, who canst lift to fortune's height
The wretch by truth and virtue scorn'd,
And crush with insolent delight,
All whom true merit rais'd, or noble birth adorn'd !

Thee, oft the murd'rous band implores,
Swift darting on its hapless prey :
Thee, wafted from fierce Afric's shores,
The Corsair Chief invokes to speed him on his way.

Thee, the wild Indian Tribes revere ;
Thy charms the roving Arab owns ;
Thee, kings, thee tranquil nations fear,
The bane of social bliss, the foe to peaceful thrones.

For, soon as thy loud trumpet calls
To deadly rage, to fierce alarms,
Just Order's goodly fabric falls,
Whilst the mad people cries, "To arms ! to arms !"

With thee Proscription, child of strife,
With Death's choice implements, is seen,
Her Murderer's gun, Assassin's knife,
And, "last not least in love," her darling *Guillotine.*

Fond Hope is thine,—the hope of Spoil,
And Faith,—such faith as ruffians keep :
They prosper thy destructive toil,
That makes the Widow mourn, the helpless Orphan weep.

Then false and hollow friends retire,
Nor yield one sigh to soothe despair ;
Whilst crowds triumphant Vice admire,
Whilst Harlots shine in robes that deck'd the Great
    and Fair.

Guard our famed Chief to Britain's strand !
Britain, our last, our deadliest foe :
Oh, guard his brave associate band !
A band to slaughter train'd, and "nursed in scenes of
    woe ".

What shame, alas ! one little Isle
Should dare its native laws maintain !
At Gallia's threats serenely smile,
And, scorning her dread power, triumphant rule the main.

For this have guiltless victims died
In crowds at thy ensanguined shrine !
For this has recreant Gallia's pride
O'erturned Religion's Fanes, and braved the Wrath
    Divine !

What Throne, what Altar, have we spared
To spread thy power, thy joys impart ?
Ah ! then, our faithful toils reward !
And let each falchion pierce some loyal Briton's heart.

[THE FOLLOWING IS A TRANSLATION, BY DUNCOMBE, OF

HORACE'S ODE TO FORTUNE,

*Of which the above Ode is a parody.*

O GODDESS, whose propitious sway
Thy Antium's favourite sons obey;
Whose voice from depth of woe recalls
The wretch, and triumphs turns to funerals;

From Thee, rich crops the needy swain
Implores. Thee, sovereign of the main,
The mariner invokes, who braves
In a Bithynian bark the Cretan waves;

Thee, Scythians, wandering far and near,
And unrelenting Dacians, fear:
The warlike sons of Italy;
Cities, and realms, and empires, worship Thee.

Mothers of barbarous monarchs dread,
And purple tyrants, lest thou tread
With spurning foot, and scatter round
The sculptured column on th' encumbered ground;

And lest the fickle crowd should break
Their bonds; and with loud clamours wake
The peaceful to assert their right
By force of arms, and quell usurping might.

Ruthless necessity prepares
The way for Thee; and ever bears
Huge nails in her strong hands of brass
The wedge, the hook, and lead's hot molten mass.

Thee Hope and white robed Faith, adore,
So rarely found!—She, when no more
Thou smil'st, attends the fallen great
Stript of his gay attire and stately seat.

But venal crowds and harlots fly:
And, if the flowing casks are dry,
When to the dregs the wine they drink,
From friendship's yoke the false associates shrink.

Thy aid for Cæsar Rome implores,
Conduct him safe to Britain's shores,
The limits of the world; and lead
Our new-raised bands against the trembling Mede.

Alas ! we mourn our crimes, our scar
And brethren slain in civil wars :
How oft have Roman youth embrued
Their savage hands in streams of social blood !

What has this Iron Age not dared ?
What Gods revered ? What Altars spared ?
O ! point again the blunted steel,
And let the Massagete our vengeance feel !—ED.]

THE following Song is recommended to be sung at all
*Convivial* Meetings, convened for the purpose of opposing
the Assessed-Tax Bill. The correspondent who has transmitted it to us informs us that he has tried it with great
success among many of his well-disposed neighbours, who
had been at first led to apprehend that the 1-20th part of
their income was too great a sacrifice for the preservation
of the remainder of their property from French Confiscation.

You have heard of REWBELL,*
That demon of hell,
And of BARRAS, his brother Director ;

[* The above verses refer to the memorable events of the
18th Fructidor, Sept. 4, 1797 (the model of Prince Louis
Napoléon's *coup d'état*, Dec. 2, 1851), when Rewbell, Barras,
and Larévellière-Lepaux, on the plea that the Republic was in
danger, got rid of their fellow-directors, Carnot (grandfather to
the present President of the French Republic) and Barthélemy,
who were replaced by Merlin and François de Neufchateau,
dispersed by military force the members of the Five Hundred
and the Ancients, fifty-three of whom were condemned to
transportation—banished the editors, &c., of forty-two newspapers—annulled the elections of forty-eight departments—
and effected other arbitrary measures without opposition. The
springs of the movement were throughout directed by Buonaparte, seconded by Hoche and Augereau. This event was the
true era of the commencement of military despotism in France.
But THIERS considers "the Directory by these means prevented civil war, and substituted an arbitrary but necessary
act of power, carried out with energy, but with all the mildness
and moderation that revolutionary times would allow ".—ED.]

Of the canting LEPAUX,
And that scoundrel MOREAU,
  Who betray'd his old friend and protector.

Would you know how these friends,
For their own private ends,
  Would subvert our Religion and Throne?—
Do you doubt of their skill
To change Laws at their will?—
  You shall hear how they treated their own.

'Twas their pleasure to look,
In a little blue book,
  At the Code of their famed legislation,
That with truth they might say,
In the space of one day
  They had broke every Law of the Nation.

The first law that they see,
Is "*the Press shall be free!*"
  The next is "*the Trial by Jury*":
Then, "*the People's free Choice*";
Then, "*the Members' free Voice*"—
  When REWBELL exclaim'd in a fury—

"On a method we'll fall
For infringing them all—
  We'll seize on each Printer and Member:
No period so fit
For a desperate hit,
  As our bloody month of *September*.

"We'll annul each election
Which wants our correction,
  And name our own creatures instead.

When once we've our will,
No blood we will spill,
  (But let CARNOT be knock'd on the head).

"To *Rochefort* we'll drive
Our victims alive,
  And as soon as on board we have got 'em,
Since we destine the ship
For no more than one trip,
  We can just make a hole in the bottom.

"By this excellent plan,
On the *true Rights of Man*,
  When we've founded our *fifth Revolution*,
Though *England's* our foe,
An army shall go
  To *improve* HER corrupt Constitution.

"We'll address to the Nation
A fine Proclamation
  With offers of friendship so warm :
Who can give BUONAPARTE
A welcome so hearty
  As the friends of a THOROUGH REFORM ? "

# No. X.

Jan. 15, 1798.

FOR the two following poems we are indebted to unknown correspondents. They could not have reached us at a more seasonable period.

The former, we trust, describes the feelings common to every inhabitant of this country. The second, we know too well, is expressive of the sentiments of our enemies.

## LINES,

### WRITTEN AT THE CLOSE OF THE YEAR 1797.

LOUD howls the storm along the neighbouring shore;
BRITAIN indignant hears the frantic roar:
Her generous sons pour forth on every side,
Firm in their country's cause—their country's pride!
See wild Invasion threats this envied land:
Swift to defend her, springs each Social Band:
Her white rocks echoing to their cheerful cry,
"GOD AND OUR KING!"—"ENGLAND AND VICTORY!"

Yes! happy BRITAIN, on thy tranquil coast
No trophies mad Philosophy shall boast!
Though thy disloyal sons, a feeble band,
Sound the loud blast of treason through the land;
Scoff at thy dangers with unnatural mirth,
And execrate the soil which gave them birth;
With jaundiced eye thy splendid triumphs view,
And give to FRANCE the palm to BRITAIN due:

Or,—when loud strains of gratulation ring,*
And lowly bending to the ETERNAL KING,
Thy SOVEREIGN bids a nation's praise arise
In grateful incense to the fav'ring skies—
Cast o'er each solemn scene a scornful glance,
And only sigh for ANARCHY and FRANCE.

Yes! unsupported *Treason's* standard falls,
*Sedition* vainly on her children calls,
While Cities, Cottages, and Camps contend,
Their King, their Laws, their Country to defend.†

Raise, BRITAIN, raise thy sea-encircled head ;
Round the wide world behold thy glory spread ;
Firm as thy guardian oaks thou still shalt stand,
The dread and wonder of each hostile land ;

---

[ * Alluding to the National Thanksgiving for the three great naval victories achieved by Lords Howe, St. Vincent, and Duncan. On this occasion the King and Queen, with their family, the Houses of Lords and Commons, &c., went in procession to St. Paul's, where Divine Service was performed. The Government Papers attributed to the Opposition Press a desire to throw discredit on this proceeding. "The consequence of the Procession to St. Paul's " (says the *Morning Post*, of Dec. 25) "was, that *one* man returned thanks to the Almighty, and *one* woman was *kicked* TO DEATH."—ED.]

[† Mary Frampton, in her journal (Dec. 20, 1797), gives a lively account of the King's attendance at St. Paul's for Duncan's Victory on the 11th Oct. "The King," she says, "stopped under the dome, and conversed for some time with Lord Duncan and the sailors ; and, to the great scandal of good church-goers, did not hold his tongue for any considerable time together during the service. . . . Pitt was attacked at Temple Bar by three ruffians, who rushed from the mob and seized upon the door of his carriage undoubtedly with an intent to drag him out, but three of the Light Horse Volunteers rode up, and backing their horses against them, sent them head over heels to the place from whence they came, rather faster than they ventured out." Page 99.—ED.]

While the dire fiends of discord idly rave,
And, mad with anguish, curse the severing wave.

QUEEN of the OCEAN, lo! she smiles serene,
'Mid the deep horrors of the dreadful scene;
With heartfelt piety to Heav'n she turns—
From Heav'n the flame of British courage burns—
She dreads no power but HIS who rules the ball,
At whose "great bidding" empires rise and fall;
In HIM, on peaceful plain, or tented field,
She trusts, secure in HIS protecting shield—
GALLIA, thy threats she scorns—BRITAIN SHALL NEVER
YIELD.
                                    AN ENGLISHWOMAN.

---

TRANSLATION OF THE NEW SONG
OF THE
"ARMY OF ENGLAND".
WRITTEN BY THE CI-DEVANT BISHOP OF AUTUN.*
WITH NOTES BY THE TRANSLATOR.

GOOD Republicans all,
The Directory's call
    Invites you to visit JOHN BULL;
Oppress'd by the rod
Of a King, and a God,†
    The cup of his misery's full.

---

[* PRINCE TALLEYRAND.—ED.]
† GENERAL DANICAN, in his Memoirs, tells us, that while he was in command, a felon, who had assumed the name of Brutus, chief of a revolutionary tribunal at Rennes, said to his colleagues, on Good Friday, "Brothers, we must put to death this day, at the same hour the counter-revolutionist Christ died, that young devotee who was lately arrested": and this young lady was guillotined accordingly, and her corpse treated with *every possible species of indecent insult*, to the infinite amusement of a vast multitude of spectators.

Old JOHNNY shall see
What makes a man FREE ;
Not parchments, nor Statutes on Paper ;
And stripp'd of his riches,
Great Charter, and breeches,
Shall cut a FREE Citizen's caper.

Then away, let us over
To *Deal*, or to *Dover*—
We laugh at his talking so big ;
He's pamper'd with feeding,
And wants a sound bleeding—
*Par Dieu!* he shall bleed like a pig !

JOHN, tied to the stake,
A grand baiting will make,
When worried by mastiffs of France ;
What REPUBLICAN FUN,
To see his blood run,
As at *Lyons, La Vendée,* and *Nantz !* *

---

* The reader will find in the works of PETER PORCUPINE [W. COBBETT] (a spirited and instructive writer) an ample and satisfactory commentary on this and the following stanza. The French themselves inform us, that by the several modes of destruction here alluded to, upwards of 30,000 persons were butchered at Lyons, and this once magnificent city almost levelled to the ground, by the command of a wretched actor (COLLOT D'HERBOIS), whom they had formerly hissed from the stage. From the same authorities we learn, that at Nantz 27,000 persons, of both sexes, were murdered ; chiefly by drowning them in plugged boats. The waters of the Loire became putrid, and were forbidden to be drunk, by the savages who conducted the massacre :—that at Paris 150,000, and in La Vendée 300,000 persons were destroyed.—Upon the whole, the French themselves acknowledge, that TWO MILLIONS of human beings (exclusive of the military) have been sacrificed to the principles of EQUALITY and the RIGHTS OF MAN : 250,000

With grape-shot discharges,
And plugs in his barges,
  With *National Razors* good store,
We'll pepper and shave him,
And in the *Thames* lave him—
  How sweetly he'll bellow and roar!

What the villain likes worse,
We'll vomit his Purse,
  And make it the guineas disgorge;
For your RAPHAELS and RUBENS
We would not give two-pence;
  Stick, stick to the PICTURES OF GEORGE.

No Venus of stone,
But of good flesh and bone,
  Will do for a true Democrat;
When weary with slaughter,
With JOHN's Wife and Daughter,
  We'll join in a little *chit-chat*.

---

of these are stated to be WOMEN, and 30,000 CHILDREN. In this
last number, however, they do not include the unborn; nor
those who started from the bodies of their agonizing parents,
and were stuck upon the bayonets of those very men who are
now to compose the "ARMY OF ENGLAND," amidst the most
savage acclamations.

[At the beginning of the revolution, some companies of
children, called *Bonsbons*, were dressed and drilled as National
Guards, as a compliment to the Dauphin, who to please the
Parisians sometimes donned that uniform. Similar companies
were afterwards formed in Brittany, and employed to shoot
those poor wretches whom the two guillotines could not
dispatch in sufficient numbers!—*Biog. Univ.*, art. *St. André.*
—ED.]

5

The Shop-keeping hoard,
The Tenant and Lord,
And the Merchants,* are excellent prey :
At our cannon's first thunder,
*Rape, pillage,* and *plunder*
The *Order* shall be *of the day.*

French fortunes and lives,
French daughters and wives,
Have *five honest men* to defend 'em !
And BARRAS and Co.
When to *England* we go,
Will kindly take JOHN's *in commendam.*

---

* At Lyons, JABOGUES, the *second* murderer (the Actor being the *first*), in his speech to the Democratic Society, used these words—" Down with the edifices raised for the profit or the pleasure of the rich ; down with them ALL. COMMERCE and ARTS are useless to a warlike people, and are the destruction of that SUBLIME EQUALITY which France is determined to spread over the globe." Such are the consequences of RADICAL REFORM ! Let any merchant, farmer, or landlord ; let any husband or father consider this, and then say, " *Shall we or shall we not contribute a moderate sum,* IN PROPORTION TO OUR ANNUAL EXPENDITURE, *for the purpose of preserving ourselves from the fate of Lyons, La Vendée, and Nantz ?* "

STYPTIC.

# No. XI.

Jan. 22, 1798.

WE have said in another part of our paper of this day, "that though we shall never begin an attack, we shall always be prompt to repel it ".

On this principle, we could not pass over in silence the EPISTLE TO THE EDITORS OF THE *Anti-Jacobin*, which appeared in the *Morning Chronicle* of Wednesday, and from which we have fortunately been furnished with a motto for this day's paper.

We assure the author of the epistle, that the answer which we have here the honour to address to him, contains our genuine and undisguised sentiments upon the merits of the poem.

Our conjectures respecting the authors and abettors of this performance may possibly be as vague and unfounded as theirs are with regard to the EDITORS of the *Anti-Jacobin*. We are sorry that we cannot satisfy their curiosity upon this subject—but we have little anxiety for the gratification of our own.

It is hardly to be expected, that the character of the epistle should be taken on trust from the editors of this volume; it is thought best, therefore, to subjoin the whole performance as it originally appeared—a mode of hostility obviously the most fair, and in respect to the combatants in the cause of Jacobinism, by much the most effectual. They are always best opposed by the arms which they themselves furnish. Jacobinism shines by its own light.

To the respectable names which the author of the following address has thought proper to connect with the " Anti-Jacobin," no apology is made for thus preserving this otherwise perishable specimen of dulness and defamation. He who has been reviled by the enemies of the " Anti-Jacobin," must feel that principles are attributed to him, of which he need not be ashamed : and when the abuse is conveyed in such a strain of feebleness and folly, he must see that those principles excite animosity only in quarters of which he need not be afraid.

It is only necessary to add, what is most conscientiously the truth, that this production, such as it is, is *by far the best* of all the attacks that the combined wits of the cause have been able to muster against the " Anti-Jacobin ".

EPISTLE TO THE EDITORS OF THE ANTI-JACOBIN.*

*Hic Niger est ; hunc tu, Romane, caveto !*

To tell what gen'rals did, or statesmen spoke,
To teach the world by truths, or please by joke ;
To make mankind grow bold as they peruse,
Judge on existing things, and—weigh the news ;
For this a PAPER first display'd its page,
Commanding tears and smiles through ev'ry age !

Hail, justly famous ! who in modern days
With nobler flight aspire to higher praise ;
Hail, justly famous ! whose discerning eyes
At once detect MISTAKES, MIS-STATEMENTS, LIES ;          10
Hail, justly famous ! who with fancy blest,
Use fiend-like virulence for sportive jest ;
Who only bark to serve your private ends—
Patrons of Prejudice, Corruption's friends !
Who hurl your venom'd darts at well-earned fame—
Virtue your hate, and Calumny your aim !

[* Probably written by the Rt. Hon. John Courtnay.]

Whoe'er ye are, all hail!—whether the skill
Of youthful CANNING guides the ranc'rous quill;
With powers mechanic far above his age,
Adapts the paragraph and fills the page;                    20
Measures the column, mends whate'er's amiss,
Rejects THAT letter, and accepts of THIS;
Or HAMMOND, leaving his official toil,
O'er this great work consume the midnight oil—
Bills, passports, letters, for the Muses quit,
And change dull business for amusing wit:—
His life of labour at one gasp is o'er,
His books forgot—his desk beloved no more!
Proceed to prop the Ministerial cause;
See consequential MORPETH nods applause;                    30
In ev'ry fair one's ears at balls and plays
The gentle GRANVILLE LEVESON whispers praise:
Well-judging Patrons, whom such works can please;
Great works, well worthy Patrons such as these!

.

Who heard, not raptured, the poetic Sage
Who sung of Gallia in a headlong rage,
And blandly drew with no uncourtly grace
The simple manners of our English race—
Extoll'd great DUNCAN, and, supremely brave,
Whelm'd BUONAPARTE's pride beneath the wave?           40
I swear by all the youths that MALMESBURY chose,
By ELLIS' sapient prominence of nose,
By MORPETH's gait, important, proud, and big—
By LEVESON GOWER's crop-imitating wig,
That, could the pow'rs which in those numbers shine,
Could that warm spirit animate my line,
Your glorious deeds which humbly I rehearse—
Your deeds should live immortal as my verse;
And, while they wonder'd whence I caught my flame,
Your sons should blush to read their fathers' shame! 50

Proceed, great men!—your office is not done;
Proceed with what you have so well begun:
Load Fox (if you by PITT would be preferr'd),
With ev'ry guilt that KENYON ever heard—
Adult'rer, gamester, drunkard, cheat and knave,
A factious demagogue and pension'd slave!

Loose, loose your cry—with ire satiric flash :
Let all the Opposition feel your lash ;
And prove them to these hot and partial times,
A combination of the worst of crimes!          60

But softer numbers softer subjects fit :
In liquid phrases thrill the praise of PITT ;
Extol in eulogies of candid truth
The Virgin Minister—the Heav'n-born Youth ;
The greatest gift that fate to England gave,
Created to support and born to save ;
Prompt to supply whate'er his country lacks—
Skilful to GAG, and knowing how to TAX !
With him companions meet in order stand—
A firm, compact, and well-appointed band ;          70
Skill'd to advance or to retreat, DUNDAS,
And bear thick battle on his front of brass ;
GRENVILLE with pond'rous head, which match'd we find
By equal ponderosity behind.——

But hold, my Muse ; nor farther these pursue !—
Great Editors, we have digress'd from you ;
From you, to whom our trivial lays belong,
From you, the sole inspirers of our song !
Proceed :—urge on the same vindictive strain,
To gain the applauses of great MALMESBURY's train ;          80
With jaundiced eyes the noblest patriot scan :
Proceed—be more opprobrious if you can ;
Proceed—be more abusive ev'ry hour ;
To be more stupid is beyond your power.

Line 10.—[One of the distinguishing features of the " ANTI-JACOBIN " was
their articles devoted to an exposure of the " Lies, Misrepresentations, and
Mistakes " of the Opposition Press.—ED.]
Line 23.—[George Hammond, at this time Canning's colleague as Under-
Secretary of State ; the latter being succeeded by John Hookham Frere.—ED.]
Line 30.—[Lord Morpeth, son of the (fifth) Earl of Carlisle who was satirized
by Byron in " English Bards and Scotch Reviewers ".—ED.]
Line 32.—[George Granville Leveson Gower, eldest son of the first Marquis
of Stafford, born in 1758, became second Marquis in 1803, and created Duke of
Sutherland in 1833. He was one of Canning's intimate college companions.—
ED.]
Line 41.—[James Harris, first Earl of Malmesbury, one of the most distin-
guished of English diplomatists. His " Diaries and Correspondence," published by his grandson, the third Earl, throw much light on the transactions of
the eventful period to which they refer.—ED.]
Line 42.—[George Ellis, the accomplished editor of the "Specimens of the
Early English Poets, and of Early English Metrical Romances," &c. In early
life he contributed to the *Rolliad*, being the author of Nos. 1 and 2, in Part I.,

and Nos. 1 and 2, in Part II. Of the *Political Eclogues* he wrote the one entitled
"Charles Jenkinson". In the *Probationary Odes*, he wrote No. II. "Ode on the
New Year, by Lord Mulgrave," and No. XX. "Irregular Ode for the King's
Birth Day, by Sir G. Howard". Afterwards, however, he became much attached
to Pitt, and acted as Secretary to Lord Malmesbury during his unsuccessful
negotiations with the French for peace, at Lisle, 1797. Horace Walpole thus
alludes to him, in a letter of 24th June, 1783 : "English people are in fashion at
Versailles. A Mr. Ellis, who wrote some pretty verses at Bath two or three
years ago, is a favourite there." Sir Walter Scott addressed to him Canto V. of
"Marmion". He died in 1815, aged 70.—ED.]
Line 71.—[The Rt. Hon. Henry Dundas (afterwards created Viscount Mel-
ville), in the Commons, and Lord Grenville in the Lords, were Pitt's most
efficient supporters.—ED.]

## TO THE AUTHOR OF THE EPISTLE TO THE EDITORS OF THE ANTI-JACOBIN.

*Nostrorum sermonum candide judex !*

BARD of the borrow'd lyre ! to whom belong
The shreds and remnants of each hackney'd song ;
Whose verse thy friends in vain for wit explore,
And count but *one good line* in eighty-four !
Whoe'er thou art, all hail ! Thy bitter smile
Gilds our dull page, and cheers our humble toil !

For *yet*—though firm and fearless in the cause
Of pure Religion, Liberty, and Laws,—
Though TRUTH approved, though fav'ring VIRTUE smiled,
Some doubts remained : WE *yet* were *unreviled*.      10

Thanks to thy zeal ! those doubts at length are o'er !
Thy suffrage crowns our wish !—WE ask no more
To stamp with sterling worth each honest line,
Than Censure, cloth'd in vapid Verse like thine !

But say—in full blown honours dost thou sit
'Midst BROOKES'S ELDERS on the BENCH OF WIT,
Where HARE, chief-justice, frames the stern decree,

While with their learned brother, sages three,
FITZPATRICK, TOWNSHEND, SHERIDAN, agree?

Or art thou One—THE PARTY's flattered fool,       20
Train'd in *Debrett's,* or *Ridgway's* civic school—
One, who with rant and fustian daily wears,
Well-natured RICHARDSON! thy patient ears;—
Who sees nor Taste nor Genius in these times,
Save PARR's *buzz* prose,* and COURTENAY's kidnapp'd
    rhymes?†

---

\* BUZZ PROSE.—The learned reader will perceive that this is
an elegant *metonymy*, by which the quality belonging to the
outside of the head is transferred to the inside. *Buzz* is an
epithet usually applied to a large wig. It is here used for
swelling, burly, bombastic writing.

There is a picture of HOGARTH's (the Election Ball, we
believe), in which there are a number of Hats thrown together
in one corner of the room; and it is remarked as a peculiar
excellence that there is not a Hat among them of which you
cannot to a certainty point out the owner among the figures
dancing, or otherwise distributed through the picture.

We remember to have seen an experiment of this kind tried
at one of the Universities with the *wig* and *writings* here alluded
to. A page taken from the most happy and elaborate part of
the writings was laid upon a table in a barber's shop, round
which a number of wigs of different descriptions and dimensions
were suspended, and among them that of the Author in question.
It was required of a young student, after reading a few sentences
in the page, to point out among the wigs that which must of
necessity belong to the Head in which such sentences had been
engendered. The experiment succeeded to a miracle. The
learned reader will now see all the beauty and propriety of the
*metonymy*.

† KIDNAPP'D RHYMES.—Kidnapp'd implies something more
than *stolen*. It is, according to an expression of Mr. Sheridan's
(in the " Critic "), *using other people's* " *thoughts as gipsies do stolen
children—disfiguring them, to make them pass for their own* ".

This is a serious charge against an author, and ought to be
well supported. To the proof then!

Or is it he,—the youth, whose daring soul
With *half a mission* sought the Frozen Pole;—
And then, returning from the unfinish'd work,
Wrote *half a letter,*—to demolish BURKE?
Studied Burke's manner,—aped his forms of speech; 30

---

In an Ode of the late LORD NUGENT'S are the following
spirited lines:

"Though CATO liv'd—though TULLY spoke—*
Though BRUTUS dealt the godlike stroke,
    Yet perish'd fated ROME!"

The author above mentioned saw these lines, and liked them
—as well he might; and as he had a mind to write about Rome
himself, he did not scruple to enlist them into his service; but
he thought it right to make a small alteration in their appearance, which he managed thus. Speaking of Rome, he says it is
the place
                "*Where* CATO liv'd":—

A sober truth! which gets rid at once of all the poetry and
spirit of the original, and reduces the sentiment from an
example of manners, virtue, patriotism, from the *vitæ exemplar
dedit* of LORD NUGENT, to a mere question of inhabitancy. *Ubi
habitavit Cato*—where he was an inhabitant-householder, paying
scot and lot, and had a house on the right-hand side of the way,
as you go down *Esquiline* Hill, just opposite to the poulterer's.
But to proceed—

        "*Where* CATO liv'd; *where* TULLY spoke,
        *Where* BRUTUS dealt the godlike stroke—
        —*By which his glory rose!!!*"

The last line is *not* borrowed.
We question whether the history of modern literature can
produce an instance of a theft so shameless, and turned to so
little advantage.

---

[* Horace Walpole, in a letter to Hannah More, quotes one word of these
verses incorrectly, writing:—"Though Cato *died*," an error which P. Cunningham allows to pass, as also another, that *Mr.*—instead of *Lord*—Nugent wrote
them.—ED.]

Though when he strives his metaphors to reach,
One luckless slip his meaning overstrains,
And loads the blunderbuss with BEDFORD's brains.*

* *And loads the blunderbuss with* BEDFORD's *brains.*—This line
is wholly unintelligible without a note. And we are afraid the
note will be wholly incredible, unless the reader can fortunately
procure the book to which it refers.

In the "Part of a Letter," which was published by MR. ROBT.
ADAIR, in answer to MR. BURKE's "Letter to the D. of B.,"
nothing is so remarkable as the studious imitation of Mr.
Burke's style.

His vehemence, and his passion, and his irony, his wild
imagery, his far-sought illustrations, his rolling and lengthened
periods, and the short quick pointed sentences in which he
often condenses as much wisdom and wit as others would expand through pages, or through volumes,—all these are carefully kept in view by his opponent, though not always very
artificially copied or applied.

But imitators are liable to be led strangely astray; and never
was there an instance of a more complete mistake of a plain
meaning, than that which this line is intended to illustrate—a
mistake no less than that of a *coffin* for a *corpse*. This is hard
to believe or to comprehend—but you shall hear.

MR. BURKE, in one of his publications, had talked of the
French "*unplumbing* the dead in order to destroy the living,"—
by which he intended, without doubt, not metaphorically, but
literally, "*stripping the dead of their* LEADEN COFFINS, *and then
making them* (*not the* DEAD *but the* COFFINS) *into bullets*". A
circumstance perfectly notorious at the time the book was
written.

But this does not satisfy our author. He determines to
retort MR. BURKE's own words upon him; and unfortunately
"reaching at a metaphor," where MR. BURKE only intended a
fact, he falls into the little mistake above mentioned, and by a
stroke of his pen transmutes the illustrious HEAD of the house
of RUSSELL into a metal, to which it is not for us to say how
near or how remote his affinity may possibly have been. He
writes thus—"*If* MR. BURKE *had been content with* '*unplumbing*'
*a dead Russell, and hewing* HIM (observe—not the coffin, but
HIM—the old dead Russell himself) *into grape and canister, to
sweep down the whole generation of his descendants*," &c., &c.

The thing is scarcely credible; but IT IS SO! We write
with the book open before us.

Whoe'er thou art—ne'er may thy patriot fire,
Unfed by praise or patronage, expire !
Forbid it, Taste !—with Compensation large
Patrician hands thy labours shall o'ercharge ! *
BEDFORD and WHITBREAD shall vast sums advance,
The *Land* and *Malt* of Jacobin Finance !

Whoe'er thou art—before thy feet we lay,        40
With lowly suit, our *Number of to-day!*
Spurn not our offering with averted eyes !
Let thy pure breath revive the extinguished *Lies!*
*Mistakes*, *Mis-statements*, now so oft o'erthrown,
Rebuild, and prop with nonsense of thy own !
Pervert our meaning, and misquote our text—
And *furnish us a motto for the next !*

---

* Qu.—Surcharge ?

Line 16.—[Brookes's Club was the grand rendezvous of the Whigs.—ED.]

Line 17.—[JAS. HARE was M.P. for Knaresborough, and one of the most brilliant wits of the Whig Party. At Eton his verses were hung up as specimens of excellence. Great expectations were raised as to his eloquence in the House of Commons. But his timidity was so great that he broke down in his first speech, and this failure, joined with delicate health, prevented a second attempt. Horace Walpole speaks of his "brilliancy and fire," and of his own inferiority to him. His *bons mots* were innumerable. He died in 1804. The following is Lord Ossory's opinion of the social talents of some of the best talkers of his day :—" Horace Walpole was an agreeable, lively man, very affected, always aiming at wit, in which he fell very short of his old friend, GEORGE SELWYN, who possessed it in the most genuine but indescribable degree. HARE's conversation abounded with wit, and perhaps of a more lively kind ; so did BURKE'S, though with much alloy of bad taste ; but, upon the whole, my brother the General [FITZPATRICK] was the most agreeable man in society of any of them."—MS., R. Vernon Smith.—ED.]

Line 19.—[General FITZPATRICK was one of Fox's most attached friends and political supporters. BOSWELL, speaking of a dinner at BEAUCLERK'S, 24th April, 1779, says, on a celebrated wit being mentioned (believed to be Fitzpatrick), "JOHNSON replied, ' I have been several times in company with him, but never perceived any strong power of wit. He produces a general effect by various means ; he has a cheerful countenance and a gay voice. Besides his trade is wit. It would be as wild in him to come into company without merriment, as for a highwayman to take the road without his pistols.' " WALPOLE (in his *Journal of the Reign of George III.*, i. 167, and ii. 560, describes him as "an agreeable young man of parts," and mentions his "genteel irony and badinage". He was Lord Shelburne's brother-in-law, at whose house Johnson might have met him, as well as in Fox's company. Rogers (*Table Talk*, p. 104) said that Fitzpatrick was at one time nearly as famous for his wit as Hare. He possessed no mean poetic talents, particularly for compositions of wit, fancy, and satire. To the *Rolliad* he contributed "Extract from the Dedication"; Nos. v. ix. and xii., in Part I. ; and No. v. in Part II. In the *Political Eclogues*, he wrote "The Liars"; and "Pindaric Ode" (No. xv.)—also, "Incantation for raising a Phantom, imitated from Macbeth," in the *Political Miscellanies*.

## GENERAL RICHARD FITZPATRICK'S EPITAPH ON HIMSELF.

### "MY OWN EPITAPH.

"Whose turn is next? This monitory Stone
Replies, vain Passenger, perhaps thy own.
If, idly curious, thou wilt seek to know
Whose relics mingle with the dust below,
Enough to tell thee, that his destin'd span
On Earth he dwelt,—and, like thyself, a Man.
Nor distant far th' inevitable day
When thou, poor mortal, shalt like him be clay.
Through life he walk'd unemulous of fame,
Nor wish'd beyond it to preserve a name.
Content, if Friendship, o'er his humble bier,
Drop but the heartfelt tribute of a tear ;
Though countless ages should unconscious glide,
Nor learn that ever he had liv'd, or died.
                     "R. F."

Such is the epitaph placed on a stone sarcophagus in the usual form, in the churchyard at Sunninghill, close to the house where Gen. Fitzpatrick's friend, G. Ellis, died.—Nichols, *Lit. Illustr.*, vol. vii., pp. 633-4.—ED.]

Line 19.—[Lord JOHN TOWNSHEND, the second son of the first Marquis Townshend. He represented Cambridge till ousted by PITT at the general election in 1784. In 1788 he became the colleague of FOX for Westminster. He afterwards represented Knaresborough for twenty-five years : his colleague in 1797 was HARE. He had great powers of wit and satire. In the *Political Eclogues* (subjoined to *The Rolliad*), he wrote the one entitled "Jekyll". To the *Probationary Odes for the Laureatship* he contributed No. xii., in ridicule of Warren Hastings's agent, Major John Scott, M.P. Also, the "Dialogue between a certain personage and his Minister," in imitation of the Ninth Ode of Horace, Book III.—ED.]

Line 20.—[Sir FRANCIS BURDETT, then M.P. for Boroughbridge.—ED.]

Line 23.—[JOHN RICHARDSON, M.P. for Newport, Cornwall, and one of the proprietors of Drury Lane Theatre. In the *Rolliad* he was the author, in Part I., of Nos. iv., x., and xi. ; and in Part II. of Nos. iii. and iv. He wrote No. iv. of *Probationary Odes*, in ridicule of Sir R. Hill, Bart. ; No. xix. on Viscount Mountmorres, and the concluding prose portion. To the *Political Miscellanies* he contributed, "This is the House that George Built," and in conjunction with Tickell, the "Epigrams by Sir Cecil Wray," "Pretymaniana," and "Foreign Epigrams". In the latter Dr. Laurence assisted them. Also "A Tale: At Brookes's once it so fell out". "Theatrical Intelligence Extraordinary." "Epigram : Who shall Expect the Country's Friend?" "A new Ballad : Billy Eden," in conjunction with Tickell. "Proclamation." He died in 1803.—ED.]

Line 25.—[The Rev. SAMUEL PARR, LL.D., was not only a great scholar, but an uncompromising Whig, and one of Fox's most enthusiastic supporters. His conversational powers were great, and his arguments were enforced by boldness, dogmatism, and arrogance, which qualities, however, did not always exempt him from stinging retorts even from the fair sex. The following, among other attacks, appears in Crabb Robinson's interesting *Diary*, ii. 457 :—

## A RECIPE.

To half of BUSBY'S skill in mood and tense
Add BENTLEY'S pleasantry, without his sense:
Of WARBURTON take all the spleen you find,
And leave his genius and his wit behind.
Squeeze CHURCHILL'S rancour from the verse it flows in,
And knead it stiff with JOHNSON'S heavy prosing.
Add all the piety of ST. VOLTAIRE,
Mix the gross compound—*Fiat* DR. PARR.

His person, in full canonicals, with capacious wig, unfailing tobacco pipe and tankard, is, with the effigies of many other noted politicians of the period, introduced into a spirited bacchanalian scene by Gillray, published in 1801, entitled *The Union Club*.

Line 25.—[JOHN COURTENAY was for many years one of the men of mark in the House of Commons for his ability, independent spirit, erudition, and coarse sarcastic wit. He was born at Carlingford, Ireland, in 1738. Having obtained the patronage of George, Viscount Townshend, Lord-Lieutenant (1767-72), he became the principal writer in the "*Batchelor*," a government paper, distinguished by genuine wit and humour, conducted by Simcox, a clergyman; Richard Marlay, afterwards Bishop of Waterford and Lismore; Robert Jephson, a dramatic poet of note; the Rev. Mr. Boroughs, and others. The chief task of these advocates of the Castle was to counteract the "*Baratarian Letters*," an Irish imitation of *Junius*, which, attacking the Lord-Lieutenant's government, received contributions from Flood, and first published Grattan's character of Chatham. At the "Coalition," 1783, he was appointed Surveyor-general of the Ordnance, and henceforward attached himself to Fox. He wrote, among other works, *A Poetical Review of the Literary and Moral Character of the late Samuel Johnson, LL.D.*, 1786; *The Rape of Pomona, an Elegiac Epistle from the Waiter at Hockrel to the Hon. Mr. Lyttelton*, 1773; *Philosophical Reflections on the late Revolution in France*; and a *Biographical Sketch of his own Life*. In his *Epistles in Rhyme* he thus ridicules Horace Walpole's *Strawberry Verses* on the two Misses Berry:—

" Who to love tunes his note, with the fire of old age,
And chirps the trim lay in a trim Gothic cage ".

Walpole, however (*Correspondence*, ix. 434-5), good-naturedly laughed at them, saying that these verses on himself were really some of the best in the whole set. Courtenay was a member of *The Literary Club*, founded by Sir Joshua Reynolds, and figures in several of Gillray's caricatures. He it was who, referring to Gay's *Beggars' Opera*, designated the author the *Orpheus of Highwaymen*. He died 24th March, 1816.—ED.]

Line 26.—[Sir ROBERT ADAIR. Some observations on his alleged mission to St. Petersburgh to counteract the measures of Government will be found on a subsequent page. The publication here satirized is entitled " Part of a Letter from Robert Adair, Esq., to the Rt. Hon. C. J. Fox; occasioned by Mr. Burke's mention of Lord Keppel in a recent publication," London, Debrett, 1796, and is by no means a contemptible composition. It is called "*Part* of a Letter," because it is a portion of a longer one, being only the part devoted to a vindication of the writer's uncle, Admiral Lord Keppel, and of Fox; with characteristic delineations of Sir G. Saville, the Marquis of Rockingham, Lord North, and George Byng, M.P., on all of whom he passes great compliments.—ED.]

# ODE TO LORD MOIRA.

### I.

IF on your head⁎ some vengeance fell,
MOIRA, for every tale you tell,
　The listening Lords to cozen ;
If but one whisker lost its hue,
Changed (like Moll Coggin's tail) to blue,
　I'd hear them by the dozen.

### II.

But still, howe'er you draw your bow,†
Your charms improve, your triumphs grow,
　New grace adorns your figure ;
More stiff your boots, more black your stock,　10
Your hat assumes a prouder cock,
　Like Pistol's (if 'twere bigger).

### III.

Tell then your stories, strange and new,
Your Fathers fame‡ shall vouch them true ;
　So shall the *Dublin Papers ;*
Swear by the stars§ that saw the sight,

---

⁎HORACE, ODE VIII., BOOK II.

#### IN BARINEM.

*Ulla si juris tibi pejerati*
*Pœna, Barine, nocuisset unquam,*
*Dente si nigro fieres, vel uno*
　　　　*Turpior ungui,*
*Crederem.* †*Sed tu simul obligásti*
*Perfidum votis caput, enitescis*
*Pulchrior multo,* juvenumque prodis
　　　　Publica cura.
‡ Expedit *matris cineres* opertos
　Fallere, et toto §*taciturna noctis*
　*Signa* cum cœlo, gelidâque Divos
　　　　Morte carentes.

'He had it from his Father, who would tell you Fifty in a breath—&c, & tell them—till he believ'd them all himself!'

LORD LONGBOW, the Alarmist, discovering the Mysteries of IRELAND.—with the grasping out of the little farthing Rush-light, &c'y story of Mall Coggin,

That infant thousands die each night,
While troops *blow out their tapers.*

IV.

SHUCKBURGH* shall cheer you with a smile,
MACPHERSON† simpering all the while,      20
With BASTARD† and with Bruin :†
And fierce NICHOLL,‡ who wields at will
Th' emphatic stick, or powerful quill,
  To prove his country's ruin.

V.

Each day new followers § crowd your board,
And lean expectants hail my Lord
  With adoration fervent :
Old THURLOW,‖ though he swore by G—
No more to own a master's nod,
  Is still your humble servant.      30

VI.

Old PULTENEY¶ too, your influence feels,
And asks from you th' Exchequer Seals,
  To tax and save the nation :

---

*Ridet hoc, inquam,* * *Venus ipsa ; rident
Simplices* † *Nymphæ, ferus et* ‡ *Cupido
Semper ardentes acuens sagittas*
              Cote cruentâ.
Adde quod pubes tibi crescit omnis,
§ *Servitus crescit nova ;* ‖ *nec priores
Impiæ tectum dominæ relinquunt,*
              Sæpe minati.

Te suis matres metuunt juvencis ;
Te ¶ *senes parci, miseræque* § *nuper
Virgines nuptæ, tua ne retardet*
              Aura Maritos.

TOOKE trembles,* lest your potent charms
Should lure CHARLES FOX § from *his* fond arms,
To YOUR Administration.                    36

---

* The trepidation of Mr. Tooke, though natural, was not
necessary; as it appeared from the ever-memorable "Letter to
Mr. M'Mahon" (which was published about this time in the
*Morning Chronicle*, and threw the whole town into paroxysms
of laughter), that in the Administration which his Lordship
was so gravely employed in forming, Mr. Fox was to have no
place !

[TRANSLATION OF HORACE, BOOK II., ODE VIII.
BY ARCHDEACON WRANGHAM.

Avenger of insulted truth,
Had Heaven, Barine, dimm'd one tooth ;
Or bade, in justice bade, thee wail
A speck upon a single nail—
I'd trust thee : but ere well the vow
Has passed those treacherous lips, there glow
New beauties mantling o'er thy cheek ;
And thee the youth, thee only seek.

It profits thee to be forsworn
By thy dead mother's hallowed urn ;
By heaven, and each mute nightly sign,
And every deathless power divine.
Yes: Venus laughs well-pleased, and lo !
The gentle Nymphs are laughing too ;
And Cupid, who his burning darts
Whets with fresh blood from lovers' hearts.

Boyhood is rising to thy sway,
Thy train of slaves augments : e'en they,
Who swore thy threshold to forsake,
Hug the fond chain they cannot break.
Thee for their sons pale mothers fear,
The frugal father for his heir ;
And plighted maidens, lest thy charms
Keep the false truants from their arms.—ED.]

### NOTES TO THE ODE TO LORD MOIRA.

[This Ode, written by GEORGE ELLIS, refers to the wish of a "Third Party"
in the House of Commons, who were dissatisfied with the conduct of the war,
the embarrassed state of the finances, and the alarming situation of the country, to have an interview with LORD MOIRA, with a view to effect a change of
Ministry. The following extracts from a letter from his Lordship to COL.
M'MAHON, dated June 15, 1797, will throw some light on this negotiation.
"They requested that I would endeavour, on the assurance of their support, to
form an administration, on the principle of excluding persons, who had on
either side made themselves obnoxious to the public. I strenuously recommended them to form an alliance with MR. FOX'S party, that might be satisfactory to themselves, and reduce to strict engagement the extent of the measures,
which MR. FOX, when brought into office by themselves, would propose.

Hitherto nobody has been designated to any particular office but SIR WILLIAM
PULTENEY. The gentleman had said that he was the person whom they should
be most gratified in seeing CHANCELLOR OF THE EXCHEQUER, and I had professed to them and to him that there was not any person with whom I could
act more confidently. I added, the introduction of LORD THURLOW, SIR W.
PULTENEY, and myself, into the Cabinet, would not assure the public of a
change of system."—ED.]
    Line 3.—[Referring to LORD MOIRA'S complaints against the Government
agents, for unnecessary cruelty to the Irish rebels.—ED.]
    Line 13.—[The following attack upon Lord Moira, "for his patriotic zeal,
and the correctness and propriety with which he gave, in the upper House of
Parliament, an account of the insurrection upon his estates, and in other parts
of Ireland," is extracted from the "*Batchelor*". These observations were there
pointed at the father of Lord Moira, but have been adapted by the Author of
the *Ode* and the Artist to the son.
    *Lord Moira.*—" My Lords, I rise to return my thanks to the Noble Lord who
spoke last. I can testify the truth of all he has asserted. At the time of the
Insurrection in the North, I had frequent and intimate conversations with that
celebrated enchanter, *Moll Coggin.* I have often seen her riding on a black ram
with a blue tail. Once I endeavoured to fire at her, but my gun melted in my
hand into a clear jelly. This jelly I tasted, and if it had been a little more acid,
it would have been most excellent. The Noble Lords may laugh ; but I declare
the fact upon my veracity, which has never been doubted. Once I pursued this
fiend into my ale cellar : she rode instantly out of my sight into the bung-hole
of a beer barrel. She was at that time mounted on her black ram with the
blue tail. Some time after, my servants were much surprised to find their ale
full of *blue hairs.* I was not surprised, as I knew the blue *hairs* were the hairs
of the ram's *blue tail.* Noble Lords may stare, but the fact is as I relate it.
This *Moll Coggin* was the fiend who raised the *Oak-boys* to rebellion. I was also
well acquainted with the two Cow-boys mentioned by the Noble Lord ; they
were my tenants, and were certainly endowed with supernatural powers. I
have known one of them tear up by the roots an Oak two hundred feet high,
and bear it upright on his head four miles! his party were on that account
called Oak-boys. Noble Lords may laugh, but I speak from certain knowledge.
The Oak-tree grew in my garden, and I have often seen five hundred Swans
perching on its boughs ; these swans were remarkable for destroying all the
snipes in the country—they flew faster than any snipe I ever saw, and you may
imagine a small bird could make but a feeble resistance in the talons of a swan.
I hope, my Lords, you will pardon my wandering a little from the present subject,"
&c.—ED.]
    Line 17.—[" One night after *nine o'clock*, a party of Soldiers saw a light in a
house by the road-side—they went and ordered it to be extinguished immediately:
the people of the house begged that the light might be suffered to remain
because there was a child belonging to the family in convulsion fits, who must
expire for want of help if the people were to be without fire and candle ; *but this
request HAD NO EFFECT.*" *Lord Moira's Speech in the House of Lords, November* 22,
1797. This statement was, however, satisfactorily disproved. The incident
forms a feature in the accompanying engraving. Notwithstanding official
denials, it has long been admitted that the conduct of the Soldiery in Ireland
was simply infamous. Billeting on Catholics and reputed malcontents of the
better class appears to have been invariably as an unlimited licence for robbery,
devastation, ravishment, and, in case of resistance, murder. Sir Ralph Abercromby, on assuming the command of the army in Ireland, declared, in general
orders, that their habits and discipline were such as to render them "formidable
to everybody but the enemy ". The just severity of this phrase was confirmed
by the subsequent experience of Lord Cornwallis.—ED.]
    Line 19.—[Sir George Augustus William Shuckburgh, distinguished by his
scientific researches, married the daughter and sole heiress of Jas. Evelyn, Esq.
of Felbridge, Surrey, by whom he had an only daughter, Julia, who became, in
1810, the wife of the Earl of Liverpool. Sir George, on the decease of his father-
in-law in 1793, assumed the additional surname of Evelyn. He died in 1804,
having been five times returned to Parliament for the county of Warwick.—ED.]

Line 20.—[Sir John Macpherson, Bart. was M.P. for Horsham, and for a shor
period Governor-General of India.—ED.]
    Line 21.—[Col. Bastard was M.P. for Devon. He was returned with Mr
Rolle, the hero of " *The Rolliad*," on the Pitt interest.—ED.]
    Line 31.—[Sir William Pulteney was M.P. for Shrewsbury, and no Member in
the House was more looked up to. He was the second son of Sir James John
stone, Bart., of Westerhall, and brother of Governor Johnstone. He married
the cousin of Lt.-Gen. Henry Pulteney, surviving brother of William Pulteney
Earl of Bath, assuming the name of Pulteney. The General left immense
wealth, "the fruits of his brother's virtues!" as Horace Walpole sarcastically
phrases it. The greater part of it he bequeathed to the said cousin. Sir Wil
liam Johnstone Pulteney died in 1805. His daughter was created Countess o
Bath.—ED.]
    Line 38.—[Of M'MAHON it is said in T. RAIKES's *Journal* (November, 1836):-
" George IV. never had any private friends : he selected his confidants from hi
minions. M'MAHON was an Irishman of low birth and obsequious manners
he was a little man, his face red, covered with pimples ; always dressed in th
blue and buff uniform, with his hat on one side, copying the air of his master
to whom he was a prodigious foil, and ready to execute any commissions, whic
in those days were somewhat complicated." He was private secretary an
keeper of the privy purse to King George IV. when Prince Regent, was swor
of the Privy Council, and created a Baronet, 7th August, 1817, with remainde
in default of male issue, to his brother. SIR JOHN died 12th September, 181'
the title devolving on his brother THOMAS, a distinguished military officer, wh
was Adjutant-General of Her Majesty's forces in India, Lieut.-Gov. of Port
mouth, Commander-in-Chief of the Bombay Army, &c.
    SIR JOHN M'MAHON left a large personal property, amounting to £90,00
One of his bequests is thus worded : "To THOMAS MARRABLE, a dear ar
esteemed friend, £2000 ; and with my last prayers for the glory and happine:
of the best-hearted man in the world, the PRINCE REGENT, I bequeath him th
said Thomas Marrable, an invaluable servant". The latter was a member
the household of King George IV., and one of his confidential agents. A fu
length portrait of him as one of the procession is given in Sir G. Nayler's histo
of the coronation of that monarch.
    Among Gillray's *Caricatures* is an amusing one, engraved but not designed l
him, published in 1804, representing the Heir-Apparent, mounted on a tall hors
with the much smaller person of M'Mahon consequentially riding on a dimin
tive steed at his side, passing the gates of Carlton House. The quotation fro
Burns engraved on it suggests that the Prince might still prove a worthy occ
pant of the throne.—ED.]

# No. XII.

Jan. 29, 1798.

THE following Ode* was dropped into the letterbox in our Publisher's window. From its title—"A BIT OF AN ODE TO MR. FOX"—we were led to imagine there was some mistake in the business, and that it was meant to have been conveyed to Mr. Wright's neighbour, Mr. Debrett, whom we recollected to have been the Publisher of the " Half of a Letter" to the same gentleman, which occasioned so much noise (of horse-laughing) in the world. Our politics certainly do not entitle us to the honourable distinction of being made the channel for communicating such a production to the public. But, for our parts, as we are " not at war with genius," on whatever side we find it, we are happy to give this Poem the earliest place in our Paper; and shall be equally ready to pay the same attention to any future favours of the same kind, and from the same quarter.

The Poem is a free translation, or rather, perhaps, imitation, of the twentieth Ode of the second Book of HORACE. We have taken the liberty to subjoin the passages of which the parallel is the most striking.

A BIT OF AN ODE TO MR. FOX.*

I.

On[1] grey goose quills sublime I'll soar
To metaphors unreach'd before,
    That scare the vulgar reader:

---

[* As if written by ROBERT ADAIR, who had previously indited
" HALF a Letter to Mr. Fox".]

With style well form'd from BURKE's best·books—
From rules of grammar (e'en HORNE TOOKE's)
    A bold and free Seceder.

II.

I² whom, dear Fox, you condescend
To call your "Honourable Friend,"
    Shall live for everlasting:
That ⁸ Stygian Gallery I'll quit,
Where printers crowd me, as I sit
    Half-dead with rage and fasting.

III.

I⁴ feel! the growing down descends,
Like goose-skin, to my fingers' ends—
    Each nail becomes a feather:
My cropp'd head⁵ waves with sudden plumes,
Which erst (like BEDFORD's, or his groom's)
    Unpowder'd, braved the weather. *

IV.

I mount, I mount into the sky,
" Sweet ⁰ bird," to ⁷ *Petersburg* I'll fly ;
    Or, if you bid, to *Paris;*
Fresh missions of the *Fox and Goose*
Successful Treaties may produce ;
    Though PITT in all miscarries.

V.

Scotch,⁸ English, Irish *Whigs* shall read
The Pamphlets, Letters, Odes I breed,
    Charm'd with each bright endeavour :

[* MR. PITT's Tax upon Hair-powder proved a faire:
many of the public declining its use. Those who continu'd it
were called " *guinea-pigs,*" the tax being a guinea per head.-ED.]

*Alarmists* [9] tremble at my strain,
E'en [10] PITT, made candid by champaign,
Shall hail ADAIR "*the clever*".

VI.

Though criticism assail my name,
And luckless blunders blot my fame,[11]
O ![12] make no needless bustle ;
As vain and idle it would be
To waste one pitying thought on me,
As to [13] "unPLUMB a RUSSELL ".*

---

[1] Non usitatâ nec tenui ferar
Pennâ biformis per liquidum æthera
Vates.
[2] ——Non ego, quem vocas
Dilecte, Mæcenas, obibo,
[3] Nec Stygiâ cohibebor undâ.
[4] Jamjam resident cruribus asperæ
Pelles, et album mutor in alitem
[5] Supernê, nascunturque leves
Per digitos humerosque plumæ.
Visam gementis littora Bosphori,
Syrtesque Gætulas,[6] canorus
Ales,[7] Hyperboreosque campos.
[8] Me Colchus, et qui [9] dissimulat metum
  \*    \*    \*
 \*    \*    \*  me peritus
Discet Iber Rhodanique [10] potor.
Absint [11] inani funere neniæ,
[12] Luctusque turpes et querimoniæ.
[13] —————— ——— sepulchri
Mitte supervacuous honores.

[\* For an explanation of this allusion, see Note at p. 74.—ED.]

## [LYRICS OF HORACE, BOOK II., ODE XX.

### TRANSLATED BY ARCHDEACON WRANGHAM

Borne on no weak or vulgar wing,
Upward through air, two-form'd, I'll spring;
Nor longer grovel here, but soar
Where Envy shall pursue no more.
Not I, from hnmble lineage sprung,
Not I, dear Patron, whom thy tongue
Summons to fame, will fear to die,
Or bound by Styx's fetters lie.

A rougher skin my legs assume ;
My upward limbs the cygnet's plume
Invests ; my shoulders, fingers feel
The feathery softness o'er them steal.

Fleeter than Icarus now I'll haste,
A tuneful swan, to Libya's waste,
And heaving sands, where Bospor's wave
Tosses, or Arctic tempests rave.
Me Colchis, Dacia me shall learn,
Who hides her fear of Marsian stern ;
Me Scythia's hordes, the well-trained son
Of Spain, and he who quaffs the Rhone.

From my mock bier be far away
The loud lament, the funeral lay ;
And, tribute to my fancied doom,
Far the vain honours of the tomb !—ED.]

[The charge of FOX'S having sent ADAIR to St. Petersburg, to counteract the measures of PITT'S government, first broached in Mr. Burke's " Letter on the Conduct of the Minority," has been vigorously contradicted, yet so late as April, 1854, it was alluded to as a fact by Lord Malmesbury in the House of Peers. It was, however, on this occasion again authoritatively denied by LORD CAMPBELL, who took occasion to observe that SIR ROBERT ADAIR was "now in his 90th year, and for many years had served his country with great assiduity and fidelity. He had been sent by successive ministers [Mr. Fox, Lord Grey, *Mr. Canning* (who assisted in libelling him so often in the pages of the present work), Lord Wellesley, Lord Palmerston, the Duke of Wellington] to Vienna, to Constantinople, to Brussels, and to Berlin, and had represented the Crown of England upon some occasions of very great importance, in which he had uniformly acquitted himself to the satisfaction of the Government and for the benefit of his country. He believed a more honourable man had not lived in this country at any time."

The following denial by Sir Robert Adair himself is copied from his autograph statement, prefixed to the *Life of Wilberforce*, published in 1838 :—" This idle story is here accredited by Mr. Wilberforce, and inserted by his sons, without due examination. It was grounded on a journey I made to Vienna and St. Petersburg in 1791. Doctor Prettyman [*sic*], Bishop of Winchester, in a work entitled *The Life of the Right Hon. William Pitt*, published by him in 1823, brought forward the fact of my having gone upon this journey as a criminal charge against Mr. Fox, who, as he pretends, sent me upon it with the intent of counteracting some negociations then carrying on between Great Britain and Russia at St. Petersburg. I answered his accusation, I trust successfully, in two letters published by Longman & Co. [*Two Letters from Mr. Adair to the Bp. of Winchester, in answer to the charge of a High Treasonable Misdemeanour brought by his Lordship against Mr. Fox and himself in his Life of the Rt. Hon. W. Pitt*, 8vo., 1821], and explained the circumstances which induced me in my travels in 1791 to visit the two capitals above mentioned.—ROBERT ADAIR : 1838."

The "Mission" was, however, firmly believed in, and PITT was urged, but in vain, by the Duke of Richmond and others of the Government, to arrest FOX for high treason.

The following extract from the *Political Memoranda of Francis, fifth Duke of Leeds, now first printed from the Originals in the British Museum; edited by Oscar Browning, for the Camden Society*, 1884, is an illustration of the rumours current at the time, and many years after.

"Saty. 24 Novr. 1792. LORD ST. HELENS dined with me. After the Ladies were gone upstairs we conversed for some time on Foreign affairs. . . . Speaking of the Russian business of last year he reprobated in the strongest terms the conduct of FOX in sending an agent, MR. ADAIR, to Petersburg to counteract the negociations of this Court at that of Russia. He told me he knew for certain that MR. ADAIR had shewn to some English merchants at Petersburg the Empress' Picture set in diamonds which had been given to him. That it was not one of the sort usually given, but of much greater value, being set round with large Brilliants, and the whole Picture covered with a Table Diamond instead of Chrystal. That this was a present seldom made but on some very particular occasion or to some great favorite (I remember to have seen such a one in the possession of P. Orlow). LD. ST. H. thought it must have been worth six or seven thousand pounds, and of too much value probably to have been meant for MR. ADAIR. The conclusion we both very naturally drew from this circumstance was not very favorable to MR. FOX."

The following additional particulars relating to the connection between FOX and ADAIR may not be thought out of place here. They are extracted from the highly interesting and important *Croker Papers, being the Correspondence and Diaries*, 1809-1830, *of the Rt. Hon. J. W. CROKER, M.P., Edited by Louis J. Jennings, M.P.*, 3 vols., 8vo., 1884.

The first is in these terms: "When ADAIR, whose father was a surgeon, went as FOX'S Ambassador to Russia, LORD WHITWORTH, then the King's Minister, made a good joke, which tended not a little to lower ADAIR, and defeat his object. 'Est-ce un homme très considérable, ce M. d'Adair?' asked the EMPRESS. 'Pas trop, Madame,' replied Lord Whitworth, 'quoique son père était grand seigneur [saigneur].' The other is taken from a very long statement on various matters, made by K. George IV., when Prince of Wales, to Croker personally. Adair's wife, the Prince said, was a Frenchwoman with whom ANDREOSSI, when here as Buonaparte's Minister, intrigued. THE DUCHESS OF DEVONSHIRE told him—the Prince of Wales—that Mrs. Adair had offered her a bribe of £10,000 down, and as much more whenever she might want it, if she would communicate the Cabinet secrets, with which the French thought she could not fail to be acquainted, through her intimacy with all the leaders of the Government. This caused a breach between FOX and ADAIR. But the former could only tell ADAIR that an obstacle—which he could neither reveal nor overcome, but which did not affect or alter FOX'S personal regard for him —prevented his appointment to be FOX'S Under-Secretary of State.—*Croker Papers*, i. 203.—ED.]

# No. XIII.

Feb. 5, 1798.

## ACME AND SEPTIMIUS; OR, THE HAPPY UNION

CELEBRATED AT THE CROWN AND ANCHOR TAVERN.

Fox,[1] with TOOKE to grace his side,
Thus address'd his blooming bride—
"Sweet! should I e'er, in power or place,
Another Citizen embrace;
Should e'er my eyes delight to look
On aught alive save JOHN HORNE TOOKE,
Doom me to ridicule and ruin,
In the coarse hug[2] of *Indian* Bruin!"
He spoke;[3] and to the left and right,
NORFOLK hiccupp'd with delight.
TOOKE,[4] his bald head gently moving,
   On the sweet patriot's drunken eyes
   His wine-empurpled lips applies,
And thus returns in accents loving:
"So, my dear[5] CHARLEY, may success
At length my ardent wishes bless,
And lead, through discord's low'ring storm,
To one grand RADICAL REFORM!
As, from this hour I love thee more
Than e'er I hated thee before!"
He spoke, and to the left and right,
NORFOLK hiccupp'd with delight.
With this good omen they proceed;[6]
Fond toasts their mutual passion feed;

In Fox's breast HORNE TOOKE prevails
Before [7] rich *Ireland* and *South Wales;* *
And Fox (unread each other book),
Is Law and Gospel to HORNE TOOKE.
When were such kindred souls united?
Or wedded pair so much delighted?

[1] Acmen Septimius suos amores
Tenens in gremio, mea, inquit, Acme,
Ni te perdite amo, &c.
[2] Cæsio veniam obvius Leoni.
[3] Hoc ut dixit, Amor sinistram, ut ante
Dextram, sternuit approbationem.
[4] At Acme leviter caput reflectens,
· Et dulcis pueri ebrios ocellos
Illo purpureo ore suaviata,
Sic, inquit, mea vita,[5] Septimille, &c.
[6] Nunc ab auspicio bono profecti
Mutuis animis amant, amantur.
Unam Septimius misellus Acmen
Mavult quam [7] Syrias Britanniasque. *

* *I.e.*, The Clerkship of the Pells in Ireland, and Auditorship
of South Wales.

[ACME AND SEPTIMIUS. FROM CATULLUS.

SEPTIMIUS said, and fondly prest
The doating ACME to his breast :—
" My Acme, if I prize not thee
With love as warm as love can be,
With passion spurning any fears
Of growing faint in length of years,
Alone may I defenceless stand
To meet, on Lybia's desert sand,
Or under India's torrid sky,
The tawny lion's glaring eye ! "
LOVE, before who utter'd still
On the left-hand omens ill,
As he ceased his faith to plight
Laugh'd propitious on the right.
Then ACME gently bent her head,
Kiss'd with those lips of cherry red
The eyes of the delightful boy,
That swam with glistening floods of joy ;
And whisper'd as she closely prest—
" SEPTIMIUS, soul of ACME'S breast,
Let all our lives and feelings own
One lord, one sovereign, Love alone !
I yield to love, and yield to thee,
For thou and love are one to me.

Though fond thy fervent heart may beat,
My feelings glow with greater heat,
And madder flames my bosom melt
Than all that thou hast ever felt."—ED.]

[The following account of the celebration of Fox's Birth-day, printed in the *Anti-Jacobin*, has not hitherto appeared in the editions of the *Poetry*. *The Song by Mr. Fox* refers to the Subscription raised, after a meeting at the Crown and Anchor, in the summer of 1793, for relieving him in his then present need, and purchasing an Annuity for him. A Caricature by GILLRAY on this meeting was published on the 12th June, 1793.

## MR. FOX'S BIRTH-DAY.

The public, distracted with the various accounts of the celebration of Mr• Fox's Birth-day, naturally turn to us for an authentic detail of that important event—from a recollection of the correct and impartial statement we gave in a former Number, of what passed at a MEETING OF THE FRIENDS OF FREEDOM [page 32].

To justify their confidence, we have had recourse to the *Morning Post* and *Morning Chronicle* (the *Courier* being too stupid for our purpose), whose statements we have carefully read, and corrected from the information of several gentlemen who were present. We are thus enabled to lay before our readers a genuine narrative of the whole proceeding, which we defy the tongue of Slander to controvert in any material point.

As Mr. Fox's reputation had been for some time on the decline, it was thought necessary by the party (who are in great want of a *Head*) to make as respectable an appearance as possible on the present occasion. It was therefore suggested (at a previous meeting of confidential friends) that if the unfortunate shyness which subsisted between the *Whig-Club* and the *Corresponding Society* could be opportunely removed by a few unimportant concessions on the part of the former, such a number of citizens might be readily procured from that respectable body as would serve to give the day an *éclat* it had not experienced since the fatal schism of 1792.

This hint, so reasonable in itself, was immediately adopted, and Sir FRANCIS BURDETT, who was well acquainted with their haunts, was ordered into the neighbourhood of Smithfield with a competent number of tickets. He was on the point of setting out, when the Editor of the *Morning Post* observed, that *forgery* * was so common at present, that he hardly thought it prudent to admit all who might come with a bit of scribbled paper : on this it was determined to distribute the price of admission amongst a certain number of people to be selected by the Envoy :—these, it was rightly concluded, would not fail to appear, from motives of vanity, as they could have no other possible chance of dining with the Premier Dupe. we would say Duke, in England. It now remained to determine the sum : this, after a short discussion, was fixed at Eight Shillings and Sixpence per head, " which," said the Editor of the *Morning Post*, " will shew we cannot be persons of mean rank, since we can afford, in hard times, to give so much for a dinner " ;† and Citizen BOSVILLE was desired to advance the money upon the credit of the Whig Fund.

Previous to the meeting, the chairman dispatched a note to Sir WILLIAM ADDINGTON, requesting that the Crown and Anchor might be exempted from the visitation of his runners during the morning of the 24th [Jan., 1798]. To this Sir WILLIAM assented, on condition that it should be recommended to the

---

[* On 7th Feb., 1796, a *forged* French newspaper called *L'Eclair*, containing false intelligence, was circulated in London for stock-jobbing purposes. On 3rd July a verdict of £100 was given against D. STUART, proprietor of *The Morning Post*, for sending the above paper to the proprietors of *The Telegraph*, by which it was discredited ; and on the following day, a verdict of £1500 was given against Mr. Dickinson, for falsely accusing Mr. Goldsmid, the money-broker, of forging the above. It announced a peace between Austria and France.—ED.]

† *Morning Post*, Jan. 25.

gentlemen, to leave their pocket-books and watches at home, that there might be as little temptation as possible to break the peace. Thus everything was arranged with a precaution that seemed to set accident at defiance.

Before four o'clock the passage to the LARGE ROOM was crammed, when, on a hint that dinner was on the point of being served, one of the head waiters advanced to the great door, and opened a wicket for the admission of the company, as fast as they paid down their money. Two or three had already passed in good order, when Mr. John Nicholls advanced, and instead of 8s. 6d., produced to the astonished receiver, *seventeen* of his PRINTED SPEECHES, which, valuing them at sixpence a-piece, he contended would make up the sum required. These "*assets*," however, were absolutely rejected; and a violent dispute was on the point of commencing, when Sir CHRISTOPHER HAWKINS stept forward, and whispering a few words, which we did not hear, obtained leave for his friend to pass. The Speeches were therefore deposited, and Mr. NICHOLLS was already got within the wicket, when the man suddenly pulled him back by the coat, and the dispute recommenced with more violence than ever. Upon inquiry into the cause of this new tumult, we found that a wag (whom we afterwards discovered to be Mr. JEKYLL) had played the member for Tregony a trick; having taken an opportunity, in the crowd, of extracting the *genuine* speeches from the pocket of the Honourable Member, and replacing them by the same number of the *spurious* ones, printed for Mr. WRIGHT, the publisher of this Paper. These the waiter very properly refused to receive, alleging, and indeed truly, that instead of *six* pence a-piece, the whole seventeen were not worth *six* farthings.

This altercation continued so long, that the company grew impatient; and Mr. BRYAN EDWARDS, a little ashamed of his friend, who still continued obstinate, offered to furnish his quota. Harmony now seemed to be restored, when all at once a cry of astonishment broke forth that beggars all description. On putting his hand into his pocket for the price of admission, Mr. E. suddenly turned pale, and exclaimed, " By G—, gentlemen, some of you have picked my pockets !" A hundred voices instantly repeated the same cry, and a dreadful scene of confusion and uproar took place.

Ardebant cuncta et fracta compage ruebant.

What the consequence would have been, it is impossible to say, had not the waiter, with an air of authority, commanded the doors to be shut at each end of the passage, and every man to exhibit the contents of his pocket. A faint cry of No! No! was over-ruled; and Sir FRANCIS BURDETT produced an old Red Cap from the bosom of his shirt, which he put into the hands of the Duke of BEDFORD, who was appointed collector-general *by acclamation*. With this his Grace went, from man to man, executing his duty with the utmost fairness and impartiality; and when he had finished, poured out the contents of the cap before them all. These, it must be confessed, were a little heterogeneous, consisting, besides a large sum of money, of a brass knocker (this was immediately claimed by the landlord), a pewter pot squeezed together, a pair of pattens, a pint decanter, a duck ready trussed for dressing, a great quantity of potatoes, and a vinegar cruet. What was most extraordinary was, that though, as his Grace afterwards declared, the money was found in very unequal portions, yet the total sum, which was £222, 5s. 6d., being divided among the company, amounting to 523 persons, produced 8s. 6d. for each individual, with the exception of the *Member* for *Tregony*, who brought nothing but his speech, and Capt. MORRIS, who pays for everything with a Song.

Nothing material occurred during the Dinner, which was allowed to be excellent of its kind, and where no such dish as Cow-heel (as maliciously reported in *The True Briton*) made its appearance.

As soon as the cloth was removed, the Duke of NORFOLK took the Chair amidst repeated plaudits,* and addressed the Company in these words :

"Three virtuous Men, Citizens, have stood up in defence of Liberty—MAXIMILIAN ROBESPIERRE, COLLOT D'HERBOIS, and CHARLES JAMES FOX :—The first is guillotined; the second transported to *Cayenne*; and the third"—— Here

---

* *Morning Chronicle*, Jan. 25.

all eyes were immediately upon Mr. FOX, who now entered the room, supported by Citizens JOHN GALE JONES and JOHN HORNE TOOKE ——"As the Right Hon. Gentleman (resumed the Duke, a little peevishly) has mistaken his cue, and appeared sooner than he ought, I shall spare his modesty the panegyric I was preparing, and shortly conclude with proposing the health of CHARLES JAMES FOX."—This was drank with three times three.

As soon as the clamour had subsided, Mr. FOX arose and said, "That language, at least any which he could boast, was inadequate to the exquisite feelings of gratitude which at once delighted and oppressed him, at the sight of so numerous and so respectable a body of free and independent Citizens, met for a purpose which would make this the proudest and the happiest day of his life". Having dwelt a little on this idea, Mr. FOX observed, "that he would not interrupt the conviviality of the day by a long Speech : he knew there were several present who came to hear him make a long Speech, but he would not make a long Speech—to what purpose should he do it?—what could he add to the Speech lately delivered by him, and so faithfully recorded in the ANTI-JACOBIN, a contemptible Publication, but one to which the praise of Accuracy could not be denied. The new and extraordinary circumstances of the times called for new and extraordinary measures: he would, therefore, if they pleased, compress what he had to say into a *Song*—(*loud applauses*)—One word only.— He owed both the *burden* and the *idea* of this Song to the *Morning Chronicle*. He had yesterday, the 23rd, found there A BEGGING ADDRESS to the Nation, with DATE OBOLUM BELISARIO prefixed to it as a Motto. This had pleased him much, and this morning at breakfast he had endeavoured to adapt it, *mutatis mutandis*, to his own circumstances : he should now have the honour of giving it."

SONG BY MR. FOX.

*To the Tune of*

" Good People of England, and all who love Ale."

Good People of England, of every degree,
Lords. Commoners, listen, O ! listen to me ;
Republicans, Royalists, all—mark my ditty—
You'll find I've a number of claims on your pity—
    Date Obolum Belisario.

Ye who heard me assert that Lord NORTH, now so mourn'd,
Was a *beast* to be shunn'd, was a *fool* to be scorn'd,
Yet who saw me, with real or fancied alarms,
Take the *fool* to my councils, the *beast* to my arms,
    Date Obolum Belisario.

Ye who heard me declare the SUBSCRIBERS of REEVES
Were a scoundrel collection of cut-throats and thieves,
Yet who saw me immediately after repair,
And SUBSCRIBE at the Long-Room in Hanover Square,
    Date Obolum Belisario.

Ye who heard—when Invasion was close at our door,
And *Parker* and Liberty rul'd at the *Nore*—
Ye who heard—no ; I mean, who DID NOT HEAR me speak,
While SHERIDAN,* damn him ! affected to *squeak*,
    Date Obolum Belisario.

Ye who heard me repeat that Resistance, at length,
Was reduc'd, by PITT'S Bill, to a question of *Strength*,
And that *prudence* alone——

We know not how far Mr. FOX might have proceeded, had he not been interrupted by a jangling of bells from the Side-table which immediately drew all eyes that way. This proceeded from Capt. MORRIS, who had fallen asleep

---

* This appears to allude to Mr. SHERIDAN'S conduct during the *Mutiny*.

during Mr. FOX'S Song, and was now nodding on his chair, with a large paper Cap on his head, ornamented with gilt tassels and bells, which one of the company had dexterously whipped on unperceived. The first motion was that of indignation; but the stupid stare of the unconscious Captain, who half opened his eyes at every sound of the bells as his head rose or fell, and immediately closed them again, *somno vinoque gravatus*, had such a powerful effect on the risible faculties of the Company, that they broke, as if by consent, into the most violent and convulsive fits of laughter; Mr. FOX himself not being exempt from the general contagion.

As soon as the Captain was made sensible of the cause of this uproar, he attempted to pull off the Cap, but was prevented by a Citizen from the *Corresponding Society*, who maintained that the Company had a right to be amused by the Captain in what manner they pleased; and that, as he seemed to amuse them more effectually in *that state* than in any other, he insisted, for one, on his continuing to wear the Cap. This was universally agreed to, with the exception of the Duke of NORFOLK. The Captain was therefore led to the upper table, with all his "jangling honours loud upon him!" Here, as soon as he was seated, his Noble Friend called upon him for a Song.

The Captain sang the "PLENIPO" in his best manner.

This was received with great applause; and then the Duke gave "The Defenders—of Ireland"—(*three times three*).

Captain MORRIS then began
    "And all the Books of Moses";—
but was interrupted, before he had finished the first line, by Mr. TIERNEY, who declared he would not sit there and hear anything like ridicule on the Bible.*— (*Much coughing and scraping.*)—Mr. Erskine took God to witness, that he thought the Captain meant no harm;—and a gentleman from Cambridge, whose name we could not learn, said, with great *naïveté*, that it was no more than was done every day by his acquaintance. Mr. TIERNEY, however, persisted in his opposition to the Song, and Captain MORRIS was obliged to substitute "Jenny Sutton" in the place of it

But the good humour of the company was already broken in upon, and Mr. TIERNEY soon after left the room (to which he did not return) with greater marks of displeasure in his face than we ever remember to have seen there.

The Duke now gave RADICAL REFORM (*three times three, followed by continued shouts of applause*).

A Counsellor JACKSON attempted to sing "Paddy Whack," but was soon silenced, on account of his stupid perversion of the words, and his bad voice.

Citizen GALE JONES then rose and said—that he was no Orator, though he got his living by oratory, being Chairman of a Debating Society. He had also written a book—which he was told had some merit. He did not rise to recommend it, but he thought it right to *hint*, that those who wished for Constitutional information might be supplied with it at the Bar; the price was trifling —Eighteen-pence was nothing to the majority of the Company;—to himself, indeed—(here Mr. HORNE TOOKE called out Order! Order! with some marks of impatience)—He begged pardon, he would say no more—there was no one whom he valued like Mr. TOOKE, there was no one indeed to whom he was under such obligations; the very shoes he had on were charged by Citizen HARDY to Mr. TOOKE'S account—Mr. TOOKE was also a great friend to a Radical Reform—he loved a Radical Reform himself; the Poor must always love Radical Reforms— he should therefore beg leave to propose the health of Mr. JOHN HORNE TOOKE. —(*Three times three.*)

Mr. TOOKE rose, and spoke nearly as follows: "You all know, Citizens, in what detestation I once held the Man whose Birth-day we are now met to commemorate. You cannot yet have forgot the 'TWO PAIR OF PORTRAITS' I formerly published, nor the glaring light in which I hung up him and his father to the execration of an indignant posterity. You must also be apprized of the charges of Corruption, Insurrection,and Murder (*much hissing and applause,*

---

* This is not the first time that we have heard of Mr. TIERNEY'S discouragement of impiety. However we may disapprove of this gentleman's political principles, we are not insensible to the merit of such conduct.

*the latter predominant*) which I brought against him, justly, as I must still think, at a former Election for Westminster. How happens it then, you will say, that I now come forward to do him honour? I will tell you. At the last Election for Westminster, I had still my suspicions of his sincerity; he appeared too anxious to preserve measures with the spruce and powdered Aristocrats who usually attended him to the Hustings; nor was it till the fourth or fifth day before the close of the Poll, that those suspicions were removed. Aware that he was losing ground among the People, he determined to make one great effort to re-establish his popularity. He therefore came forward, and addressed the free and independent Electors in front of the Hustings, in a Speech, of which the remembrance yet warms my heart. From that moment, I marked him as my own! Retractation was impossible; and the panegyric he lately delivered on a Radical Reform, in a House which I despise too much to name, was the natural and inevitable consequence of that day's declaration. You may remember, that when I addressed my Friends, I only said, 'Gentlemen, Mr. FOX has spoken my sentiments; he has even gone beyond them—but I thank him'.— What I then said I now repeat, with regard to his Speech on a late occasion— 'I AM MOST PERFECTLY SATISFIED WITH HIS CONDUCT; NOR DO I WISH TO ADVANCE ONE STEP IN THE CAUSE OF REFORM, BEYOND WHAT MR. FOX HAS PLEDGED HIMSELF TO GO!!!'"*

Mr. TOOKE then begged leave to propose Mr. FOX's health for the second time, and sat down amidst a thunder of applause.†

The Duke of NORFOLK observed to the Company, that as they had drunk the health of a Man dear to the People, he would now call upon them to drink the health of their Sovereign!—here a hiccup interrupted his Grace, and a most violent cry of "No Sovereign! no Sovereign!" resounded through the room, and continued for several minutes, notwithstanding the earnest entreaties of the Duke to be heard. Order was, however, restored at length, when his Grace gently chid the Company for taking advantage of a slight infirmity of nature, to impute a design to him which was wholly foreign from his heart—(*loud applause*). He augured well, however, of their patriotism, and would now afford them an opportunity of repairing the injury they had done him, by giving the Toast as he intended—"THE HEALTH OF OUR SOVEREIGN—THE MAJESTY OF THE PEOPLE".§ —(*Loud and incessant shouts of applause.*)

A disgusting scene of uproar and confusion followed, which we shall not attempt to detail. The Chairman sank under the table in a state of stupefaction, and the rest of the Company, maddened alike with noise and wine, committed a thousand outrages, till they were literally turned into the streets by the Waiters. As many of them as could speak were conducted home by the watchmen; others were conveyed "in silent majesty" to the Round-house; and not a few of them slept out the remainder of the night upon the steps of the neighbouring houses. The Reporters of the Jacobin Papers were sought out, and conveyed home by the pressmen, devils, &c., and one poor youth, whom we afterwards found to be a Writer in the *Morning Chronicle* (hired for the day by *The True Briton*) || had his pockets picked of a clean white Handkerchief and a Notebook, after being severely beaten for deserting his former Employers.

---

* *Morning Post*, Jan. 25.    † *Morning Chronicle*, Jan. 25.

‡ *Morning Chronicle, Morning Post, Morning Herald*, &c.

§ The Company seem to have recollected (had *his Grace* forgotten?) that the DUKE of NORFOLK has *another* SOVEREIGN, to whom he has recently, more than once, sworn Allegiance; and under whom he *now* holds the LIEUTENANCY of the WEST RIDING of the COUNTY OF YORK, and the Command of a REGIMENT of MILITIA.

|| See *The True Briton*, of Thursday, Jan. 25.

The LOYAL TOAST.

# No. XIV.

Feb. 12, 1798.

IT has been our invariable custom to suppress such of our correspondents' favours as conveyed any compliments to ourselves; and we have deviated from it in the present instance, not so much out of respect to the uncommon excellence of the Poem before us, as because it agrees so intimately with the general design of our paper—to expose the deformity of the French Revolution, to counteract the detestable arts of those who are seeking to introduce it here, and above all, to invigorate the exertions of our countrymen against every Foe, foreign and domestic, by showing them the immense and inexhaustible resources they yet possess in British Courage and British Virtue !

TO

~ THE AUTHOR OF THE ANTI-JACOBIN.

FOE TO THY COUNTRY'S FOES ! 'tis THINE to claim
From Britain's genuine sons a British fame—
Too long French manners our fair isle disgraced ;
Too long French fashions shamed our native taste.
Still prone to change, we half-resolved to try
The proffered charms of FRENCH FRATERNITY.

Fair was her form, and FREEDOM's honour'd name
Conceal'd the horrors of her secret shame :
She claim'd some kindred with that guardian pow'r,
Long worshipp'd here in Britain's happier hour :
Virtue and Peace, she said, were in her train,
The long-lost blessings of ASTRÆA's reign—
But soon the vizor dropp'd—her haggard face
Betray'd the FURY lurking in the GRACE—

The false attendants that behind her press'd,
In vain disguised, the latent guilt confess'd :
PEACE dropt her snow-white robe, and shudd'ring show'd
AMBITION's mantle reeking fresh with blood ;
Presumptuous FOLLY stood in REASON's form,
Pleased with the power to ruin,—not reform ;
PHILOSOPHY, proud phantom, undismay'd,
With cold regard the ghastly train survey'd ;
Saw PERSECUTION gnash her iron teeth,
While *Atheists* preach'd the *eternal sleep of death ;*
Saw ANARCHY the social chain unbind,
And DISCORD sour the blood of human kind ;
Then talk'd of Nature's Rights, and Equal Sway ;
And saw her system safe—AND STALK'D AWAY !

Foil'd by our ARMS, where'er in ARMS we met,
With ARTS LIKE THESE the foe assails us yet.
Hopeless the fort to storm, or to surprise,
More secret wiles his envious malice tries ;
Diseas'd himself, spread wide his own despair,
Pollutes the fount, and taints the wholesome air.

While many a Chief, to glory not unknown,
Alarms each hostile shore, and guards our own,
'Tis THINE, the latent treachery to proclaim ;
An humbler warfare, but the cause the same.
In vain had POMPEY crush'd the PONTIC HOST,
And chas'd the pirate swarm from every coast ;
The crew that leagu'd their country to o'erthrow ;
The base confederates of a GALLIC * foe ;

---

* Conjuravere Cives nobilissimi Patriam incendere—*Gallorum* gentem infestissimam nomini Romano in bellum arcessunt— Dux Hostium cum exercitu supra caput est.—ORAT. CATON. ap. SALLUST.

Had not the Civic Consul's watchful eye
Track'd through the windings of conspiracy,
Exposed, confounded, shamed, and forced away,
The "JACOBIN REFORMER * of his day ".

'Tis THINE a subtler mischief to pursue,
And drag a deeper, darker, plot to view ;
Whate'er its form, still ready to engage,
Detect its malice, or resist its rage ;
Whether it whispers low, or raves aloud,
In sneers profane, or blasphemies avow'd ; †
Insults its King, reviles its Country's cause,
And, 'scaped from Justice, braves the lenient Laws :
Whate'er the hand in desperate faction bold,
By native hate inspired, or foreign gold ;
Traitors absolved, and libellers released,
The recreant Peer, or renegado Priest ; ‡
The *Sovereign-people's* cringing, crafty slave,
The dashing fool, and instigating knave,
Each claims thy care ; nor think the labour vain—
VERMIN HAVE SUNK THE SHIP THAT RULED THE MAIN.

---

* Tum Catilina polliceri tabulas novas, proscriptionem locu-
pletium, Magistratus, Sacerdotia, rapinas, alia omnia quæ
bellum atque lubido Victorum fert.—SALLUST.

[ † "A Correspondent cautions us against making a profane
use of MR. WILBERFORCE's appearance on Sunday; that gentleman would not have been so ungodly as to gallop there without
a sufficient reason—it was the fulfilment of some Prophecy ;
and the horse he rode might be related to the White Horse of
the Revelations."—*Morning Chronicle*, Jan. 11, 1798.—ED.]

[‡ This refers to Charles Howard, eleventh DUKE OF NORFOLK,
(who gave, at a public dinner, the famous toast of " Our Sovereign's health, the Majesty of the People,") and to John Horne
Tooke, who was a regularly ordained clergyman, and had been
tried for High Treason and acquitted.—ED.]

7

'Tis THINE, with Truth's fair shield to ward the blow,
And turn the weapon back upon the foe :
To trace the skulking fraud, the candid cheat,
That can retract the falsehood, yet repeat ;
To wake the listless, slumb'ring as they lie,
Lapt in th' embrace of soft security ;
To rouse the cold, re-animate the brave,
And shew the cautious all they have to save.

Erect that standard ALFRED first unfurl'd,
Britain's just pride, the wonder of the world ;
Whose staff is Freedom's spear, whose blazon'd field
Beams with the CHRISTIAN CROSS, the REGAL SHIELD ;
That standard which the PATRIOT BARONS bore,
Restored, from RUNIMEDE's resounding shore ;
Which since consign'd to WILLIAM's guardian hand,
Waved in new splendour o'er a grateful land ;
Which oft in vain by force or fraud assail'd,
Has stood the shock of ages—and prevail'd.

Yes! the BRIGHT SUN OF BRITAIN yet shall shine—
The clouds are earth-born, but his fire divine ;
That temperate splendour, and that genial heat,
Shall still illume, and cherish Empire's Seat ;
While the red Meteor, whose portentous glare
Shot plagues infectious through the troubled air ;
Admired, or fear'd no more, shall melt away,
Lost in the radiance of HIS BRIGHTER DAY!

DESIGN FOR THE NEW GALLERY OF BUSTS AND PICTURES.

## LINES.

*Written under the Bust of Charles Fox at the Crown
and Anchor.*

I'll not sell Uncle NOLL, Charles Surface cries ;—
I'll not sell CHARLEY Fox, John Bull replies :
Sell him, indeed! who'll find me such another?—
Fox is above all price; so hold your pother.

*Morning Post, Feb.* 6.

To make our readers some amends for this miserable
doggrel, we will present them, in our turn, with some
lines written *under a bust*, NOT *at the Crown and Anchor*,
by an ENGLISH TRAVELLER just returned from Petersburgh. We believe they are more just; we are certain
they are more poetical.

## LINES.

*Written by a Traveller at Czarco-zelo under the Bust of a certain
Orator, once placed between those of Demosthenes and Cicero.*

I.

THE GRECIAN Orator of old,
With scorn rejected PHILIP's laws,
Indignant spurn'd at foreign gold,
And triumph'd in his country's cause.

II.

A foe to every wild extreme,
'Mid civil storms, the Roman Sage
Repress'd Ambition's frantic scheme,
And check'd the madding people's rage.

III.

Their country's peace, and wealth and fame,
With patriot zeal their labours sought,

And Rome's or Athens' honoured name
Inspired and govern'd every thought.

### IV.

Who now, in this presumptuous hour,
Aspires to share the Athenian's praise?
—The advocate of foreign power,
The Æschines of later days.

### V.

What chosen name to Tully's join'd,
Is thus announced to distant climes?
—Behold, to lasting shame consign'd,
The *Catiline* of modern times! *

---

[* These lines allude to the Empress Catherine's plac:
in her gallery the bust of Fox between those of Demosthei
and Cicero, as a token of gratitude for his exertions in ‹
feating the project of PITT, who, in conjunction with Prus
and Holland, had, in 1791, prepared a powerful armame
to compel her to give up Ockzakow, which she had seiz
The Court party delighted in stigmatizing Fox as the mod‹
*Catiline.* " But the part which he took in parliament sub
quent to 1793, (says *Sir N. W. Wraxall*), and the eulogiu
lavished by him on the French Revolution, soon changed t
Empress's tone. She caused the bust to be removed ; a
when reproached with such a change in her conduct, she repli
' C'étoit Monsieur Fox de *Quatre-vingt-onze* que j'ai placé d‹
mon cabinet '."—*Wraxall's Posthumous Memoirs*, vol. 1., pp. 4
436.

" It seems to have escaped general notice, (says Sir Jan
Prior in his Life of Burke), that the misfortunes of Poland
her final partition may be, in some degree, attributed, howe·
undesignedly on their part, to Mr. Fox and the Oppositi
in the strong and unusual means made use of to thwart I
Pitt in the business of Ockzakow. They lay claim, it is tr
to the merit of having prevented war on that occasion. I
if war had then taken place with England for one act of ‹
lence comparatively trivial, Russia, in all probability, wo
not have ventured upon a second and still greater aggressi
involving the existence of a nation, with the certainty o:

second war. Nothing, after all, might have saved Poland from the combination then on foot against her ; but it is certain that Mr. Pitt, from recent experience, had little encouragement to make the attempt."

It is a curious circumstance that, though the *plate* illustrating these *Lines* was published, according to its inscription, on the 17th March, 1792, the five stanzas engraved on it are identical with those which appeared in the *Anti-Jacobin* of 12th Feb., 1798, though these were introduced as written " by an English Traveller just [*sic*] returned from Petersburgh ".

Assuming the date on the engraving to be correct, we might account for the *parachronism* on the supposition that the author of the earlier *plate-stanzas* availed himself of the appearance of the *Lines written under the Bust of Charles Fox at the Crown and Anchor to reproduce them*—six years afterwards—with a few verbal alterations, to adapt them to a later period—and with an equivocal statement as to the period of their first production.

The following are the alterations in the reprinted version :—

Stanza 2 line 3, frantic *for* lawless.
    ,,   3  ,,  1, their country's *for* domestic.
    ,,   3  ,,  1, and wealth and *for* external.
    ,,   3  ,,  3, honoured *for* sacred.
    ,,   4  ,,  1, now *for* then.
    ,,   4  ,,  3, advocate *for* tool confessed.
    ,,   4  ,,  4, later *for* modern.
    ,,   5  ,,  2, thus *for* now.
    ,,   5  ,,  4, Catiline *for* Cataline.
    ,,   5  ,,  4, modern *for* later.—ED.]

# No. XV.

Feb. 19, 1798.

## THE PROGRESS OF MAN.*

𝕬 𝕯idactic 𝕻oem,

IN FORTY CANTOS, WITH NOTES CRITICAL AND EXPLANATORY :
CHIEFLY OF A PHILOSOPHICAL TENDENCY.

DEDICATED TO R. P. KNIGHT, ESQ.

### CANTO FIRST.

CONTENTS.—The Subject proposed.—Doubts and Wavering;
—Queries not to be answered.—Formation of the stupendou
Whole.—Cosmogony; or the Creation of the World :—th
Devil—Man—Various Classes of Being :—ANIMATED BEING
—Birds—Fish—Beasts—the Influence of the Sexual Appe
tite—on Tigers—on Whales—On Crimpt Cod—on Perch-
on Shrimps—on Oysters.—Various Stations assigned to dif
ferent Animals :—Birds—Bears—Mackerel.—Bears remark
able for their fur—Mackerel cried on a Sunday—Birds d
not graze—nor Fishes fly—nor Beasts live in the Water.-
Plants equally contented with their lot :—Potatoes—Cabbag
—Lettuce—Leeks—Cucumbers.—MAN only discontented-
born a Savage ; not choosing to continue so, become
polished—resigns his Liberty—Priest-craft—King-craft-
Tyranny of Laws and Institutions. — Savage Life — de
scription thereof :—The Savage free—roaming Woods—feed
on Hips and Haws—Animal Food—first notion of it fror
seeing a Tiger tearing his prey—wonders if it is good-
resolves to try—makes a Bow and Arrow—kills a Pig-
resolves to roast a part of it—lights a fire—APOSTROPHE t
fires—Spits and Jacks not yet invented.—Digression.-
CORINTH—SHEFFIELD.—Love, the most natural desire afte
Food.—Savage Courtship.—Concubinage recommended.-
Satirical Reflections on Parents and Children—Husband

[* Written to ridicule Richard Payne Knight's *Progress* (
*Civil Society*, a Didactic Poem, in Six Books. London, 179(
4to.—ED.]

and Wives—against collateral Consanguinity.—FREEDOM the
only Morality, &c. &c. &c.

WHETHER some great, supreme o'er-ruling Power
Stretch'd forth its arm at Nature's natal hour,
'Composed this mighty whole with plastic skill,
Wielding the jarring elements at will?
Or whether, sprung from Chaos' mingling storm,  5
The mass of matter started into form?
Or Chance o'er earth's green lap spontaneous fling
The fruits of autumn and the flowers of spring?
Whether material substance unrefined,
Owns the strong impulse of instructive mind,  10
Which to one centre points diverging lines,
Confounds, refracts, invig'rates, and combines?
Whether the joys of earth, the hopes of heaven,
By man to God, or God to man, were given?
If virtue leads to bliss, or vice to woe?  15
Who rules above, or who reside below?

---

*Ver.* 3. A modern author of great penetration and judgment
observes very shrewdly, that "the cosmogony of the world
has puzzled the philosophers of all ages. What a medley of
opinions have they not broached upon the creation of the
world. Sanconiathon, Manetho, Berosus, and Ocellus Lucanus
have all attempted it in vain. The latter has these words—
*Anarchon ara kai ateleutaion to pan*—which imply, that all things
have neither beginning nor end." See Goldsmith's *Vicar of
Wakefield:* see also Mr. Knight's Poem on the *Progress of Civil
Society.*

*Ver.* 12. The influence of Mind upon Matter, comprehending
the whole question of the Existence of Mind as independent
of Matter, or as co-existent with it, and of Matter considered
as an intelligent and self-dependent Essence, will make the
subject of a larger Poem in 127 Books, now preparing under
the *same* auspices.

*Ver.* 14. See Godwin's *Enquirer;* Darwin's *Zoonomia;* Paine;
Priestley, &c. &c.; also all the French Encyclopædists.

*Ver.* 16. *Quæstio spinosa et contortula.*

Vain questions all—shall man presume to know?
On all these points, and points obscure as these,
Think they who will,—and think whate'er they please!

   Let us a plainer, steadier theme pursue—     20
Mark the grim savage scoop his light canoe;
Mark the dark rook, on pendent branches hung,
With anxious fondness feed her cawing young.—
Mark the fell leopard through the desert prowl,
Fish prey on fish, and fowl regale on fowl;—     25
How Lybian tigers' chawdrons love assails,
And warms, 'midst seas of ice, the melting whales;—
Cools the crimpt cod, fierce pangs to perch imparts,
Shrinks shrivell'd shrimps, but opens oysters' hearts;—
Then say, how all these things together tend     30
To one great truth, prime object, and good end?

   First—to each living thing, whate'er its kind,
Some lot, some part, some station is assign'd.
The feather'd race with pinions skim the *air*—
Not so the mackerel, and still less the bear;     35
*This* roams the *wood*, carniv'rous for his prey!
*That* with soft roe pursues his *watery* way:

---

*Ver.* 26. "Add thereto a tiger's chawdron."—Macbeth.
*Ver.* 26, 27. "In softer notes bids Lybian lions roar,
        And warms the whale on Zembla's frozen shore."
        *Progress of Civil Society,* Book I. ver. 98.
   *Ver.* 29. "An oyster may be crossed in love."—Mr. Sheridan's
*Critic.*
   *Ver.* 34. Birds fly.
   *Ver.* 35. But neither fish, nor beasts—particularly as here
exemplified.
   *Ver.* 36. The bear.
   *Ver.* 37. The mackerel—there are also *hard-roed* mackerel.
*Sed de his alio loco.*

*This*, slain by hunters, yields his shaggy hide;
*That*, caught by fishers, is on *Sundays* cried.—

But each contented with his humble sphere,              40
Moves unambitious through the circling year;
Nor e'er forgets the fortune of his race,
Nor pines to quit, or strives to change his place.
Ah! who has seen the mailed lobster rise,
Clap her broad wings, and soaring claim the skies?     45
When did the owl, descending from her bow'r,
Crop, 'midst the fleecy flocks, the tender flow'r;
Or the young heifer plunge, with pliant limb,
In the salt wave, and fish-like strive to swim?

The same with plants—potatoes 'tatoes breed.—         50
Uncostly cabbage springs from cabbage seed;
Lettuce to lettuce, leeks to leeks succeed;
Nor e'er did cooling cucumbers presume
To flow'r like myrtle, or like violets bloom.
—Man, only,—rash, refined, presumptuous man,          55
Starts from his rank, and mars creation's plan.

*Ver.* 38. Bear's *grease*, or *fat*, is also in great request; being
supposed to have a *criniparous*, or hair-producing quality.
*Ver.* 39. There is a special Act of Parliament which permits
mackerel to be cried on Sundays.
*Ver.* 45 to 49. Every animal contented with the lot which
it has drawn in life. A fine contrast to man, who is always
discontented.
*Ver.* 49. *Salt wave*—wave of the sea—"*briny wave*".—Poetæ
passim.
*Ver.* 50. A still stronger contrast, and a greater shame to
man, is found in plants;—they too are contented—he restless
and changing. *Mens agitat mihi, nec placida contenta quiete est.*
*Ver.* 50. *Potatoes 'tatoes breed.* Elision for the sake of verse,
not meant to imply that the root degenerates.—Not so with man—
Mox daturus
Progeniem vitiosiorem.

Born the free heir of nature's wide domain,
To art's strict limits bounds his narrow'd reign ;
Resigns his native rights for meaner things,
For faith and fetters—laws, and priests, and kings.    60

*( To be continued.)*

We are sorry to be obliged to break off here. The
remainder of this admirable and instructive Poem is in
the press, and will be continued the first opportunity.

THE EDITOR.

[The following is the commencement of Knight's poem :—

    Whether primordial motion sprang to life
    From the wild war of elemental strife ;
    In central chains the mass inert confined,
    And sublimated matter into mind :
    Or, whether one great all-pervading soul
    Moves in each part and animates the whole ;
    Unnumbered worlds to one great centre draws,
    And governs all by pre-established laws :
    Whether in fates' eternal fetters bound,
    Mechanic nature goes her endless round :
    Or ever varying, acts but to fulfil
    The sovereign mandates of Almighty will ;—
    Let learned folly seek, or foolish pride,
    Rash in presumptuous ignorance, decide.—ED.]

[Eminent as Richard Payne Knight was as a classical scholar and archæologist, his poetical powers were not highly appreciated by his literary contemporaries, as is amusingly shown in a letter from Horace Walpole, dated 22nd
March, 1796, to the Rev. W. Mason, in which he declares how much he is
"offended and disgusted by Mr. Knight's new, insolent, and self-conceited
poem ". He winds up thus : "I send you a parody on two lines of Mr. Knight,
which will show you that his poem is seen in its true light by a young man of
allowed parts, MR. CANNING, whom I never saw. The originals are the two
first lines at the top of page 5 :"—

    "Some fainter irritations seem to feel,
      Which o'er its languid fibres gently steal ".—KNIGHT.

    " Cools the crimp'd cod, to pond-perch pangs imparts,
      Thrills the shelled shrimps, and opens oysters' hearts."—CANNING.

It is evident from this that Canning had thought of parodying the poem immediately after its publication, and that Walpole had seen a specimen in manuscript, nearly two years before its publication in the *Anti-Jacobin*, in which the
two lines (28, 29) are thus altered :—

    " Cools the crimpt cod, fierce pangs to perch imparts,
      Shrinks shrivell'd shrimps, but opens oysters' hearts ".

By an oversight, Peter Cunningham, in his edition of Walpole's Letters, attributes the latter's attack to a previous production of Knight's, published in
1794, entitled *The Landscape ; a didactic Poem in three Books*, a work which had
excited Walpole's high indignation by expressing opinions opposed to his
own.—ED.]

## No. XVI.

Feb. 26, 1798.

THE specimen of the poem on the "Progress of Man," with which we favoured our Readers in our last Number, has occasioned a variety of letters, which we confess have not a little surprised us, from the unfounded, and even contradictory charges they contain. In one, we are accused of Malevolence, in bringing back to notice a work that had been quietly consigned to oblivion;—in another, of Plagiarism, in copying its most beautiful passages;—in a third, of Vanity, in striving to imitate what was in itself inimitable, &c., &c. But why this alarm? has the author of the " *Progress of Civil Society* ". an exclusive patent for fabricating *Didactic* poems? or can we not write against Order and Government without incurring the guilt of Imitation? We trust we were not so ignorant of the nature of a didactic poem (so called from *didaskein*, to teach, and *poema*, a poem ; because it teaches nothing, and is not poetical) even before the " *Progress of Civil Society* " appeared, but that we were capable of such an undertaking.

We shall only say further, that we do not intend to proceed regularly with our Poem ; but having the remaining thirty-nine Cantos by us, shall content ourselves with giving, from time to time, such extracts as may happen to suit our purpose.

The following passage, which, as the reader will see by turning to the Contents prefixed to the head of the Poem, is part of the First Canto, contains so happy a deduction of MAN's present state of Depravity, from the first slips and failings of his Original State, and inculcates so forcibly the mischievous consequences of *social* or *civilized*, as opposed to *natural* society, that no dread of imputed imitation can prevent us from giving it to our readers.

## PROGRESS OF MAN.

Lo ! the rude savage, free from civil strife,
Keeps the smooth tenour of his guiltless life ;
Restrain'd by none, save Nature's lenient laws,
Quaffs the clear stream, and feeds on hips and haws.
Light to his daily sports behold him rise !                    65
The bloodless banquet health and strength supplies.
Bloodless not long—one morn he haps to stray
Through the lone wood—and close beside the way
Sees the gaunt tiger tear his trembling prey ;
Beneath whose gory fangs a leveret bleeds,                     70
Or pig—such pig as fertile China breeds.

Struck with the sight, the wondering savage stands,
Rolls his broad eyes, and clasps his lifted hands !
Then restless roams—and loaths his wonted food ;
Shuns the salubrious stream, and thirsts for blood.            75

By thought matured, and quicken'd by desire,

---

*Ver.* 61—66. Simple state of savage life—previous to the pastoral, or even the hunter state.
*Ver.* 66. First savages disciples of Pythagoras.
*Ver.* 67, &c. Desire of animal food natural only to beasts, or to man in a state of civilized society. First suggested by the circumstances here related.
*Ver.* 71. Pigs of the *Chinese* breed most in request.
*Ver.* 76. First formation of a bow. Introduction of the science of archery.

New arts, new arms, his wayward wants require.
From the tough yew a slender branch he tears,
With self-taught skill the twisted grass prepares ;
Th' unfashioned bow, with labouring efforts bends        80
In circling form, and joins th' unwilling ends.
Next some tall reed he seeks—with sharp-edg'd stone
Shapes the fell dart, and points with whiten'd bone.

Then forth he fares.   Around in careless play,
Kids, pigs, and lambkins unsuspecting stray ;        85
With grim delight he views the sportive band,
Intent on blood, and lifts his murderous hand.
Twangs the bent bow—resounds the fateful dart,
Swift-wing'd, and trembles in a porker's heart.

Ah, hapless porker! what can now avail        90
Thy back's stiff bristles, or thy curly tail?
Ah! what avail those eyes so small and round,
Long pendent ears, and snout that loves the ground?

Not unreveng'd thou diest!—in after times
From thy spilt blood shall spring unnumber'd crimes. 95
Soon shall the slaught'rous arms that wrought thy woe,
Improved by malice, deal a deadlier blow ;

---

*Ver.* 79. Grass twisted, used for a string, owing to the want
of other materials not yet invented.

*Ver.* 83. Bone—fish's bone found on the sea-shore, shark's
teeth, &c. &c.

*Ver.* 90. Ah! what avails, &c.—See Pope's *Description of the
death of a Pheasant.*

*Ver.* 93. "With leaden eye that loves the ground."

*Ver.* 94. The first effusion of blood attended with the most
dreadful consequences to mankind.

*Ver.* 97. *Social* Man's wickedness opposed to the simplicity
of savage life.

When *social* man shall pant for nobler game,
And 'gainst his fellow man the vengeful weapon aim.

As love, as gold, as jealousy inspires,    100
As wrathful hate, or wild ambition fires,
Urged by the statesman's craft, the tyrant's rage,
Embattled nations endless wars shall wage,
Vast seas of blood the ravaged field shall stain,
And millions perish—that a *king* may reign !    105

For blood once shed, new wants and wishes rise ;
Each rising want invention quick supplies.
To roast his victuals is man's next desire,
So two dry sticks he rubs, and lights a fire.
Hail fire, &c. &c.

---

*Ver.* 100, 101. Different causes of war among men.
*Ver.* 106. Invention of fire--first employed in cookery, and
produced by rubbing dry sticks together.

# No. XVII.

March 5, 1798.

WE are obliged to a learned correspondent for the following ingenious imitation of BION.—We will not shock the eyes of our fair readers with the original Greek, but the following *Argument* will give them some idea of the nature of the Poem here imitated.

## ARGUMENT.

Venus is represented as bringing to the Poet, while sleeping, her son Cupid, with a request that he would teach him Pastoral Poetry—Bion complies, and endeavours to teach him the rise and progress of that art:—Cupid laughs at his instructions, and in his turn teaches his master the Loves of Men and Gods, the Wiles of his Mother, &c.— "Pleased with his lessons," says BION, "I forgot what I lately taught Cupid and recollect in its stead only what Cupid taught me."

## IMITATION, &c.*

WRITTEN AT ST. ANNE'S HILL.

SCARCE had sleep my eyes o'erspread,
Ere Alecto sought my bed ;
In her left hand a torch she shook,
And in her right led JOHN HORNE TOOKE.
O thou ! who well deserv'st the bays,
Teach him, she cried, Sedition's lays—
She said, and left us ; I, poor fool,

---

[* Written in the character of C. J. Fox, at his seat, St. Anne's Hill, near Chertsey, during his secession from Parliament from 1797 to 1802. His fondness for the Greek Poets is well known.—ED.]

Began the wily priest to school;
Taught him how MOIRA sung of lights,
Blown out by troops o' stormy nights; *
How ERSKINE, borne on rapture's wings,
At clubs and taverns sweetly sings
Of *self*—while yawning Whigs attend—
*Self* first, last, midst, and without end; †
How BEDFORD piped, ill-fated Bard; ‡
Half-drown'd, in empty Palace-yard;
How LANSDOWNE, nature's simple child,

[* Alluded to at page 79.—ED.]

[† Erskine was noted for his intense vanity, which procured him the nickname of *Ego.* Sir John Bowring, who knew him well, gives in his *Autobiography* several instances of this peculiarity, one of which is here inserted. "The master-string of his mind was vanity; its vibrations trembling to the very end of his existence. He said, 'When the Emperor Alexander came to England, Lord Granville told me that the Emperor wished to see me. I went. He received me with particular attention, and said he was very anxious to make my acquaintance. He spoke English as well as you do. "You are a friend and correspondent," he said, "of my most valued friend La Harpe?" "Yes, sire." "Is he a regular correspondent?" "Yes, a very kind one." "Has he been so of late?" "Well, if your Majesty will cross-examine me, I must own he owes me a letter." He put his hand into his pocket, and drew forth a letter addressed to me. "Yes, there is his answer. I intercepted it that I might have the pleasure of knowing Lord Erskine." I gave Alexander all my writings and speeches, which he received with many expressions of satisfaction.' "—ED.]

[‡ On April 3, 1797, an open-air meeting of the inhabitants of Westminster was held in Palace Yard, during very inclement weather (Westminster Hall having been shut against them by order of the keeper), to consider of an address to his Majesty to dismiss PITT's ministry. Fox and the Duke of Bedford took part in the proceedings. Meetings were held about the same time all over the country for the same object.—ED.]

At Bowood trills his wood-notes wild—*
How these and more (a phrenzied choir)
Sweep with bold hand Confusion's lyre,
Till madding crowds around them storm
"FOR ONE GRAND RADICAL REFORM!"

TOOKE stood silent for a while,
Listening with sarcastic smile;
Then in verse of calmest flow,
Sung of treasons, deep and low,
Of rapine, prisons, scaffolds, blood,
Of war against the great and good;
Of Venice, and of Genoa's doom,
And fall of unoffending Rome;
Of monarchs from their station hurl'd,
And one waste desolated world.

Charm'd by the magic of his tongue,
I lost the strains I lately sung,
While those he taught, remain impress'd
For ever on my faithful breast.

DORUS.

---

[* After Lord Shelburne's resignation of the office of Prime
Minister, consequent on the coalition of Fox and Lord North,
he was created Marquis of Lansdowne, and withdrew almost
entirely from public life, passing his time principally at his
magnificent seat, Bowood, near Calne, Wiltshire.—ED.]

[BION. IDYLLIUM III. THE TEACHER TAUGHT.

TRANSLATED BY FAWKES.

As late I slumbering lay, before my sight
Bright VENUS rose in visions of the night:
She led young Cupid; as in thought profound
His modest eyes were fixed upon the ground;
And thus she spoke: "To thee, dear swain, I bring
My little son; instruct the boy to sing".

8

No more she said; but vanished into air,
And left the wily pupil to my care:
I,—(sure I was an idiot for my pains),
Began to teach him old bucolic strains;
How PAN the pipe, how PALLAS formed the flute,
PHŒBUS the lyre, and MERCURY the lute:
LOVE, to my lessons quite regardless grown,
Sang lighter lays, and sonnets of his own,
Th' amours of men below, and gods above,
And all the triumphs of the queen of love.
I, sure the simplest of all shepherd swains,
Full soon forgot my old bucolic strains;
The lighter lays of LOVE my fancy caught,
And I remembered all that Cupid taught.—ED.]

———————

SOMETHING like the same idea seems to have dictated the following Stanzas, which appear to be a loose imitation of the beautiful Dialogue of Horace and Lydia, and for which, though confessedly in a lower style of poetry, and conceived rather in the *slang*, or *Brentford* dialect, than in the classical Doric of the foregoing Poem, we have many thanks to return to an ingenious academical correspondent.

## THE NEW COALITION.[1]

### I.

Fox.—When erst I coalesced with North
And brought my *Indian bantling* forth [2]
In place—I smiled at faction's storm,
Nor dreamt of *radical reform*.

### II.

TOOKE.—While yet no patriot project pushing,
Content I thump'd old Brentford's cushion,
I pass'd my life so free and gaily ; .
Not dreaming of that d——d *Old Bailey.*

III.

Fox.—Well! now my favourite preacher's *Nickle*,³
He keeps for PITT a rod in pickle;
His gestures fright th' astonish'd gazers,
His sarcasms cut like Packwood's razors.

IV.

TOOKE.—*Thelwall's*⁴ my man for state alarm;
I love the rebels of *Chalk Farm;*
Rogues that no statutes can subdue,
Who'd bring the French, and head them too.

V.

Fox.—A whisper in your ear, JOHN HORNE,⁵
For *one great end* we both were born,
Alike we roar, and rant, and bellow—
Give us your hand, my honest fellow.

VI.

TOOKE.—Charles, for a shuffler long I've known thee:
But come—for once, I'll not disown thee;
And since with patriot zeal thou burnest,
With thee I'll live—or hang *in earnest.*

[HORACE. BOOK III., ODE IX.

HORACE.—Whilst I was fond, and you were kind,
Nor any dearer youth, reclined
On your soft bosom, sought to rest,
Not Persia's monarch was so blest.

LYDIA.—Whilst you adored no other face,
Nor loved me in the second place,
Your Lydia's celebrated fame
Outshone the Roman Ilia's name.

HORACE.—Me *Chloe* now possesses whole;
Her voice and lyre command my soul:
Nor would I death itself decline,
Could I redeem her life with mine.

LYDIA.—For me young lovely *Calaïs* burns,
And warmth for warmth my heart returns.
Twice would I life for him resign,
Could *his* be ransomed thus with *mine*.

HORACE.—What if the God, whose bands we broke,
Again should tame us to the yoke !
What if my *Chloe* cease to reign,
And *Lydia* her lost power regain !

LYDIA.—Though Phosphor be less fair than *he;*
*Thou* wilder than the raging sea;
Lighter than down; yet gladly I
With *thee* would live, with *thee* would die.—ED.]

[Another version of this Ode published in the *Anti-Jacobin Review*, vol. 1, pp. 597-8 (the successor to the *Anti-Jacobin*), may perhaps not be considered out of place here. It was written by the Rev. C. E. Stewart, a constant contributor to the former journal.

### THE HONEY-MOON OF FOX AND TOOKE.

*Donec gratus eram tibi.*

FOX.—Since Fox of his Tooke is possest,
No sorrows my bosom can harass ;
What Director was ever so blest ?
I'm greater, far greater than Barras.

TOOKE.—If Fox to his consort is true,
And this blest Coalition sincere,
I'll engage as a private with you,
Nor envy thy fame, Robespierre.

FOX.—You once were the worst of my foes,
E'en Pitt I detested not more,
When you dar'd my Election oppose,
And eternal antipathy swore.

TOOKE.—Not to you was my hatred confin'd,
Your father I styled " The Defaulter,"
Drew a portrait of both, and consign'd
Both father and son to the halter.

Fox.—Drive these hated reflections away;
    For you I would gladly resign.
    Jockey Norfolk, big Bedford, and Grey;
    But they answer your purpose and mine.

Tooke.—Whate'er you attempt or intend,
    I am yours, and will bring at your call,
    Binns, Gurney, Scott, Ferguson, Frend,
    Corresponding Society—all.

Both.—Thus reconcil'd, fond, and delighted,
    Together we'll ride in the storm,
    While Jacobin Clubs, all united,
    Make a radical, perfect Reform.—Ed.]

---

## Notes to the "New Coalition".

[1 The Secret History of Fox's coalition with Lord North, his former adversary,—a proceeding which entailed on him much odium,—was first brought to light by the publication of the "Memorials and Correspondence of Charles James Fox," begun by the late Lord Holland, and edited by Earl Russell. It was occasioned by his disgust at the conduct of the Earl of Shelburne, for while Fox as one of the Secretaries of State under the Rockingham Administration was treating with Dr. Franklin for peace with the United States through the agent of the Cabinet (Thomas Grenville) Lord Shelburne, the other Secretary of State, was, through *his* agent Oswald, privately thwarting his measures, and that with the concurrence of the King! The consequence of the Coalition was the fall of Lord Shelburne's ministry, and Fox and Lord North's "taking the Treasury by storm".—Ed.]

[2 The *India Bill* brought in by Fox, shortly after his accession to office, was the signal for his downfall. The Bill passed the House of Commons by large majorities, but when it reached the Lords, the King, who hated Fox, empowered Earl Temple to declare that he would consider everyone who supported the measure as personally his enemy. The Bill was consequently lost on the second reading by a majority of eighty-seven against twenty-nine. The Coalition Ministry resigned, and Pitt, then in his 23rd year, became Prime Minister.]

[³ JOHN NICHOLLS, M.P. for Tregony, was blind of one eye, and altogether remarkably ugly. His delivery was ungraceful, and his action generally much too vehement. He wrote *Recollections and Reflections during the Reign of George III.*, 2 vols. 8vo., 1822. His hostile pamphlet on the *Income Tax* is marked by great ability.—ED.]

[⁴ On the 14th April, 1794, THELWALL was in the chair at a supper of one of the Divisions of the Reformers, and blowing off the head of a pot of porter said, " This is the way I would have all kings served ".—ED.]

[⁵ JOHN HORNE TOOKE was educated for the Church, and in 1760 became vicar of *New Brentford*. Resigning this he studied the Law, but being a clergyman was refused admission to the Bar. At first he supported PITT, then a *promising* Reformer, publishing in 1788 his "Two Pair of Portraits," disadvantageously contrasting Fox and his father with Pitt and his father. But Pitt not fulfilling his hopes, he became his bitter opponent and softened his animosity towards Fox. In 1775 he was imprisoned for a libel on the king's troops in America. In 1790 he was an unsuccessful candidate for Westminster; the other candidates being Fox and Admiral Sir Alan Gardner. In 1794 he was tried, in company with THELWALL and others, for high treason, when all were acquitted. In 1796 he again stood for Westminster, and failed; but in 1801 he obtained a seat in Parliament for Old Sarum, on the nomination of Lord Camelford. A remarkable memoir of him was contributed to the *Quarterly Review*, vol. 7, by Lord Dudley, Secretary for Foreign Affairs in Canning's administration, 1827-8.—ED.]

# No. XVIII.

March 12, 1798.

WE are indebted for the following exquisite imitation of one of the most beautiful Odes of Horace, to an unknown hand. All that we can say is, that it came to us in a blank cover sealed with a ducal coronet, and that it appears evidently to be the production of a mind not more classical than convivial.

## ODE.

WHITHER, O Bacchus, in thy train,*
Dost thou transport thy votary's brain
    With sudden inspiration?
Where dost thou bid me quaff my wine,
And toast new measures to combine
    The *Great* and *Little Nation?*

Say, in what tavern I shall raise †
My mighty voice in Charley's praise,
    And dream of future glories,
When Fox, with salutary sway
(Terror the Order of the Day),
    Shall reign o'er King and Tories?

HOR. LIB. III., CARM. XXV.
DITHYRAMBUS.
*Quo me, Bacche, rapis, tui
Plenum? quæ nemora, aut quos agor in specus,
Velox mente novâ?
    † Quibus
Antris egregii Cæsaris audiar
Eternum meditans decus
Stellis inserere, et consilio Jovis?

My mighty feelings must have way !*
A toast I'll give—a thing I'll say,
    As yet unsaid by any,—
"OUR SOV'REIGN LORD!"—let those who doubt
My honest meaning, hear me out—
    "HIS MAJESTY—THE MANY!"

Plain folks may be surprised, and stare,†
As much surprised as BOB ADAIR
    At Russia's wooden houses ;
And Russian snows, that lie so thick ; ‡
And Russian boors § that daily kick,
    With barbarous foot, their spouses.

What joy, when drunk, at midnight's hour,‖
To stroll through Covent Garden's bow'r,
    Its various charms exploring ;
And, 'midst its shrubs and vacant stalls,
And proud Piazza's crumbling walls,
    Hear trulls and watchmen snoring !

---

* Dicam insigne, recens, adhuc
Indictum ore alio.
    † Non secus in jugis
Exsomnis stupet Evias,
Hebrum prospiciens,
    ‡ et nive candidam
Thracen, ac *pede barbaro*
*Lustratam Rhodopen.*
§ There appears to have been some little mistake in the
Translator here—*Rhodope* is not, as he seems to imagine, the
name of a woman, but of a mountain, and not in *Russia.* Pos-
sibly, however, the Translator may have been misled by the
inaccuracy of the traveller here alluded to.
    ‖ Ut mihi devio
Rupes, et vacuum nemus
Mirari libet !

Parent of wine, and gin, and beer,*
The nymphs of Billingsgate you cheer ;
Naiads robust and hearty ;
As Brookes's chairmen fit to wield
Their stout oak bludgeons in the field,
To aid our virtuous party.

Mortals! no common voice you hear ; †
*Militia Colonel, Premier Peer*,
*Lieutenant of a County !*
I speak high things! yet, god of wine,
For thee, I fear not to resign
These gifts of royal bounty.

---

\* O Naiadum potens
Baccharumque valentium
Proceras manibus vertere fraxinos.
† Nil parvum, aut humili modo,
Nil mortale loquar.  Dulce periculum est,
O Lenæe, sequi deum
Cingentem viridi tempora pampino.

---

[HORACE.  BOOK III., ODE XXV.  TO BACCHUS.
TRANSLATED BY FRANCIS.

Whither in sacred ecstasy,
BACCHUS, when full of thy divinity,
Dost thou transport me ?  To what glades ?
What gloomy caverns, unfrequented shades ?
In what recesses shall I raise
My voice to sacred Cæsar's deathless praise,
Amid the stars to bid him shine,
Ranked in the councils of the powers divine ?
Some bolder song shall wake the lyre,
And sounds unknown its trembling strings inspire.
Thus o'er the steepy mountains' height,
Starting from sleep, thy priestess takes her flight :
Amazed, behold the Thracian snows,
With languid streams where icy Heber flows
Or Rhodopé's high-towering head,

Where frantic choirs barbarian measures tread.
O'er pathless rocks, through lonely groves,
With what delight my raptured spirit roves!
O thou, who rul'st the Naiad's breast;
By whom the Bacchanalian maids, possessed
With sacred rage inspired by thee,
Tear from the bursting glebe th' uprooted tree;
Nothing or low, or mean, I sing,
No mortal sound shall shake the swelling string.
The venturous theme my soul alarms;
But warmed by thee the thought of danger charms.
When vine-crowned Bacchus leads the way,
What can his daring votaries dismay?—ED.]

[The preceding Ode, written in the character of Charles Howard, eleventh
DUKE OF NORFOLK, refers to the famous toast, "Our Sovereign's health—THE
MAJESTY OF THE PEOPLE," proposed by his Grace at a Banquet at the "Crown
and Anchor Tavern," Strand, on the 24th January, 1798, given to celebrate the
birthday of C. J. FOX. For this toast and other sentiments promulgated at
the meeting, his Grace a few days after received notice of his dismissal from
the Lord-Lieutenancy of the West Riding of Yorkshire and his Colonelcy in
the Militia, and on the 6th of February Earl Fitzwilliam was gazetted to the
former office, vice the Duke of Norfolk, *resigned*. But sixteen years earlier, this
*Toast* was not considered seditious; for in the *General Advertiser* of the 13th of
April, 1782, then edited by Perry (afterwards the eminent proprietor of the
*Morning Chronicle*), we find an account of a dinner of the electors of Westminster
held the preceding day at the Shakespeare Tavern, *Earl Fitzwilliam* in the
chair. The first toast given by his Lordship was, "THE MAJESTY OF THE
PEOPLE". It was drunk by the Earl of Effingham, the Earl of Surrey (afterwards Duke of Norfolk, and the subject of the present remarks), Mr. Secretary
Fox, Burke, Windham, Dean Jebb, J. Churchill, Brand Hollis, Dr. Brocklesby,
&c. Thus the identical toast was proposed and drunk by the Earl of Fitzwilliam, to whom the Lord-Lieutenancy now taken from the Duke of Norfolk
was given. It is not a little remarkable that Lord Fitzwilliam himself was
dismissed by his new Tory allies, Oct. 23, 1819, from the same Lord-Lieutenancy
of the West Riding of Yorkshire, having signed the requisition for the York
meeting, at which resolutions were passed condemning the measures of Ministers
(Lords Liverpool, Eldon, Bathurst, Castlereagh, Palmerston, &c.), respecting
the Manchester Reform Meeting, called by Henry Hunt, on 16th August, at
which occurred what is known as the "Peterloo Massacre".—ED.]

["THE MAJESTY OF THE PEOPLE," AS GIVEN ON FOX'S BIRTHDAY.

The company was a very large one, but the estimated number of 2000 diners
is surely an error. The Duke of Norfolk presided, supported by the Duke of
Bedford, the Earls of Lauderdale and Oxford, Sheridan, Tierney, Erskine,
Capt. Morris (who produced three new songs for the occasion), and Horne
Tooke; the latter became reconciled to Fox by the explanation the latter gave
of his sentiments on parliamentary reform. On the cloth being removed, he
rose and said, "We are met in a moment of most serious difficulty to celebrate
the birth of a man dear to the friend of freedom. I shall only recall to your
memory that not twenty years ago, the illustrious GEORGE WASHINGTON
had not more than two thousand men to rally round him when his country
was attacked. America is now free. This day full two thousand men are
assembled in this place. I leave the application to you. I propose to you the
health of CHARLES JAMES FOX."
In the course of the evening the Duke's health was drunk with great en-

thusiasm. He returned thanks, and concluded his speech with these words, "Give me leave to call on you to drink, Our Sovereign's health,

"THE MAJESTY OF THE PEOPLE".

After this toast had been drunk and warmly applauded, the Duke gave successively, "The Rights of the People," "Constitutional Redress of the Wrongs of the People," "A speedy and effectual Reform in the Representation of the People in Parliament," "The genuine Principles of the British Constitution," "The People of Ireland, and may they be speedily restored to the Blessings of Law and Liberty".

On the 6th of February, the next monthly meeting of the *Whig Club* was held at the London Tavern, Ludgate Hill. The DUKE OF NORFOLK presided. He gave as a toast, "The Man who dares be honest in the worst of times—

"CHARLES JAMES FOX".

FOX returned thanks, and then toasted

"THE SOVEREIGNTY OF THE PEOPLE".

He subsequently proposed the health of the Duke of Norfolk in a most powerful speech. He adverted to the dismissal of the DUKE. "No reason had been officially assigned; it was, however, generally understood that it had arisen from the eulogium pronounced on GENERAL WASHINGTON. Was it to be wondered at, that the noble Duke, who had uniformly opposed the American war, should have done so? What Englishman, what man of any country, whose heart was animated with a love of freedom, did not venerate the name of that illustrious patriot? It seems also "a toast" has given offence—the Majesty of the People. I do not know upon what times we are fallen, but the sovereignty of the people of Great Britain is surely a thing not new to the language, to the feelings, nor the hearts of Englishmen. It is the basis of the whole system of our Government. It is an opinion, which if it be not true, King William was an usurper. By what right did the glorious and immortal King William the Third, whose portrait is placed on our chair, come to the throne of these realms, if not by that of the sovereignty of the people? . . . The King holds his title by an Act of Parliament. Who called that Parliament? King William the Third. By what right did he obtain it? By a Convention representing the sovereignty of the people. The Convention of Representatives in fact did the thing. It is whimsical enough to deprive the noble Duke of his appointments for an offence which, if he had not committed during the reigns of George I. and George II., would have subjected him to the charge of being a Jacobite, and an adherent of the exiled family. . . . Of the persons of his Majesty's Ministers I will not say a word. There are several of them to whom I may fairly say this sentiment is not new. One member of the Cabinet (the Duke of Portland) is still a member of this club; another (Mr. Windham) was a member; and a third (Earl Spencer) long gloried in holding the same tenets. How often with the two first have we drunk the sentiment in this room! What did they mean when they drank the Sovereignty of the People? What, but that they recognised by this approved and customary method a truth which belongs to all people in reality, but is the avowed basis of the Government of England, that the people of every country are its legitimate Sovereign, and that all authority is delegated from and for them? I should be ashamed, on account of my old respect for those persons, if they did not honestly avow this to be their sense of the sentiment."

While adverting, on this occasion, to the dismissal of the DUKE OF NORFOLK from his Lord-Lieutenancy and Colonelcy of Militia, FOX remarked, "I have nothing the Ministers can take from me. I am still indeed a Privy Councillor, at least I know nothing to the contrary; and if this sentiment entitles the Noble Duke to this animadversion, I shall certainly feel that I am equally entitled to this mark of his Majesty's displeasure." This anticipation was verified shortly afterwards.

On the 1st of May following, at the Freemasons' Tavern, another dinner of the *Whig Club* took place. FOX was in the chair, and gave, as the first toast—

"THE SOVEREIGNTY OF THE PEOPLE OF GREAT BRITAIN".

The Duke of Norfolk proposed "The Health of the Man who dares be Honest in the worst of Times—

"CHARLES JAMES FOX".

FOX responded in a most impressive speech. He said: "On any other occasion, he should have contented himself with returning thanks, but in the very peculiar embarrassments in which the country was now plunged, he thought it necessary to say a few words in the only place in which he thought it might be useful for him to deliver his sentiments. The circumstances and events of public affairs of late had induced him and many of his friends to abstain from their usual assiduous attendance in Parliament. Their exertions for the preservation of the Constitution had been of no avail; two years ago they had seen the repeal of the Bill of Rights carried by a triumphant majority; they had seen the functions of the Constitutional Law suspended, on alarm created by the Ministers themselves; and however well-founded the alarm might now be, he scorned the idea that it was necessary for him to attend in his place in the House of Commons, for the purpose only of vindicating himself from the vulgar calumny that he was not an enemy to a foreign invasion. It would be an insult on his whole life if such a declaration could be expected from him. He believed there was not a voice in the assembly he addressed which was not in unison with his own—namely, that every man who heard him was both ready and willing to stand forth in defence of his country, with the spirit that belongs to Englishmen. He found no fault with those who thought it necessary to make these professions elsewhere. Thus much only would he say in this place for himself. *The present Government of the country, he had no hesitation in saying, was a Government of Tyranny. They had adopted the principles of Robespierre, and their object was to establish tyranny in England.* Look at the situation of the Sister Kingdom; our own will soon be the same. He had no remedy to recommend but that the friends of freedom should be united and firm, and wait for better times. Tyranny was now the order of the day in every country in Europe. Notwithstanding the arbitrary proceedings of our own Ministers, he was persuaded the unanimous feeling of the country, the universal determination of every man in it was to be ready to take the field against a foreign foe; and, indeed, they had a powerful motive to do so, for if they were united, they had a better chance to get rid of the tyranny of their own Ministers than they could possibly have by the success of a foreign invasion. Even in his present retirement he should be ready to come forward, in every constitutional effort, to regain our lost liberties; and he should be in the foremost of the ranks to repel the invasion of a daring enemy."

This speech led to a most important consequence—the erasing from the Privy Council Book the name of one of the most illustrious statesmen which had ever adorned it. FOX'S name was struck out by the King on the 9th of May.

On the 6th of June, after the dinner at the *Whig Club*, the DUKE OF BEDFORD proposed "THE HEALTH OF CHARLES FOX," and remarked in severe terms on Ministers having caused the King to strike his name out of the list of the Privy Council. FOX said: "It would be most unfit for him to say a word respecting the Noble Duke's allusion to a circumstance personal to himself. Would to God the time of the Ministers had been always employed in such *frivolous fooleries* as settling who should be *Honourable* and who *Right Honourable*, and deliberating on the titles most befitting their friends and supporters." FOX, with some of his supporters, seceded from Parliament in 1797, and returned to the House of Commons in 1802 to defend the Peace of Amiens, and he was persuaded to continue his parliamentary attendance by the urgent request of friends, with whose wishes he felt himself bound to comply.—ED.]

# No. XIX.

March 19, 1798.

FOR the authenticity of the enclosed Ballad we refer our readers to a volume of MS. Poems discovered upon the removal of some papers, during the late alterations which have taken place at the Tax-office, in consequence of the Reports of the Finance Committee.

It has been communicated to our printer by an ingenious friend of his, who occasionally acts for the Deputy Collector of the Parish of St. Martin in the Fields; but without date, or any other mark, by which we are enabled to guess at the particular subject of the composition.

## CHEVY CHASE.*

GOD prosper long our noble king,
Our lives and safeties all:
A woeful story late there did
In Britain's Isle befall.

DUKE SMITHSON, of NORTHUMBERLAND,
A vow to God did make,
The choicest gifts in fair England,
For him and his to take.

[* This clever parody has reference to the attempt made by the DUKE OF NORTHUMBERLAND to evade payment of PITT's Income-tax. To mitigate the severity of the pressure on persons with large families, a deduction of ten per cent. was allowed to persons who had above a certain number of children. Among others the Duke was not ashamed to avail himself of this clause.—ED.]

" Stand fast, my merry men," he cried,
" By Moira's Earl and me,
And we will gain place, wealth and pow'r,
As arm'd neutrality.

"Excise and Customs, Church and Law,
I've begg'd from *Master* Rose ;
The Garter too—but still *the Blues*
I'll have, or I'll oppose."

" Now God be with him," quoth the King,
" Sith 'twill no better be ;
I trust we have within our realm
Five hundred good as he."

The Duke then join'd with Charley Fox,
A leader ware and tried,
And Erskine, Sheridan, and Grey
Fought stoutly by his side.

Throughout the English Parliament,
They dealt full many a wound ;
But in his king's and country's cause,
Pitt firmly stood his ground.

And soon a law like arrow keen,
Or spear, or curtal-axe,
Struck poor Duke Smithson to the heart,
In shape of *Powder-tax.**

Sore leaning on his crutch, he cried,
" Crop, crop, my merry men all ;
No guinea for your head I'll pay,
Though Church and State should fall ".

---

[*See Note at p. 84 in "*A Bit of an Ode to Mr. Fox*," line 18.—Ed.]

Again the taxing-man appear'd—
No deadlier foe could be ;
A schedule of a cloth-yard long,
Within his hand bore he.

" Yield thee, DUKE SMITHSON, and behold
The assessment thou must pay ;
Dogs, horses, houses, coaches, clocks,
And servants in array."

" Nay," quoth the DUKE, " in thy black scroll
Deductions I espye—
For those who, poor, and mean, and low,
With children burthen'd lie.

"And though full sixty thousand pounds
My vassals pay to me,
From Cornwall to *Northumberland*,
Through many a fair countée ;

" Yet England's church, its king, its laws,
Its cause, I value not,
Compar'd with this, my constant text,
*A penny sav'd, is got.*

" No drop of princely PERCY's blood
Through these cold veins doth run ;
With *Hotspur's* castles, blazon, name,
I still am *poor* SMITHSON.

" Let England's youth unite in arms,
And every liberal hand,
With honest zeal, subscribe their mite,
To save their native land :

" I at *St. Martin's* Vestry Board,
To swear shall be content,
That I have children eight, and claim
*Deductions ten per cent.*"

God bless us all from factious foes,
And French fraternal kiss ;
And grant the king may never make
Another *Duke* like this.*

---

[* SIR HUGH SMITHSON married Lady Eliz. Seymour, great-granddaughter of Joceline, eleventh Earl of Northumberland, who was the last of the male Percies. He was created DUKE OF NORTHUMBERLAND in 1766. The hero of this Ballad was his son, who died in 1817.—ED.]

# No. XX.

## ODE TO JACOBINISM.

March 26, 1798.

### I.

DAUGHTER of Hell, insatiate power,
Destroyer of the human race,
Whose iron scourge and madd'ning hour
Exalt the bad, the good debase ;
Thy mystic force, despotic sway,
Courage and innocence dismay,
And patriot monarchs vainly groan
With pangs unfelt before, unpitied and alone !

### II.

When first to scourge the sons of earth,
Thy sire his darling child design'd,
Gallia. receiv'd the monstrous birth—
VOLTAIRE inform'd thy infant mind ;
Well-chosen nurse ! his sophist lore
He bade thee many a year explore !
He mark'd thy progress, firm though slow,
And statesmen, princes, leagued with their invet'rate foe.

### III.

Scared at thy frown terrific, fly
The morals (antiquated brood) ;
Domestic Virtue, social Joy,
And Faith that has for ages stood :
Swift they disperse, and with them go
The friend sincere, the gen'rous foe.—

9

Traitors to God and man avow'd,
By thee now rais'd aloft, now crush'd beneath the crowd.

IV.

Revenge, in blood-stain'd robe arrayed,
    Immersed in gloomy joy profound;
Ingratitude, by guilt dismay'd,
    With anxious eye wild glancing round,
Still on thy frantic steps attend:
With Death, thy victim's only friend,
    Injustice, to the truth severe,
And Anguish, dropping still the life-consuming tear.

V.

Oh swiftly on my country's head,
    Destroyer, lay thy ruthless hand;
Nor yet in Gallic terrors clad,
    Nor circled by the *Marseilles band*,
    (As by th' initiate thou art seen),
With thund'ring cannon, *guillotine*,
    With screaming Horror's funeral cry,
Fire, Rapine, sword, and chains, and ghastly Poverty.

VI.

Thy sophist veil, dread goddess, wear,
    Falsehood insidiously impart;
Thy philosophic train, be there,
    To taint the mind, corrupt the heart;
The gen'rous virtues of our isle,
Teach us to hate and to revile;
    Our glorious Charter's faults to scan,
Time-sanction'd truths despise, and preach THY RIGHTS
    OF MAN.
                                AN ENGLISH JACOBIN.

[The original poem, of which the above is an imitation, is subjoined :—

## HYMN TO ADVERSITY.

### BY THOMAS GRAY.

Daughter of Jove, relentless power,
Thou tamer of the human breast,
Whose iron scourge, and torturing hour,
The bad affright, afflict the best !
Bound in thy adamantine chain,
The proud are taught to taste of pain,
And purple tyrants vainly groan,
With pangs unfelt before, unpitied and alone.

When first thy sire to send on earth
Virtue, his darling child, designed,
To thee he gave the heavenly birth,
And bade thee form her infant mind,
Stern, rugged nurse ! thy rigid lore
With patience many a year she bore :
What sorrow was, thou bad'st her know,
And from her own she learnt to melt at others' woe.

Scared at thy frown terrific, fly
Self-pleasing Folly's idle brood,
Wild Laughter, Noise, and thoughtless Joy,
And leave us leisure to be good.
Light they disperse, and with them go
The summer friend, the flattering foe ;
By vain prosperity received,
To her they vow their truth, and are again believed.

Wisdom, in sable garb arrayed,
Immersed in rapturous thought profound,
And Melancholy, silent maid,
With leaden eye that loves the ground,
Still on thy solemn steps attend :
Warm Charity, the general friend,
With Justice, to herself severe,
And Pity, dropping soft the sadly-pleasing tear.

O, gently on thy suppliant's head,
Dread goddess, lay thy chastening hand !
Not in thy Gorgon terrors clad,
Nor circled with the vengeful band

(As by the impious thou art seen),
With thundering voice, and threatening mien,
With screaming Horror's funeral cry,
Despair, and fell Disease, and ghastly Poverty.

Thy form benign, O goddess! wear,
Thy milder influence impart,
Thy philosophic train be there,
To soften not to wound my heart.
The generous spark extinct revive;
Teach me to love and to forgive;
Exact my own defects to scan,
What others are, to feel, and know myself a man.—ED.]

# No. XXI.

April 2, 1798.

WE promised in our Sixteenth Number, that though we should not proceed regularly with the publication of the Didactic Poem, the PROGRESS OF MAN,—a work which, indeed, both from its bulk, and from the erudite nature of the subject, would hardly suit with the purposes of a Weekly Paper, — we should, nevertheless, give from time to time such extracts from it as we thought were likely to be useful to our readers, and as were in any degree connected with the topics or events of the times.

The following extract is from the 23rd Canto of this admirable and instructive Poem;—in which the author (whom, by a series of accidents, which we have neither the space, nor indeed the liberty, to enumerate at present, we have discovered to be MR. HIGGINS, of *St. Mary Axe*) describes the vicious refinement of what is called civilized society, in respect to marriage; contends with infinite spirit and philosophy against the factitious sacredness and indissolubility of that institution; and paints in glowing colours the happiness and utility (in a moral as well as political view) of an arrangement of an opposite sort, such as prevails in countries which are yet under the influence of pure and unsophisticated nature.

In illustration of his principles upon this subject, the author alludes to a popular production of the German Drama, the title of which is the " REFORMED HOUSE-

KEEPER" [*The Stranger*], which he expresses a hope of seeing transfused into the language of this country.

# THE PROGRESS OF MAN.

## CANTO TWENTY-THIRD.

### CONTENTS.

ON MARRIAGE.—Marriage being indissoluble the cause of its being so often unhappy.—Nature's laws not consulted in this point.—Civilized nations mistaken.—OTAHEITE : Happiness of the natives thereof—visited by Captain Cook, in his Majesty's Ship *Endeavour*—Character of Captain Cook.— Address to Circumnavigation.—Description of His Majesty's Ship *Endeavour*—Mast, rigging, sea-sickness, prow, poop, mess-room, surgeon's mate—History of one.—Episode concerning naval chirurgery.—Catching a Thunny Fish.—Arrival at Otaheite—cast anchor—land—Natives astonished.—Love —Liberty—Moral—Natural—Religious—Contrasted with European manners.—Strictness—License—Doctor's Commons.—Dissolubility of MARRIAGE recommended—Illustrated by a game at Cards—Whist—Cribbage—Partners changed— Why not the same in Marriage?—Illustrated by a River.— Love free.—Priests, Kings.—German Drama.—KOTZEBUE'S "Housekeeper Reformed".—Moral employments of Housekeeping described—Hottentots sit and stare at each other —Query, WHY?—Address to the Hottentots—History of the Cape of Good Hope.—Resumé of the Arguments against Marriage.—Conclusion.

# PROGRESS OF MAN.

### EXTRACT.

HAIL! beauteous lands* that crown the Southern Seas ;
Dear happy seats of Liberty and Ease!
Hail! whose green coasts the peaceful ocean laves,

---

* The ceremony of invocation (in didactic poems especially) is in some measure analogous to the custom of drinking toasts; the corporeal representatives of which are always supposed to be absent, and unconscious of the irrigation bestowed upon their names. Hence it is, that our Author addresses himself to the natives of an island who are not likely to hear, and who, if they did, would not understand him.

Incessant washing with its watery waves!
Delicious islands! to whose envied shore
Thee, gallant Cook! the ship *Endeavour*\* bore.

There laughs the sky, there zephyr's frolic train,
And light-wing'd loves, and blameless pleasures reign :
There, when two souls congenial ties unite,
No hireling *Bonzes* chant the mystic rite;
Free every thought, each action unconfin'd,
And light those fetters which no rivets bind.

There in each grove, each sloping bank along,
And flow'rs and shrubs and odorous herbs among,
Each shepherd clasp'd, with undisguis'd delight,
His yielding fair one,—in the Captain's sight;
Each yielding fair, as chance or fancy led,
Preferr'd new lovers to her sylvan bed.†

Learn hence, each nymph, whose free aspiring mind
Europe's cold laws,‡ and colder customs§ bind—
O! learn, what Nature's genial laws decree—
What Otaheite ‖ is, let Britain be!

   *   *   *   *   *

---

\* His Majesty's ship *Endeavour.*

† In justice to our Author we must observe, that there is a delicacy in this picture, which the words, in their common acceptation, do not convey. The amours of an English shepherd would probably be preparatory to marriage (which is contrary to our Author's principles), or they might disgust us by the vulgarity of their object. But in Otaheite, where the place of a shepherd is a perfect sinecure (there being no sheep on the island), the mind of the reader is not offended by any disagreeable allusion.

‡ Laws made by parliaments or kings.

§ Customs voted or imposed by ditto, not the customs here alluded to.

‖ M. Bailly and other astronomers have observed, that in

Of WHIST or CRIBBAGE mark th' amusing game—
The partners *changing*, but the SPORT the *same*.
Else would the gamester's anxious ardour cool,
Dull every deal, and stagnant every pool.
—Yet must *one* * Man, with one unceasing Wife,
Play the LONG RUBBER of connubial life.

Yes! human laws, and laws esteem'd divine,
The generous passion straiten and confine ;
And, as a stream, when art constrains its course,
Pours its fierce torrent with augmented force,
So, Passion† narrowed to one channel small,
*Unlike* the former, does not flow at all.
—For Love *then* only flaps his purple wings,
When uncontroll'd by priestcraft or by kings.

Such the strict rules, that, in these barbarous climes,
Choke youth's fair flow'rs, and feelings turn to crimes ;
And people every walk of polish'd life‡
With that two-headed monster, MAN and WIFE.

Yet bright examples sometimes we observe,
Which from the general practice seem to swerve ;

consequence of the varying obliquity of the Ecliptic, the climates of the circumpolar and tropical climates may, in process of time, be materially changed. Perhaps it is not very likely that even by these means Britain may ever become a small island in the South Seas. But this is not the meaning of the verse—the similarity here proposed relates to manners, not to local situation.

* The word *one* here, means all the inhabitants of Europe (excepting the French, who have remedied this inconvenience), not any particular individual. The Author begs leave to disclaim every allusion that can be construed as personal.

† As a stream—simile of dissimilitude, a mode of illustration familiar to the ancients.

‡ Walks of polished life, see "Kensington Gardens," a poem.

Such as presented to Germania's* view,
A KOTZEBUE'S bold emphatic pencil drew :
Such as, translated in some future age,
Shall add new glories to the British stage ;
—While the moved audience sit in dumb despair,
" Like Hottentots,+ *and at each other stare* ".

With look sedate, and staid beyond her years,
In matron weeds a *Housekeeper* appears.
The jingling keys her comely girdle deck—
Her 'kerchief colour'd, and her apron *check*.
Can that be Adelaide, that " soul of whim,"
*Reform'd* in practice, and in manner prim ?
—On household cares intent,‡ with many a sigh
She turns the pancake, and she moulds the pie ;
Melts into sauces rich the savoury ham ;
From the crush'd berry strains the lucid jam ;
Bids brandied cherries,§ by infusion slow,
Imbibe new flavour, and their own forego,
Sole cordial of her heart, sole solace of her woe !
While, still responsive to each mournful moan,
The saucepan simmers in a softer tone.

*     *     *     *     *

* Germania—Germany ; a country in Europe, peopled by the Germani : alluded to in Cæsar's Commentaries, page 1, vol. ii. edit. prin. See also several Didactic Poems.
† A beautiful figure of German literature. The Hottentots remarkable for staring at each other—God knows why.
‡ This delightful and instructive picture of domestic life is recommended to all keepers of boarding-schools, and other seminaries of the same nature.
§ It is a singular quality of brandied cherries that they exchange their flavour for that of the liquor in which they are immersed.—See Knight's *Progress of Civil Society*.

[The following extracts will give some idea of PAYNE KNIGHT'S poem.

Hail! happy States, that fresh in vigour rise
From Europe's wrecks beneath Atlantic skies!
Long may ye feel the blessings ye bestow ;
Nor e'er your parents' sickly symptoms know!
But when that parent, crush'd beneath the weight
Of debts and taxes, yields herself to fate ;
May you her hapless fugitives receive,
Comfort their sorrows, and their wants relieve !
For come it will—th' inevitable day,
When Britain must corruption's forfeit pay,
Beneath a despot's, or a rabble's sway.

After a glowing description of the amours of a shepherd and shepherdess,
he thus speaks of *Marriage :*—

Bless'd days of youth, of liberty, and love !
How short, alas ! your transient pleasures prove !
Just as we think the sweet delights our own,
We strive to fix them, and we find them flown :—
For fix'd by laws, and limited by rules,
Affection stagnates and love's fervour cools ;
Shrinks like the gather'd flower, which, when possess'd,
Droops in the hand, or withers on the breast :
Feels all its native bloom and fragrance fly,
And death's pale shadows close its purple dye.
While mutual wishes form love's only vows,
By mutual interests nursed, the union grows ;
Respectful fear its rising power maintains,
And both preserve, when each may break, its chains.
But when in bands indissoluble join'd,
Securely torpid sleeps the sated mind ;
No anxious hopes or fears arise, to move
The flagging wings, or stir the fires of love :
Benumb'd, the soul's best energies repose,
And life in dull unvaried torpor flows ;
Or only shakes off lethargy to teaze
Whom once its only pleasure was to please.—ED.]

In illustration of these peculiar doctrines of Love and Marriage, the authors
of the present Parody introduced into the first twenty lines of the preceding
" Extract," the very free statements on these subjects which appear in Chapters
8, 12, 14, 16, 17, of the narrative of Cook's First Voyage to the Pacific in the
" Endeavour," in 1708, derived, by the editor, Dr. John Hawkesworth, from the
Diary of Mr. (afterwards Sir Joseph) Banks, who accompanied Captain Cook.—
ED.]

[LORD ERSKINE, after dinner, inveighed bitterly against Marriage ; and
smarting, I suppose, under the recollection of his own unsuccessful choice, concluded by saying that a wife was *a tin canister tied to a man's tail,* which very
much excited the indignation of Lady Ann Culling Smith, who was of the
party. " Monk " Lewis took a sheet of paper, and wrote the following neat
epigram on the subject, which he presented to Her Royal Highness [the Duchess
of York] :—

" Lord Erskine at marriage presuming to rail,
Says, *a wife's a tin canister tied to one's tail ;*
And the fair Lady Ann, while the subject he carries on,
Feels hurt at his Lordship's degrading comparison.
But wherefore degrading? if taken aright,
A tin canister's useful, and polished, and bright,
And if dirt its original purity hide,
'Tis the fault of the puppy to whom it is tied."
　　　　　　　　　　　　　　*—Journal of T. Raikes,* ii. 56.—ED.]

[RICHARD PAYNE KNIGHT, eminent as he was as a classical scholar and archæologist, was not successful as a poet or moralist, and this is shown in an amusing manner in a letter from Horace Walpole to the Rev. W. Mason, dated 22nd March, 1796, in which he declares how much he is offended and disgusted by Knight's " *new* insolent and self-conceited poem," alluding to his *Progress of Civil Society*,—the former one being " *The Landscape*, a didactic poem in three books," 4to, pub. 1794, of which mention has already been made.

In 1816 he was examined before a Select Committee of the House of Commons on the proposed purchase by the Government of the Elgin Marbles ; but his estimate of their value as works of the highest art was much below that of other artistic witnesses, such as Flaxman, Westmacott, Chantrey, B. West, and others. For these statements he was severely criticised in vol. 14 of the *Quarterly Review*, and in a squib, reprinted in the *New Whig Guide* in 1819. He valued the collection at £25,000 ; Gavin Hamilton's estimate was £60,800, and Lord Aberdeen's £35,000 ; for which latter sum they were obtained by the Government. He bequeathed his collection of ancient Bronzes, Greek Coins, &c.—valued at £50,000—to the British Museum.

He represented Ludlow till 1806. He was a supporter of Fox, upon whom he wrote a Monody. He was never married, and he was succeeded in his fine property, including Downton Castle, near Ludlow, &c., on his death in 1824, by his brother, Thomas Andrew Knight, one of the most scientific of horticulturists, and he in turn was succeeded by his grandson, Andrew Johnes Rouse Boughton, second son of the late Sir W. E. Rouse Boughton, Bart., who added by royal license in 1856 the name of Knight to his patronymic.—ED.]

[The drama (here nicknamed *The Reformed Housekeeper*), but entitled by the author " *Misanthropy and Repentance*," was produced at Drury Lane Theatre, Sheridan being then lessee, as " *The Stranger*," on the 24th March, 1798. The following was the cast :—*The Stranger*, J. P. Kemble ; *Baron Steinfort*, John Palmer ; *Francis*, R. Palmer ; *Peter*, Suett ; *Tobias*, J. Aikin ; *Solomon*, Wewitzer ; *Count Wintersen*, Barrymore ; *Mrs. Haller*, Mrs. Siddons ; *Countess Wintersen*, Mrs. Goodall ; *Charlotte*, Miss Stuart. It was considered by competent authorities as one of Kemble's finest efforts, and was performed on twenty-six successive nights. Some of our most eminent actors and actresses have essayed the principal parts. Miss O'Neill made her last appearance on the stage in the character of Mrs. Haller, 13th of July, 1818.

The acting version purported to be altered from the German by Benj. Thompson (afterwards Count Rumford), but it is likely that all or most of the alterations came from the skilful hands of Sheridan, assisted by Kemble. The pathetic song introduced, " *I have a silent sorrow here*," was written by the former. Two other versions of the drama appeared in the year 1798—one by A. Schinck, and the other by G. Papendick—but neither has been acted.

Kotzebue tells us in his *Autobiography* that this play of his was acted at the Imperial Palace of *The Hermitage*, St. Petersburg, under his superintendence while manager of the Imperial Company of German Comedians, and excited visible emotion in the Emperor Paul. He himself saw it acted at Tobolsk during his exile in Siberia. The vast and splendid palace of *The Hermitage* is now given up to the Arts. It contains the enormous collection of Pictures accumulated by the Russian sovereigns (including the Houghton Gallery formed by Sir Robert Walpole), together with a Gallery of Sculpture, one of the finest assortments of Antique Gems in the world, a museum of Grecian and Etruscan Antiquities, and a library of rare Books and Manuscripts.

An awful event took place during the performance of this play a short time after its production. John Palmer, an eminent comedian, while acting the principal character, at Liverpool, on the 2nd of August, 1798, expired on the stage. He had recently suffered severe domestic bereavements, which are supposed to have given a painful application to some passages in the third act in which he had to utter the words : " There is another and a better world ". In the first scene of the fourth act, his agitation increased ; he fell into the arms of the performer of the part of Baron Steinfort, and died without a groan. A narrative of this shocking event, published immediately afterwards, by the same performer, disposes of the generally-received but more emotional tradition that

Palmer's earthly career was terminated while pronouncing the above words. He was in his fifty-seventh year.

This is not the only instance of so impressive an end, for a similar death-stroke overtook Joseph Peterson, an excellent actor, in October, 1758, while representing *The Duke* in *Measure for Measure.* In act 3, sc. 1, in reciting the words—

> "—Reason thus with life :
> If I do lose thee, I do lose a thing
> That none but fools would keep : a breath thou art—"

he dropped into the arms of Moody, who personated *Claudio*, and never spoke more !—ED.]

["One other noted character we visited—the one who, according to William Taylor of Norwich, was the greatest of all. This was AUGUST VON KOTZEBUE, the very popular dramatist, whose singular fate it was to live at variance with the great poets of his country, while he was the idol of the mob. He was at one time (about this time (1801) and a little later) a favourite in all Europe. One of his plays, *The Stranger*, I have seen acted in German, English, Spanish, French, and, I believe, also Italian. He was the pensioner of Prussia, Austria, and Russia. The odium produced by this circumstance, and the imputation of being a spy, are assigned as the cause of his assassination by [C. L. Sand] a student of Jena, a few years after our visit [March 3, 1819]. He was living, like Goethe, in a large house and in style. I drank tea with him, and found him a lively little man, with small black eyes. He had the manners of a *petit-maître.*"— *Crabb Robinson's Diary* (1801), i. 115.—ED.]

## No. XXII.

April 9, 1798.

TO THE EDITOR OF THE ANTI-JACOBIN.

SIR,—I saw, with strong approbation, your specimen of ancient Sapphic measure in English, which I think far surpasses all that Abraham Fraunce, Richard Stany-hurst, or Sir Philip Sidney himself, have produced in that style—I mean, of course, your sublime and beautiful *Knife-Grinder*, of which it is not too high an encomium to say, that it even rivals the efforts of the fine-eared democratic poet, Mr. Southey. But you seem not to be aware, that we have a genuine Sapphic measure belonging to our own language, of which I now send you a short specimen.

### THE JACOBIN.

I AM a hearty Jacobin,
Who own no God, and dread no sin,
Ready to dash through thick and thin
   For freedom :

And when the teachers of Chalk-Farm
Gave Ministers so much alarm,
And preach'd that kings did only harm,
   I fee'd 'em.

By BEDFORD's cut I've trimm'd my locks,
And coal-black is my knowledge-box,
Callous to all, except hard knocks
   Of thumpers ;

My eye a noble fierceness boasts,
My voice as hollow as a ghost's,
My throat oft washed by factious toasts
            In bumpers.

Whatever is in France, is right;
Terror and blood are my delight;
Parties with us do not excite
            Enough rage.

Our boasted laws I hate and curse,
Bad from the first, by age grown worse,
I pant and sigh for univers-*
            al suffrage.

WAKEFIELD [1] I love—adore HORNE TOOKE,
With pride on JONES [2] and THELWALL [3] look,
And hope that they, by hook or crook,
            Will prosper.

But they deserve the worst of ills,
And all th' abuse of all our quills,
Who form'd of strong and *gagging Bills* [4]
            A cross pair.

Extinct since then each speaker's fire,
And silent ev'ry daring lyre,†
Dum-founded they whom I would hire
            To lecture.

---

* This division of the word is in the true spirit of the English
as well as the ancient Sapphic. See the " Counter-Scuffle,"
" Counter-Rat," and other poems in this style.

† There is a doubt, whether this word should not have been
written *liar*.

Tied up, alas! is ev'ry tongue
On which conviction nightly hung,*
And THELWALL looks, though yet but young,
A spectre.⁵

B. O. B.

---

\* These words, of *conviction* and *hanging*, have so ominous a sound, it is rather odd they were chosen.

[(1) The Rev. Gilbert Wakefield wrote several pamphlets against government, of which no notice was taken, until his Letter to the Bishop of Llandaff appeared, when the Attorney-General instituted a prosecution against him. He was found guilty and imprisoned; during which imprisonment a subscription of £3000 among his friends supported his wife and family very comfortably.—ED.]

[(2) John Gale Jones was an active political agitator for many years. In 1810, he was the conductor of the debating club, denominated the "British Forum," which at one of its meetings discussed the propriety of the exclusion of strangers from the House of Commons during the debates on the Walcheren Expedition. For his observations the House, disregarding his apology, committed him to Newgate.—ED.]

[(3) "John Thelwall left his shop (that of a silk mercer) to be one of the Re- formers of the age. After his acquittal he went about the country lecturing. Sometimes he was attended by numerous admirers, but more frequently hooted and pelted by the mob. In order to escape prosecution for sedition, he took as his subject Greek and Roman history, and had ingenuity enough to give such a colouring to events and characters, as to render the application to living persons and present events an exciting mental exercise. I heard one or two of these lectures, and thought very differently of him then from what I thought after- wards. When, however, he found his popularity on the wane, and more strin- gent laws had been passed, to which he individually gave occasion, he came to the prudent resolution of abandoning his vagrant habits, and leading a farmer's life in a beautiful place near Brecon. . . . He was an amiable man in private life, an affectionate husband, and a fond father. He altogether mistook his talents—he told me without reserve that he believed he should establish his name among the epic poets of England; and it is a curious thing considering his own views that he thought the establishment of Christianity, and the British Constitution, very appropriate subjects for his poem. . . . THELWALL, unlike Hardy, had the weakness of vanity; but he was a perfectly honest man, and had a power of declamation which qualified him to be a mob orator. He used to say that if he were at the gallows with liberty to address the people for half- an-hour, he should not fear the result; but he was sure he could excite them to a rescue. I became acquainted with him soon after his acquittal, and never ceased to respect him for his sincerity, though I did not think highly of his understand- ing."—*Crabb Robinson's Diary*, 1790 and 1799.—ED.] ·

[(4) These "Gagging Bills," of 1796, required that notice should be given to the magistrate of any public meeting to be held on political subjects; he was authorized to be present, and empowered to seize those guilty of sedition on the spot; and a second offence against the act was punishable with transportation. So exasperated were the Opposition with this measure that Fox and a large part of the minority withdrew altogether for a considerable time from the House.—ED.]

[(5) The hero of the above song was Charles Howard, eleventh Duke of Nor- folk, who both as a member of the House of Commons (while Earl of Surrey), and afterwards as a peer, was one of Fox's most strenuous supporters. SIR N. WRAXALL thus describes him: "Nature, which cast him in her coarsest mould, had not bestowed on him any of the external insignia of high descent. His person, large, muscular, and clumsy, was destitute of grace or dignity, though he possessed much activity. At a time when men of every description wore hair-powder and a queue, he had the courage to cut his hair short, and to renounce powder, which he never used except when going to court. In his youth he led a most licentious life, having frequently passed the whole night in excesses of every kind, and even lain down, when intoxicated, occasionally to sleep in the streets, or on a block of wood. In cleanliness he was negligent to so great a degree that he rarely made use of water for the purpose of bodily refreshment and comfort. Complaining one day to Dudley North that he was a martyr to the rheumatism, and had ineffectually tried every remedy for its relief, "Pray, my lord," said he, "did you ever try a clean shirt?" It must not be forgotten, however, that he was a munificent patron of literature, for he defrayed the entire expense of printing Taylor's Translation of Plato, 5 vols. 4to.; Dallaway's History of Sussex, 2 vols. 4to.; and Duncumb's History of Herefordshire, 2 vols. The initials B. O. B. refer to *Mr.* (afterwards *Sir Robert*) *Adair*, who is often alluded to in these pages.—ED.]

# No. XXIII.

April 16, 1798.

WE cannot better explain to our readers the design of the poem from which the following extracts are taken, than by borrowing the expressions of the author, Mr. HIGGINS, of *St. Mary Axe*, in the letter which accompanied the manuscript.

We must premise, that we had found ourselves called upon to remonstrate with Mr. H. on the freedom of some of the positions laid down in his other didactic poem, the "Progress of Man"; and had in the course of our remonstrance hinted something to the disadvantage of the *new principles* which are now afloat in the world, and which are, in our opinion, working so much prejudice to the happiness of mankind. To this Mr. H. takes occasion to reply—*

"What you call the *new principles* are, in fact, nothing less than *new*. They are the principles of primeval nature, the system of original and unadulterated man.

---

[* These observations are directed against Godwin's work on "Political Justice," which, on its first appearance, excited extraordinary attention. His aim was to represent the whole system of society as radically and essentially wrong, and to extirpate all those principles which uphold its present constitution. The existence of the Deity is spoken of as an hypothesis, and the ethics are worthy of the religion. HOLCROFT reviewed it in the "Monthly Review," but was doubtful whether to praise or blame it.—ED.]

["I noticed (says CRABB ROBINSON in 1811) the infinite superiority of GODWIN over the French writers in moral feeling and tendency. I had learned to hate Helvetius and Mirabeau, and yet retained my love for GODWIN. This was agreed to as a just sentiment."—ED.]

10

"If you mean by my addiction to *new principles* that the object which I have in view in my larger work [meaning the 'Progress of Man'] and in the several other *concomitant* and *subsidiary* didactic poems which are necessary to complete my plan, is to restore this first, and pure simplicity; to rescue and to recover the interesting nakedness of human nature, by ridding her of the cumbrous establishments which the folly, and pride, and self-interest of the worst part of our species have heaped upon her;—you are right. Such is my object. I do not disavow it. Nor is it mine alone. There are abundance of abler hands at work upon it. *Encyclopedias, Treatises, Novels, Magazines, Reviews,* and *New Annual Registers,* have, as you are well aware, done their part with activity and with effect. It remained to bring the *heavy* artillery of a didactic poem to bear upon the same object.

"If I have selected your paper as the channel for conveying my labours to the public, it was not because I was unaware of the hostility of your principles to mine, of the bigotry of your attachment to 'things as they are,' but because, I will fairly own, I found some sort of cover and disguise necessary for securing the favourable reception of my sentiments; the usual pretexts of humanity, and philanthropy, and fine feeling, by which we have for some time obtained a passport to the hearts and understandings of men, being now worn out or exploded. I could not choose but smile at my success in the first instance, in inducing *you* to adopt my poem as your own.

"But you have called for an explanation of these principles of ours, and you have a right to obtain it.

. Our first principle is, then—the reverse of the trite
·· and dull maxim of Pope—' *Whatever is, is right*'. We
contend, that ' *Whatever is, is wrong*'; that institutions,
civil and religious, that social order (as it is called
in *your* cant) and regular government, and law, and I
know not what other fantastic inventions, are but so
many cramps and fetters on the free agency of man's
*natural intellect* and *moral sensibility*; so many badges
of his degradation from the primal purity and excellence
of his nature.

" Our second principle is, the ' *eternal and absolute
perfectibility of man*'. We contend, that if, as is demon-
strable, we have risen from a level with the *cabbages
of the field* to our present comparatively intelligent and
dignified state of existence, by the mere exertion of
our own *energies;* we should, if these *energies* were not re-
pressed and subdued by the operation of prejudice,
and folly, by KING-CRAFT and PRIEST-CRAFT, and the
other evils incident to what is called civilized society,
continue to exert and expand ourselves in a proportion
infinitely greater than anything of which we yet have
any notion :—in a *ratio* hardly capable of being calculated by any science of which we are now masters :
but which would in time raise man from his present
biped state to a rank more worthy of his endowments
and aspirations ; to a rank in which he would be, as it
were, *all* MIND ; would enjoy unclouded perspicacity and
perpetual vitality; feed on *oxygene*, and never die, but
*by his own consent.*

" But though the poem of the PROGRESS OF MAN
alone would be sufficient to teach this system and
enforce these doctrines, the whole practical effect of

them cannot be expected to be produced, but by the
gradual perfecting of each of the sublimer sciences ;—
at the husk and shell of which we are now nibbling and
at the kernel whereof, in our present state, we cannot
hope to arrive. These several sciences will be the
subjects of the several *auxiliary* DIDACTIC POEMS which
I have now in hand (one of which, entitled THE LOVES
OF THE TRIANGLES, I herewith transmit to you), and for
the better arrangement and execution of which, I
beseech you to direct your bookseller to furnish me with
a handsome Chambers's Dictionary ; in order that I may
be enabled to go through the several articles alphabeti-
cally, beginning with *Abracadabra*, under the first letter,
and going down to *Zodiac*, which is to be found under
the last.

" I am persuaded that there is no science, however
abstruse, nay, no trade or manufacture, which may not
be taught by a didactic poem. In that before you, an
attempt is made (not unsuccessfully, I hope) to *enlist the
imagination under the banners of Geometry. Botany* I found
done to my hands. And though the more rigid and unbending stiffness of a mathematical subject does not
admit of the same appeals to the warmer passions,
which naturally arise out of the *sexual* (or, as I have
heard several worthy gentlewomen of my acquaintance,
who delight much in the poem to which I allude, term
it, by a slight misnomer no way difficult to be accounted
for—the *sensual*) system of Linnæus ;—yet I trust that
the range and variety of illustration with which I have
endeavoured to ornament and enlighten the arid truths
of Euclid and Algebra, will be found to have smoothed
the road of Demonstration, to have softened the rugged

features of Elementary Propositions, and, as it were, to have strewed the *Asses' Bridge* with flowers."

Such is the account which Mr. HIGGINS gives of his own undertaking, and of the motives which have led him to it. For our parts, though we have not the same sanguine persuasion of the *absolute perfectibility* of our species, and are in truth liable to the imputation of being more satisfied with *things as they are*, than Mr. HIGGINS and his associates ;—yet, as we are, in at least the same proportion, less convinced of the practical influence of didactic poems, we apprehend little danger to our readers' morals from laying before them Mr. HIGGINS's doctrine in its most fascinating shape. The poem abounds, indeed, with beauties of the most striking kind, —various and vivid imagery, bold and unsparing impersonifications ; and similitudes and illustrations brought from the most ordinary and the most extraordinary occurrences of nature—from history and fable—appealing equally to the heart and to the understanding, and calculated to make the subject of which the poem professes to treat rather amusing than intelligible. We shall be agreeably surprised to hear that it has assisted any young student at either University in his mathematical studies.

We need hardly add, that the plates illustrative of this poem (the engravings of which would have been too expensive for our publication) are to be found in Euclid's Elements, and other books of a similar tendency.

# LOVES OF THE TRIANGLES.*

## ARGUMENT OF THE FIRST CANTO.

Warning to the profane not to approach—Nymphs and Deities of Mathematical Mythology—Cyclois of a pensive turn— Pendulums, on the contrary, playful—and why?—Senti- mental Union of the Naiads and Hydrostatics—Marriage of Euclid and Algebra.—Pulley the emblem of Mechanics— Optics of a licentious disposition—distinguished by her tele- scope and green spectacles.—Hyde-Park Gate on a Sunday morning—Cockneys—Coaches.—Didactic Poetry—Nonsensia —Love delights in Angles or Corners—Theory of Fluxions explained—Trochais, the Nymph of the Wheel—Smoke-Jack described—Personification of elementary or culinary Fire.— Little Jack Horner—Story of Cinderella—Rectangle, a Magi- cian, educated by Plato and Menecmus—in love with Three Curves at the same time—served by Gins, or Genii—trans- forms himself into a Cone—the Three Curves requite his passion—Description of them—Parabola, Hyperbola, and Ellipsis — Asymptotes — Conjugated Axes. — Illustrations — Rewbell, Barras, and Lepaux, the three virtuous Directors— Macbeth and the Three Witches—the Three Fates—the Three Graces—King Lear and his Three Daughters—Derby Diligence—Catherine Wheel.—Catastrophe of Mr. Gingham, with his Wife and Three Daughters overturned in a One-horse Chaise—Dislocation and Contusion two kindred Fiends—Mail Coaches—Exhortation to Drivers to be careful—Genius of the Post-Office — Invention  of  Letters — Digamma — Double Letters—Remarkable Direction of one—Hippona the God- dess of Hack-horses—Parameter and Abscissa unite to over- power the Ordinate, who retreats down the Axis-Major, and forms himself in a Square—Isosceles, a Giant—Dr. Rhomboides —Fifth Proposition, or Asses' Bridge—Bridge of Lodi— Buonaparte — Raft  and  Windmills — Exhortation  to  the recovery of our Freedom—Conclusion.

[* Written in ridicule of Dr. DARWIN'S *Loves of the Plants.*]

# THE LOVES OF THE TRIANGLES.

𝔄 𝔐athematical and 𝔓hilosophical 𝔓oem,

INSCRIBED TO DR. DARWIN.

## CANTO I.

STAY your rude steps, or e'er your feet invade
The Muses' haunts, ye sons of War and Trade!
Nor you, ye legion fiends of Church and Law,
Pollute these pages with unhallow'd paw!
Debased, corrupted, grovelling, and confined,          5
No DEFINITIONS touch *your* senseless mind;
To *you* no POSTULATES prefer their claim,
No ardent AXIOMS *your* dull souls inflame;
For *you* no TANGENTS touch, no ANGLES meet,
No CIRCLES join in osculation sweet!                   10

For *me*, ye CISSOIDS, round my temples bend
Your wandering curves; ye CONCHOIDS extend;

---

Ver. 1—4. Imitated from the introductory couplet to the
*Economy of Vegetation:*
"Stay your rude steps, whose throbbing breasts infold
    The legion fiends of glory and of gold".
This sentiment is here expanded into four lines.
    Ver. 6. *Definition*—A distinct notion explaining the genesis
of a thing.—*Wolfius.*
    Ver. 7. *Postulate*—A self-evident proposition.
    Ver. 8. *Axiom*—An indemonstrable truth.
    Ver. 9. *Tangents*—So called from touching, because they
touch circles, and never cut them.
    Ver. 10. *Circles*—See Chambers's Dictionary, article "Circle".
    Ver. 10. *Osculation*—For the *osculation*, or kissing of circles
and other curves, see Huygens, who has veiled this delicate
and inflammatory subject in the decent obscurity of a learned
language.
    Ver. 11. *Cissois*—A curve supposed to resemble the sprig of
ivy, from which it has its name, and therefore peculiarly
adapted to poetry.
    Ver. 12. *Conchois*, or *Conchylis*—A most beautiful and pictur-

Let playful PENDULES quick vibration feel,
While silent CYCLOIS rests upon her wheel;
Let HYDROSTATICS, simpering as they go,                    15
Lead the light Naiads on fantastic toe;
Let shrill ACOUSTICS tune the tiny lyre;
With EUCLID sage fair ALGEBRA conspire;
The obedient pulley strong MECHANICS ply,
And wanton OPTICS roll the melting eye!                    20

I see the fair fantastic forms appear,
The flaunting drapery, and the languid leer;
Fair sylphish forms—who, tall, erect, and slim,
Dart the keen glance, and stretch the length of limb;
To viewless harpings weave the meanless dance,            25
Wave the gay wreath, and titter as they prance.

Such rich confusion charms the ravish'd sight,
When vernal Sabbaths to the Park invite.

---

esque curve; it bears a fanciful resemblance to a *conch,* shell.
The conchois is capable of infinite extension, and presents a
striking analogy between the animal and mathematical creation
—every individual of this species containing within itself a
series of *young* conchoids for several generations, in the same
manner as the Aphides and other insect tribes are observed to do.
    Ver. 15. *Hydrostatics*—Water has been supposed, by several
of our philosophers, to be capable of the passion of love.  Some
later experiments appear to favour this idea.  Water, when
pressed by a moderate degree of heat, has been observed to
*simper,* or *simmer,* as it is more usually called.  The same does
not hold true of any other element.
    Ver. 17. *Acoustics*—The doctrine or theory of sound.
    Ver. 18. *Euclid and Algebra*—The loves and nuptials of these
two interesting personages, forming a considerable episode in
the third canto, are purposely omitted here.
    Ver. 19. *Pulley*—So called from our Saxon word to PULL,
signifying to pull or draw.
    Ver. 23. *Fair sylphish forms*—*Vide* modern prints of nymphs
and shepherds dancing to nothing at all.
    Ver. 27. *Such rich confusion*—Imitated from the following

Mounts the thick dust, the coaches crowd along,
Presses round Grosvenor Gate th' impatient throng ; 30
White-muslined misses and mammas are seen,
Linked with gay cockneys, glittering o'er the green :
The rising breeze unnumbered charms displays,
And the tight ankle strikes th' astonished gaze.

But chief, thou Nurse of the Didactic Muse, 35
Divine NONSENSIA, all thy soul infuse ;
The charms of *Secants* and of *Tangents* tell,
How Loves and Graces in an *Angle* dwell ;
How slow progressive *Points* protract the *Line*,
As pendent spiders spin the filmy twine ; 40
How lengthened *Lines*, impetuous sweeping round,
Spread the wide *Plane*, and mark its circling bound ;

---

genteel and sprightly lines in the first canto of the " Loves of
the Plants " :
"So bright its folding canopy withdrawn,
Glides the gilt landau o'er the velvet lawn,
Of beaux and belles displays the glittering throng,
And soft airs fan them as they glide along ".

Ver. 38. *Angle*—Gratus puellæ risus ab Angulo.—*Hor.*

Ver. 39. *How slow progressive Points*--The Author has reserved
the picturesque imagery which the *theory of fluxions* naturally
suggested for his " Algebraic Garden," where the *fluents* are
described as rolling with an even current between a margin of
*curves* of the higher order over a pebbly channel, inlaid with
*differential calculi.*

In the following six lines he has confined himself to a strict
explanation of the theory, according to which lines are supposed
to be generated by the motion of points, planes by the lateral
motion of lines, and solids from planes, by a similar process.

*Quære*—Whether a practical application of this theory would
not enable us to account for the genesis or original formation of
space itself, in the same manner in which Dr. Darwin has
traced the whole of the organized creation to his six filaments
—Vide *Zoonomia.* We may conceive the whole of our present
universe to have been originally concentred in a single point;

How *Planes*, their substance with their motion grown,
Form the huge *Cube*, the *Cylinder*, the *Cone*.

we may conceive this primeval point, or *punctum saliens* of the
universe, evolving itself by its own energies, to have moved
forward in a right line, *ad infinitum*, till it grew tired ; after
which the right line which it had generated would begin to put
itself in motion in a lateral direction, describing an area of
infinite extent. This area, as soon as it became conscious of
its own existence, would begin to ascend or descend, according
as its specific gravity might determine it, forming an immense
solid space filled with vacuum, and capable of containing the
present existing universe.

Space being thus obtained, and presenting a suitable nidus,
or receptacle for the generation of chaotic matter, an immense
deposit of it would gradually be accumulated ; after which, the
filament of *fire* being produced in the chaotic mass by an *idio-
syncrasy*, or self-formed habit, analogous to fermentation, *explosion* would take place ; *suns* would be shot from the central
chaos ; *planets* from *suns;* and *satellites* from *planets.* In this
state of things the filament of *organization* would begin to exert
itself in those independent masses which, in proportion to their
bulk, exposed the greatest surface to the action of *light* and *heat.*
This filament, after an infinite series of ages, would begin to
*ramify*, and its viviparous offspring would diversify their forms
and habits, so as to accommodate themselves to the various
*incunabula* which Nature had prepared for them. Upon this
view of things it seems highly probable that the first effort of
Nature terminated in the production of vegetables, and that
these, being abandoned to their own *energies*, by degrees
detached themselves from the surface of the earth, and supplied
themselves with wings or feet, according as their different pro-
pensities determined them in favour of aerial and terrestrial
existence. Others, by an inherent disposition to society and
civilization, and by a stronger effort of *volition*, would become
men. These, in time, would restrict themselves to the use of
their *hind feet;* their *tails* would gradually rub off by sitting
in their caves or huts, as soon as they arrived at a domesti-
cated state ; they would invent *language* and the use of *fire,*
with our present and hitherto imperfect system of *society.*
In the meanwhile, the *Fuci* and *Algæ*, with the *Corallines*
and *Madrepores*, would transform themselves into *fish*, and
would gradually populate all the submarine portion of the
globe.

Lo! where the chimney's sooty tube ascends,        45
The fair TROCHAIS from the corner bends!
Her coal-black eyes upturned, incessant mark
The eddying smoke, quick flame, and volant spark;
Mark with quick ken, where flashing in between,
Her much-loved *Smoke-Jack* glimmers thro' the scene; 50
Mark, how his various parts together tend,
Point to one purpose,—in one object end;
The spiral *grooves* in smooth meanders flow,
Drags the long *chain*, the polished axles glow,
While slowly circumvolves the piece of beef below;   55
The conscious fire with bickering radiance burns,
Eyes the rich joint, and roasts it as it turns.

So youthful Horner rolled the roguish eye,
Cull'd the dark plum from out his Christmas pie,
And cried, in self-applause—"How good a boy
am I".                                             60

So she, sad victim of domestic spite,
Fair Cinderella, pass'd the wintry night,
In the lone chimney's darksome nook immured,
Her form disfigured, and her charms obscured.
Sudden her godmother appears in sight,             65
Lifts the charmed rod, and chants the mystic rite.
The chanted rite the maid attentive hears,

Ver. 46. *Trochais*—The Nymph of the Wheel, supposed to be
in love with Smoke-Jack.
Ver. 56. *The conscious fire*—The sylphs and genii of the
different elements have a variety of innocent occupations
assigned them; those of fire are supposed to divert themselves
with writing *Kunkel* in phosphorus.—See *Economy of Vegetation:*
    "Or mark, with shining letters, Kunkel's name
    In the pale *phosphor's* self-consuming flame".

And feels new ear-rings deck her listening ears;
While 'midst her towering tresses, aptly set,
Shines bright, with quivering glance, the smart
  aigrette;                                          70
Brocaded silks the splendid dress complete,
And the Glass Slipper grasps her fairy feet.
Six cock-tailed mice transport her to the ball,
And liveried lizards wait upon her call.
Alas! that partial Science should approve
The sly RECTANGLE's too licentious love!
For *three* bright nymphs, &c., &c.

(To be continued.)

---

Ver. 68. *Listening ears*—Listening, and therefore peculiarly
suited to a pair of diamond ear-rings. See the description of
Nebuchadnezzar in his transformed state—

"Nor flattery's self can pierce his *pendent ears*".

In poetical diction, a person is said to "*breathe the* BLUE *air*,"
and to "*drink the* HOARSE *wave!*"—not that the colour of the
sky or the noise of the water has any reference to drinking or
breathing, but because the poet obtains the advantage of thus
describing his subject under a *double relation*, in the same
manner in which material objects present themselves to our
different senses at the same time.

Ver. 73. *Cock-tailed mice*—Coctilibus Muris. *Ovid.*—There
is reason to believe that the *murine*, or *mouse* species, were
anciently much more numerous than at the present day. It
appears from the sequel of the line, that Semiramis surrounded
the city of Babylon with a number of these animals.

Dicitur altam<br>Coctilibus Muris cinxisse Semiramis urbem.

It is not easy at present to form any conjecture with respect
to the end, whether of ornament or defence, which they could
be supposed to answer. I should be inclined to believe, that in
this instance the mice were dead, and that so vast a collection
of them must have been furnished by way of tribute, to free the

country from these destructive animals. This superabundance of the *murine* race must have been owing to their immense fecundity, and to the comparatively tardy reproduction of the *feline* species. The traces of this disproportion are to be found in the early history of every country.—The ancient laws of Wales estimate a cat at the price of as much corn as would be sufficient to cover her, if she were suspended by the tail with her fore-feet touching the ground.—See Howel Dha.—In Germany, it is recorded that an army of rats, a larger animal of the *mus* tribe, was employed as the ministers of divine vengeance against a feudal tyrant; and the commercial legend of our own Whittington might probably be traced to an equally authentic origin.

# No. XXIV.

April 23, 1798.

## THE LOVES OF THE TRIANGLES.

𝔄 𝔐𝔞𝔱𝔥𝔢𝔪𝔞𝔱𝔦𝔠𝔞𝔩 𝔞𝔫𝔡 𝔓𝔥𝔦𝔩𝔬𝔰𝔬𝔭𝔥𝔦𝔠𝔞𝔩 𝔓𝔬𝔢𝔪.

(*Continued.*)

### CANTO I.

ALAS! that partial Science should approve      75
The sly RECTANGLE's too licentious love!
For *three* bright nymphs the wily wizard burns;—
*Three* bright-eyed nymphs requite his flame by turns.
Strange force of magic skill! combined of yore
With Plato's science and Menecmus' lore.      80
In *Afric's* school, amid those sultry sands
High on its base where Pompey's pillar stands,
This learnt the Seer; and learnt, alas! too well,
Each scribbled talisman, and smoky spell:

---

Ver. 76. *Rectangle*—"A figure which has one angle, or more, of ninety degrees". *Johnson's Dictionary.*—It here means a right-angled triangle, which is therefore incapable of having more than one angle of ninety degrees, but which may, according to our author's *Prosopopœia*, be supposed to be in love with three, or any greater number of nymphs.

Ver. 80. *Plato's and Menecmus' lore*—Proclus attributes the discovery of the conic sections to Plato, but obscurely. Eratosthenes seems to adjudge it to Menecmus. "*Neque Menecmeos necesse erit in cono secare ternarios.*" (Vide *Montucla.*) From Greece they were carried to Alexandria, where (according to our author's beautiful fiction) *Rectangle* either did or might learn magic.

What muttered charms, what soul-subduing arts,     85
Fell Zatanai to his sons imparts.

GINS—black and huge ! who in Dom-Daniel's cave
Writhe your scorched limbs on sulphur's azure wave ;
Or, shivering, yell amidst eternal snows,
Where cloud-capp'd Caf protrudes his granite toes ;   90
(Bound by his will, *Judæa's* fabled king,
Lord of *Alaʹddin's* lamp and mystic ring.)
Gins ! ye remember !—for your toil conveyed
Whate'er of drugs the powerful charm could aid ;
Air, earth, and sea ye searched, and where below     95
Flame embryo lavas, young volcanoes glow,—

---

Ver. 86. *Zatanai*—Supposed to be the same with Satan.—
Vide the *New Arabian Nights*, translated by Cazotte, author of
" *Le Diable amoureux* ".

Ver. 87. *Gins*—the Eastern name for Genii.—Vide *Tales of
ditto*.

Ver. 87. *Dom-Daniel*—a sub-marine palace near Tunis, where
Zatanai usually held his court.—Vide *New Arabian Nights*.

Ver. 88. *Sulphur*—A substance which, when cold, reflects
the yellow rays, and is therefore said to be yellow. When
raised to a temperature at which it *attracts oxygene* (a process
usually called *burning*), it emits a blue flame. This may be
beautifully exemplified, and at a moderate expense, by igniting
those *fasciculi* of brimstone *matches*, frequently sold (so frequently, indeed, as to form one of the London cries) by women
of an advanced age, in this metropolis. They will be found to
yield an *azure*, or blue light.

Ver. 90. *Caf*—the Indian *Caucasus.*—Vide *Bailly's Lettres sur
l'Atlantide*, in which he proves that this was the native country
of Gog and Magog (now resident in Guildhall), as well as of the
Peris, or fairies, of the Asiatic romances.

Ver. 91. *Judæa's fabled king*—Mr. HIGGINS does not mean to
deny that Solomon was really king of Judæa. The epithet
*fabled* applies to that empire over the Genii, which the retro-
spective generosity of the Arabian fabulists has bestowed upon
this monarch.

Ver. 96. *Young volcanoes*—The genesis of burning mountains
was never, till lately, well explained. Those with which we are

Gins! ye beheld appall'd th' enchanter's hand
Wave in dark air th' *Hypothenusal* wand;
Saw him the mystic *Circle* trace, and wheel
With head erect, and far-extended heel;　　　　　　100
Saw him, with speed that mocked the dazzled eye,
Self-whirled, in quick gyrations eddying fly:
Till done the potent spell—behold him grown
Fair *Venus'* emblem—the *Phœnician* CONE.

---

best acquainted are certainly not viviparous; it is therefore
probable, that there exists, in the centre of the earth, a considerable reservoir of their eggs, which, during the obstetrical
convulsions of general earthquakes, produce new volcanoes.

Ver. 100. *Far-extended heel*—The personification of *Rectangle,*
besides answering a poetical purpose, was necessary to illustrate Mr. HIGGINS's philosophical opinions. The ancient
mathematicians conceived that a cone was generated by the
revolution of a triangle; but this, as our author justly observes,
would be impossible, without supposing in the triangle that
*expansive nisus,* discovered by Blumenbach, and improved by
Darwin, which is peculiar to animated matter, and which alone
explains the whole mystery of organization. Our enchanter sits
on the ground, with his heels stretched out, his head erect, his
wand (or *hypothenuse*) resting on the extremities of his feet and
the tip of his nose (as is finely expressed in the engraving in the
original work), and revolves upon his bottom with great velocity.
His skin, by magical means, has acquired an indefinite power of
expansion, as well as that of assimilating to itself all the *azote*
of the air, which he decomposes by expiration from his lungs—
an immense quantity, and which, in our present unimproved
and uneconomical mode of breathing, is quite thrown away.
By this simple process the transformation is very naturally
accounted for.

Ver. 104. *Phœnician Cone*—It was under this shape that
Venus was worshipped in Phœnicia. Mr. HIGGINS thinks it
was the *Venus Urania,* or Celestial Venus; in allusion to which,
the Phœnician grocers first introduced the practice of preserving
sugar-loaves in blue or sky-coloured paper—he also believes
that the *conical* form of the original grenadier's cap was typical
of the loves of Mars and Venus.

Triumphs the Seer, and now secure observes 105
The kindling passions of the *rival* CURVES.

And first, the fair PARABOLA behold,
Her timid arms, with virgin blush, unfold !
Though, on one *focus* fixed, her eyes betray
A heart that glows with love's resistless sway ; 110
Though, climbing oft, she strives with bolder grace
Round his tall neck to clasp her fond embrace,
Still ere she reach it, from his polished side
Her trembling hands in devious *Tangents* glide.

Not thus HYPERBOLA ;—with subtlest art 115
The blue-eyed wanton plays her changeful part ;
Quick as her *conjugated axes* move
Through every posture of luxurious love,
Her sportive limbs with easiest grace expand ;
Her charms unveiled provoke the lover's hand ; 120
Unveiled, except in many a filmy ray,
Where light *Asymptotes* o'er her bosom play,
Nor touch her glowing skin, nor intercept the day.

Yet why, ELLIPSIS, at thy fate repine ?
More lasting bliss, securer joys are thine. 125

---

Ver. 107. *Parabola*—The curve described by projectiles of
all sorts, as bombs, shuttlecocks, &c.
Ver. 115. *Hyperbola*—Not figuratively speaking, as in rhetoric,
but mathematically ; and therefore blue-eyed.
Ver. 122. *Asymptotes*—" Lines, which though they may approach still nearer together till they are nearer than the least
assignable distance, yet being still produced infinitely, will never
meet ".—*Johnson's Dictionary.*
Ver. 124. *Ellipsis*—A curve, the revolution of which on its
axis produces an ellipsoid, or solid resembling the eggs of birds,
particularly those of the gallinaceous tribe. *Ellipsis* is the only
curve that embraces the cone.

11

Though to each fair his treacherous wish may stray,
Though each, in turn, may seize a transient sway,
'Tis thine with mild coercion to restrain,
Twine round his struggling heart, and bind with endless
    chain.

Thus, happy France ! in thy regenerate land,          130
Where TASTE with RAPINE saunters hand in hand ;
Where, nursed in seats of innocence and bliss,
REFORM greets TERROR with fraternal kiss ;
Where mild PHILOSOPHY first taught to scan
The *wrongs* of PROVIDENCE, and *rights* of Man ;          135
Where MEMORY broods o'er FREEDOM's earlier scene,
The *Lantern* bright, and brighter *Guillotine ;*
*Three* gentle swains evolve their longing arms,
And woo the young REPUBLIC's virgin charms ;
And though proud *Barras* with the fair succeed,          140
Though not in vain th' Attorney *Rewbell* plead,
Oft doth th' impartial nymph their love forego,
To clasp thy crooked shoulders, blest *Lepaux !*

So, with dark dirge athwart the blasted heath,
*Three* Sister Witches hailed the appalled Macbeth.          145

So, the *Three* Fates beneath grim Pluto's roof,
Strain the dun warp, and weave the murky woof ;
'Till deadly Atropos with fatal shears
Slits the thin promise of the expected years,
While 'midst the dungeon's gloom or battle's din,          150
Ambition's victims perish, as they spin.

Thus, the *Three* Graces on the Idalian green
Bow with deft homage to Cythera's Queen ;

Her polished arms with pearly bracelets deck,
Part her light locks, and bare her ivory neck ;    155
Round her fair form ethereal odours throw,
And teach th' unconscious zephyrs where to blow,
Floats the thin gauze, and glittering as they play,
The bright folds flutter in phlogistic day,

So, with his daughters *Three*, th' unsceptered Lear 160
Heaved the loud sigh, and poured the glistering tear :
His daughters *Three*, save one alone, conspire
(Rich in his gifts) to spurn their generous sire ;
Bid the rude storm his hoary tresses drench,
Stint the spare meal, the hundred knights retrench ; 165
Mock his mad sorrow, and with altered mien
Renounce the daughter, and assert the queen.
A father's griefs his feeble frame convulse,
Rack his white head, and fire his feverous pulse ;
Till kind Cordelia soothes his soul to rest,    170
And folds the parent-monarch to her breast.

Thus some fair spinster grieves in wild affright,
Vexed with dull megrim, or vertigo light ;
Pleased round the fair, *Three* dawdling doctors stand,
Wave the white wig, and stretch the asking hand,    175
State the grave doubt, the nauseous draught decree,
And all receive, though none deserve, a fee.

So down thy hill, romantic Ashbourn,* glides
The Derby dilly, carrying *Three* INSIDES.

[* " Romantic Ashbourn." The road down Ashbourn Hill
winds in front of Ashbourn Hall, then the residence of the Rev.
Mr. Leigh, who married a relation of CANNING's, and to whom
the latter was a frequent visitor.    A clever parodical application
of this couplet was made by O'CONNELL to LORD STANLEY's sec-
tion of a party of six, who wished to hold the balance of power,

One in each corner sits, and lolls at ease, 180
With folded arms, propt back, and outstretched knees;
While the pressed *Bodkin*, punched and squeezed to
death,
Sweats in the midmost place, and scolds, and pants for
breath.*

(*To be continued.*)

during PEEL's short administration in 1835. He altered it to
"The Derby Dilly," carrying *six* insides.—See the Greville
Memoirs, vol. 3, pp. 236, &c.—ED.]

[* Thus sings Dr. Darwin of the Loves of the Plants:
"*Two* brother swains, of Collins' gentle name,
The same their features, and their forms the same,
With rival love for fair Collinia sigh,
Knit the dark brow, and roll the unsteady eye.
With sweet concern the pitying beauty mourns,
And soothes with smiles the jealous pair by turns.
"Woo'd with long care, Curcuma, cold and shy,
Meets her fond husband with averted eye.
*Four* beardless youths the obdurate beauty move
With soft attentions of Platonic love."—ED.]

# No. XXV.

April 30, 1798.

## BRISSOT'S GHOST.*

As at the Shakespeare Tavern dining,
O'er the well replenished board
Patriotic chiefs reclining,
Quick and large libations poured ;
While, in fancy, great and glorious,
'Midst the democratic storm,
Fox's crew, with shout victorious,
Drank to *Radical Reform ;*

Sudden, up the staircase sounding,
Hideous yells and shrieks were heard ;
Then, each guest with fear confounding,
A grim train of Ghosts appeared :
Each a head, with anguish gasping,
(Himself a trunk deformed with gore),
In his hand, terrific, clasping,
Stalked across the wine-stained floor.

On them gleamed the lamp's blue lustre,
When stern BRISSOT's grizzly shade
His sad bands was seen to muster,
And his bleeding troops arrayed.

---

[* BRISSOT was one of the first movers in the outbreak of the French Revolution, and with twenty other Girondists suffered death under the guillotine, October 30, 1793. He was one of the most virtuous as well as most accomplished *littérateurs* of the time.—ED.]

Through the drunken crowd he hied him,
Where the chieftain sate enthroned,
There, his shadowy trunks beside him,
-    Thus in threatening accents groaned :

" Heed, oh heed our fatal story,
(I am BRISSOT's injured Ghost),
You who hope to purchase glory
In that field where I was lost !
Though dread PITT's expected ruin
Now your soul with triumph cheers,
When you think on our undoing,
You will mix your hopes with fears.

" See these helpless, headless spectres,
Wandering through the midnight gloom :
Mark their Jacobinic lectures
Echoing from the silent tomb ;
These, thy soul with terror filling,
Once were Patriots fierce and bold "—
(Each his head, with gore distilling,
Shakes, the whilst his tale is told).

" Some from that dread engine's carving
In vain contrived their heads to save—
See BARBAROUX and PÉTION * starving
In the Languedocian cave !

---

* Such was the end of these worthies. They were found
starved to death in a cave in Languedoc. Vide *Barrère's Rep*.

[CHARLES BARBAROUX was one of the most distinguished and
energetic of the Girondists. As he opposed the party of Marat
and Robespierre, he was, in 1793, proscribed as a Royalist and
an enemy of the Republic. He wandered about the country,
hiding himself as he best could for thirteen months, when he
was taken, and perished by the guillotine, June 25, 1794.—ED.]
JÉROME PÉTION DE VILLENEUVE was a prominent member

See, in a higgler's* hamper buckled,
How LOUVET's soaring spirit lay !
How virtuous ROLAND,† helpless cuckold,
Blew what brains he had away.

" How beneath the power of MARAT,
CONDORCET, blaspheming, fell,
Begged some laudanum of GARAT,‡
Drank ;—and slept,— to wake in hell !

---

of the Jacobin Club, and a great ally of Robespierre. Being
elected MAIRE DE PARIS in Bailly's stead, he encouraged the
demonstrations of the lowest classes, and the arming of the
populace. He then joined the Girondists. On their defeat by
the army of the Convention, he fled in July, 1793, into Bretagne.
A short time after the corpses of himself and Buzot were found
in a corn-field near St. Émilion, partly devoured by wolves.
They were supposed to have died by their own hands. He was
extremely virtuous in all his domestic relations ; but his public
career shows him to have been weak, shallow, ostentatious, and
vain.—ED.]
    * See LOUVET's *Récit de mes Périls*.
    † This philosophic coxcomb is the idol of those who admire
the French Revolution *up to a certain point*.
    ‡ This little anecdote is not generally known.—It is strikingly
pathetic.—GARAT has recorded this circumstance in a very
eloquent sentence—" O toi, qui arrêtas la main avec laquelle tu
traçais le progrès de l'esprit humain, pour porter sur tes lèvres
le breuvage mortel, d'autres pensées et d'autres sentimens ont
incliné ta volonté vers le tombeau, dans ta dernière délibéra-
tion.—(GARAT, it seems, did not choose to poison *himself.*)—Tu
as rendu à la liberté éternelle ton âme Républicaine par ce
poison qui avait été partagé entre nous comme le pain entre des
frères."
    "Oh you, who stayed the hand with which you were tracing
the progress of the human mind, to carry the mortal mixture
to your lips—it was by other thoughts and other sentiments
that your judgment was at length determined in that last deli-
berated act. You restored your republican spirit to an eternal
freedom, by that poison which we had shared together, like a
morsel of bread between two brothers."

Oh that, with worthier souls uniting,
    I in my country's cause had shone !
Had died my Sovereign's battle fighting,
    Or nobly propp'd his sinking throne !—

"But hold !—I scent the gales of morning—
    Covent-Garden's clock strikes One !
Heed, oh heed my earnest warning,
    Ere England is, like France, undone !
To St. Stephen's quick repairing,
    Your dissembled mania end ;
And, your errors past forswearing,
    Stand at length your Country's Friend !"

[The preceding ballad is parodied from the one by Glover, entitled—

### ADMIRAL HOSIER'S GHOST.

As near Porto-Bello lying
    On the gently swelling flood,
At midnight with streamers flying,
    Our triumphant navy rode :
There while VERNON sat all-glorious
    From the Spaniard's late defeat,
And his crews, with shouts victorious,
    Drank success to England's fleet :

On a sudden, shrilly sounding,
    Hideous yells and shrieks were heard,
Then each heart with fear confounding,
    A sad troop of ghosts appeared :
All in dreary hammocks shrouded,
    Which for winding-sheets they wore,
And with looks by sorrow clouded,
    Frowning on that hostile shore.

On them gleam'd the moon's wan lustre,
    When the shade of HOSIER brave
His pale bands was seen to muster,
    Rising from their wat'ry grave :
O'er the glimmering wave he hied him,
    Where the Burford rear'd her sail,
With three thousand ghosts beside him,
    And in groans did VERNON hail.

Heed, O heed, our fatal story,
    I am HOSIER'S injured ghost,
You who now have purchas'd glory,
    At this place where I was lost ;
Though in Porto-Bello's ruin
    You now triumph free from fears,

When you think on our undoing,
    You will mix your joy with tears.
See these mournful spectres sweeping
    Ghastly o'er this hated wave,
Whose wan cheeks are stain'd with weeping,
    These were English Captains brave.
Mark those numbers pale and horrid,
    Those were once my sailors bold,
See each hangs his drooping forehead,
    While his dismal tale is told.

I by twenty sail attended
    Did this Spanish town affright,
Nothing then its wealth defended
    But my orders not to fight.
O! that in this rolling ocean
    I had cast them with disdain,
And obey'd my heart's warm motion
    To have quell'd the pride of Spain.

For resistance I could fear none,
    But with twenty ships had done
What thou, brave and happy VERNON,
    Hast achiev'd with six alone.
Then the Bastimentos never
    Had our foul dishonour seen,
Nor the sea the sad receiver
    Of this gallant train had been.

Thus, like thee, proud Spain dismaying,
    And her galleons leading home,
Though condemned for disobeying,
    I had met a traitor's doom:
To have fallen, my country crying
    He has play'd an English part,
Had been better far than dying
    Of a griev'd and broken heart.

Unrepining at thy glory,
    Thy successful arms we hail;
But remember our sad story,
    And let HOSIER'S wrongs prevail.
Sent in this foul clime to languish,
    Think what thousands fell in vain,
Wasted with disease and anguish,
    Not in glorious battle slain.

Hence with all my train attending
    From their oozy tombs below,
Through the hoary foam ascending,
    Here I feed my constant woe.
Here the Bastimentos viewing,
    We recal our shameful doom,
And our plaintive cries renewing,
    Wander through the midnight gloom.

O'er these waves for ever mourning,
    Shall we roam deprived of rest,
If to Britain's shores returning,
    You neglect my just request;
After this proud foe subduing,
    When your patriot friends you see,
Think on Vengeance for my ruin,
    And for England sham'd in me.]

# No. XXVI.

May 7, 1798.

## LOVES OF THE TRIANGLES.

THE frequent solicitations which we have received for a continuation of the LOVES OF THE TRIANGLES have induced us to lay before the public (with Mr. Higgins's permission) the concluding lines of the Canto. The catastrophe of Mr. and Mrs. Gingham, and the episode of Hippona, contained, in our apprehension, several reflections of too free a nature. The conspiracy of Parameter and Abscissa against the Ordinate is written in a strain of poetry so very splendid and dazzling as not to suit the more tranquil majesty of diction which our readers admire in Mr. Higgins. We have therefore begun our extract with the Loves of the Giant Isosceles, and the Picture of the Asses-Bridge, and its several illustrations.

CANTO I.

EXTRACT.

'Twas thine alone, O youth of giant frame,
Isosceles ! * that rebel heart to tame !
In vain coy Mathesis † thy presence flies :
Still turn her fond hallucinating ‡ eyes ;

---

\* *Isosceles*—An equi-crural triangle—It is represented as a *Giant*, because Mr. HIGGINS says he has observed that procerity is much promoted by the equal length of the legs, more especially when they are long legs.

† *Mathesis*—The doctrine of mathematics—Pope calls her *mad Mathesis.*—Vide *Johnson's Dictionary.*

‡ *Hallucinating*—The disorder with which Mathesis is affected is a disease of *increased volition,* called *erotomania,* or *sentimental love.* It is the fourth species of the second genus of the first

Thrills with *Galvanic* fires * each tortuous nerve,
Throb her blue veins, and dies her cold reserve.
—Yet strives the fair, till in the giant's breast
She sees the mutual passion's flame confessed :
Where'er he moves, she sees his tall limbs trace
*Internal Angles*† *equal at the base ;*
Again she doubts him : but *produced at will,*
She sees *th' external Angles equal still.*

Say, blest Isosceles ! what favouring power,
Or love, or chance, at night's auspicious hour,
While to the Asses-Bridge‡ entranced you strayed,
Led to the Asses-Bridge the enamoured maid?—

---

order and third class ; in consequence of which, Mr. Hackman
shot Miss Reay in the lobby of the playhouse.—Vide *Zoonomia,*
vol. ii., pp. 363, 365.

* *Galvanic fires*—Dr. Galvani is a celebrated philosopher at
Turin. He has proved that the electric fluid is the proximate
cause of nervous sensibility ; and Mr. HIGGINS is of opinion
that by means of this discovery, the sphere of our disagreeable
sensations may be, in future, considerably enlarged. " Since
dead frogs (says he) are awakened by this fluid to such a degree
of posthumous sensibility as to jump out of the glass in which
they are placed, why not men, who are sometimes so much more
sensible when alive ? And if so, why not employ this new
stimulus to deter mankind from dying (which they so perti-
naciously continue to do) of various old-fashioned diseases, notwithstanding all the brilliant discoveries of modern philosophy,
and the example of Count Cagliostro ?

† *Internal Angles, &c.*—This is an exact versification of
Euclid's fifth theorem.—Vide *Euclid in loco.*

‡ *Asses-Bridge*—Pons Asinorum—The name usually given to
the before-mentioned theorem—though, as Mr. Higgins thinks,
absurdly. He says, that having frequently watched companies
of asses during their passage of a bridge, he never discovered in
them any symptoms of geometrical instinct upon the occasion.
But he thinks that with Spanish asses, which are much larger
(vide *Townsend's Travels through Spain*), the case may possibly be
different.

The Asses-Bridge, for ages doomed to hear
The deafening surge assault his wooden ear,
With joy repeats sweet sounds of mutual bliss,
The soft susurrant sigh, and gently-murmuring kiss.

So thy dark arches, *London Bridge*, bestride
Indignant Thames, and part his angry tide,
There oft—returning from those green retreats,
Where fair *Vauxhallia* decks her sylvan seats ;—
Where each spruce nymph, from city compters free,
Sips the froth'd syllabub, or fragrant tea ;
While with sliced ham, scraped  beef, and burnt cham-
    pagne,
Her 'prentice lover soothes his amorous pain ;—
There oft, in well-trimmed wherry, glide along
Smart beaux and giggling belles, a glittering throng :
Smells the tarr'd rope—with undulation fine
Flaps the loose sail—the silken awnings shine ;
" Shoot we the bridge !" the venturous boatmen cry ;
" Shoot we the bridge !" the exulting fare* reply.
—Down the steep fall the headlong waters go,
Curls the white foam, the breakers roar below.
The veering helm the dexterous steersman stops,
Shifts the thin oar, the fluttering canvas drops ;
Then with closed eyes, clenched hands, and quick-drawn
    breath,
Darts at the central arch, nor heeds the gulf beneath.
Full 'gainst the pier the unsteady timbers knock,
The loose planks, starting, own the impetuous shock ;

---

* *Fare* –A person, or a number of persons, conveyed in a
hired vehicle by land or water.

The shifted oar, dropp'd sail, and steadied helm,
With angry surge the closing waters whelm—
Laughs the glad Thames, and clasps each fair one's
  charms,
That screams and scrambles in his oozy arms.
Drench'd each smart garb, and clogged each straggling
  limb,
Far o'er the stream the Cockneys sink or swim;
While each badged boatman,* clinging to his oar,
Bounds o'er the buoyant wave, and climbs the applauding
  shore.

So, towering Alp! from thy majestic ridge †
Young Freedom gazed on Lodi's blood-stained *Bridge;*
Saw, in thick throngs, conflicting armies rush,
Ranks close on ranks, and squadrons squadrons crush;
Burst in bright radiance through the battle's storm,
Waved her broad hands, displayed her awful form;
Bade at her feet regenerate nations bow,
And twined the wreath round BUONAPARTE's brow.
Quick with new lights, fresh hopes, and altered zeal,
The slaves of despots dropp'd the blunted steel:
Exulting Victory owned her favourite child,
And freed Liguria clapp'd her hands, and smiled.

---

* *Badged boatman*—Boatmen sometimes wear a *badge*, to distinguish them, especially those who belong to the Watermen's Company.

† *Alp*, or *Alps*—A ridge of mountains which separate the North of Italy from the South of Germany. They are evidently primeval and volcanic, consisting of granite, toadstone, and basalt, and several other substances, containing animal and vegetable recrements, and affording numberless undoubted proofs of the infinite antiquity of the earth, and of the consequent falsehood of the Mosaic chronology.

Nor long the time ere Britain's shores shall greet
The warrior-sage, with gratulation sweet :
Eager to grasp the wreath of naval fame,
The GREAT REPUBLIC plans the *Floating Frame!*
O'er the huge plane gigantic *Terror* stalks,
And counts with joy the close-compacted balks :
Of young-eyed *Massacres* the Cherub crew,
Round their grim chief the mimic task pursue ;
Turn the stiff screw,* apply the strengthening clamp,
Drive the long bolt, or fix the stubborn cramp,
Lash the reluctant beam, the cable splice,
Join the firm dove-tail with adjustment nice,
Through yawning fissures urge the willing wedge,
Or give the smoothing adze a sharper edge.
Or group'd in fairy bands, with playful care,
The unconscious bullet to the furnace bear ;—
Or gaily tittering, tip the match with fire,
Prime the big mortar, bid the shell aspire ;
Applaud, with tiny hands, and laughing eyes,
And watch the bright destruction as it flies.

Now the fierce forges gleam with angry glare—
The windmill † waves his woven wings in air ;

---

* *Turn the stiff screw*, &c.—The harmony and imagery of these
lines are imperfectly imitated from the following exquisite
passage in the *Economy of Vegetation :*
> " Gnomes, as you now dissect, with hammers fine,
> The granite rock, the noduled flint calcine ;
> Grind with strong arm the circling Chertz betwixt,
> Your pure Ka—o—lins and Pe—tunt—ses mixt.
> *Canto* ii. line 297.

[† *The windmill,* &c.—This line affords a striking instance of the
sound conveying an echo to the sense. I would defy the most
unfeeling reader to repeat it over without accompanying it by
some corresponding gesture imitative of the action described.—
EDITOR.]

Swells the proud sail, the exulting streamers fly,
.Their nimble fins unnumber'd paddles ply :
Ye soft airs breathe, ye gentle billows waft,
And, fraught with Freedom, bear the expected Raft !
Perch'd on her back, behold the Patriot train,
MUIR, ASHLEY, BARLOW, TONE, O'CONNOR, PAINE !
While TANDY's hand directs the blood-empurpled rein.

Ye Imps of Murder ! guard her angel form,
Check the rude surge, and chase the hovering storm ;
Shield from contusive rocks her timber limbs,
And guide the sweet Enthusiast* as she swims !

And now, with web-foot oars, she gains the land,
And foreign footsteps press the yielding sand :
The Communes spread, the gay Departments smile,
Fair Freedom's Plant o'ershades the laughing isle :
Fired with new hopes, the exulting peasant sees
The Gallic streamer woo the British breeze ;†
While, pleased to watch its undulating charms,
The smiling infant‡ spreads his little arms.

---

* *Sweet Enthusiast*, &c.—A term usually applied in allegoric
or technical poetry to any person or object to which no other
qualifications can be assigned.—*Chambers's Dictionary.*

[† ANNE PLUMPTRE, who made herself known as one of the
first introducers of German plays, said: "*People are talking
about an Invasion. I am not afraid of an Invasion ; I believe the
country would be all the happier if* BUONAPARTE *were to effect a
landing and overturn the Government. He would destroy the Church
and the Aristocracy, and his government would be better than the
one we have*". Crabb Robinson's *Diary* (1810), i. 298.—ED.]

‡ *The smiling infant*—Infancy is particularly interested in
the diffusion of the new principles. See the "Bloody Buoy".
See also the following description and prediction :
"Here Time's huge fingers grasp his giant mace,
And dash proud Superstition from her base ;
Rend her strong towers and gorgeous fanes, &c.
*       *       *       *       *       *

Ye sylphs of DEATH ! on demon pinions flit
Where the tall Guillotine is raised for PITT :
To the poised plank tie fast the monster's back,*
Close the nice slider, ope the expectant sack ;
Then twitch, with fairy hands, the frolic pin—
Down falls the impatient axe with deafening din ;
The liberated head rolls off below,†
And simpering Freedom hails the happy blow !

---

While each light moment, as it passes by,
With feathery foot and pleasure-twinkling eye,
Feeds from its baby-hand with many a kiss
The callow-nestlings of domestic bliss."—*Botanic Garden.*
* *The monster's back*—Le Monstre Pitt, l'ennemi du genre hu-
main. See *Debates of the legislators of the Great Nation, passim.*
† Atque illud prono præceps agitur decursus.—*Catullus.*

[The following lines of Dr. Darwin's, in Canto ii., gave great
offence to the Government :—

So, borne on sounding pinions to the west,
When tyrant-power had built his eagle nest ;
While from his eyry shriek'd the famish'd brood,
Clench'd their sharp claws, and champ'd their beaks for
    blood,
Immortal FRANKLIN watch'd the callow crew,
And stabb'd the struggling vampires, ere they flew.
—The patriot-flame with quick contagion ran,
Hill lighted hill, and man electris'd man :
Her heroes slain awhile Columbia mourn'd,
And crown'd with laurels Liberty return'd.

The warrior, Liberty, with bending sails,
Helm'd his bold course to fair Hibernia's vales ;
Firm as he steps along the shouting lands,
Lo ! Truth and Virtue range their radiant bands ;
Sad Superstition wails her empire torn,
Art plies his oar, and Commerce pours her horn.

Long had the giant-form on Gallia's plains
Inglorious slept, unconscious of his chains ;
Round his large limbs were wound a thousand strings
By the weak hands of confessors and kings ;

O'er his closed eyes a triple veil was bound,
And steely rivets lock'd him to the ground ;
While stern Bastile with iron-cage inthralls
His folded limbs, and hems in marble walls.—ED.]

NOTES TO LOVES OF THE TRIANGLES.

[The general features of Dr. Darwin's extraordinary poems, the "*Loves of the
Plants,*" and the "*Economy of Vegetation,*" which are so admirably ridiculed in
the preceding pages, may be gathered from the following specimens :—

ARGUMENT.

THE Genius of the place invites the Goddess of Botany—She descends—is received by Spring and the Elements—Addresses the Nymphs of Fire—Love created
the Universe—Chaos explodes—All the Stars revolve—Colours of the Morning
and Evening Skies—Exterior Atmosphere of inflammable Air—Fires at the
Earth's Centre—Animal Incubation—Venus visits the Cyclops—Phosphoric
Lights in the Evening--Bolognian Stone—Ignis fatuus—Eagle armed with
Lightning—Discovery of Fire—Medusa—The Chemical Properties of Fire—
Lady in Love—Gunpowder—Steam-engine—Labours of Hercules—Halo round
the Heads of Saints—Fairy rings—Death of Professor Richman—Cupid snatches
the thunderbolt from Jupiter—The great Egg of Night—Naiad released—Frost
assailed—Whale attacked—Ice-Islands navigated into the Tropic Seas—Rainy
Monsoons--Elijah on Mount Carmel—Departure of the Nymphs of Fire like
sparks from Artificial Fireworks, &c.

" Nymphs ! you disjoin, unite, condense, expand,
  And give new wonders to the Chemist's hand ;
On tepid clouds of rising steam aspire,
Or fix in sulphur all its solid fire ;
With boundless spring elastic airs unfold,
Or fill the fine vacuities of gold ;
With sudden flash vitrescent sparks reveal,
By fierce collision from the flint and steel ;
Or mark with shining letters Kunkel's name
In the pale phosphor's self-consuming flame.
So the chaste heart of some enchanted maid
Shines with insidious light, by love betray'd ;
Round her pale bosom plays the young desire,
And slow she wastes by self-consuming fire."

These poems, produced in that dreary time for English poetry which elapsed
between the disappearance of Cowper and Burns and the advent of Scott and
Byron, had, in spite of their glaring absurdities, no lack of warm admirers.
Miss Seward, in her *Life of Dr. Darwin,* published in 1804, sets no limits to her
admiration :—" We are presented," she says, " with an highly imaginative and
splendidly descriptive poem, whose successive pictures alternately possess the
sublimity of Michael Angelo, the correctness and elegance of Raphael, with the
glow of Titian ; whose landscapes have, at times, the strength of Salvator, and
at others the softness of Claude ; whose numbers are of stately grace, and artful
harmony ; while its allusions to ancient and modern history and fable, and its
interspersion of recent and extraordinary anecdotes, render it extremely entertaining. * * * Each part is enriched by a number of philosophical notes.
They state a great variety of theories and experiments in Botany, Chemistry,
Electricity, Mechanics, and in the various species of Air, salubrious, noxious,
and deadly," &c.]

THE SCOTTISH "POLITICAL MARTYRS".

[THOMAS MUIR, the younger, of Hunter's Hill, a promising young advocate
of the Scottish Bar, and of high respectability, was tried at Edinburgh, 30th
and 31st of August, 1793, before Lord Justice Clerk (Braxfield), Lords Hender-

land, Swinton, Dunsinnan, and Abercromby, for Sedition. The weightiest
charge against him was that of "*lending*" a copy of Paine's *Rights of Man* to a
person who begged a reading of that popular book. He was found guilty, and
sentenced to fourteen years' transportation. On the 17th of the ensuing
month, the Rev. THOS. FYSHE PALMER, a Unitarian Minister of Dundee, and an
ex-fellow of Queen's College, Cambridge, was tried at Perth for publishing a
seditious Address, and sentenced to seven years' transportation. On their
arrival at Woolwich, in a revenue cutter, they were put on board separate
hulks, and assisted at the common labour on the banks of the river. MUIR,
soon after his arrival in New South Wales, effected his escape, in an American
vessel, to South America, whence he proceeded to Spain. During this voyage,
in an action with a British frigate, he received a wound in the head, from
which he recovered; but on his arrival at his destination, he was imprisoned
by the Spanish authorities, until, on the application of M. de Talleyrand in the
name of the then government of France, he obtained his release. He then
went to France, and died at Bourdeaux [or Chantilly] in 1799; aged 33.
PALMER served out his seven years, but died on the homeward voyage.

Other Trials soon followed. At the close of December, 1793, MR. SKIRVING,
MR. GERRALD, and MR. MARGAROT were tried at Edinburgh on similar charges
of seditious practices, and were all sentenced to fourteen years' transportation.
The former two died soon after reaching New South Wales. MAURICE MAR-
GAROT, who appears to have conducted himself throughout with the most
abandoned and shameless profligacy, was the only one of these convicts—his
fourteen years over—who ever set foot again in Britain.

GERRALD was a man of very superior ability, and a favourite pupil of Dr.
Parr's, as is mentioned by De Quincey in his famous essay on that noted Whig
pedagogue.

On the Scottish "political martyrs" Lord Cockburn, in his posthumous
*Examination of the Trials for Sedition in Scotland*, published in 1888, which deals
with the twenty-five trials of the above-named five and of thirty-two others, between 1793 and 1849, passes his deliberate verdict, that, with the exception of
Muir, not one of them was guiltless. But, like ordinary criminals, they were
entitled to a fair and impartial trial; and their trials were, one and all, iniquitous. Of the six judges who presided in the first fourteen (1793-94), five were
dull, timid nonentities; the sixth, Lord Justice Clerk Braxfield, was, says
Lord Cockburn, "a profound practical lawyer, and a powerful man; coarse
and illiterate . . . utterly devoid of judicial decorum, and though pure in the
administration of civil justice, when he was exposed to no temptation, with no
other conception of principle in any political case except that the upholding of
his party was a duty attaching to his position. Over the five weak men who sat
beside him, this coarse and dexterous ruffian predominated as he chose." But
Jedburgh—no, nor the Bloody Assize itself—could scarcely match one scene in
Gerrald's trial :—"'After all,' he was urging in his defence, 'the most useful
discoveries in philosophy, the most important changes in the moral history of
man, have been innovations. The Revolution was an innovation, Christianity
itself was an innovation.' Instantly upon this, the following interruption took
place :—Lord Braxfield: 'You would have been stopped long before this, if
you had not been a stranger. All that you have been saying is sedition. And
now, my Lords, he is attacking Christianity.' Lord Henderland: 'I allow him
all the benefit of his defence. But . . . I cannot sit here as a judge without
saying that it is a most indecent defence. . . .' The juries were packed as
never, surely, before, or afterwards."

With such judges, such juries, and, at least, in two cases, false witnesses, it
might seem easy to anticipate the result; but the result transcends anticipation.
In almost every case a light sentence would have amply met the requirements
of justice; but the judges all shared Lord Swinton's opinion that "it is impossible to punish Sedition adequately, now that torture has been abolished". So
they strove to supply the deficiency by Transportation, a punishment unwar-
ranted by precedent.

With respect to Margarot's trial at Edinburgh, the following is a vivid
memory of Lord Cockburn's boyhood :—

"MARGAROT came from the Black Bull [in Leith Street] to be tried, attended by a procession of the populace and his Convention friends, with banners and what was called a tree of liberty. This tree was in the shape of the letter M, about twenty feet high and ten wide. The honour of bearing it up by carrying the two upright poles was assigned to two eminent Conventionalists, and the little culprit walked beneath the circular placard in the centre, which proclaimed liberty and equality, &c. I was looking out of a window in the old Post-Office, which was then the northmost house on the west side of the North Bridge. I think I see the scene yet. The whole North Bridge, from the Tron Church to the Register Office, was quite empty at first; not a single creature venturing on that bit of sand, over which the waves were so soon to break from both ends. The Post-Office and the adjoining houses had been secretly filled with constables, and sailors from a frigate in the roads (I think *The Hind*, Capt. Cochrane), all armed with sticks and batons. No soldier appeared, it being determined that this civic insurrection should be put down by the civil force, unaided, at least, by scarlet. As soon as the tree, which led the van, emerged from Leith Street, and appeared at the north end of the bridge, Provost Elder and the Magistrates issued from some place they had retired to (I believe the Tron Church), and appeared, all robed, at the south end. The day was good. There was still not one person—I doubt if there was even a dog—on any part of the space, being the whole length of the bridge, between the two parties. But the rear of each was crammed with people, who filled up every inch as those in front moved on. The Magistrates were in a line across the street, with the Provost in the centre, the city officers behind this line, and probably a hundred loyal gentlemen in the rear of the officers. The two parties advanced steadily towards each other, and in perfect silence, till they met just about the Post-Office. The Provost stepped forward about a pace, so that he almost touched the front line of the rebels, when, advancing his cane, he commanded them to retire. This order probably would not have been obeyed; but, at any rate, it could not have been obeyed speedily, from the crowd behind. However, all this was immaterial; for, without waiting one instant to see whether they meant to retire or not, the houses vomited forth their bludgeoned contents, and in almost two minutes the tree was demolished and thrown over the bridge, the street covered with the knocked down, the accused dragged to the bar, and the insurrection was over."

On February 20th, 1837, a meeting took place at the Crown and Anchor Tavern, Strand, for commencing a subscription to erect monuments in London and Edinburgh to the memory of the above five Reformers. Joseph Hume, M.P. was in the chair; Colonel Perronet Thompson, Mr. Dan. Whittle Harvey, and fifteen other members of Parliament were present. A lofty obelisk was erected on the Calton Hill to the memory of the "Scottish Martyrs," but London did not sympathize with the movement.—ED.]

---

## JOEL BARLOW.

[JOEL BARLOW, born in 1756 in Connecticut, was educated as a Presbyterian minister, but afterwards turned Deist. Before this change he translated the Psalms into metre, and his version is still used in the churches of New England. He now adopted the Law, and engaged in periodicals—one, *The Anarchist*, which was political in its character, and exercised great influence. In 1788, after visiting England, he went to Paris, where he joined the Girondists. In 1791, he returned to England, where he published the first part of his *Advice to the Privileged Orders*, in which he assails the whole system of Government pursued in monarchical Europe, the Church establishments, the standing armies, the judicial organisations, and the financial systems which belong to the old governments. In February, 1792, he published a political poem, which he entitled *The Conspiracy of Kings;* also a Letter to the *Convention* advising the separation of Church and State. So great did his reputation become that he was fixed on by the London Constitutional Society to present their Address to the *Convention*. After various political transactions in the interest of France, and also in commercial speculations which made him a rich man, he left Paris in 1805, living on his estate in America till 1811, when he was sent as Minister

Plenipotentiary to Paris. But Napoleon being on his Russian Expedition, he followed him to Wilna; but the fatiguing journey proved fatal: he died 26th December, 1812. He wrote at an early age a poem, *The Vision of Columbus*, which acquired great popularity, and which he afterwards enlarged as *The Columbiad*. Among other works he published (in 1796) a mock-heroic poem, *Hasty Pudding*, which is generally considered his best work.—ED.]

## THEOBALD WOLFE TONE.

[THEOBALD WOLFE TONE, the founder of the ASSOCIATION OF UNITED IRISH-MEN, was born in Dublin in 1764, and, after passing through Trinity College, came to London to prosecute his legal studies, which he soon forsook for politics, being induced thereto by the indignation excited in his breast by the persecution of the Irish Catholics, whose cause, although himself a Protestant, he warmly advocated. With the view of getting their grievances redressed, he founded the society of UNITED IRISHMEN, which gave great alarm to the English Government. His liberty being menaced, he went to America, and thence to France, where he arranged with Gen. Hoche the expeditions to Bantry Bay and the Texel. Being appointed Adjutant-General, he served in several of the French armies, and lastly in Gen. Hardi's expedition in October, 1798. The vessel he was aboard of was captured by the English, and he was conveyed to Dublin, tried by a Court-Martial, and sentenced to be hanged. He anticipated his execution, however, by committing suicide in prison, 19th November, 1798.—ED.]

## ARTHUR O'CONNOR.

[On the 21st and 22nd May, 1798, ARTHUR O'CONNOR (proprietor of a Dublin newspaper, *The Press*), JOHN BINNS (an active member of the *London Corresponding Society*), JOHN ALLEN, JEREMIAH LEARY, and JAS. O'COIGLY, *alias* Jas. Quigley, *alias* Jas. John Fivey (a Priest), were tried at Maidstone for High Treason. ROBERT FERGUSSON was counsel for Allen. O'COIGLY only was found Guilty, and was executed 7th June, on Pennenden Heath. After being suspended for ten minutes, he was cut down and his head severed from his body : the disgusting remainder of his sentence was remitted. He met his death with great fortitude, and denying to the last the charge of treasonable correspondence abroad. In the *State Trials*, vols. 26 and 27, are included the Life of the prisoner; Observations on his Trial; Address to the People of Ireland; and Letters, all written by himself during his confinement in Maidstone Gaol. His real name, he says, was the Rev. Jas. Coigly, and his age 36. "Can you imagine a man more treacherous and profligate than O'COIGLY ?" said Sir James Mackintosh to DR. PARR. "Yes, Sir, he might have been worse : he was a parson—he might have been a lawyer ; he was a traitor—he might have been an apostate ; he was an Irishman—he might have been a Scotchman." When it is recollected that Mackintosh was a Scotchman and a lawyer, and that he had written in defence of the French Revolution against Burke, these observations of Dr. Parr were both insolent and uncalled for.

A Portrait of "Arthur O'Connor, late Member in the Irish Parliament for Borough of Philipstown, painted by J. Dowling, engraved by W. Ward," was published in London, 18th April, 1798. Another Portrait in military uniform is to be found in Barrington's *Memoirs of the Union*. He figures also in several of GILLRAY'S *Caricatures*.

In the *Birmingham Daily Post* of April 2, 1888, it is stated that THE HON. R. E. O'CONNOR, M.A., barrister-at-law, the latest addition to the Legislative Council of New South Wales, is a grandson of ARTHUR O'CONNOR, one of the leaders of the United Irishmen, who died a General in the service of France.

When O'CONNOR was acquitted by the Jury, on the above-named occasion, but before the Judge had given orders for his release, a strange scene occurred in court, an attempt being made, as it was alleged, by SACKVILLE, EARL OF THANET, ROBERT FERGUSSON (in after years known as CUTLAR FERGUSSON, Judge-Advocate-General), and others to facilitate his escape in order to avoid further charges about to be preferred against him, Binns also being implicated for this exploit, which was unsuccessful, but attended with violence. These confederates were tried at the Bar of the Court of King's Bench, 25th April, 1799. The Counsel for the Crown were Sir John Scott [Lord Eldon], Law [Lord Ellenborough], Sir W. Garrow, Sir C. Abbot, &c., while the defendants had the powerful advocacy of Erskine and others. His Lordship and Mr. Fergusson were found guilty after a long and ingenious defence by the latter, which presaged his future eminence as a Counsel. LORD THANET was ordered to pay a fine of £1000; to be imprisoned in the Tower for a year; and to give security for good behaviour for seven years on the expiration of the sentence; himself in £10,000, and two sureties in £5000 each. FERGUS-SON was ordered to pay a fine of £100; to be imprisoned in the King's Bench prison for one year; to give security for good behaviour for seven years from the expiration of the sentence; himself in £500, and two sureties in £250 each. —See State Trials, vols. 26 and 27.—ED.]

## JAMES NAPPER TANDY.

["A person who afterwards made a considerable figure in the local affairs of Ireland raised himself about this time into considerable notoriety by his patriotic exertions. This was Mr. JAMES NAPPER TANDY, a gentleman in the middle station of life, without talent or natural influence, had become a warm advocate in the corporation of Dublin; he debated zealously in public, he argued strenuously in private, and persevered in both with indefatigable ardour. His person was ungracious—his language neither eloquent nor argumentative—his address neither graceful nor impressive—but he was sincere and persevering—and though in many instances erroneous and violent, he was considered to be honest. His private character furnished no ground to doubt the integrity of his public one—and, like many of those persons who occasionally spring up in revolutionary periods, he acquired celebrity without being able to account for it, and possessed influence without rank or capacity. In 1796, Mr. Tandy lost all his popularity, and nearly his life, by his apparent want of courage in an affair between him and Mr. Toler, then Solicitor-General, afterwards Lord Norbury, and Chief Justice of the Common Pleas. Mr. Tandy having signified to Mr. Toler his desire to fight him, the Chief Justice readily accepted the offer. Both parties manœuvred very skilfully; but Mr. Tandy delaying his ultimatum too long for the impatience of the Solicitor-General, he brought him before the House of Commons for a breach of privilege, and pro-secuted him for sedition. Mr. Tandy escaped to the Continent, entered the French Service, invaded Ireland, was, with his confederates, arrested by the British Envoy at Hamburg, 24 Nov., 1798, contrary to the law of nations: the Minister of France claimed them as French citizens, and the Senate, un-willing to offend either power, came to no decision on the subject. Tandy was thereupon taken to Ireland and condemned to be hanged—was pardoned by Lord Cornwallis, and sent back to France, where he died a French General." —Barrington's Memoirs of the Union, vol. 1, where is a portrait of Tandy.—ED.]

# No. XXVII.

May 14, 1798.

THE gallant defence of the ISLES OF ST. MARCOU would justify a more serious celebration than is attempted in the following poem ; and the modest and unassuming manner in which LIEUTENANT PRICE gives the account of services so highly meritorious, adds to the hope which we entertain that he will meet a more solid reward than any verse of ours or of our correspondent's could bestow.

CITIZEN MUSKEIN, if he understands Horace, and can read English, will be amply rewarded for the victory of which he has, no doubt, by this time, made a pompous report to the Directory, by the perusal of the 14th Ode of the 1st Book, for which we have to return our thanks to a classical correspondent.

## A CONSOLATORY ADDRESS TO HIS GUNBOATS.

BY CITIZEN MUSKEIN.

*O navis ! referent in mare te novi fluctus.*

O GENTLE GUN-BOATS, whom the Seine
Discharged from Havre to the main ;
Now leaky, creaking, blood-bespattered,
With rudders broken, canvas shattered—
O tempt the treacherous sea no more,
But gallantly regain the shore.

Scarce could our guardian goddess, Reason,
Ensure your timbers through the season.
Though built of wood from famed Marseilles,
Well-manned from galleys, and from jails,

Though with LEPAUX's and REWBELL's aid,
By PLEVILLE's * skill your keel was laid ;
Though lovely STAEL, and lovelier STONE,*
Have worked their fingers to the bone,
And cut their petticoats to rags     .
To make your bright three-coloured flags ;
Yet sacrilegious grape and ball
Deform the works of STONE and STAEL,
And trembling, without food or breeches,
Our sailors curse the *painted* ———.†

Children of Muskein's anxious care,
Source of my hope and my despair,
GUN-BOATS—unless you mean hereafter
To furnish food for British laughter—
Sweet GUN-BOATS, with your gallant crew,
Tempt not the rocks of SAINT MARCOU ;
Beware the Badger's bloody pennant,
And that d——d invalid LIEUTENANT !

---

* STONE.—Better known by the name of WILLIAMS.
† We decline printing this rhyme at length, from obvious reasons of delicacy ; at the same time that it is so accurate a translation of *pictis puppibus*, that we know not how to suppress it, without doing the utmost injustice to the general spirit of the poem.

## LYRICS OF HORACE. ODE XIV., BOOK I.

### TRANSLATED BY ARCHDEACON WRANGHAM.

O Ship, fresh billows soon again
Shall bear thee to the boisterous main !
Firm, keep the port. See, see thy side,
Without a single oar to guide !
Wounded by tempests is thy mast :
Thy sail-yards groan beneath the blast ;
Nor can thy keel, uncabled, brave
The swelling of th' imperious wave.

Torn are thy sails ! nor Gods hast thou,
When danger threats, to hear thy vow.
Though born of noblest wood, 'twas thine
To tower a vigorous Pontic pine ;
'Tis vain thy race, thy name, to prize :
Nought on his painted stern relies
The trembling seaman. Storms afar
Thicken to mock thy strength : beware.

Thou, who wast late my anxious fear,
Thou now my fondest, tenderest care :
O shun, dear Ship, those tossing seas
Which part the white-cliff'd Cyclades !

[MUSKEIN was an inhabitant of Antwerp, whom the Directory not only
appointed to superintend the construction of the flat-bottomed boats for the
invasion of Great Britain (usually called by the French sailors " *bateaux à la
Muskein* "), but made a " *capitaine de vaisseau* ". An attack was ordered to be
made upon the two small islands of SAINT MARCOUF (each not more than 200
yards in length), of which, in July, 1795, SIR SIDNEY SMITH, with the Diamond
frigate, had taken unobstructed possession, and which were considered to give
to the English great facility in intercepting between the ports of Hâvre and
Cherbourg. The islands are situated off the river Isigny, on the coast of Nor-
mandy, and about four miles distant from the French shore. After being
garrisoned with about 500 seamen and marines, including a great proportion of
invalids, these small islands were placed under the command of LIEUT.
CHARLES PAPPS PRICE, of *The Badger*, a cruiser-converted Dutch hoy, mounting
four, or at most six, guns.
    On the 8th April, 1798, MUSKEIN, with 33 flat-bottomed boats, with a body
of troops on board, and a few gun-brigs, was about to make a combined attack
on the two islands, but was driven off by two British frigates, THE DIAMOND,
*Capt. Sir R. J. Strachan*, and THE HYDRA, *Capt. Sir Francis Laforey*, and stood
into Caen river. While there for three weeks, repairing damages, he was joined
by seven heavy gun-brigs, and about 40 flat-boats and armed fishing vessels,
bringing with them additional troops.
    On the 6th May, LIEUT. PRICE received information that an attack was
meditated during the night. By 10 p.m., owing to the prevailing calm, the
small naval force on the station, consisting of the 50-gun ship, ADAMANT, *Capt.
Wm. Hotham*, 24-gun ship. EURYDICE, *Capt. John Talbot*, and 18-gun brig-sloop,
ORESTES, *Capt. W. Haggitt*, had not been able to approach nearer to the islands
than six miles—precisely what the assailants wanted. The attacking force
consisted of 52-gun brigs and flat-bottomed boats, having on board, as was reported, about 6000 men. At day-break, on the 7th, the flotilla was seen drawn
up in a line opposite to the south-west front of the western redoubt ; and
instantly was opened, upon the brigs and flats composing it, a fire from 17
pieces of cannon, consisting of four 4, two 6, and six 24 pounder long guns, and
three 24 and two 32-pounder carronades, being all the guns that would bear.
The brigs remained at a distance of from 300 to 400 yards, in order to batter the
redoubt with their heavy long guns, while the boats, with great resolution,
rowed up until within musket-shot of the battery. But the guns of the latter,
loaded with round, grape, and canister, soon poured destruction amongst these,
cutting several of the boats "into chips," and compelling all that could keep
afloat to seek their safety in flight. Six or seven boats were seen to go down,
and one small flat, No. 13, was afterwards towed in, bottom upwards. She
appeared, by some pieces of paper found in her, to have had 144 persons on
board, including 129 of the second company of the Boulogne battalion.
    The loss sustained by the British garrison amounted to one private-marine

killed, and two private-marines and two seamen wounded. According to one French account, the invaders lost about 900 in killed or drowned, and between 300 and 400 wounded. As a reward for their conduct on this occasion, Lieutenants PRICE and BOURNE were each promoted to the rank of Commander. The former died a Post Captain, at Hereford, in 1813, aged 62.—*James's Naval History*, vol. ii., pp. 128-131 : ed. 1886.—ED.]

[M. PLÉVILLE was Minister of Marine, and, shortly after this unsuccessful *début* of the famous flotilla, was succeeded by Rear-Adm. Bruix, who directed Rear-Adm. La Crosse to take the command, and to make a second attack upon the islands. This, however, the French Government declined to make.—ED.]

## HELEN MARIA WILLIAMS.

HELEN MARIA WILLIAMS.—[" Among the literary celebrities of the French Revolution was Helen Maria Williams, at whose house were wont to assemble the most distinguished of the liberal writers of France, her own reputation giving considerable *éclat* to these meetings. She wrote some of the most beautiful hymns in our language, was a prisoner under the *reign of terror*, and published a work on the French Revolution which is full of the most touching incidents, and adorned with specimens of the ardent and pathetic poetry, the product of French genius under the excitement of those most mysterious days. A. Humboldt was much attached to her, and committed to her care the translation and publication of some of his most elaborate works.

"She had two nephews, ATHANAS and CHARLES COQUEREL, whom she educated, and who both attained considerable fame, one in the theological and the other in the political field. Athanas was for some time the preacher in the Protestant Church at Amsterdam, and married the daughter of a Swiss gentleman, the only person I have ever known on the Continent to adopt the dress and profess the opinions of an English Quaker. Miss Williams maintained intimate relations with her English friends, was familiar with the great lights of the Revolution, and her conversation was most instructive, entertaining, and varied. All her sympathies were on the side of freedom, and though she was not so prominent as to be persecuted by the Emperor, like Madame de Staël, she was the object of a good deal of suspicion and narrowly watched by the police."—*Autobr. Recollections by Sir John Bowring*, pp. 353-4.—ED.]

[MISS WILLIAMS, for some years, wrote that portion of the *New Annual Register* which relates to France. Among many other productions she was the author of the song *Evan Banks* (to the tune of *Savourna Delish*), which has often been attributed to Burns ; a novel called *Julia*, and a *Tour in Switzerland*. Horace Walpole called her in his *Correspondence* a "scribbling trollop ".

She lived for many years, and until the death of that gentleman—in Paris, 1818—under the *protection* of JOHN HURFORD STONE, a man of letters, who in the early part of the French Revolution had removed with his wife to Paris, where he formed an intimacy with Miss Williams. She was born about 1762, and died in Paris in 1827 as a friend to the Bourbons, and the enemy of the Revolution !

This MR. STONE was born at Tiverton in 1763. While in Paris he was in the confidence of the Directory, and became one of the chief printers there. In 1805, he brought out an edition of the *Geneva Bible*, and published several English reprints ; also Miss Williams's translation of HUMBOLDT'S *Travels*. His brother, WM. STONE, was tried in 1796 for High Treason, for holding treasonable correspondence with him.—ED.]

---

# ELEGY

## ON THE DEATH OF JEAN BON ST. ANDRÉ.

The following exquisite tribute to the memory of an unfortunate republican is written with such a touching sensibility, that those who can command salt tears must prepare to shed them. The narrative is simple and un-affected ; the event in itself interesting ; the moral obvious and awful.—We have only to observe, that as this account of the transaction is taken from the French papers, it may possibly be somewhat partial.—The DEY's own statement of the affair has not yet been received. Every friend of humanity will join with us in expressing a candid and benevolent hope, that this busi-ness may not tend to kindle the flames of war between these two unchristian powers ; but that, by mutual con-cession and accommodation, they may come to some point (short of the restoration of JEAN BON's head on his shoulders, which in this stage of the discussion is hardly practicable) by which the peace of the Pagan world may be preserved. For our part, we pretend not to decide from which quarter the concessions ought principally to be made. It is but candid to allow that there are pro-bably faults on *both sides*, in this, as in most other cases. For the character of the DEY we profess a sincere re-spect on the one hand ; and on the other, we naturally wish that the head of JEAN BON ST. ANDRÉ should be reserved for his own guillotine.


ELEGY ; OR, DIRGE.

I.

ALL in the town of TUNIS,
In Africa the torrid,
    On a Frenchman of rank
    Was played such a prank,
As LEPAUX must think quite horrid.

II.

No story half so shocking,
By kitchen fire or laundry,
  Was ever heard tell,—
  As that which befel
The great JEAN BON ST. ANDRÉ.*

III.

Poor John was a gallant Captain,
In battles much delighting;
  He fled full soon
  On the first of June—
But he bade the rest keep fighting.

IV.

To Paris then returning,
And recovered from his panic,
  He translated the plan
  Of *Paine's Rights of Man*,
Into language Mauritanic.

V.

He went to teach at Tunis—
Where as Consul he was settled—

---

[* Jean Bon St. André, deputy to the Convention for the Department of Lot, during the reign of Terror, rivalled Marat and Robespierre in cruelty. Having been appointed to re-model the Republican Navy, he was present at the action of June 1, 1794, in which he shewed excessive cowardice. He was afterwards Consul at Smyrna, where he was arrested by the Turks, but released on the peace. Napoleon subsequently commissioned him to organise the four departments of the Rhine, in which he succeeded. He was created a Baron, a Chevalier of the Legion of Honour and Prefect of Maure. He died in 1813 of a contagious malady caught while performing charitable offices for the sick !—ED.]

Amongst other things,
" That the people are kings ! "
Whereat the DEY was nettled.

VI.

The Moors being rather stupid,
And in temper somewhat mulish,
Understood not a word
Of the doctrine they heard,
And thought the Consul foolish.

VII.

He formed a *Club* of *Brothers*,
And moved some resolutions—
" Ho ! ho ! (says the DEY),
" So this is the way
" That the French make *Revolutions* ".

VIII.

The DEY then gave his orders
In Arabic and Persian—
" Let no more be said—
But bring me his head !
These *Clubs* are my aversion ".

IX.

The Consul quoted WICQUEFORT,
And PUFFENDORF and GROTIUS ;
And proved from VATTEL
Exceedingly well,
Such a deed would be quite atrocious.

X.

'Twould have moved a Christian's bowels
To hear the doubts he stated ;—

But the Moors they did
As they were bid,
And strangled him while he prated.

XI.

His head with a sharp-edged sabre
They severed from his shoulders,
And stuck it on high,
Where it caught the eye,
To the wonder of all beholders.

XII.

This sure is a doleful story
As e'er you heard or read of ;—
If at Tunis you prate
Of matters of state,
Anon they cut your head off !

XIII.

But we hear the French Directors
Have thought the point so knotty ;
That the DEY having shown
He dislikes JEAN BON,
They have sent him BERNADOTTÉ.

On recurring to the French papers to verify our Correspondent's statement of this singular adventure of
JEAN BON ST. ANDRÉ, we discovered, to our great morti-
fication, that it happened at ALGIERS, and not at TUNIS.
We should have corrected this mistake, but for two
reasons—first, that ALGIERS would not stand in the
verse ; and, secondly, that we are informed by the young
man who conducts the Geographical Department of the
*Morning Chronicle*, that both the towns are in Africa, or

Asia (he is not quite certain which), and, what is more to the purpose, that both are peopled by Moors. TUNIS, therefore, may stand.

[MARSHAL BERNADOTTÉ, the French *Prince of Monté Corvo*, died as CHARLES JOHN XIV., *King of Sweden*, 8th March, 1844, in his eighty-first year. He married, in 1798, EUGENIA-BERNARDINA-DÉSIRÉE DE CLARY, daughter of a Marseilles merchant, and sister of MADAME JOSEPH BUONAPARTE (Queen of Spain). "She, who was not a common-place person," says MADAME DE RÉMUSAT, in her valuable *Memoirs*, "had before her marriage been very much in love with Napoleon, and appears to have always preserved the memory of that feeling! It has been supposed that her hardly extinguished passion caused her obstinate refusal to leave France." She survived her husband many years, and died in Paris, in the Rue d'Anjou Saint Honoré. Her husband was succeeded on the throne of Sweden by their son, OSCAR I., who married JOSÉPHINE, *daughter of* EUGÈNE BEAUHARNAIS, Duc de Leuchtenberg, and *granddaughter of the* EMPRESS JOSEPHINE.

BERNADOTTÉ owed his elevation to the throne to the misgovernment of Gustavus IV., who had brought the nation to the verge of ruin, and who was deposed in 1809, when his uncle, the Duke of Sudermania, became king as Charles XIII. ; and the next year, BERNADOTTÉ was elected *Crown Prince*, and successor to the throne.

In 1813, he rendered great assistance to the Allies, for, as Crown Prince, he joined the confederacy against France with 30,000 men ; and, after defeating Marshal Ney, with great loss, on the 6th September, he, on the 18th October, with the co-operation of Blücher, again defeated him at the decisive Battle of Leipsic ; and, on the 19th, the Emperor Alexander, the King of Prussia, and the Crown Prince, entered the great square of Leipsic, amidst the acclamations of the inhabitants. He was a decided democrat, and hated by Napoleon, but was the only sovereign of the revolutionary branch who was permitted to retain his dominions after the great reaction in 1814. The choice made of this great soldier of fortune excited the surprise of all Europe at the time, but the wisdom of it was soon demonstrated by his prudent conduct. He had distinguished himself from all Napoleon's other marshals by his clemency in victory. For half a century before his accession, Sweden had not known the peace and prosperity in which he left the country on his death.

In T. RAIKES'S *Diary* will be found some interesting anecdotes of BERNA-DOTTÉ'S gratitude for services rendered him while a young subaltern. But one is of a more startling nature, as it records his narrow escape from the death intended for him by the widow of the late king, who had purposely prepared a poisoned cup of coffee for him, which she herself presented to him at her own table. Having been suddenly warned, he succeeded in forcing it upon her. She resolutely accepted her fate, and died during the night.—ED.

# No. XXVIII.

May 21, 1798.

WE have received the following letter, with the poem that accompanies it, from a gentleman whose political opinions have hitherto differed from our own ; but who appears to feel, as every man who loves his country must, that there can be but one sentiment entertained by Englishmen at the present moment.

Were we at liberty, we should be happy to do justice to the author, and credit to ourselves, by mentioning his name.

TO THE EDITOR OF THE "ANTI-JACOBIN".

SIR,—However men may have differed on the political or constitutional questions which have of late been brought into discussion—whatever opinions they may have held on the system or conduct of administration— there can surely be now but one sentiment as to the instant necessity of firm and strenuous union for the preservation of our very existence as a people ; and if degrees of obligation could be admitted, where the utmost is required from all, it should seem that in this cause the opposers of administration stand doubly pledged ; for with what face of consistency can men pretend to stickle for points of constitutional liberty at home, who will not be found amongst the foremost at their posts to defend their country from the yoke of foreign slavery ?

That there should be any set of men so infatuated as not to be convinced that the object of the enemy must be the utter destruction of these countries, after making the largest allowance for the effects of prejudice and passion, it is not easy to conceive. Such, however, we are told, there are. They believe, then, that after a long series of outrage, insult, and injury, in the height of their animosity and presumptión, these moderate, mild, disinterested conquerors will invade us in arms, out of pure love and kindness, merely for our good, only to make us wiser, and better, and happier, and more prosperous than before !

Future events lie hid in the volume of Fate, but the intentions of men may be known by almost infallible indications. Passion and interest, the two mighty motives of human action, determine the Government of France to attempt the abolition of the British Empire ! and if, abandoned by God and our right arm, we should flinch in the conflict, that destruction will be operative to the full of their gigantic and monstrous imaginations ! —Harbours filled up with the ruins of their towns and arsenals, the Thames rendered a vast morass, by burying the Imperial City in her bosom—but I will not proceed in the horrible picture.

Are we then, it may be asked, to wage eternal war ?— No ; a glorious resistance leads to an honourable peace. The French people have been long weary of the war ; their spirit has been forced by a system which must end in the failure of the engagement to give them the plunder of this country. They will awake from their dream, and raise a cry for peace, which their government will not dare to resist. The monarchs of Europe must now begin clearly to perceive that their fate hangs on the destiny of England ; they will unite to compel a satisfactory peace on a broad foundation ; and peace, when war has been tried to the utmost, will probably be permanent. A few years of wise economy and redoubled industry will place us again on the rising scale ; and if the pressure of the times may have rendered it necessary sometimes to have cast a temporary veil over the statue of Liberty, she may again safely be shown in an unimpaired lustre.

Of the following verses I have nothing to say : if it should be decided that the greatness of the object cannot bear out the mediocrity of the execution, I will not appeal from the decision.

## ODE TO MY COUNTRY.
### MDCCXCVIII.
#### S. 1.

BRITONS ! hands and hearts prepare :
The angry tempest threatens nigh,
Deep-toned thunders roll in air,
Lightnings thwart the livid sky ;
Throned upon the wingéd storm,
Fell DESOLATION rears her ghastly form,
Waves her black signal to her Hell-born brood,
And lures them thus with promised blood :

#### A. 1.

" Drive, my sons, the storm amain !
Lo, the hated, envied land,
Where PIETY and ORDER reign,
And Freedom dares maintain her stand.
Have ye not sworn, by night and hell,
These from the earth for ever to expel ?

13

Rush on, resistless, to your destined prey,
Death and rapine point the way."

### E. 1.

Britons! stand firm! with stout and dauntless heart
  Meet unappall'd the threatening boaster's rage ;
Yours is the great, the unconquerable part,
  For your loved hearths and altars to engage,
And sacred LIBERTY, more dear than life—
Yours be the triumph in the glorious strife.
Shall theft and murder braver deeds excite
Than honest scorn of shame and heavenly love of right?

### S. 2.

Turn the bright historic page !
  Still in glory's tented field,
Albion's arms, for many an age,
  Have taught proud Gallia's bands to yield.
Are not WE the sons of those
Whose steel-clad sires pursued the insulting foes,
E'en to the centre of their wide domain,
And bowed them to a BRITON's reign ? *

### A. 2.

Kings, in modest triumph led,
  Graced the SABLE VICTOR's arms : †
His conquering lance, the battle's dread ;—
  His courtesy the conquered charms.
The lion-heart soft pity knows,
To raise with soothing cares his prostrate foes ;

---

* Henry VI. crowned at Paris.    † The Black Prince.

The vanquished head true valour ne'er oppress'd,
Nor shunn'd to succour the distress'd.

### E. 2.

Spirit of great ELIZABETH ! inspire
High thoughts, high deeds, worthy our ancient fame ;
Breathe through our ardent ranks the patriot fire,
Kindled at Freedom's ever-hallowed flame ;
Baffled and scorned, the Iberian tyrant found,
Though half a world his iron sceptre bound,
The gallant Amazon could sweep away,
Armed with her people's love, the " INVINCIBLE " array. *

### S. 3.

The BOLD USURPER † firmly held
The sword by splendid treasons gained ;
And Gallia's fiery genius quelled,
And Spain's presumptuous claims restrained :
When lust of sway, by flattery fed, ‡
To venturous deeds the youthful monarch led,
In the full flow of victory's swelling tide
Britain checked his power and pride.

### A. 3.

To the great BATAVIAN's name §
Ceaseless hymns of triumph raise !
Scourge of tyrants, let his fame
Live in songs of grateful praise.
Thy turrets, BLENHEIM,‖ glittering to the sun,
Tell of bright fields from warlike Gallia won ;

---

* The Spanish Armada. † Oliver Cromwell. ‡ Louis XIV.
§ William III. ‖ Blenheim, Ramilies, &c., &c.

Tell how the mighty monarch mourned in vain
His impious wish the world to chain.

## E. 3.

And ye famed heroes, late retired to heaven,
 Whose setting glories still the skies illume,
Bend from the blissful seats to virtue given—
 Avert your long-defended country's doom.
Earth from her utmost bounds shall wondering tell
How victory's meed ye gained, or conquering fell ;
Britain's dread thunders bore from pole to pole,
Wherever man is found, or refluent oceans roll.

## S. 4.

Names embalmed.in honour's shrine,
 Sacred to immortal praise,
Patterns of glory, born to shine
 In breathing arts or pictured lays :
See WOLFE, by yielding numbers pressed,
Expiring smile, and sink on victory's breast !
See MINDEN'S plains and BISCAY'S billowy bay
Deeds of deathless fame display.

## A. 4.

O ! tread with awe the sacred gloom,
 Patriot Virtue's last retreat ;
Where Glory, on the trophied tomb,
 Joys their merit to repeat ;
There CHATHAM lies, whose master-hand
Guided through seven bright years the mighty band,
That round his urn, where grateful Memory weeps,
Each in his hallowed marble sleeps.

## E. 4.

Her brand accursed when civil discord hurled,*
Britain alone the united world withstood,
RODNEY his fortune-favoured sails unfurled,
And led three nation's chiefs to Thames's flood.
Firm on his rock the VETERAN HERO† stands;
Beneath his feet unheeded thunders roar;
Smiling in scorn, he sees the glittering bands
Fly with repulse and shame old CALPE's hopeless
shore.

## S. 5.

Heirs or partners of their toils,
Matchless heroes still we own;
Crowned with honourable spoils
From the leagued nations won.
On their high prows they proudly stand,
The godlike guardians of their native land;
Lords of the mighty deep triumphant ride,
Wealth and victory at their side.

## A. 5.

Loyal, bold, and generous bands,
Strenuous in their country's cause,
Guard their cultivated lands,
Their altars, liberties, and laws.
On his firm, deep-founded throne,
Great BRUNSWICK sits—a name to fear unknown,
With brow erect commands the glorious strife,
Unawed, and prodigal of life.

---

* American War.      † Lord Heathfield.

## E. 5.

Sons of fair Freedom's long-descended line,
To Gallia's yoke shall Britons bend the neck?—
No; in her cause though fate and hell combine
To bury all in universal wreck,
Of this fair Isle to make one dreary waste,
Her greatness in her ruins only traced,—
Arts, commerce, arms, sunk in one common grave—
The man who dares to die will never live a slave.

# No. XXIX.

May 28, 1798.

In a former number, we were enabled, by the communication of a classical correspondent, to compliment CITIZEN MUSKEIN with an Address to his Gun-boats, imitated from a favourite Ode of Horace. Another (or perhaps the same) hand has obligingly furnished us with a composition, which we have no doubt will be equally acceptable to the citizen to whom it is addressed.

## ODE TO THE DIRECTOR MERLIN.

### HORACE, B. I., O. V.

WHO now from Naples, Rome, or Berlin,
Creeps to thy blood-stained den, O MERLIN,
  With diplomatic gold?—to whom
  Dost thou give audience *en costume ?*

*King Citizen !*—How sure each state
That bribes thy love shall feel thy hate ;
  Shall see the democratic storm
  Her commerce, laws, and arts deform.

How credulous, to hope the bribe
Could purchase peace from MERLIN's tribe !
  Whom, faithless as the waves or wind,
  No oaths restrain, no treaties bind.

For us—beneath yon SACRED ROOF,
The NAVAL FLAGS and arms of proof,
  By British valour nobly bought,
  Show how true safety must be sought !

[THIERS, in his *History of the French Revolution*, frequently asserts the incorruptibility (with the exception of BARRAS) of the French Directory. But ALISON, in his History, exposes the extraordinary conduct of M. DE TALLEYRAND, then Minister of Foreign Affairs, towards the Envoys from the United States of America, who complained that an immense number of American vessels had been seized by the French Government under a decree of Jan., 1798, which directed that all ships having for their cargoes, in whole or in part, any English merchandise, should be held lawful prize, whoever was the proprietor thereof, from the single circumstance of its coming from England or its foreign settlements. The Envoys were told that nothing could be done till their Government had advanced a sum equal to 1,280,000*l.* as a loan, and 50,000*l.* as a douceur to the Directors. These terms were, of course, indignantly rejected. The Hanse Towns, too, only obtained licenses to navigate the high seas by the secret payment of 150,000*l.* to the Republican rulers.—ED.]

---

[LYRICS OF HORACE.   BOOK I., ODE V.

TRANSLATED BY ARCHDEACON WRANGHAM.

What slender youth, all essenced o'er,
In sweet alcove or rosy bower,
Now woos thee, Pyrrha, to be kind?
For whom these tresses dost thou bind,
Thus simply neat?   O how shall he,
Poor youth! bewail the boisterous sea,
Rough with black tempests!   How accuse
Capricious Gods, and broken vows!

Fond dupe! he hopes—so sweet that kiss—
Thou'lt still be witching, still be his!   ·
What treacherous gales beset his way,
Ah! little knows he!   Hapless they,
Who ne'er thy faithless smiles have tried!
—That I have 'scaped the whelming tide,
A tablet and my dripping vest,
Hung up in Neptune's fane, attest.—ED.]

# No. XXX.

June 4, 1798.

OUR ingenious correspondent, MR. HIGGINS, has not been idle. The deserved popularity of the extracts which we have been enabled to give from his two didactic poems, the *Progress of Man*, and the *Loves of the Triangles*, has obtained for us the communications of several other works which he has in hand, all framed upon the same principle, and directed to the same end. The propagation of the New System of Philosophy forms, as he has himself candidly avowed to us, the main object of all his writings. A system, comprehending not politics only and religion, but morals and manners, and generally whatever goes to the composition or holding together of human society; in all of which a total change and revolution is absolutely necessary (as he contends) for the advancement of our common nature to its true dignity, and to the summit of that perfection which the combination of matter, called MAN, is by its innate energies capable of attaining.

Of this system, while the sublimer and more scientific branches are to be taught by the splendid and striking medium of didactic poetry, or *ratiocination in rhyme*, illustrated with such paintings and portraitures of essences and their attributes as may lay hold of the imagination while they perplex the judgment;—the more ordinary parts, such as relate to the conduct of common life and the regulation of social feelings, are naturally the subject of a less elevated style of writing;

of a style which speaks to the eye as well as to the ear,
—in short, of dramatic poetry and scenic representation.
" With this view," says Mr. HIGGINS (for we love to
quote the very words of this extraordinary and indefatigable writer),—" with this view," says he, in a letter
dated from his study in St. Mary Axe, the window of
which looks upon the parish pump,—" with this view I
have turned my thoughts more particularly to the
German stage, and have composed—in imitation of the
most popular pieces of that country, which have already
met with so general reception and admiration in this—a
Play; which, if it has a proper run, will, I think, do
much to unhinge the present notions of men with regard
to the obligations of civil society, and to substitute, in
lieu of a sober contentment, and regular discharge of the
duties incident to each man's particular situation, a wild
desire of undefinable latitude and extravagance,—an
aspiration after shapeless somethings that can neither be
described nor understood,—a contemptuous disgust at
all that *is*, and a persuasion that nothing is as it ought
to be;--to operate, in short, a general discharge of every
man (in his own estimation) from every tie which laws,
divine or human, which local customs, immemorial
habits, and multiplied examples, impose upon him; and
to set them about doing what they like, where they like,
when they like, and how they like,—without reference to
any law but their own will, or to any consideration of
how others may be affected by their conduct.

" When this is done, my dear sir," continues Mr. H.
(for he writes very confidentially)—" you see that a great
step is gained towards the dissolution of the frame of
every existing community. I say nothing of *Governments*,

as *their* fall is of course implicated in that of the social system;—and you have long known that I hold every Government (that acts by coercion and restriction—by laws made by the few to bind the many) as a *malum in se*,—an evil to be eradicated,—a nuisance to be abated, —by force, if force be practicable; if not, by the artillery of reason, by pamphlets, speeches, toasts at club-dinners, and though last, not least, by didactic poems.

" But where would be the advantage of the destruction of this or that Government, if the form of Society itself were to be suffered to continue such as that another must necessarily arise out of it and over it?—Society, my dear sir, in its present state, is a *hydra*. Cut off one head,—another presently sprouts out, and your labour is to begin again. At best you can only hope to find it a *polypus;*—where, by cutting off the *head*, you are sometimes fortunate enough to find a *tail* (which answers all the same purposes) spring up in its place. This, we know, has been the case in France; the only country in which the great experiment of regeneration has been tried with anything like a fair chance of success.

" Destroy the frame of society,—decompose its parts, —and see the elements fighting one against another,— insulated and individual,—every man for himself (stripped of prejudice, of bigotry, and of feeling for others) against the remainder of his species;—and there is then some hope of a totally new *order of things*,—of a *Radical Reform* in the present corrupt system of the world.

" The German Theatre appears to proceed on this judicious plan. And I have endeavoured to contribute my mite towards extending its effect and its popularity. There is one obvious advantage attending this mode of teaching;—that it can proportion the infractions of law, religion, or morality, which it recommends, to the capacity of a reader or spectator. If you tell a student, or an apprentice, or a merchant's clerk, of the virtue of a Brutus, or of the splendour of a La Fayette, you may excite his *desire* to be equally conspicuous; but how is he to set about it? Where is he to find the tyrant to murder? How is he to provide the monarch to be imprisoned, and the national guards to be reviewed on a white horse?—But paint the beauties of *forgery* to him in glowing colours;—show him that the presumption of virtue is in favour of rapine and occasional murder on the highway—and he presently understands you. The highway is at hand—the till or the counter is within reach. These *haberdashers' heroics* come home to the business and the bosoms of men.—And you may readily make ten *footpads*, where you would not have materials nor opportunity for a single *tyrannicide*.

"The subject of the piece which I herewith transmit to you is taken from common or middling life; and its merit is that of teaching the most lofty truths in the most humble style, and deducing them from the most ordinary occurrences. Its moral is obvious and easy; and is one frequently inculcated by the German dramas which I have had the good fortune to see; being no other than '*the reciprocal duties of one or more husbands to one or more wives, and to the children who may happen to arise out of this complicated and endearing connection*'. The plot, indeed, is formed by the combination of the plots of *two* of the most popular of these plays (in the same way as Terence was wont to combine two stories of Menander's). The characters are such as the admirers of these plays will recognise for their familiar acquaintances. There are the usual ingredients of imprisonments, post-houses and horns, and appeals to angels and devils. I have omitted only the *swearing*, to which English ears are not yet sufficiently accustomed.

"I transmit at the same time a *Prologue*, which in some degree breaks the matter to the audience. About the song of Rogero, at the end of the first Act, I am less anxious than about any other part of the performance, as it is, in fact, literally translated from the composition of a young German friend of mine, an *Illuminé*, of whom I bought the original for three-and-sixpence. It will be a satisfaction to those of your readers who may not at first sight hit upon the tune, to learn that it is setting by a hand of the first eminence.—I send also a rough sketch of the plot, and a few occasional notes.—The *geography* is by the young gentleman of the *Morning Chronicle*."

# THE ROVERS; OR, THE DOUBLE ARRANGEMENT.

### Dramatis Personæ.

PRIOR of the ABBEY of QUEDLINBURGH, very corpulent and cruel.

ROGERO, a prisoner in the Abbey, in love with MATILDA POTTINGEN.

CASIMERE, a Polish emigrant, in Dembrowsky's legion, married to CECILIA, but having several children by MATILDA.

PUDDINGFIELD and BEEFINGTON, English noblemen, exiled by the tyranny of King John, previous to the signature of Magna Charta.

RODERIC, Count of SAXE WEIMAR, a bloody tyrant, with red hair, and an amorous complexion.

GASPAR, the minister of the Count—author of ROGERO's confinement.

YOUNG POTTINGEN, brother to MATILDA.
MATILDA POTTINGEN, in love with ROGERO, and mother to CASIMERE'S children.
CECILIA MÜCKENFELD, wife to CASIMERE.
Landlady, Waiter, Grenadiers, Troubadours, &c., &c.
PANTALOWSKY and BRITCHINDA, children of MATILDA, by CASIMERE.
JOACHIM, JABEL, and AMARANTHA, children of MATILDA, by ROGERO.
CHILDREN OF CASIMERE AND CECILIA, with their respective Nurses.
SEVERAL CHILDREN—fathers and mothers unknown.

*The Scene lies in the town of Weimar, and the neighbourhood of the Abbey of Quedlinburgh.*

*Time from the 12th to the present century.*

# PROLOGUE.*

### IN CHARACTER.

Too long the triumphs of our early times,
With civil discord and with regal crimes,
Have stain'd these boards; while Shakespeare's pen has shown
Thoughts, manners, men, to modern days unknown.
Too long have Rome and Athens been *the rage;*
                                          [*Applause.*
And classic Buskins soil'd a British stage.

To-night our bard, who scorns pedantic rules,
His plot has borrow'd from the German schools;
The German schools—where no dull maxims bind
The bold expansion of the electric mind.

---

[ * Parodied from Pope's Prologue to *Cato.*—ED.]

Fix'd to no period, circled by no space,
He leaps the flaming bounds of time and place.
Round the dark confines of the forest raves,
With *gentle* Robbers* stocks his gloomy caves;
Tells how Prime Ministers† are shocking things,
And *reigning Dukes* as bad as tyrant Kings;
How to *two* swains‡ *one* nymph her vows may give,
And how *two* damsels‡ with *one* lover live!
Delicious scenes!—such scenes *our* bard displays,
Which, crown'd with German, sue for British, praise.

Slow are the steeds, that through Germania's roads
With hempen rein the slumbering post-boy goads;
Slow is the slumbering post-boy, who proceeds
Thro' deep sands floundering on those tardy steeds;
More slow, more tedious, from his husky throat,
Twangs through the twisted horn the struggling note.

These truths confess'd—Oh! yet, ye travell'd few,
Germania's *plays* with eyes unjaundiced view!

---

* See *The Robbers*, a German tragedy [by SCHILLER], in which robbery is put in so fascinating a light, that the whole of a German University went upon the highway in consequence of it.

† See *Cabal and Love*, a German tragedy [by SCHILLER], very severe against prime ministers and reigning Dukes of Brunswick. This admirable performance very judiciously reprobates the hire of German troops for the *American* war in the reign of Queen Elizabeth, a practice which would undoubtedly have been highly discreditable to that wise and patriotic princess, not to say wholly unnecessary—there being no American war at that particular time.

‡ See *The Stranger; or, Reformed Housekeeper*, in which the former of these morals is beautifully illustrated; and *Stella*, a genteel German comedy [by GOETHE], which ends with placing a man *bodkin* between *two wives*, like *Thames* between his *two banks* in *The Critic*. Nothing can be more edifying than these two dramas. I am shocked to hear that there are some people who think them ridiculous.

View and approve!—though in each passage fine
The faint translation* mock the genuine line;
Though the nice ear the erring sight belie,
For *U twice dotted* is pronounced like *I;*\*     [*Applause*.
Yet oft the scene shall nature's fire impart,
Warm *from* the breast, and glowing *to* the heart!

Ye travell'd few, attend!—On *you* our bard
Builds his fond hope! Do you his genius guard!
                                              [*Applause*.
Nor let succeeding generations say
A British audience *damn'd* a German play!
                    [*Loud and continued Applauses*.

*Flash of lightning.—The ghost of* PROLOGUE'S GRANDMOTHER
*by the Father's side, appears to soft music, in a white tiffany
riding-hood.* PROLOGUE *kneels to receive her blessing, which
she gives in a solemn and affecting manner, the audience clapping and crying all the while.—Flash of lightning.—*PROLOGUE
*and his* GRANDMOTHER *sink through the trap-doors.*

## THE ROVERS; OR, THE DOUBLE ARRANGEMENT.

### ACT I. SCENE I.

*Scene represents a room at an inn, at Weimar—On one side of
the stage the bar-room, with jellies, lemons in nets, syllabubs,*

---

* These are the warnings very properly given to readers, to
beware how they judge of what they cannot understand. Thus
if the translation runs, "*lightning of my soul, fulgation of angels,
sulphur of hell,*" we should recollect that this is not coarse or
strange in the German language when applied by a lover to his
mistress; but the English has nothing precisely parallel to the
original 𝕸𝖚𝖑𝖕𝖈𝖍𝖆𝖚𝖘𝖊 𝕬𝖗𝖈𝖍𝖆𝖓𝖌𝖊𝖑𝖎𝖈𝖍𝖊𝖓, which means rather *emanation of the archangelic nature*—or to 𝕾𝖒𝖊𝖑𝖑𝖒𝖕𝖓𝖐𝖊𝖗𝖓 𝖁𝖆𝖓𝖐𝖊𝖑𝖋𝖊𝖗, which,
if literally rendered, would signify *made of stuff of the same odour
whereof the devil makes flambeaux.* See Schüttenbrüoh on the
German idiom.

*and part of a cold roast fowl, &c.—On the opposite side, a window looking into the street, through which persons (inhabitants of Weimar) are seen passing to and fro in apparent agitation—* MATILDA *appears in a great coat and riding-habit, seated at the corner of the dinner-table, which is covered with a clean huckaback cloth; plates and napkins, with buck's-horn-handled knives and forks, are laid as if for four persons.*

MAT. Is it impossible for me to have dinner sooner?

LAND. Madam, the Brunswick post-waggon is not yet come in, and the ordinary is never before two o'clock.

MAT. [*With a look expressive of disappointment, but immediately recomposing herself.*] Well, then, I must have patience. [*Exit Landlady.*] Oh Casimere!—How often have the thoughts of thee served to amuse these moments of expectation!—What a difference, alas!—Dinner—it is taken away as soon as over, and we regret it not!—It returns again with the return of appetite.—The beef of to-morrow will succeed to the mutton of to-day, as the mutton of to-day succeeded to the veal of yesterday. But when once the heart has been occupied by a beloved object, in vain would we attempt to supply the chasm by another. How easily are our desires transferred from dish to dish!—Love only, dear, delusive, delightful love, restrains our wandering appetites, and confines them to a particular gratification! . . . . . .

*Post-horn blows; re-enter* LANDLADY.

LAND. Madam, the post-waggon is just come in with only a single gentlewoman.

MAT. Then show her up—and let us have dinner instantly; [*Landlady going*] and remember—[*after a moment's recollection, and with great earnestness*] —remember the toasted cheese. [*Exit Landlady.*

14

CECILIA *enters, in a brown cloth riding-dress, as if just
alighted from the post-waggon.*

MAT. Madam, you seem to have had an unpleasant
journey, if I may judge from the dust on your riding-
habit.

CEC. The way was dusty, madam, but the weather
was delightful.   It recalled to me those blissful moments
when the rays of desire first vibrated through my soul.

MAT. [*Aside.*] Thank Heaven! I have at last found
a heart which is in unison with my own.   [*To Cecilia*]
—Yes, I understand you—the first pulsation of sentiment—the silver tones upon the yet unsounded harp. . . . .

CEC. The dawn of life—when this blossom [*putting her
hand upon her heart*] first expanded its petals to the pene-
trating dart of love!

MAT. Yes—the time—the golden time, when the first
beams of the morning meet and embrace one another!—
The blooming blue upon the yet unplucked plum! . . . . .

CEC. Your countenance grows animated, my dear
madam.

MAT. And yours too is glowing with illumination.

CEC. I had long been looking out for a congenial
spirit!—my heart was withered—but the beams of yours
have rekindled it.

MAT. A sudden thought strikes me—Let us swear an
eternal friendship.

CEC. Let us agree to live together!

MAT. Willingly.            [*With rapidity and earnestness.*

CEC. Let us embrace.                    [*They embrace.*

MAT. Yes; I too have loved!—you, too, like me, have
been forsaken.

[*Doubtingly, and as if with a desire to be informed.*

CEC. Too true!

BOTH. Ah these men! these men!

LANDLADY *enters, and places a leg of mutton on the table, with sour krout and prune sauce; then a small dish of black puddings—* CECILIA *and* MATILDA *appear to take no notice of her.*

MAT. Oh, Casimere!

CEC. [*Aside.*] Casimere! that name!—Oh, my heart, how it is distracted with anxiety.

MAT. Heavens! Madam, you turn pale.

CEC. Nothing—a slight megrim—with your leave, I will retire—

MAT. I will attend you.

[*Exeunt* MATILDA *and* CECILIA; *Manent* LANDLADY *and* WAITER, *with the dinner on the table.*

LAND. Have you carried the dinner to the prisoner in the vaults of the abbey?

WAITER. Yes—Pease soup, as usual—with the scrag end of a neck of mutton. The emissary of the Count was here again this morning, and offered me a large sum of money if I would consent to poison him.

LAND. Which you refused? [*With hesitation and anxiety.*

WAITER. Can you doubt it? [*With indignation.*

LAND. [*Recovering herself, and drawing up with an expression of dignity.*] The conscience of a poor man is as valuable to him as that of a prince . . .

WAITER. It ought to be still more so, in proportion as it is generally more pure.

LAND. Thou say'st truly, Job.

WAITER. [*With enthusiasm.*] He who can spurn at wealth when proffered as the price of crime, is greater than a prince.

*Post-horn blows.—Enter* CASIMERE (*in a travelling dress, a light blue great coat with large metal buttons, his hair in a long queue, but twisted at the end; a large Kevenhuller hat; a cane in his hand*).

CAS. Here, Waiter, pull off my boots, and bring me a pair of slippers. [*Exit Waiter.*] And hark'ye, my lad, a basin of water [*rubbing his hands*] and a bit of soap. I have not washed since I began my journey.

WAITER. [*Answering from behind the door.*] Yes, Sir.

CAS. Well, Landlady, what company are we to have?

LAND. Only two gentlewomen, Sir.—They are just stept into the next room—they will be back again in a minute.

CAS. Where do they come from?

[*All this while the* WAITER *re-enters with the basin and water;* CASIMERE *pulls off his boots, takes a napkin from the table, and washes his face and hands.*

LAND. There is one of them, I think, comes from Nuremburgh.

CAS. [*Aside.*] From Nuremburgh! [*with eagerness*] her name!

LAND. Matilda.

CAS. [*Aside.*] How does this idiot woman torment me! —What else?

LAND. I can't recollect.

CAS. Oh, agony!          [*In a paroxysm of agitation.*

WAITER. See here, her name upon the travelling trunk —Matilda Pottingen.

CAS. Ecstasy! ecstasy!          [*Embracing the Waiter.*

LAND. You seem to be acquainted with the lady—shall I call her?

CAS. Instantly—instantly—tell her her loved, her long-lost—tell her——

LAND. Shall I tell her dinner is ready?

CAS. Do so—and in the meanwhile I will look after my portmanteau. [*Exeunt severally.*

*Scene changes to a subterranean vault in the Abbey of Quedlinburgh, with coffins, 'scutcheons, death's heads and crossbones—toads and other loathsome reptiles are seen traversing the obscurer parts of the stage.—*ROGERO *appears, in chains, in a suit of rusty armour, with his beard grown, and a cap of a grotesque form upon his head—beside him a crock, or pitcher, supposed to contain his daily allowance of sustenance.—A long silence, during which the wind is heard to whistle through the caverns.—*ROGERO *rises, and comes slowly forward, with his arms folded.*

ROG. Eleven years! it is now eleven years since I was first immured in this living sepulchre—the cruelty of a Minister—the perfidy of a Monk—yes, Matilda! for thy sake—alive amidst the dead—chained—coffined—confined—cut off from the converse of my fellow-men. Soft! —what have we here! [*stumbles over a bundle of sticks.*] This cavern is so dark that I can scarcely distinguish the objects under my feet. Oh—the register of my captivity. Let me see; how stands the account? [*Takes up the sticks, and turns them over with a melancholy air; then stands silent for a few minutes, as if absorbed in calculation.*]—Eleven years and fifteen days!—Hah! the twenty-eighth of August! How does the recollection of it vibrate on my heart! It was on this day that I took my last leave of my Matilda. It was a summer evening; her melting hand seemed to dissolve in mine, as I prest it to my bosom. Some demon whispered me that I should never see her more. I stood gazing on the hated vehicle which

was conveying her away for ever. The tears were petri-
fied under my eyelids. My heart was crystallized with
agony. Anon—I looked along the road. The diligence
seemed to diminish every instant; I felt my heart beat
against its prison, as if anxious to leap out and overtake
it. My soul whirled round as I watched the rotation of
the hinder wheels. A long trail of glory followed after
her, and mingled with the dust; it was the emanation of
Divinity, luminous with love and beauty, like the splendour of the setting sun; but it told me that the sun of
my joys was sunk for ever. Yes, here in the depths of
an eternal dungeon, in the nursing cradle of hell, the
suburbs of perdition, in a nest of demons, where despair
in vain sits brooding over the putrid eggs of hope; where
agony wooes the embrace of death; where patience, beside the bottomless pool of despondency, sits angling for
impossibilities. Yet, even *here*, to behold her, to embrace
her! Yes, Matilda, whether in this dark abode, amidst
toads and spiders, or in a royal palace, amidst the more
loathsome reptiles of a court, would be indifferent to me;
angels would shower down their hymns of gratulation
upon our heads, while fiends would envy the eternity of
suffering love. . . . . . . . Soft, what air was that? it
seemed a sound of more than human warblings. Again!
[*listens attentively for some minutes.*] Only the wind; it is
well, however; it reminds me of that melancholy air,
which has so often solaced the hours of my captivity.
Let me see whether the damps of this dungeon have not
yet injured my guitar. [*Takes his guitar, tunes it, and
begins the following air, with a full accompaniment of violins
from the orchestra.*

[*Air, Lanterna Magica.*]
# SONG.
### BY ROGERO.[1]

### I.

Whene'er with haggard eyes I view
This dungeon that I'm rotting in,
I think of those companions true
Who studied with me at the U—
—niversity of Gottingen—
—niversity of Gottingen.

[*Weeps, and pulls out a blue kerchief, with which he
wipes his eyes; gazing tenderly at it, he proceeds—*

### II.

Sweet kerchief, check'd with heavenly blue,
Which once my love sat knotting in !—
Alas ! Matilda *then* was true !
At least I thought so at the U—
—niversity of Gottingen—
—niversity of Gottingen.

[*At the repetition of this line* ROGERO *clanks his
chains in cadence.*

### III.

Barbs ! Barbs ! alas ! how swift you flew
Her neat post-waggon trotting in !
Ye bore Matilda from my view;
Forlorn I languish'd at the U—
—niversity of Gottingen—
—niversity of Gottingen.

### IV.

This faded form ! this pallid hue !
This blood my veins is clotting in,

My years are many—they were few
When first I entered at the U—
—niversity of Gottingen—
—niversity of Gottingen.

V.

There first for thee my passion grew,
Sweet! sweet Matilda Pottingen!
Thou wast the daughter of my tu—
—tor, law professor at the U—
—niversity of Gottingen —
—niversity of Gottingen.

VI.

Sun, moon, and thou vain world, adieu,
That kings and priests are plotting in:
Here doomed to starve on water gru—
—el,* never shall I see the U—-
—niversity of Gottingen—
—niversity of Gottingen.

> [*During the last stanza* ROGERO *dashes his head repeatedly against the walls of his prison; and, finally, so hard as to produce a visible contusion; he then throws himself on the floor in an agony. The curtain drops; the music still continuing to play till it is wholly fallen.*]

---

* A manifest error, since it appears from the Waiter's conversation (p. 211) that Rogero was not doomed to starve on water-gruel, but on pease-soup, which is a much better thing. Possibly the length of Rogero's imprisonment had impaired his memory ; or he might wish to make things appear worse than they really were; which is very natural, I think, in such a case as this poor unfortunate gentleman's.—*Printer's Devil.*

[The character of ROGERO is a quiz upon SIR ROBERT ADAIR,

who received his education at Göttingen, and fell in love with
his tutor's daughter. His relative, LORD ALBEMARLE, says in
his *Reminiscences:* "Throughout life my kinsman was an enthusiastic admirer of the fair sex, which he generally 'loved, not
wisely, but too well'". He married, in 1805, Mdlle. Angélique
Gabrielle, daughter of the Marquis d'Hazincourt and the Com-
tesse de Champagne.

ADAIR was the son of Mr. Robert Adair, sergeant-surgeon to
K. George III., by his wife LADY CAROLINE KEPPEL, daughter
of Wm. Anne, second Earl of Albemarle. He was educated at ,
Westminster School and Göttingen University; called to the
Bar, but never practised. He contested Camelford in 1796;
and was M.P. for Appleby, 1799-1802, for Camelford, 1802-1812.
He was sent by Fox as Minister Plenipotentiary to Vienna in
1806; and by his old adversary CANNING to Constantinople in
1808; and also to Berlin. He was Ambassador to Constantinople, 1809-11, and to Belgium, 1831-5. He was a facile writer,
and wrote several spirited pamphlets, including defences of his
relatives, Francis, Duke of Bedford, and Admiral Keppel, Fox,
and other Whigs. He contributed to the *Political Eclogues* a
poem called *Margaret Nicholson,* in which George III., Pitt,
Jenkinson, &c., were ridiculed, and the *Song of Scrutina* (on the
"Westminster Scrutiny"), in the style of Ossian, in the *Probationary Odes for the Laureateship.* He was the author also of an
account of his *Mission to the Court of Vienna;* and his *Negotiations for the Peace of the Dardanelles:* 3 vols., 8vo. For his services in the latter business he was made G.C.B. He was born
24th May, 1763, and died 3rd Oct., 1855.

There is a curious circumstance connected with the composition of this song, the first five stanzas of which were written
by CANNING. Having been accidentally seen, previous to its
publication, by PITT, who was cognisant of the proceedings of
the "Anti-Jacobin" writers, he was so amused with it, that he
took up a pen and composed the last stanza on the spot.—ED.]

[This drama was produced at the Haymarket Theatre, July
26, 1811, with alterations and additions, and some introductory
matter, which contained smart hits at the Quadrupeds, which
then desecrated the stage of Covent Garden Theatre. Liston
performed *Rogero;* Munden, *Casimere;* Mrs. Glover, *Matilda;*
Mrs. Gibbs, *Cecilia.* The following Prologue, written by George
Colman the younger, in imitation of Pope's prologue to *Cato,*
was spoken by Elliston:—

> To lull the soul by spurious strokes of art,
> To warp the genius, and mislead the heart;

To make mankind revere wives gone astray,*
Love pious sons who rob on the highway ; †
For this the foreign muses trod our stage
Commanding *German schools* to be the rage.
Hail to such schools !   Oh, fine *false feeling,* hail !
Thou badst *non-natural nature* to prevail ;
Through thee, *soft super-sentiment* arose,
Musk to the mind like civet to the nose ;
Till fainting taste (as invalids do wrong),
Snuff'd the sick perfume, and grew weakly strong.
Dear Johnny Bull ! you boast much resolution,
With, thanks to Heaven ! a glorious Constitution :
Your taste, recovered half from foreign quacks,
Takes airings, now, on English horses' backs ;
While every modern bard may raise his name,
If not on *lasting praise,* on *stable fame.*
Think that to Germans you have given no check,
Think how each actor hors'd has risk'd his neck ;
You've shewn them favour : Oh, then, once more shew it
To this night's *Anglo-German, Horse-Play* Poet !—ED.]

* Vide *The Stranger.*          † *Lovers' Vows.*

# No. XXXI.

June 11, 1798.

WE have received, in the course of the last week, several long, and to say the truth, dull letters, from unknown hands, reflecting in very severe terms on MR. HIGGINS, for having, as it is affirmed, attempted to pass upon the world, as a faithful sample of the productions of the German theatre, a performance no way resembling any of those pieces which have so late excited, and which bid fair to engross, the admiration of the British public.

As we cannot but consider ourselves as the guardians of MR. HIGGINS's literary reputation, in respect to every work of his which is conveyed to the world through the medium of our paper (though, what we think of the danger of his principles we have already sufficiently explained for ourselves, and have, we trust, succeeded in putting our readers upon their guard against them)—we hold ourselves bound not only to justify the fidelity of the imitation, but (contrary to our original intention) to give a further specimen of it in our present uumber, in order to bring the question more fairly to issue between our author and his calumniators.

In the first place we are to observe, that MR. HIGGINS professes to have taken his notion of German plays wholly from the translations which have appeared in our language.   If *they* are totally dissimilar from the originals, Mr. H. may undoubtedly have been led into error ; but the fault is in the translators, not in him.   That he does not differ widely from the models which he proposed to himself, we have it in our power to prove satisfactorily, and might have done so in our last number, by subjoining to each particular passage of his play the scene in some one or other of the German plays which he had in view when he wrote it. These parallel passages were faithfully pointed out to us by Mr. H. with that candour which marks his character ; and if they were suppressed by us (as in truth they were), on our heads be the blame, whatever it may be. Little, indeed, did we think of the imputation which the omission would bring upon Mr. H., as in fact our principal reason for it was the apprehension that, from the extreme closeness of the imitation in most instances, he would lose in praise for invention more than he would gain in credit for fidelity.

The meeting between Matilda and Cecilia, for example, in the first act of *The Rovers*, and their sudden intimacy, has been censured as unnatural. Be it so. It is taken, *almost word for word*, from *Stella*, a German (or professedly a German) piece now much in vogue; from which also the catastrophe of Mr. HIGGINS's play is in part borrowed, so far as relates to the agreement to which the ladies come, as the reader will see by and bye, to share Casimere between them.

The dinner-scene is copied partly from the published translation of *The Stranger*, and partly from the first ·scene of *Stella*. The song of Rogero, with which the first act concludes, is admitted on all hands to be in the very first taste ; and if no German original is to be found for it, so much the worse for the credit of German literature.

An objection has been made by one anonymous letter-writer to the names of Puddingfield and Beefington, as little likely to have been assigned to English characters by any author of taste or discernment. In answer to this objection we have, in the first place, to admit, that a small, and we hope not an unwarrantable, alteration has been made by us since the MS. has been in our hands. These names stood originally Puddincrantz and Beefinstern, which sounded to our ears as being liable, especially the latter, to a ridiculous inflection—a difficulty that could only be removed by furnishing them with English terminations. With regard to the more substantial syllables of the names, our author proceeded, in all probability, on the authority of Goldoni, who, though not a German, is an Italian writer of considerable reputation ; and who, having heard that the English were distinguished for their love of liberty and beef, has judiciously compounded the two words *Runnymede* and *Beef*, and thereby produced an English nobleman, whom he styles *Lord Runnybeef.*

To dwell no longer on particular passages, the best way perhaps of explaining the whole scope and view of Mr. H.'s imitation will be to transcribe the short sketch of the plot which that gentleman transmitted to us, together with his drama, and which it is perhaps the more necessary to give at length, as, the limits of our paper not allowing of the publication of the whole piece, some general knowledge of its main design may be acceptable to our readers, in order to enable them to judge of the several extracts which we lay before them.

## PLOT.

Rogero, son of the late minister of the Count of Saxe Weimar, having while he was at college, fallen desperately in love with Matilda Pottingen, daughter of his tutor, Doctor Engel-

bertus Pottingen, Professor of Civil Law; and Matilda evidently
returning his passion, the Doctor, to prevent ill consequences,
sends his daughter on a visit to her aunt in Wetteravia, where
she becomes acquainted with Casimere, a Polish Officer, who
happens to be quartered near her aunt's, and has several children by him.

Roderic, Count of Saxe Weimar, a prince of a tyrannical and
licentious disposition, has for his Prime Minister and favourite
Gaspar, a crafty villain, who had risen to his post by first ruin-
ing, and then putting to death, Rogero's father.    Gaspar,
apprehensive of the power and popularity which the young
Rogero may enjoy at his return to Court, seizes the occasion of
his intrigue with Matilda (of which he is apprized officially by
Doctor Pottingen) to procure from his master an order for the
recall of Rogero from college, and for committing him to the
care of the Prior of the Abbey of Quedlinburgh, a priest,
rapacious, savage, and sensual, and devoted to Gaspar's interests
—sending at the same time private orders to the Prior to confine him in a dungeon.

Here Rogero languishes many years.    His daily sustenance
is administered to him through a grated opening at the top of
a cavern, by the landlady of the Golden Eagle at Weimar, with
whom Gaspar contracts, in the prince's name, for his support;
intending, and more than once endeavouring, to corrupt the
waiter to mingle poison with the food, in order that he may get
rid of Rogero for ever.

In the meantime, Casimere, having been called away from
the neighbourhood of Matilda's residence to other quarters,
becomes enamoured of and marries Cecilia, by whom he has
a family ; and whom he likewise deserts after a few years' co-
habitation, on pretence of business which calls him to Kamtschatka.

Doctor Pottingen, now grown old and infirm, and feeling the
want of his daughter's society, sends young Pottingen in search
of her, with strict injunctions not to return without her ; and
to bring with her either her present lover Casimere, or, should

that not be possible, Rogero himself, if he can find him; the Doctor having set his heart upon seeing his children comfortably settled before his death. Matilda, about the same period, quits her aunt's in search of Casimere; and Cecilia, having been advertised (by an anonymous letter) of the falsehood of his Kamtschatka journey, sets out in the post-waggon on a similar pursuit.

It is at this point of time the Play opens—with the accidental meeting of Cecilia and Matilda at the Inn at Weimar. Casimere arrives there soon after, and falls in first with Matilda, and then with Cecilia. Successive *éclaircissements* take place, and an arrangement is finally made, by which the two ladies are to live jointly with Casimere.

Young Pottingen, wearied with a few weeks' search, during which he has not been able to find either of the objects of it, resolves to stop at Weimar, and wait events there. It so happens that he takes up his lodgings in the same house with Puddingfield and Beefington, two English noblemen, whom the tyranny of King John has obliged to fly from their country; and who, after wandering about the continent for some time, have fixed their residence at Weimar.

The news of the signature of Magna Charta arriving, determines Puddingfield and Beefington to return to England. Young Pottingen opens his case to them, and entreats them to stay to assist him in the object of his search.—This they refuse; but coming to the Inn where they are to set off for Hamburgh, they meet Casimere, from whom they had both received many civilities in Poland.

Casimere, by this time tired of his " DOUBLE ARRANGEMENT," and having learnt from the waiter that Rogero is confined in the vaults of the neighbouring abbey *for love*, resolves to attempt his rescue, and to make over Matilda to him as the price of his deliverance. He communicates his scheme to Puddingfield and Beefington, who agree to assist him; as also does young Pottingen. The Waiter of the Inn, proving to be a *Knight Templar* in disguise, is appointed leader of the expedition. A band of

Troubadours, who happen to be returning from the Crusades, and a company of Austrian and Prussian Grenadiers returning from the Seven Years' War, are engaged as troops.

The attack on the Abbey is made with success. The Count of Weimar and Gaspar, who are feasting with the Prior, are seized and beheaded in the refectory. The Prior is thrown into the dungeon from which Rogero is rescued. Matilda and Cecilia rush in. The former recognises Rogero, and agrees to live with him. The children are produced on all sides—and young Pottingen is commissioned to write to his father, the Doctor, to detail the joyful events which have taken place, and to invite him to Weimar to partake of the general felicity.

# THE ROVERS; OR, THE DOUBLE ARRANGEMENT.

## ACT II.

*Scene, a Room in an ordinary Lodging-house at Weimar—* PUDDINGFIELD *and* BEEFINGTON *discovered sitting at a small deal table, and playing at All-fours—Young* POTTINGEN, *at another table in the corner of the room, with a pipe in his mouth, and a Saxon mug of a singular shape beside him, which he repeatedly applies to his lips, turning back his head, and casting his eyes towards the firmament—at the last trial he holds the mug for some moments in a directly inverted position ; then replaces it on the table with an air of dejection, and gradually sinks into a profound slumber—the pipe falls from his hand, and is broken.*

BEEF. I beg.

PUDD. [*Deals three cards to* BEEFINGTON.]　Are you satisfied ?

BEEF. Enough ; what have you ?

PUDD. High, low, and the game.

BEEF. D——n ! 'Tis my deal. [*Deals ; turns up a knave.*]　One for his heels ! [*Triumphantly.*

PUDD. Is king highest ?

BEEF. No.   [*Sternly*]   The game is mine.   The knave
gives it me.

PUDD. Are knaves so prosperous?

BEEF. Aye, marry are they in this world.   They have
the game in their hands.   Your kings are but *noddies* * to
them.

PUDD. Ha! ha! ha!   Still the same proud spirit,
Beefington, which procured thee thine exile from
England.

BEEF. England! my native land! when shall I revisit
thee?

> [*During this time* PUDDINGFIELD *deals, and
> begins to arrange his hand.*

BEEF. [*Continues.*] Phoo, hang All-fours; what are they
to a mind ill at ease?   Can they cure the heartache?
Can they soothe banishment?   Can they lighten
ignominy?   Can All-fours do this?   O, my Puddingfield!
thy limber and lightsome spirit bounds up against afflic-
tion with the elasticity of a well-bent bow; but mine—
O! mine—

> [*Falls into an agony, and sinks back in his chair. Young*
> POTTINGEN, *awakened by the noise, rises, and advances with
> a grave demeanour towards* BEEFINGTON *and* PUDDINGFIELD.
> *The former begins to recover.*

---

* This is an excellent joke in German; the point and spirit
of which is but ill-*Rendered* in a translation.   A NODDY, the
reader will observe, has two significations, the one a *knave at
All-fours*, the other a *fool* or *booby*.   See the translation by Mr.
Render of *Count Benyowsky, or the Conspiracy of Kamschatka*, a
German Tragi-Comi-Comi-Tragedy, where the play opens with
a scene of a game at chess (from which the whole of this scene
is copied), and a joke of the same point, and merriment about
pawns, *i.e.*, boors being a *match* for kings.

Y. Pot. What is the matter, comrades,* you seem agitated. Have you lost or won?

Beef. Lost! I have lost my country.

Y. Pot. And I my sister. I came hither in search of her.

Beef. O, England!

Y. Pot. O, Matilda!

Beef. Exiled by the tyranny of an usurper, I seek the means of revenge, and of restoration to my country.

Y. Pot. Oppressed by the tyranny of an Abbot, persecuted by the jealousy of a Count, the betrothed husband of my sister languishes in a loathsome captivity; her lover is fled no one knows whither, and I, her brother, am torn from my parental roof, and from my studies in chirurgery, to seek him and her, I know not where—to rescue Rogero, I know not how. Comrades, your counsel. My search fruitless—my money gone—my baggage stolen! what am I to do? In yonder Abbey—in these dark, dank vaults, there, my friends, there lies Rogero—there Matilda's heart.

SCENE II.

*Enter* Waiter.

Waiter. Sir, here is a person who desires to speak with you.

Beef. [*Goes to the door and returns with a letter, which he opens. On perusing it his countenance becomes illuminated, and expands prodigiously.*] Ah, my friend, what joy!

[*Turning to* Puddingfield.

---

* This word in the original is strictly *fellow-lodgers*—" Co-occupants of the same room in a house let out at a small rent by the week". There is no single word in English which expresses so complicated a relation, except perhaps the cant term of *chum*, formerly in use in our Universities.

PUDD. What? tell me—let your Puddingfield partake it.

BEEF. See here. [*Produces a printed paper.*

PUDD. What? [*With impatience.*

BEEF. [*In a significant tone.*] A newspaper!

PUDD. Ah, what sayst thou?—A newspaper!

BEEF. Yes, Puddingfield, and see here [*shows it partially*], from England.

PUDD. [*With extreme earnestness.*] Its name?

BEEF. The *Daily Advertiser.*

PUDD. Oh, ecstasy!

BEEF. [*With a dignified severity.*] Puddingfield, calm yourself—repress those transports—remember that you are a man.

PUDD. [*After a pause, with suppressed emotion.*] Well, I will be—I am calm—yet tell me, Beefington, does it contain any news?

BEEF. Glorious news, my dear Puddingfield—the Barons are victorious—King John has been defeated—Magna Charta, that venerable immemorial inheritance of Britons, was signed last Friday was three weeks, the third of July, Old Style.

PUDD. I can scarce believe my ears—but let me satisfy my eyes—show me the paragraph.

BEEF. Here it is, just above the advertisements.

PUDD. [*Reads.*] "The great demand for Packwood's Razor Straps"—

BEEF. Pshaw!—what, ever blundering!—you drive me from my patience. See here, at the head of the column.

PUDD. [*Reads.*]

"A hireling print, devoted to the court,
Has dared to question our veracity

Respecting the events of yesterday;
But by to-day's accounts, our information
Appears to have been perfectly correct.
The Charter of our Liberties received
The royal signature at five o'clock,
When messengers were instantly dispatched
To Cardinal Pandulfo; and their majesties,
After partaking of a cold collation,
Returned to Windsor."—I am satisfied.

BEEF. Yet here again—there are some further particulars [*turns to another part of the paper*]. "Extract of
a letter from Egham—My dear friend, we are all here in
high spirits—the interesting event which took place this
morning at Runnymede, in the neighbourhood of this
town "—

PUDD. Ah, Runnymede ! enough — no more — my
doubts are vanished—then are we free indeed !

BEEF. I have, besides, a letter in my pocket from our
friend, the immortal Bacon, who has been appointed
Chancellor. Our outlawry is reversed!—What says my
friend—shall we return by the next packet?

PUDD. Instantly, instantly !

BOTH. Liberty ! Adelaide ! revenge !

[*Exeunt—Young* POTTINGEN *following and waving his
hat, but obviously without much consciousness of the
meaning of what has passed.*

*Scene changes to the outside of the Abbey.—A Summer's Evening ;
Moonlight.*

*Companies of Austrian and Prussian Grenadiers march across the
stage confusedly, as if returning from the Seven Years' War.—
Shouts and martial music.*

*The Abbey Gates are opened; the Monks are seen passing in pro-
cession, with the* PRIOR *at their head; the choir is heard chanting*

*vespers.—After which a pause; then a bell is heard, as if ringing for supper; soon after, a noise of singing and jollity.*
*Enter from the Abbey, pushed out of the gates by the* PORTER, *a* TROUBADOUR, *with a bundle under his cloak, and a Lady under his arm ;* TROUBADOUR *seems much in liquor, but caresses the* FEMALE MINSTREL.

FEM. MIN. Trust me, Gieronimo, thou seemest melancholy. What hast thou got under thy cloak?

TROU. Pshaw! women will be inquiring. Melancholy! not I. I will sing thee a song, and the subject of it shall be the question—"What have I got under my cloak?" It is a riddle, Margaret—I learnt it of an almanac-maker at Gotha—if thou guessest it after the first stanza, thou shalt have never a drop for thy pains. Hear me—and, d'ye mark! twirl thy thingumbob while I sing.

FEM. MIN. 'Tis a pretty tune, and hums dolefully.
[*Plays on her balalaika.*

TROU. I bear a secret comfort *here,* *
[*Putting his hand on the bundle.*
A joy I'll ne'er impart ;
It is not wine, it is not beer,
But it consoles my heart.

---

**᾽** [* The above song is a parody on that pathetic one—given below—written by Sheridan, and introduced into Kotzebue's drama of *The Stranger*, to be overheard by the latter. It was sung by Mrs. Bland—as Annetta—to a melody by the Duchess of Devonshire, in a manner, it is said, that thrilled every heart.

"I have a silent sorrow here,
A grief I'll ne'er impart ;
It breathes no sigh, it sheds no tear,
But it consumes my heart.
This cherish'd woe, this lov'd despair,
My lot for ever be ;
So my soul's lord, the pangs I bear
Be never known by thee !

FEM. MIN. [*Interrupting him.*] I'll be hang'd if you don't mean the bottle of cherry-brandy that you stole out of the vaults in the abbey cellar.

TROU. I mean!—Peace, wench; thou disturbest the current of my feelings—

[FEM. MIN. *attempts to lay hold on the bottle;* TROUBADOUR *pushes her aside, and continues singing without interruption.*

This cherry-bounce, this loved noyau,
  My drink for ever be ;
But, sweet my love, thy wish forego ;
  I'll give no drop to thee !

[*Both together.*]

TROU. { This }
F. M. { That } cherry-bounce { this } loved noyau,
                      { that }

TROU. { My }
F. M. { Thy } drink for ever be ;

TROU. }
F. M. } But, sweet my love, { thy wish forego !
                         { one drop bestow,

TROU. { I }
F. M. { Nor } keep it all for { me !
                         { thee !

[*Exeunt struggling for the bottle, but without anger or animosity, the* FEM. MIN. *appearing by degrees to obtain a superiority in the contest.*

END OF ACT II.

"And when pale characters of death
  Shall mark this alter'd cheek ;
When my poor wasted trembling breath
  My life's last hope would speak ;
I shall not raise my eyes to heaven,
  Nor mercy ask for me,
My soul despairs to be forgiv'n,
  Unpardon'd, love, by thee !"—ED.

ACT THE THIRD—contains the éclaircissements and final arrangement between CASIMERE, MATILDA, and CECILIA; which so nearly resemble the concluding act of *Stella*, that we forbear to lay it before our readers.

ACT IV.

*Scene, the Inn door; Diligence drawn up.*—CASIMERE *appears superintending the package of his portmanteaus, and giving directions to the* PORTERS.

*Enter* BEEFINGTON *and* PUDDINGFIELD.

PUDD. Well, Coachey, have you got two inside places?

COACH. Yes, your Honour.

PUDD. [*seems to be struck with* CASIMERE'S *appearance. He surveys him earnestly without paying any attention to the* COACHMAN, *then doubtingly pronounces*] Casimere!

CAS. [*turning round rapidly, recognizes* PUDDINGFIELD, *and embraces him.*] My Puddingfield!

PUDD. My Casimere!

CAS. What, Beefington too! [*discovering him*] —then is my joy complete.

BEEF. Our fellow-traveller, as it seems!

CAS. Yes, Beefington—but wherefore to Hamburgh?

BEEF. Oh, Casimere*—to fly—to fly—to return—England—our country—Magna Charta—it is liberated—a

---

* See *Count Benyowsky;* where Crustiew, an old gentleman of much sagacity, talks the following nonsense :

Crustiew [*with youthful energy, and an air of secrecy and confidence*]. "To fly, to fly, to the isles of Marian—the island of Tinian—a terrestrial paradise. Free—free—a mild climate—a new-created sun—wholesome fruits—harmless inhabitants—and liberty—tranquillity."

new æra—House of Commons—Crown and Anchor—
Opposition—

CAS. What a contrast! you are flying to liberty and
your home—I, driven from my home by tyranny, and
exposed to domestic slavery in a foreign country.

BEEF. How domestic slavery?

CAS. Too true—two wives— [*slowly, and with a dejected
air—then after a pause*]—you knew my Cecilia?

PUDD. Yes, five years ago.

CAS. Soon after that period I went upon a visit to a
lady in Wetteravia—my Matilda was under her protection. Alighting at a peasant's cabin, I saw her on a
charitable visit, spreading bread-and-butter for the
children, in a light-blue riding-habit. The simplicity of
her appearance—the fineness of the weather—all con-
spired to interest me—my heart moved to hers--as if by
magnetic sympathy. We wept, embraced, and went
home together : she became the mother of my Pantalowsky. But five yèars of enjoyment have not stifled the
reproaches of my conscience—her Rogero is languishing
in captivity—if I could restore her to *him!*

BEEF. Let us rescue him.

CAS. Will without power * is like children playing at
soldiers.

BEEF. Courage without power † is like a consumptive
running footman.

CAS. Courage without power is a contradiction. ‡ Ten
brave men might set all Quedlinburgh at defiance.

---

* See *Count Benyowsky*, as before.    † See *Count Benyowsky*.

‡ See *Count Benyowsky* again ; from which play this and the
preceding references are taken word for word. We acquit the
Germans of such reprobate silly stuff. It must be the translator's.

BEEF. Ten brave men—but where are they to be found?

CAS. I will tell you—marked you the waiter?

BEEF. The waiter? [*doubtingly.*

CAS. [*in a confidential tone*]. No waiter, but a *Knight Templar.* Returning from the Crusade, he found his Order dissolved, and his person proscribed. He dissembled his rank, and embraced the profession of a waiter. I have made sure of him already. There are, besides, an Austrian, and a Prussian grenadier. I have made them abjure their national enmity, and they have sworn to fight henceforth in the cause of freedom. These with young Pottingen, the waiter, and ourselves, make seven—the Troubadour, with his two attendant minstrels, will complete the ten.

BEEF. Now then for the execution. [ *With enthusiasm.*

PUDD. Yes, my boys—for the execution.

[*Clapping them on the back.*

WAITER. But hist ! we are observed.

TROU. Let us by a song conceal our purposes.

RECITATIVE ACCOMPANIED.*

CAS.   Hist ! hist ! nor let the airs that blow
From night's cold lungs our purpose know !
PUDD. Let Silence, mother of the dumb,
BEEF. Press on each lip her palsied thumb !
WAIT. Let Privacy, allied to sin,
That loves to haunt the tranquil inn—

---

* We believe this song to be copied, with a small variation in metre and meaning, from a song in *Count Benyowsky ; or, the Conspiracy of Kamschatka,* where the conspirators join in a chorus, *for fear of being overheard.*

GREN. ) And Conscience start, when she shall view
TROU. ) The mighty deed we mean to do !

GENERAL CHORUS—*Con spirito.*

Then friendship swear, ye faithful bands,
Swear to save a shackled hero !
See where yon abbey frowning stands !
Rescue, rescue, brave Rogero !

CAS.     Thrall'd in a monkish tyrant's fetters
Shall great Rogero hopeless lie ?

Y. POT. In my pocket I have letters,
Saying, "Help me, or I die !"

*Allegro Allegretto.*

CAS. BEEF. PUDD. GREN.
TROU. WAITER, AND POT.
*with enthusiasm.*
) Let us fly, let us fly,
) Let us help, ere he die !

[*Exeunt omnes, waving their hats.*

*Scene, the Abbey Gate, with Ditches, Drawbridges, and Spikes; Time, about an hour before Sunrise.—The conspirators appear as if in ambuscade, whispering and consulting together, in expectation of the signal for attack.—The* WAITER *is habited as a Knight Templar, in the dress of his Order, with the Cross on his breast, and the scallop on his shoulder.—*PUDDINGFIELD *and* BEEFINGTON *armed with blunderbusses and pocket-pistols; the* GRENADIERS *in their proper uniforms.—The* TROUBADOUR *with his attendant minstrels bring up the rear; martial music: the conspirators come forward, and present themselves before the Gate of the Abbey.—Alarum; firing of pistols; the Convent appear in Arms upon the Walls; the Drawbridge is let down; a body of choristers and lay-brothers attempt a sally, but are beaten back, and the Verger killed.—The besieged attempt to raise the Drawbridge;* PUDDINGFIELD *and* BEEFINGTON *press forward with alacrity, throw themselves upon the Drawbridge, and by the exertion of their weight preserve it in a state of depression; the other besiegers join them, and attempt to* *force the entrance, but without effect.*—PUDDINGFIELD *makes the signal for the battering-ram.*—*Enter* QUINTUS CURTIUS *and* MARCUS CURIUS DENTATUS *in their military habits, preceded by the Roman Eagle; the rest of their Legion are employed in bringing forward a battering-ram, which plays for a few minutes to slow time, till the entrance is forced.*—*After a short resistance, the besiegers rush in with shouts of Victory.*

*Scene changes to the interior of the Abbey.*—*The inhabitants of the Convent are seen flying in all directions.*

*The* COUNT OF WEIMAR *and the* PRIOR, *who had been found feasting in the Refectory, are brought in manacled. The* COUNT *appears transported with rage, and gnaws his chains.*—*The* PRIOR *remains insensible, as if stupefied with grief.*—BEEFINGTON *takes the keys of the Dungeon, which are hanging at the* PRIOR's *girdle, and makes a sign for them both to be led away into confinement.*— *Exeunt* PRIOR *and* COUNT, *properly guarded.*—*The rest of the conspirators disperse in search of the Dungeon where* ROGERO *is confined.*

END OF ACT THE FOURTH.

# No. XXXII.

June 18, 1798.

WE are indebted for the following imitation of CATULLUS to a literary correspondent. Whether it will remove the doubts we formerly expressed, of CITIZEN MUSKEIN's acquaintance with the classics, from the minds of our readers, we cannot pretend to say. It is given to us as a faithful translation from the French—as such, we present it to our readers; premising only, that though the *Citizen Imitator* seems to have *Sans-culottized* the original in two or three places, yet he everywhere expresses himself with a *naïveté* and truth in his verse that we seek for in vain in many of his countrymen who have recorded their victories and defeats in very vulgar prose.

## AN AFFECTIONATE EFFUSION OF CITIZEN MUSKEIN TO HAVRE-DE-GRACE.

FAIREST of cities,* which the Seine
Surveys 'twixt Paris and the main,
Sweet HAVRE! sweetest HAVRE, hail!
How gladly with my tatter'd sail,†
Yet trembling from this wild adventure,
Do I thy friendly harbour enter!

AD SIRMIONEM PENINSULAM.

\* Peninsularum Sirmio, Insularumque,
  Ocelle! quascunque in liquentibus stagnis,
  Marique vasto fert uterque Neptunus;
† Quam te libenter, quamque lætus inviso,
  Vix mi ipse credens Thyniam, atque Bithynos

Well—now I've leisure, let me see
What boats are left me ; one, two, three—
Bravo ! the better half remain ;
And all my heroes are not slain.
And if my senses don't deceive,
I too am safe,*—yes, I believe,
Without a wound I reach thy shore
(For I have felt myself all o'er) ;
I've all my limbs, and, be it spoken
With honest triumph, no bone broken.

How pleasing is the sweet transition †
From this vile Gun-boat Expedition ;
From winds and waves, and wounds and scars,
From British soldiers, British tars,
To his own house, where, free from danger,
MUSKEIN may live at rack and manger ;
May stretch his limbs in his own cot, ‡
Thankful he has not gone to pot ;
Nor for the bubble Glory strive,
But bless himself that he's alive !

HAVRE, § sweet Havre ! hail again,
O ! bid thy sons (a frolic train, ||
Who under CHÉNIER welcomed in,
With dance and song, the *Guillotine* ).

Liquisse campos,* et videre te in tuto.
† O quid solutis est beatius curis
  Cum mens onus reponit, ac peregrino
  Labore fessi venimus larem ad nostrum.
‡ Desideratoque acquiescimus lecto ?
  Hoc est, quod unum est pro laboribus tantis.
§ Salve ! O venusta Sirmio ! atque hero gaude ;
  Gaudete ! vosque Lydiæ lacus undæ ;
  Ridete|| quicquid est domi cachinnorum !

In long procession seek the strand ;
For MUSKEIN now prepares to land,
'Scaped, Heav'n knows how, from that cursed crew
That haunt the rocks of SAINT MARCOU.

---

[TO THE PENINSULA OF SIRMIO.

UPON THE RETURN OF THE POET TO HIS COUNTRY HOUSE THERE.

*Translated from* CATULLUS.

SIRMIO, of all the shores the gem,
   The isles where circling Neptune strays;
   Whether the vast and boisterous main
Or lake's more limpid waves they stem,
   How gladly on thy waves I gaze !
   How blest to visit thee again !

I scarce believe, while rapt I stand,
   That I have left the Thynian fields
   And all Bithynia far behind,
And safely view my favourite land.
   Oh bliss, when care dispersing yields
   To full repose the placid mind !

Then when the mind its load lays down ;
   When we regain, all hazards past,
   And with long ceaseless travel tired,
Our household god again our own ;
   And press in tranquil sleep at last
   The well-known bed so oft desired—

This can alone atonement make
   For every toil.  Hail, Sirmio sweet !
   Be gay, thy lord hath ceased to roam !
Ye laughing waves of Lydia's lake,
   Smile all around ! thy master greet
   With all thy smiles, my pleasant home !—ED.]

# No. XXXIII.*

June 25, 1798.

AFTER the splendid account of BUONAPARTE's successes in the East, which our readers will find in another part of this paper, † and which they will peruse with equal wonder and apprehension, it is some consolation to us to have to state, not only from authority, but in verse, that our government has not been behindhand with that of France; but that aware of the wise and enterprising spirit of the enemy, and of the danger which might arise to our distant possessions from the export of learning and learned men being entirely in their hands, ministers have long ago determined on an expedition of a similar nature, and have actually embarked at Portsmouth on board one of the East India Company's ships taken up for that purpose (the ship *Capricorn*, Mr. Thomas Truman, Commander), several tons of *savans*, the growth of this country. The whole was conducted with the utmost secrecy and dispatch, and it was not till we were favoured with the following copy of a letter (obligingly communicated to us by the Tunisian gentleman to whom it is addressed) that we had any suspicion of the extent and nature of the design, or indeed of any such design being in contemplation.

[ * The following *Letter* probably alludes to the *Association for promoting the Discovery of the interior parts of Africa*, of which Sir John Sinclair was the presiding genius. "The result of their labours," says Hugh Murray, in his Account of African Discoveries, "has thrown new lustre on the British name, and widely extended the boundaries of human knowledge."—ED.]

[† Buonaparte's Bulletin.—ED.]

The several great names which are combined to render this Expedition the most surprising and splendid ever undertaken, could not indeed have been spared from the country to which they are an ornament for any other purpose than one the most obviously connected with the interests of the empire, and the most widely beneficial to mankind.

The secrecy with which they have been withdrawn from the British public, without being so much as missed or enquired after, reflects the highest honour on the planners of the enterprise. Even the celebrity of DOCTOR PARR has not led to any discovery or investigation : the silent admirers of that great man have never once thought of asking what was become of him ; till it is now all at once come to light, that he has been for weeks past on shipboard, the brightest star in the bright constellation of talents which stud the quarter-deck of the *Capricorn*, Mr. T. Truman (as before mentioned), Commander.

The resignation of the late worthy President of a certain Agricultural Board * might indeed have taught mankind to look for some extraordinary event in the world of science and adventure ; and those who had the good fortune to see the deportation from his house, of the several wonderful anomalies which had for years formed its most distinguished inmates,—the stuffed ram, the dried boar, the cow with three horns, and other fanciful productions of a like nature, could not but speculate with some degree of seriousness on the purpose of their removal, and on the place of their destination.

[* SIR JOHN SINCLAIR, the celebrated author of the *History of the Public Revenue*, the *Statistical Account of Scotland*, and many useful agricultural and other works.—ED.]

It now appears that there was in truth no light object
in view. They were destined, with the rest of the *savans*,
on whom this country prides itself (and long may it have
reason to indulge the honest exultation), to undertake a
voyage of no less grandeur than peril ; to counteract the
designs of the Directory, and to frustrate or forestal the
conquests of Buonaparte.

The young gentleman who writes the following letter
to his friend in London is, as may be seen, interpreter to
the Expedition. We have understood, further, that he is
connected with the young man who writes for the
*Morning Chronicle*, and conducts the *Critical*, *Argumenta-*
*tive*, and *Geographical* departments. Some say it is the
young man himself, who has assumed a feigned name,
and, under the disguise of a Turkish dress and circum-
cision, is gone, at the express instigation of his em-
ployers, to improve himself in geographical knowledge.
We have our doubts upon this subject, as we think we
recognise the style of this deplorable young man in an
article of last week's *Morning Chronicle*, which we have
had occasion to answer in a preceding column of our
present paper. Be that as it may, the information contained in the following letter may be depended upon.

We cannot take leave of the subject without remarking
what a fine contrast and companion the vessel and cargo
described in the following poem affords [*sic*] to the " Navis
Stultifera," the " Shippe of Fooles " of the celebrated
Barclay ; and we cannot forbear hoping that the *Argenis*
of an author of the same name may furnish a hint for an
account of this stupendous Expedition in a learned
language, from the only pen which in modern days is
capable of writing Latin with a purity and elegance

16

worthy of so exalted a theme, and that the author of a classical *preface*\* may become the writer of a no less celebrated voyage.

## TRANSLATION OF A LETTER,

(IN ORIENTAL CHARACTERS)

## FROM BAWBA-DARA-ADUL-PHOOLA,†

DRAGOMAN TO THE EXPEDITION,

## TO NEEK-AWL-ARETCHID-KOOEZ,

SECRETARY TO THE TUNISIAN EMBASSY.

DEAR NEEK-AWL,

YOU'LL rejoice, that at length I am able,
To date these few lines from the captain's own table.
Mr. Truman himself, of his proper suggestion,
Has in favour of science decided the question ;
So we walk the main-deck, and are mess'd with the captain,
I leave you to judge of the joys we are wrapt in.

At Spithead they embark'd us, how precious a cargo !
And we sail'd before day to escape the embargo.
There was SHUCKBOROUGH,‡ the wonderful mathematician ;
And DARWIN, the poet, the sage, and physician ;
There was BEDDOES, and BRUIN, and GODWIN, whose trust is,

---

[\* Dr. Parr's noted Latin Preface to his edition of *Bellendenus de Statu*. T. De Quincey, in his famous dissection of Dr. Parr and his writings, beseeches the "gentle reader" of Bellendenus to pronounce the penultimate syllable *short*, and *not long*, as is usually done.—ED.]

[† *I.e.*, from BOB ADAIR, *a dull fool*, to NICHOLL [Nicholls], *a wretched goose.*—ED.]

[‡ Sir Geo. Aug. Wm. Shuckburgh, M.P., F.R.S., author of papers in the Phil. Trans.—ED.]

He may part with his work on *Political Justice*
To some Iman or Bonze, or Judaical Rabbin ;
So with huge quarto volumes he piles up the cabin.
There was great DR. PARR whom we style *Bellendenus*,
The Doctor and I have a hammock between us.
'Tis a little unpleasant thus crowding together,
On account of the motion and heat of the weather ;
*Two* souls in one berth they oblige us to cram,
And Sir John * *will* insist on a place for his ram.
Though the Doctor, I find, is determined to think
'Tis the animal's hide that occasions the stink ;
In spite of th' experienced opinion of Truman,
Who contends that the scent is exclusively human.
But BEDDOES and DARWIN engage to repair
This slight inconvenience with *oxygen air*.

Whither bound? (you will ask). 'Tis a question, my
  friend,
On which I long doubted ; my doubt's at an end.
To Arabia the Stony, Sabæa the gummy,
To the land where each man that you meet is a mummy ;
To the mouths of the Nile, to the banks of Araxes,
To the *Red* and the *Yellow*, the *White* and the *Black* seas,
With telescopes, globes, and a quadrant and sextant,
And the works of all authors whose writings are extant ;
With surveys and plans, topographical maps,
Theodolites, watches, spring-guns and steel-traps,
Phials, crucibles, air-pumps, electric machinery,
And pencils for painting the natives and scenery.
In short, we are sent to oppose all we know
To the knowledge and mischievous arts of the foe,

[* Sir John Sinclair.—ED.]

Who, though placing in arms a well-grounded reliance,
Go to war with a flying artillery of science.

The French *savans*, it seems, recommended this
measure,
With a view to replenish the national treasure.
First, the true *Rights of Man* they will preach in all
places,
But chief (when 'tis found) in the Egyptian Oasis :
And this doctrine, 'tis hoped, in a very few weeks
Will persuade the wild Arabs to murder their cheiks,
And, to aid the *Great Nation's* beneficent plans,
Plunder pyramids, catacombs, towns, caravans,
Then enlist under Arcolé's gallant commander,
Who will conquer the world like his model ISKANDER.
His army each day growing bolder and finer,
With the Turcoman tribes he subdues Asia Minor,
Beats Paul and his Scythians, his journey pursues
Cross the Indus, with tribes of Armenians and Jews,
And Bucharians, and Affghans, and Persians, and
Tartars,—
Chokes the wretched Mogul in his grandmother's garters,
And will hang him to dry in the Luxembourg hall,
'Midst the plunder of Carthage and spoils of Bengal.

Such, we hear, was the plan; but I trust, if we meet 'em,
That *savant* to *savant*, our cargo will beat 'em.
Our plan of proceeding I'll presently tell ;—
But soft—I am call'd—I must bid you farewell :
To attend on our *savans* my pen I resign,
For, it seems, that they *duck* them on *crossing* the Line.

───────────

We deeply regret this interruption of our oriental poet,

and the more so, as the prose letters which we have received from a less learned correspondent do not enable
us to explain the tactics of our belligerent philosophers
so distinctly as we could have wished. It appears, in
general, that the learned Doctor who has the honour of
sharing the hammock of the amiable oriental, trusted
principally to his superior knowledge in the Greek
language, by means of which he hoped to entangle his
antagonists in inextricable confusion. DR. DARWIN proposed (as might be expected) his celebrated experiment
of the Ice-island,[1] which, being towed on the coast of
Africa, could not fail of spoiling the climate, and immediately terrifying and embarrassing the sailors of
Buonaparte's fleet, accustomed to the mild temperature
and gentle gales of the Mediterranean, and therefore ill
qualified to struggle with this new importation of
tempests. DR. BEDDOES was satisfied with the project
of communicating to Buonaparte a consumption, of the
same nature with that which he formerly tried on himself, but superior in virulence, and therefore calculated to
make the most rapid and fatal ravages in the hectic constitution of the Gallic hero. The rest of the plan is quite
unintelligible, excepting a hint about Sir J. S.'s intention
of proceeding with his ram to the celebrated Oasis, and
of bringing away, for the convenience of the Bank, the
treasures contained in the temple of Jupiter Ammon.

---

[1] The following are Dr. Darwin's instructions for the *transportation* of *Ice Islands*:—

"There, Nymphs! alight, array your dazzling powers,
With sudden march alarm the torpid hours;
On ice-built isles expand a thousand sails,
Hinge the strong helms, and catch the frozen gales.
The winged rocks to feverish climates guide,
Where fainting zephyrs pant upon the tide;

Pass, where to Ceuta Calpé's thunder roars,
And answering echoes shake the kindred shores ;
Pass, where with palmy plumes, Canary smiles,
And in her silver girdle binds her isles ;
Onward, where Niger's dusky Naiad laves
A thousand kingdoms with prolific waves,
Or leads o'er golden sands her threefold train
In steamy channels to the fervid main ;
While swarthy nations crowd the sultry coast,
Drink the fresh breeze, and hail the floating frost :
Nymphs ! veil'd in mist, the melting treasure steer,
And cool with arctic snows the tropic year."

"If the nations who inhabit this hemisphere of the globe, instead of destroying their seamen and exhausting their wealth in unnecessary wars, could
be induced to unite their labours to navigate these immense masses of ice into
the more southern oceans, two great advantages would result to mankind, the
tropic countries would be much cooled by their solution, and our winters in
this altitude would be rendered much milder, for perhaps a century or two, till
the masses of ice became again enormous."—Ed.]

—————

[Dr. Thomas Beddoes, born at Shiffnal in 1760, was a scientific Physician
far in advance of his age ; his *Popular Essay on Consumption*, 1779, his tracts
entitled *Hygeia*, 1801, &c., may still be studied with profit. He paid particular
attention to the medical use of the permanently Elastic Fluids, and avows that
as "one rash experiment on a patient would demolish a plan on which the hope
of relieving mankind from much of their misery is founded," he made preliminary experiments on himself in the case of *Oxygene* and *Consumption*, as
alluded to in the text. A *propos* of the artificial distribution of disease, it may
be mentioned that in *The Batchelor*, p. 189, is a method for "discharging the
Plague".

He wrote much on the political topics of the day, always taking the liberal
side, and attacking Pitt with great virulence and eloquence. The principles of
the French Revolution were at first advocated by him with the utmost
enthusiasm, but he was soon disgusted by the excesses committed. He was a
student of German literature, and much admired by Immanuel Kant. He was
also an intimate friend of Darwin's, whose political opinions he shared, and
whose works were intrusted to his revision in manuscript. A few months after
the publication of Darwin's *Botanic Garden*, its magnificent imagery and har-
monious versification inspired some admirers to say that the style of this work
was a style *sui generis*, and that it defied imitation. Dr. Beddoes maintained
an opposite opinion. Much as he admired the poem in question, he thought
that the Darwinian structure of verse might be imitated by a writer possessed
of inferior poetical powers, and in a few days he produced in the same circle
part of the manuscript of *Alexander's Expedition to the Indian Ocean* as an un-
published work of the author of the *Botanic Garden*. The deception completely
succeeded, and some enthusiastic admirers of the latter work pointed out with
triumph "certain passages as proofs of the position that the author in his happier efforts defied imitation". Beddoes's success was the more extraordinary, as
in the "Introduction" to a considerable extract from his poem which he printed
in the *Annual Anthology* for 1796, he states that he had never before written
twice as many lines of verse as the composition under notice consisted of.

As Beddoes's imitation of Darwin is seldom met with, it may not be out of
character in a work of the present nature to give a specimen of it.

AN IMITATION OF DARWIN.

" Now the new Lord of Persia's wide domain,
Down fierce Hydaspes seeks the Indian main :
High on the leading prow the Conqueror stands,
Eyes purer skies and marks diverging strands.

A thousand sails attendant catch the wind,
And yet a thousand press the wave behind ;
Two veteran hosts, outstretched on either hand,
Wide wave their wings and sweep the trembling land.
Each serried phalanx Terror stalks beside,
And shakes o'er crested helms his blazing pride ;
While Victory, still companion of his way,
Sounds her loud trump and flaunts her banners gay."

Further on, the Hero's attention is attracted to the surrounding landscape,
which he thus apostrophizes :—

"Ye fields for ever fair ! Thou mighty stream !
Bright regions ! blessed beyond the muse's dream !
Thou fruitful womb of ever-teeming earth !
Ye fostering skies that rear each beauteous birth !
Trees, that aloft uprear your stately height,
Whose sombrous branches shed a noontide night !
Groves, that for ever wear the smile of spring !
Gay birds that wave the many-tinted wing !
Of reptiles, fishes, brutes, stupendous forms !
And ye, of nameless insects glittering swarms !
Sons of soft toil, whose shuttle beauty throws,
Whose tints the Graces' earnest hands dispose,
Whose guileless bosom Care avoid and Crime,
Gay as your groves, and cloudless as your clime !
Primæval piles, that rose in massive pride,
Ere Western Art her first faint efforts tried !
Ye Brachmans old, whom purer æras bore,
Ere Western Science lisped her infant lore !
How will your wonders flush the Athenian sage ?
How ray with glory my historic page ?"

In a letter to Hannah More, Horace Walpole says : " The poetry is most admirable ; the similes beautiful, fine, and sometimes sublime ; the author is a great
poet, and could raise the passions, and possesses all the requisites of the art ". In
another lively epistle to the Misses Berry (28th April, 1789), he says : " I send
you the most delicious poem upon earth. I can read this Second Part over and
over again for ever ; for though it is so excellent, it is impossible to remember
anything so disjointed, except you consider it as a collection of short enchanting
poems. 'The Triumph of Flora,' beginning at the fifty-ninth line, is most
beautifully and enchantingly imagined, and the twelve verses that by miracle
describe and comprehend the creation of the universe out of chaos, are, in my
opinion, the most sublime passage in any author, or in any of the few languages
with which I am acquainted."—ED.]

[Darwin was acquainted with Rousseau. He was a man of great bodily and
intellectual vigour, irascible and imperious, a strong advocate of temperance, and
for many years an almost total abstainer. His professional fame was such that
George III. said he would take him as his physician if he would come to London.
He formed a botanical garden at Lichfield, about which Miss Seward wrote
some verses which suggested his *Botanic Garden*. The *Loves of the Plants* had a
singular success, and was praised in a joint poem by Cowper and Hayley.
It was translated into French, Portuguese, and Italian. Darwin himself is said
by Edgeworth to have admired the parody (*Monthly Magazine*, June and Sept.,
1802, p. 115). Coleridge (*Biographia Literaria*, 1817, p. 19) speaks of the impression
which it made even upon good judges.

In the *Anti-Jacobin Review*, vol. i. (1799), pp. 718-721, appear some Latin verses
[by Ben. Frere] which are thus introduced : " Among the copies of verses which
are annually produced as a public exercise called TRIPOS, at Cambridge, we
have selected the following as a beautiful composition. The subject is Dr.
BEDDOES'S *Factitious Air applied to the Case of Consumptions*."—ED.]

# FOREIGN INTELLIGENCE EXTRAORDINARY.*

The Priority of Intelligence which has ever distinguished OUR PAPER will, We trust, receive additional lustre from the extraordinary News which We now lay before the Public. We received it by a Neutral Ship, which arrived in the River last night; and feel ourselves much indebted to the attention of our Correspondent, a Currant Merchant at *Zante*, for its early communication. Without arrogating to ourselves that merit which is (perhaps) justly our due, We think ourselves justified in asserting that it is not only the earliest, but, if We are not much mistaken, the only account which will appear in the Prints of this Day respecting the Successes of BUONAPARTÉ.

---

## COPY OF A LETTER FROM GENERAL BUONAPARTÉ TO THE COMMANDANT AT ZANTÉ.

"*Athens*, 18 *Prairial.*

"CITIZEN GENERAL,

"Victory still attends us. I inclose you a Copy of a Letter which I have this day written to the Directory. Health and Fraternity.

"BUONAPARTÉ."

"*Head-Quarters*, Salamis, 18 *Prairial.*

"Citizens directors,

"The brave Soldiers, who conferred Liberty on *Rome*, have continued to deserve well of their Country. *Greece* has joyfully received her Deliverers. The Tree of Liberty is planted on the *Piræus*. Thirty thousand Janizaries, the Slaves of Despotism, had taken possession of the Isthmus of *Corinth*. Two Demi-brigades opened us a passage. After ten days' fighting, we have driven the *Turks* from the *Morea*. The *Peloponnesus* is now free. Every step in my power has been taken to revive the antient spirit of *Sparta*. The Inhabitants of that celebrated City, seeing *black broth* of my Troops, and the scarcity of specie to which we have been long accustomed, will, I doubt not, soon acquire the frugal virtues of their Ancestors. As a proper measure of precaution, I have removed all PITT's gold from the Country.

"Off this Island we encountered the Fleet of the SULTAN. The Mahometan Crescent soon fled before the three-coloured flag. Nine Sail of the Line are the fruits of this Victory. The CAPTAIN PACHA's Ship, a second rate, struck to a National Corvette. My Aide-de-Camp will present you with the model of a *Trireme*, which was found among the Archives of *Athens*. Vessels of this description draw so little water, that our Naval Architects may perhaps think them more eligible than Rafts, for the conveyance of the *Army of England*. Liberty will be sufficiently avenged, if the ruins of a Grecian City furnish us with the means of transporting the Conquerors of *Rome* to *Britain*.

"On landing at this Island, I participated in a Scene highly interesting to Humanity. A poor Fisherman, of the family of THEMISTOCLES, attended by his Wife, a descendant of the virtuous PHRYNE, fell at my feet. I received him

---

[* This piece has not hitherto formed a portion of the editions of *The Poetry*. —ED.]

with the Fraternal embrace, and promised him the protection of the Republic. He invited me to supper at his Hut, and in gratitude to his Deliverer presented me with a memorable *Oyster Shell*, inscribed with the Name of his illustrious Ancestor. As this curious piece of antiquity may be of service to some of the DIRECTORY, I have inclosed it in my Dispatches,together with a Marble Tablet, containing the proper form for pronouncing the Sentence of *Ostracism* on *Royalist Athenians*.

"KLÉBER, whom I had ordered to *Constantinople*, informs me that the Capital of Turkey has proved an easy conquest. *Santa-Sophia* has been converted into a Temple of Reason ; the *Seraglio* has been purified by *Theo-Philanthropists*, and the liberated Circassians are learning from our Sailors the lessons of Equality and Fraternity. A Detachment has been sent to Troy, for the purpose of organizing the Department of *Mount Ida*. The Tomb of ACHILLES has been repaired, and the Bust of BRISEIS (which formed part of the Pedestal) restored to its original state, at the expense of the Female Citizen BUONAPARTÉ.

"The Division of the Fleet destined for Egypt has anchored in the Port of *Alexandria*. BERTHIER, who commands this Expedition, informs me that this Port will soon be restored to its ancient pre-eminence ; and that its celebrated *Pharos* will soon be fit to receive the *Reverbères* which have been sent from the *Rue St. Honoré*.

"BARAGUAY D'HILLIERS, with the Left Wing of the *Army of Egypt*, has fixed his Head-quarters at *Jerusalem*. He is charged to restore the Jews to their ancient Rights. Citizens Jacob Jacobs, Simon Levi, and Benjamin Solomons, of Amsterdam, have been provisionally appointed Directors. The Palace of *Pontius Pilate* is re-building for their residence. All the vestiges of Superstition in *Palestine* have been carefully destroyed.

"I beg you will ratify a grant which I have made of the *Temple of the Sun* at *Palmyra* to a Society of *Illuminati* from *Bavaria*. They may be of service in extending our future conquests.

"I have received very satisfactory accounts from DESAIX, who had been sent by BERTHIER with a Demi-brigade into the interior of *Africa*. That fine Country has been too long neglected by Europeans. In manners and civilization it much resembles France, and will soon emulate our virtues. Already does the Torrid Zone glow with the ardour of Freedom. Already has the Altar of Liberty been reared in the *Caffrarian* and *Equinoctial Republics*. Their regenerated inhabitants have sworn eternal amity to us at a Civic Feast, to which a detachment of our Army was invited. This memorable day would have terminated with the utmost harmony, if the CAFFRARIAN COUNCIL of ANCIENTS had not devoured the greatest part of General Desaix's État-Major for their supper. I hope our Ambassador will be instructed to require that Civic Feasts of this nature be omitted for the future. The Directory of the *Equinoctial Republic* regret that the scarcity of British Cloth in Africa, and the great heat of the climate, prevent them from adopting our *costume*.

"We hope soon to liberate the *Hottentots*, and to drive the perfidious *English* from the extremities of Africa and of Europe. *Asia*, too, will soon be free. The three-coloured flag floats on the summit of Caucasus ; the *Tigrine Republic* is established ; the *Cis* and *Trans-Euphratean Conventions* are assembled ; and soon shall *Arabia*, under the mild influence of *French Principles*, resume her ancient appellation, and be again denominated 'the HAPPY'.

"In the course of the next Decade I shall sail to the Canal which is now cutting across the *Isthmus* of *Suez*. The Polytechnic School and Corps of Geographical Engineers are employed in devising means for conveying my heavy artillery across the great Desert. Soon shall *India* hail us as her Deliverers, and those proud Islanders, the *Tyrants of Calcutta*, fall before the *Heroes of Arcola*.

"The Members of the National Institute who accompanied the Squadron to Egypt, have made a large collection of Antiquities for the use of the Republic. Among the scattered remains of the Alexandrine Library, they have found a curious Treatise, in Arabic, respecting *Camels*, from which it appears that Human Beings, by proper treatment, may, like those useful animals, be trained to support thirst and hunger without complaining. Many reams of papyrus have been collected, as it is thought that during the present scarcity of linen and old rags in France, it may answer all the purposes of paper. CLEOPATRA'S celebrated Obelisk has been shipped on board the Admiral's Ship *L'Orient*, cidevant *Sans Culottes*: Another man-of-war has been freighted with the *Sphinx*, which our Engineers removed from *Grand Cairo*, and which, I trust, will be thought a proper ornament for the Hall of Audience of the Directory.—The cage in which BAJAZET was confined, has been long preserved at *Bassora*; it will be transmitted to Paris as a proper model for a new *Cayenne Diligence*.—I beg leave to present to the Director MERLIN, a very curious book, bound in Morocco leather, from Algiers. It is finely illuminated with gold; and contains lists of the various fees usually received by Deys and their Ministers from Foreign Ambassadors. A broken Column will be sent from *Carthage*. It records the downfall of that Commercial City; and is sufficiently large for an Inscription (if the Directory should think proper to place it on the Banks of the *Thames*), to inform posterity that it marks the spot where *London once stood*.

> " Health and Respect,
> "BUONAPARTÉ."

# No. XXXIV.

July 2, 1798.

## ODE TO A JACOBIN.

FROM SUCKLING'S ODE TO A LOVER.

### I.

UNCHRISTIAN JACOBIN whoever,
If, of thy God thou cherish ever
One wavering thought; if e'er HIS word
Has from one crime thy soul deterr'd,—
    Know this,
    Thou think'st amiss;
    And to think true,
Thou must renounce HIM all, and think anew.

### II.

If, startled at the *guillotine*,
Trembling thou touch the dread machine;
If, leading sainted Louis to it,
Thy steps drew back, thy heart did rue it,—
    Know this,
    Thou think'st amiss;
    And to think true,
Must rise 'bove weak remorse, and think anew.

### III.

If, callous, thou dost not mistake,
And murder for mild Mercy's sake;
And think thou followest Pity's call,
When slaughtered thousands round thee fall,—

Know this,
Thou think'st amiss;
And to think true,
Must conquer prejudice, and think anew.

IV.

If, when good men are to be slain,
Thou hear'st them plead, nor plead in vain;
Or, when thou answerest, if it be
With one jot of humanity,—
Know this,
Thou think'st amiss;
And to think true,
Must pardon leave to fools, and think anew.

V.

If, when all kings, priests, nobles hated,
Lie headless, thy revenge is sated,
Nor thirsts to load the reeking block
With heads from thine own murd'rous flock,—
Know this,
Thou think'st amiss;
And to think true,
Thou must go on in blood, and think anew.

VI.

If, thus, by love of executions,
Thou provest thee fit for revolutions;
Yet one achieved, to *that* art true,
Nor wouldst begin to change anew,—
Know this,
Thou think'st amiss;
Deem, to think true,
All constitutions bad, but those bran new.

[The preceding "ODE TO A JACOBIN" is parodied from the following

# ODE TO A LOVER,

BY SIR JOHN SUCKLING.

### I.

Honest lover whosoever,
If in all thy love was ever
One wav'ring thought; if e'er thy flame
Were not still even, still the same,—
    Know this,
    Thou lov'st amiss;
    And to love true,
Thou must begin again, and love anew.

### II.

If, when she appears i' th' room,
Thou dost not quake, and art struck dumb;
And, in striving this to cover,
Dost not speak thy words twice over,—
    Know this,
    Thou lov'st amiss;
    And to love true,
Thou must begin again, and love anew.

### III.

If, fondly, thou dost not mistake,
And all defects for graces take,
Persuad'st thyself that jests are broken,
When she has little or nothing spoken,—
    Know this,
    Thou lov'st amiss;
    And to love true,
Thou must begin again, and love anew.

IV.

If, when thou appear'st to be within,
Thou let'st not men ask and ask again;
And when thou answer'st, if it be
To what was ask'd thee, properly,—
Know this,
Thou lov'st amiss;
And to love true,
Thou must begin again, and love anew.

V.

If, when thy stomach calls to eat,
Thou cut'st not fingers 'stead of meat;
And with much gazing on her face,
Dost not rise hungry from the place,—
Know this,
Thou lov'st amiss;
And to love true,
Thou must begin again, and love anew.

VI.

If, by this thou dost discover
That thou art no perfect lover;
And desiring to love true,
Thou dost begin to love anew,—
Know this,
Thou lov'st amiss;
And to love true,
Thou must begin again, and love anew.—ED.]

# No. XXXV.

July 9, 1798.

THE following popular song is said to be in great vogue among the loyal troops in the North of Ireland. The air and the turn of the composition are highly original. It is attributed (as our correspondent informs us) to a fifer in the Drumballyroney Volunteers.

## BALLYNAHINCH.*

A NEW SONG.

I.

A CERTAIN great Statesman † whom all of us know,
In a certain assembly, no long while ago,

---

[* This spirited song refers to LORD MOIRA'S motion in the Irish House of Commons, 19th of February, 1798, for an address to the Lord Lieutenant, complaining of the excesses committed by the government authorities, civil and military, and recommending that conciliatory measures should be devised. He took occasion to praise the loyalty of his own tenants at BALLYNAHINCH ; but, unfortunately for him, shortly after, an insurrection broke out at this very place, and a large number of pikes were found secreted by the peasantry in his own woods. On June 12, General Nugent attacked the rebels, 5000 strong, commanded by Munro, near Ballynahinch, and routed them with great slaughter. This victory quelled the rebellion in the north.—ED.]

[† The EARL OF MOIRA was a gallant soldier, an eloquent orator, and a sagacious as well as honest statesman. Having early in life achieved much reputation for skill and courage during the American War, and afterwards in Flanders, he subsequently turned his attention to politics, particularly those of Ireland, his native country, which drew on him repeated attacks from the Ministerial press. In 1812 he was appointed Governor-General of India, and created MARQUIS OF HASTINGS. He was the patron of THOMAS MOORE on his arrival in London. He died in 1825.—ED.]

Declared from this maxim he never would flinch,
" That no town was so *loyal* as Ballynahinch ".

## II.

The great statesman, it seems, had perused all their
faces,
And been mightily struck with their loyal grimaces;
While each townsman had sung, like a throstle or finch,
" We are all of us *loyal* at Ballynahinch ".

## III.

The great statesman return'd to his speeches and
readings ;
And the Ballynahinchers resumed their proceedings;
They had most of them sworn, " *We'll be true to the
Frinch*," *
So *loyal* a town was this Ballynahinch !

## IV.

Determined their landlord's fine words to make good,
They hid pikes in his haggard, cut staves in his
wood ;
And attack'd the king's troops—the assertion to clinch,
That no town is so *loyal* as Ballynahinch.

## V.

O ! had we but trusted the *rebels'* professions,
Met their cannon with smiles, and their pikes with con-
cessions ;
Tho' they still took an *ell* when we gave them an
*inch*,
They would all have been *loyal*—like Ballynahinch.

---

* *Hibernice pro* French.

Viri Eruditi,

Si vobis hocce poematium, de navali laude Britanniæ, paucis annis ante conscriptum, nuperrimè recensitum atque emendatum, forté arrideat, quærite in proximis vestris tabulis locum quendam secretum atque securum, ubi repositum suâ sorte perfruatur. Quod si in me hanc gratiam contuleritis, devinctus vobis ero et astrictus beneficio.

Etonensis.

## DE NAVALI LAUDE BRITANNIÆ.

Successu si freta brevi, fatisque secundis,
Europæ sub pace vetet requiescere gentes,
Inque dies ruat ulteriús furialibus armis
Gallia, tota instans à sedibus eruere imis
Fundamenta, quibus cultæ Commercia vitæ
Firmant se subnixa;—tuisne, Britannia, regnis
Ecquid ab hoste times; dum te tua saxa tuentur,
Dum pelagus te vorticibus spumantibus ambit?

Tu medio stabilita mari, atque ingentibus undis
Cincta sedes; nec tu angusto, Vulcania tanquam
Trinacris, interclusa sinu; nec faucibus arctis
Septa freti brevis, impositisque coercita claustris.
Liberiora Tibi spatia, et porrecta sine ullo
Limite regna patent (quanto neque maxima quondam
Carthago, aut Phœnissa Tyros, ditissima tellus
Floruit imperio) confiniaque ultima mundi.

Ergone formidabis adhuc, ne se inferat olim,
Et campis impuné tuis superingruat hostis?
Usque adeone parúm est, quod laté litora cernas
Præruptisturrita jugis, protentaque longo

17

Circuitu, et tutos passim præbentia portus?
Præsertim australes ad aquas, Damnoniaque arva,
Aut ubi Vecta viret, secessusque insula fidos
Efficit objectu laterum ; saxosave Dubris
Velivolum laté pelagus, camposque liquentes
Aeria, adversasque aspectat desuper oras.

Nec levibus sanè auguriis, aut omine nullo
Auguror hinc fore perpetuum per secula nomen :
Dum nautis tam firma tuis, tam prodiga vitæ
Pectora, inexpletâ succensa cupidine famæ,
Nec turpi flectenda metu ; dum maxima quercus,
Majestate excelsa suâ, atque ingentibus umbris,
Erigitur, vasto nodosa atque aspera trunco ;
Silvarum regina. Hæc formidabilis olim
Noctem inter mediam nimborum, hyemesque sonantes,
Ardua se attollit super æquora ; quam neque fluctûs
Spumosi attenuat furor, aut violentia venti
Frangere, et in medio potis est disrumpere ponto.

Viribus his innixa, saloque accincta frementi,
Tu media inter bella sedes ; ignara malorum,
Quæ tolerant obsessæ urbes, cúm jam hostica clausas
Fulminat ad portas acies, vallataque circúm
Castra locat, sævisque aditus circumsidet armis.

Talia sunt tibi perpetuæ fundamina famæ,
Ante alias diis cara, BRITANNIA ! Prælia cerno
Inclyta, perpetuos testes quid maxima victrix,
Quid possis preclara tuo, maris arbitra, ponto.

Hæc inter, sanctas æternâ laude calendas
Servandas recolo, quibus illa, immane minata
Gentibus excidium, totum grassata per orbem
Ausaque jam imperiis intactum amplectier æquor,

Illa odiis lymphata, et libertate recenti
GALLIA, disjectam ferali funere classem
Indoluit devicta, et non reparabile vulnus.
Tempore quo instructas vidit longo ordine puppes
Rostratâ certare acie, et concurrere ad arma,
Ætheraque impulsu tremere, Uxantisque per undas
Lugubre lumen agi, atque rubentem fulgere fumum.

Cerno triumphatas acies, quo tempore IBERÛM
Disjectos fastus, lacerisque aplustria velis
Horruit Oceanus :—quali formidine Gades
Intremere, ut fractâ classem se mole moventem
Hospitium petere, et portus videre relictos !

Quid referam, nobis quæ nuper adorea risit,
Te rursús superante, die quo decolor ibat
Sanguine BELGARUM Rhenus, fluctusque minores
Volvebat, frustra indignans polluta cruore
Ostia, et Angliaco tremefactas fulmine rupes.

Cerno pias ædes procúl, et regalia quondam
Atria, cæruleis quæ preterlabitur undis
Velivolus Thamesis ; materno ubi denique nautas
Excipis amplexu, virtus quoscumque virilis
Per pelagi impulerit discrimina, quælibet ausos
Pro Patriâ. Híc rude donantur, dulcique senescunt
Hospitio emeriti, placidâque quiete potiti
Vulnera præteritos jactant testantia casus.

Macte ideó decus Oceani ! macte omne per ævum
Victrix, æquoreo stabilita BRITANNIA regno !
Litoribusque tuis ne propugnacula tantúm
Præsidio fore, nec saxi munimina credas,
Nec tantúm quæ mille acies in utrumque parantur,
Aut patriam tutari, aut non superesse cadenti ;

Invictæ quantúm metuenda tonitrua CLASSIS,
Angliacæ CLASSIS ;—quæ majestate verendâ
Ultrix, inconcussa, diú dominabitur orbi,
Hostibus invidiosa tuis, et sæpe triumphis
Nobilitata novis, pelagi Regina subacti.

---

TRANSLATION OF THE PRECEDING POEM.*

By the late A. F. Westmacott, Esq.

MEN OF LEARNING,

    If by chance the following little poem, on the naval glory
of Britain, written a few years since, and very lately revised
and corrected, please you, look in your nearest tablets for some
private and secure place, where it may be placed to enjoy its
good fortune. Should you confer on me this favour, I shall be
bound to you by the obligation of your kindness.

ETONIAN.

ON THE NAVAL GLORY OF BRITAIN.

If buoy'd by short success and fav'ring chance,
Wide Europe's peace-destroyer, restless France,
Each day still onward rush with fresh alarms,
And threaten ruin with her furious arms;
Ruin to all whereon is based the throne
That life's sweet charities have made their own;
Fearest thou, Britain, for thy rock-girt realm,
With seas that foam around and whirlpools to o'erwhelm?

Still in the midst of ocean firmly placed,
Circled by mighty waves thy seat is based!
Not by a strait enclosed, as that fair soil
Where Fabled Vulcan plies his fiery toil;
Within no narrow bay thy waters roll,
No yawning gulf, no barrier rocks control.
Wider thy space, thy realm no limit knows,
Not Tyre so rich, not Tyrian Carthage rose.

---

[* A quite literal translation of this poem would be out of the question. The
fact is, the sentiment is superior to the execution. CANNING could write much
better if he chose. He might wish to fabricate an ultra-patriotic schoolboy,
and so wrote like one ; but it is certain that as a schoolboy he has written far
better things. Either he wrote in a hurry, or cooked up a school exercise ; the
introduction looks like it, and the Latin Prose is as prosy as the verse is common-place.—A. F. W.]

Wilt thou yet fear, lest here the haughty foe,
Thy fields o'er-run, and still unpunished go!
Is it then nought to view th' extended strand
O'er which stern crags like beetling turrets stand,
And countless ports in safe embrace expand?
Look to thy southern waves, to Devon's fields,
Or where green Vectis * trusty harbour yields,
Spreading her friendly arms; or Dover's height
Looks on the sea with widespread canvas white,
And, perched on high, the liquid plain surveys,
And adverse cliffs that bound the wat'ry ways.

Not by vague augury, nor omen slight,
I view thy name through endless ages bright;
While thy firm crews still prodigal of life
Insatiate burn for fame and dare the strife.
No coward fear they know, while stands erect
The mighty oak with boughs umbrageous decked;
Majestic, high, with knotted trunk, the Queen
Of woods! Hereafter, o'er the waters seen
'Mid the dim midnight of the sounding storm
Aloft 'twill rear the terrors of its form;
In vain the roaring surges round it break,
In vain the winds their uncurbed vengeance wreak,
Throned on such pow'rs, surrounded by the sea,
The circling waves have scarce one fear for thee.
Thou know'st not ills that towns besieged await,
When hostile columns thunder at the gate;
Pitch their dread camp with fatal ramparts round,
And with fierce arms enclose the leaguered ground.

Such is to thee the base of lasting fame,
To Heav'n Britannia still the dearest name!
Gladly I view the glories of the fight,
Perpetual witnesses of deathless might,
To show, bright conqueress, nations yet to be,
What dared, what did the mistress of the sea.

'Mid these the day with praise eternal blest
Earns memory's tribute most, when, direful pest,
Denouncing ruin to the world, while she
Dared grasp the sceptre of the unconquer'd sea,
Wild with new license, mad with hatred's heat
France, grieved and humbled, viewed her ruined fleet!

---

* The Isle of Wight.

Saw how all hopes one fatal wound could mar
When well-manned squadrons armed their prows for war!
When the sky trembled, and o'er Ushant's tide
Red glared the smoke and sickly light supplied.

I see the conquered lines, what time proud Spain
With tattered sailcloths thickly strewed the main;
How Cadiz quailed when back the shattered fleet
Sought, in the port it left, a safe retreat.
Why should I tell what smile of Vict'ry beamed,
When Rhine's fair wave with Belgic slaughter gleamed;
When humbled waters tow'rds the sea it sped,
Mad that its mouths with native blood were red,
While England's thunders rolled above its rocky bed?

I see afar the domes that crown the tide,
Where Thames uncounted sails in triumph glide:
Here, the brave souls whom manly courage drove
Through the deep's perils in a holy love
Of country, find in thy maternal breast
Their toil rewarded and their daring blest!
Dismissed at length from duty nobly done
They wane in quiet 'neath the noontide sun,
Recal the dangers of their byegone wars,
And boast appealing to their manhood's scars.

On in thy race of glory, conqueress, on!
For every age thy sea-girt realm is won!
Think not the fortress which thy shores uprear,
Nor thy rock bulwarks shall inspire such fear,
Nor the brave thousands who obey thy call,
With thee to rise, or not survive thy fall,
As the dread thunders of that untamed host:
Thy fleet, Britannia, is thy proudest boast;
Awful, majestic, firm; its flag unfurl'd
Shall long wave lordly o'er the conquered world;
Hateful to foes for triumphs yet to be,
The rightful Sovereign of the subject sea.—ED.]

# No. XXXVI.*

MONDAY, July 9, 1798.

*We shall miss thee ;*
*But yet thou shalt have freedom—*
*—So ! to the Elements*
*Be free, and fare thou well.*

—THE TEMPEST.

WE have now completed our Engagement with the Public. The ANTI-JACOBIN has been conducted to the close of the Session in strict conformity with the Principles upon which it was first undertaken.

Its reception with the Public has been highly favourable :—it certainly has been out of proportion to any merit which has appeared in the execution of the Work. This is not said in the mere cant of Authorship. We are sensible that much of our success has been owing to the improved state of the Public mind ;—an improvement existing from other causes, and to which, if We have in any degree contributed, it has in return operated to our advantage, by a re-action more than equal to any impression which our exertions could have produced. There is, however, one species of merit to which We lay claim without hesitation :—We mean that of the Spirit and Principles upon which We have acted. That Spirit, We trust We shall leave behind us. The SPELL of *Jacobin invulnerability* is now broken.†

---

[* This valedictory Address, and the portion entitled FOREIGN INTELLIGENCE which follows the Poem, have never hitherto formed a part of editions of the Poetry.—ED.]

† We see with some pleasure, that what we anticipated is beginning to take effect. A NEW MAGAZINE and REVIEW is

We know from better authority than that of CAMILLE JORDAN, that one of our Daily Papers was, *early* in the French Revolution, purchased by France, and devoted to the dissemination of tenets, which, at the period to which We allude, seemed necessary to the success of the Ruling Party.

For some time matters went on swimmingly. The Editors of the favoured Prints divided their time and their attention between *London* and *Paris ;* and the superiority of the governing Party in France, over its Opponents, was as duly, and as strenuously maintained in the English Papers, as in the " *Journal du Père de Chêne,*" * " *Journal par L'Ami du Peuple,*" † or any other Journal that issued from the Presses of the Jacobin Society.

As the principles of the Revolution, however, acquired consistency in France, the struggle between the Governing Party and its Opponents became an object of less moment, and the Jacobins had leisure, as they long had had inclination, to turn their views to this Country.

A State, enjoying under a Government which they had proscribed as utterly incapable of producing either, as much freedom and happiness as comport with the nature of Man, was too bitter a satire on the decision of these new SOLONS, to be regarded with patience ; and the pens which had been so industriously employed in celebrating the plunderers and perturbators of France, were now

---

already advertised, under the same Name which We had adopted, and professedly on the same Principles. We have no knowledge of the undertaking, but from report, which speaks favourably of it ; but We heartily wish this, and every work of a similar kind, a full and happy success.

    * Published by HÉBERT.         † Published by MARAT.

engaged in the benevolent design of recommending their principles, and their plans of ameliorating the condition of the human race by Atheism and Plunder, to the serious notice of the People of *Great Britain*.

Affairs seemed rapidly hastening to a crisis : *France* saw with delight the numbers seduced by the sophistry of her Writers, and by the alluring prospects of proscription and plunder ; and her Agents, who snuffed the scent of blood like Vultures, already anticipated the Revolution which they now believed inevitable ; when the Ministry, who had viewed the progress of the evil with an anxious but unterrified eye, roused themselves into unexampled energy, and called on the Nation to rally round the Constitution which they had received from their Forefathers.

The call was gloriously answered ;—Thousands and tens of thousands sprung forth in its defence ; and the barbarous hordes which so lately threatened its destruction, overawed by their numbers, shrunk from the contest without a struggle, and vanished from the field.

But the nature of a Jacobin is restless. His hatred of all subordination is unbounded, and his thirst of plunder and blood urgent and insatiable. In arms he found himself infinitely too weak to obtain his purpose ; he must, therefore, have recourse again to artifice ; and by fallacies and lies, endeavoured to subvert and betray the judgment of those he could not openly hope to subdue.

For this purpose, the Press was engaged, and almost monopolized in all its branches : Reviews, Registers, Monthly Magazines, and Morning and Evening Prints, sprung forth in abundance.

Of these last (the only Publications with which We have any immediate concern), it is not too much to say, that they have laboured in the cause of infamy, with a perseverance which no sense of shame could repress, and no dread of punishment overcome. The objects committed to their charge were multifarious. They were to revile all Religions, but particularly the Christian, whose DIVINE FOUNDER was to be blasphemously compared to *Bacchus*, and represented as equally ideal, or, if real, more bestial and besotted! They were to magnify the power of *France* on all occasions; to deny her murders; to palliate her robberies; to suppress all mention of her miseries, and to hold her forth to the unenlightened Englishman as the mirror of justice, and truth, and generosity, and meekness, and humanity, and modera-tion, and tender forbearance :—and, on the other hand, they were to depreciate the spirit, and the courage, and the resources of *England:* they were to impede, if possible, and if not, to ridicule and revile, every measure which the honour, the prosperity, or the safety of the Country might imperiously require ; they were to repre-sent the Government as insidiously aiming to enslave the Nation, by every attempt to maintain its Independence ; and the majority of both Houses, the great body of Pro-prietors, as anxious to scatter and confound that wealth, which *their* Patrons alone, the respectable sweepings of *Craven-House*, and the *Crown* and *Anchor* Tavern, were solicitous to augment and preserve.

These, our readers will allow, were no common objects, and if they have looked into the *Morning Chronicle, Morn-ing Post*, and *Courier* Journals to which our attention has been chiefly directed, they must have seen that their attainment was sought by no common means ; by an *invariable* course of Falsehood and Misrepresentation—

such, at least, was our idea on the first perusal of these Papers, an idea which every succeeding one served to strengthen and confirm.

To detect and expose this Falsehood, and to correct this Misrepresentation, became at length an object of indispensable necessity : a variety of applications of the most malignant nature had obtained currency and credit, from the unblushing impudence with which they were first obtruded on the Public by the Agents of Sedition, and the apathy with which they were suffered to pass uncontradicted by those who despised them for their atrocity, or ridiculed them for their folly :—these were unfortunately operating on the less enlightened part of the Nation ; and it was from a full conviction of the pernicious effects they were calculated to produce, that we finally determined to step forth (after patiently waiting to see whether the business would not be taken up by abler hands), and to oppose such anti-dotes to the evil, as a regard for truth, and a sincere love and veneration for the Constitution under which we have flourished for ages, could supply.

How we have succeeded must be left to the judgment of the Public. If we might venture, indeed, to conjecture from the support which we have experienced, the result would be flattering in an unusual degree. Three com-plete Editions of our Paper (a circumstance, we believe, as yet without a precedent) have been disposed of, and the demand for them still increases.

But the motives of Profit, as will readily, we believe, be granted to us, have little influence on our minds : we contemplate the extensive circulation of our Paper with pleasure, solely from the consideration of the VAST

NUMBERS of our Countrymen whom we have fortified by our animadversions against the profligate attacks of the Agents of Sedition, whether furnished by the *Whig Club*, the *Corresponding Society*, or the *Directory of France*. Calculation was not originally our delight. Nor was it till after we saw the wonderful effects which it produced in the pages of the Jacobinical Arithmeticians that we were tempted to adopt it. Our first Essay, however, was crowned with the most complete success. In our Seventh Number, we gave (still following the laudable example of the Jacobins, who, when a Ship is to be fitted out, or a Regiment raised, for the purpose of defending our Country from an insolent and barbarous foe, nicely calculate how many idle mouths might be fed by the sums required)—We gave, we say, as accurate a statement as we could form, of the number of People that might be supplied with wholesome food for one day, by the SURCHARGE levied on the DUKE OF BEDFORD—a statement which, we are happy to add, placed the matter in so clear a light that we have since had no occasion to repeat it.

Our Readers will not *now* be surprised if we again have recourse to *Calculation* to prove the advantages which (we love to flatter ourselves) have been derived from our Paper. Our Sale (to say nothing of the new Editions which have been disposed of) has regularly amounted to *Two Thousand Five Hundred* a week ; on an average of several Papers, we find the Lies which have been detected to amount to *six*, and the Misrepresentations and Mistakes to *an equal number*. This furnishes a total of *twelve*, which, multiplied by *thirty-five*, the number of the last ANTI-JACOBIN, gives a total of *four hundred and twenty*.

If we now take the number of Subscribers (2500) and multiply them by seven, a number of which every one's family may be reasonably supposed to consist, we shall have a product of 17,500 ; but as many of these have made a practice, which we highly approve, and cannot too earnestly recommend, of lending our Papers to their poorer Neighbours, We must make our addition to the sum which We evidently take too low at 32,500. We have thus an aggregate of 50,000 People, a most respectable minority of the Readers of the whole Kingdom, who have been put effectually on their guard, by our humble though earnest endeavours, against the artifices of the seditious, and the more open attacks of the profligate and abandoned Foes of their Constitution, their Country, and their God.

Further, if we multiply 50,000, the number of Readers, by 420, the exact number of Falsehoods detected—say 500 —for We ought to take in bye-blows, and odd refutations in notes, &c.—the total of Twenty-five Millions will represent the aggregate of Falsehood which We have sent out of the World.

We have more than once repeated that we entered upon this part of our task, not from any vain hope of convincing the Writers themselves. We knew this to be impossible ; the forehead of a *Jacobin*, like the shield of AJAX, is formed of seven bull-hides, and utterly incapable of any impression of shame or remorse—but we are convinced that we have rescued, as we stated above, Fifty Thousand persons from their machinations, and taught them not only a salutary distrust, but a contempt and disbelief, of every laboured article which appears in the Papers of this description.

Nor can We be accused of presumption in this declaration, when it is considered that the conviction on which We so confidently rely is not the effect of a *solitary* impression on our Readers' minds, but of one four hundred and twenty times repeated (this being the fair amount of the number of Lies, &c., We have detected)— an agglomeration of impulse which no prejudice could resist and no pre-conceived partialities weaken or remove.

Here then We rest. We trust We have "done the State some service";—We have driven the Jacobins from many strongholds to which they most tenaciously held.* We have exposed their Principles, detected their Motives, weakened their Authority, and overthrown their Credit. We have shewn them in every instance, ignorant, and designing, and false, and wicked, and turbulent, and anarchical—various in their language, but united in their plans, and steadily pursuing through hatred and contempt, the destruction of their Country.

With this impression on the Minds of our Readers WE TAKE OUR LEAVE of them. Their welfare is in their own hands; if they suffer the Jacobins to regain any of the influence of which We have deprived them, they will compromise their own Safety; but WE shall be blameless—*Liberavimus animas nostras.*—WE HAVE DONE OUR DUTY.

---

* See the Remarks on the Treaties of *Pilnitz* and *Pavia*, &c.; on TATE's Manifesto; on Neutral Navigation; on the Treatment of Prisoners; on the Continuation of the War for a Spice Island, &c., &c., &c.

POETRY.

*New Morality.*

From mental mists to purge a nation's eyes;
To animate the weak, unite the wise;
To trace the deep infection that pervades
The crowded town, and taints the rural shades;
To mark how wide extends the mighty waste
O'er the fair realms of Science, Learning, Taste;
To drive and scatter all the brood of lies,
And chase the varying falsehood as it flies;
The long arrears of ridicule to pay,
To drag reluctant dulness back to day;              10
Much yet remains.—To you these themes belong,
Ye favoured sons of virtue and of song!

Say, is the field too narrow? are the times
Barren of folly, and devoid of crimes?

Yet, venial vices, in a milder age,
Could rouse the warmth of POPE's satiric rage:
The doating miser, and the lavish heir,
The follies and the foibles of the fair,
Sir Job, Sir Balaam, and old Euclio's thrift,
And Sappho's diamonds with her dirty shift,          20
Blunt, Charteris, Hopkins,—meaner subjects fired
The keen-eyed Poet; while the Muse inspired
Her ardent child—entwining, as he sate,
His laurel'd chaplet with the thorns of hate.

But say,—indignant does the Muse retire,
Her shrine deserted, and extinct its fire?
No pious hand to feed the sacred flame,
No raptured soul a poet's charge to claim?

Bethink thee, GIFFORD ; when some future age
Shall trace the promise of thy playful page ;—     30
" * The hand which brushed a swarm of fools away
Should rouse to grasp a more reluctant prey ! "—
Think then, will pleaded indolence excuse
The tame secession of thy languid Muse ?

Ah ! where is now that promise ? why so long
Sleep the keen shafts of satire and of song ?
Oh ! come, with taste and virtue at thy side,
With ardent zeal inflamed, and patriot pride ;
With keen poetic glance direct the blow,
And empty all thy quiver on the foe :—     40
No pause—no rest—till weltering on the ground
The poisonous hydra lies, and pierced with many a
    wound.

Thou too ! — the nameless Bard, † — whose honest
    zeal
For law, for morals, for the public weal,
Pours down impetuous on thy country's foes
The stream of verse, and many-languaged prose ;
Thou too ! though oft thy ill-advised dislike
The guiltless head with random censure strike,—
Though quaint allusions, vague and undefined,
Play faintly round the ear, but mock the mind ;—     50

---

* See the motto prefixed to *The Baviad*, a satirical poem,
by W. Gifford, Esq., unquestionably the best of its kind since
the days of Pope :
          Nunc in ovilia
          Mox in reluctantes dracones.
   † The author of *The Pursuits of Literature*. [Now known
to be T. J. Mathias, editor of various Italian works, and teacher
of Italian to the family of K. George III.—ED.]

Through the mix'd mass yet truth and learning shine,
And manly vigour stamps the nervous line;
And patriot warmth the generous rage inspires,
And wakes and points the desultory fires!

Yet more remain unknown:—for who can tell
What bashful genius, in some rural cell,
As year to year, and day succeeds to day,
In joyless leisure wastes his life away?
In him the flame of early fancy shone;
His genuine worth his old companions own;            60
In childhood and in youth their chief confess'd,
His master's pride, his pattern to the rest.
Now, far aloof retiring from the strife
Of busy talents, and of active life,
As from the loop-holes of retreat he views
Our stage, verse, pamphlets, politics, and news,
He loathes the world,—or, with reflections sad,
Concludes it irrecoverably mad;
Of taste, of learning, morals, all bereft,
No hope, no prospect to redeem it left.              70

Awake! for shame! or e'er thy nobler sense
Sink in th' oblivious pool of indolence!
Must wit be found alone on falsehood's side,
Unknown to truth, to virtue unallied?
Arise! nor scorn thy country's just alarms;
Wield in her cause thy long-neglected arms:
Of lofty satire pour th' indignant strain,
Leagued with her friends, and ardent to maintain
'Gainst Learning's, Virtue's, Truth's, Religion's foes,
A kingdom's safety, and the world's repose.          80
18

If Vice appal thee,—if thou view with awe
Insults that brave, and crimes that 'scape the law;
Yet may the specious bastard brood, which claim
A spurious homage under Virtue's name,
Sprung from that parent of ten thousand crimes,
The *New Philosophy* of modern times,—
Yet, these may rouse thee!—With unsparing hand,
Oh, lash the vile impostures from the land!

First, stern PHILANTHROPY :—not she, who dries
The orphan's tears, and wipes the widow's eyes;    90
Not she, who sainted Charity her guide,
Of British bounty pours the annual tide :—
But *French* PHILANTHROPY ;—whose boundless mind
Glows with the general love of all mankind ;—
PHILANTHROPY,—beneath whose baneful sway
Each patriot passion sinks, and dies away.

Taught in her school to imbibe thy mawkish strain,
CONDORCET, filtered through the dregs of PAINE,
Each pert adept disowns a Briton's part,
And plucks the name of ENGLAND from his heart.    100

What! shall a name, a word, a sound, control
Th' aspiring thought, and cramp th' expansive soul?
Shall one half-peopled Island's rocky round
A love, that glows for all creation, bound?
And social charities contract the plan
Framed for thy freedom, UNIVERSAL MAN!
No—through th' extended globe his feelings run
As broad and general as th' unbounded sun!
No narrow bigot *he ;—his* reason'd view
Thy interests, *England*, ranks with thine, *Peru*!    110

*France* at our doors, *he* sees no danger nigh,
But heaves for *Turkey's* woes th' impartial sigh ;
A steady patriot of the world alone,
The friend of every country—but his own.

Next comes a gentler Virtue.—Ah ! beware
Lest the harsh verse her shrinking softness scare.
Visit her not too roughly ;—the warm sigh
Breathes on her lips ;—the tear-drop gems her eye.
Sweet SENSIBILITY, who dwells enshrined
In the fine foldings of the feeling mind ;                    120
With delicate *Mimosa's* sense endued,
Who shrinks instinctive from a hand too rude ;
Or, like the *Anagallis*, prescient flower,
Shuts her soft petals at the approaching shower.

Sweet child of sickly FANCY !—her of yore
From her loved *France* ROUSSEAU to exile bore ;
And, while 'midst lakes and mountains wild he ran,
Full of himself, and shunn'd the haunts of man,
Taught her o'er each lone vale and Alpine steep
To lisp the story of his wrongs, and weep ;                    130
Taught her to cherish still in either eye,
Of tender tears a plentiful supply,
And pour them in the brooks that babbled by ;
Taught by nice scale to mete her feelings strong,
False by degrees, and exquisitely wrong ;
For the crush'd beetle, *first*,—the widow'd dove,
And all the warbled sorrows of the grove ;
*Next* for poor suff'ring *Guilt ;* and *last* of all,
For parents, friends, a king and country's fall.

Mark her fair votaries, prodigal of grief,                    140
With cureless pangs, and woes that mock relief,

Droop in soft sorrow o'er a faded flower ;
O'er a dead Jack-Ass pour the pearly shower ;
But hear, unmoved, of *Loire's* ensanguined flood,
Choked up with slain ; of *Lyons* drenched in blood ;
Of crimes that blot the age, the world, with shame,
Foul crimes, but sicklied o'er with Freedom's name ;
Altars and thrones subverted ; social life
Trampled to earth,—the husband from the wife,
Parent from child, with ruthless fury torn,—　　150
Of talents, honour, virtue, wit, forlorn,
In friendless exile,—of the wise and good
Staining the daily scaffold with their blood,—
Of savage cruelties, that scare the mind,
The rage of madness with hell's lusts combined,—
Of hearts torn reeking from the mangled breast,—
They hear,—and hope that ALL IS FOR THE BEST.

Fond hope! but JUSTICE sanctifies the prayer—
JUSTICE ! here, Satire, strike ! 'twere sin to spare !
Not she in British Courts that takes her stand,　　160
The dawdling balance dangling in her hand,
Adjusting punishments to fraud and vice,
With scrupulous quirks, and disquisition nice :
But firm, erect, with keen reverted glance,
Th' avenging angel of regenerate *France*,
Who visits ancient sins on modern times,
And punishes the POPE for CÆSAR's crimes.*

---

* The Manes of Vercengetorix are supposed to have been
very much gratified by the invasion of Italy and the plunder of
the Roman territory. The defeat of the Burgundians is to be
revenged on the modern inhabitants of Switzerland. But the
Swiss were a free people, defending their liberties against a
tyrant. Moreover, they happened to be in alliance with
France at the time. No matter ; *Burgundy* is since become

Such is the liberal JUSTICE which presides
In these our days, and modern patriots guides ;—
JUSTICE, whose blood-stain'd book one sole decree,     170
One statute, fills—" the People shall be Free ! "
Free ! By what means ?—by folly, madness, guilt,
By boundless rapines, blood in oceans spilt ;
By confiscation, in whose sweeping toils
The poor man's pittance with the rich man's spoils,
Mix'd in one common mass, are swept away,
To glut the short-lived tyrant of the day ;—
By laws, religion, morals, all o'erthrown :—
Rouse, then, ye sovereign people, claim your own :
The license that enthrals, the truth that blinds,     180
The wealth that starves you, and the power that grinds !
So JUSTICE bids.—'Twas her enlighten'd doom,
LOUIS, thy holy head devoted to the tomb !
'Twas JUSTICE claim'd, in that accursèd hour,
The fatal forfeit of too lenient power.
Mourn for the Man we may ;—but for the King,—
Freedom, oh ! Freedom's such a charming thing !

   "Much may be said on both sides."—Hark ! I hear
A well-known voice that murmurs in my ear,—
The voice of CANDOUR.—Hail ! most solemn sage,     190
Thou drivelling virtue of this moral age,
CANDOUR, which softens party's headlong rage.
CANDOUR,—which spares its foes ;—nor e'er descends
With bigot zeal to combat for its friends.

---

a province of France, and the French have acquired a property
in all the injuries and defeats which the people of that country
may have sustained, together with a title to revenge and retalia-
tion to be exercised in the present or any future centuries, as
may be found most glorious and convenient.

CANDOUR,—which loves in see-saw strain to tell
Of *acting foolishly*, but *meaning well ;*
Too nice to praise by wholesale, or to blame,
Convinced that *all* men's *motives* are the same ;
And finds, with keen discriminating sight,
BLACK's not *so* black ;—nor WHITE *so very* white.        200

" Fox, to be sure, was vehement and wrong :
But then, PITT's words, you'll own, were *rather* strong.
Both must be blamed, both pardon'd ; 'twas just so
With Fox and PITT full forty years ago !
So WALPOLE, PULTENEY ;—factions in all times
Have had their follies, ministers their crimes."

Give me th' avow'd, th' erect, the manly foe,
Bold I can meet—perhaps may turn his blow ;
But of all plagues, good Heav'n, thy wrath can send,
Save, save, oh ! save me from the *Candid Friend !*        210

" BARRAS loves plunder, MERLIN takes a bribe,—
What then ! — shall CANDOUR these good] men[ pro-
  scribe ?
No ! ere we join the loud-accusing throng,
Prove,—not the facts,—but, that *they thought them
  wrong.*

" Why hang O'QUIGLEY?—he, misguided man,
In sober thought his country's weal *might* plan :
And, while his deep-wrought Treason sapp'd the throne,
*Might* act from *taste in morals,* all his own."

Peace to such Reasoners! let them have their way ;
Shut their dull eyes against the blaze of day ;        220
PRIESTLEY's a Saint, and STONE a Patriot still ;
And LA FAYETTE a Hero, if they will.

I love the bold uncompromising mind,
Whose principles are fix'd, whose views defined;
Who scouts and scorns, in canting CANDOUR's spite,
All *taste in morals*, innate sense of right,
And Nature's impulse, all uncheck'd by art,
And feelings fine, that float about the heart :
Content, for good men's guidance, bad men's awe,
On moral truth to rest, and Gospel law.                    230
Who owns, when Traitors feel th' avenging rod,
Just retribution, and the hand of GOD ;
Who hears the groans through *Olmütz'* roofs that ring,
Of him who mock'd, misled, betray'd his King—
Hears unappall'd, though Faction's zealots preach,
Unmov'd, unsoften'd by FITZPATRICK's Speech.*

That Speech on which the melting Commons hung,
"While truths divine came mended from *his* tongue";

---

* The speech of GENERAL FITZPATRICK, on his motion for
an Address of the House of Commons to the Emperor of Germany, to demand the deliverance of M. LA FAYETTE from the
prison of Olmütz, was one of the most dainty pieces of oratory
that ever drew tears from a crowded gallery, and the clerks at
the table. It was really quite moving to hear the General talk
of religion, conjugal fidelity, and "such branches of learning".
There were a few who laughed indeed, but that was thought
hard-hearted, and immoral, and irreligious, and God knows
what. Crying was the *order of the day*. Why will not the
OPPOSITION try these topics again? LA FAYETTE indeed (the
more's the pity) is out. But why not a motion for a general
gaol-delivery of all state prisoners throughout Europe? [This
was FITZPATRICK's master-speech, and extorted the applauses of
PITT himself, who nevertheless resisted its arguments. BURKE
said that LA FAYETTE, "instead of being termed an 'illustrious
exile,' ought always to be considered, as he now was, an outcast
of society; who, having no talents to guide or influence the storm
which he had laboured to raise, fled like a dastard from the blood-
shed and massacre in which he had involved so many thousands
of unoffending persons and families".—ED.]

How loving husband clings to duteous wife,—
How pure Religion soothes the ills of life,— 240
How Popish ladies trust their pious fears
And naughty actions in their chaplains' ears.—
Half novel and half sermon, on it flow'd ;
With pious zeal THE OPPOSITION glow'd ;
And as o'er each the soft infection crept,
Sigh'd as he whin'd, and as he whimper'd, wept ;—
E'en CURWEN * dropt a sentimental tear,
And stout ST. ANDREW yelp'd a softer " Hear ! "

———

Oh ! nurse of crimes and fashions ! which in vain
Our colder servile spirits would attain, 250
How do we ape thee, *France !* but, blundering still,
Disgrace the pattern by our want of skill.
The borrow'd step our awkward gait reveals :
(As clumsy COURTENAY † mars the verse he steals.)
How do we ape thee, *France !*—nor claim alone
Thy arts, thy tastes, thy morals, for our own, 260
But to thy WORTHIES render homage due,
Their ‡ " hair-breadth scapes " with anxious interest
view ;

———

* " Now all the while did not this stony-hearted CUR shed one
tear."— *Merchant of Venice.* [JOHN CURWEN – member for the
city of Carlisle, from 1786 till 1812. He was a skilful agricul-
turist, and his operations may be said to have given a new
character to the business of farming. He died in 1828, aged
73.— ED.]

† See page 72, in the note, for a theft more shameless, and
an application of the thing stolen more stupid, than any of
those recorded of Irish story-tellers by Joe Miller.

‡ See *Récit de mes Périls,* by LOUVET ; *Mémoires d'un Détenu,*
by RIOUFFE, &c. The avidity with which these productions

Statesmen and Heroines whom this age adores,
Though plainer times would call them Rogues and
    Whores.                                      260

   See LOUVET, patriot, pamphleteer, and sage,
Tempering with amorous fire his virtuous rage.
Form'd for all tasks, his various talents see,
The luscious Novel, the severe Decree.
Then mark him welt'ring in his nasty sty,
Bare his lewd transports to the public eye.
Not *his* the love in silent groves that strays,
Quits the rude world, and shuns the vulgar gaze.
In LODOISKA's full possession blest,
One craving void still aches within his breast;   270
Plunged in the filth and fondness of her arms,
Not to himself alone he stints her charms;
Clasp'd in each other's foul embrace they lie,
But know no joy, unless the World stands by.
The fool of vanity, for her alone
He lives, loves, writes, and dies but to be known.

   His widow'd mourner flies to poison's aid,
Eager to join her LOUVET's parted shade
In those bright realms where sainted lovers stray,
But harsh emetics tear that hope away.*       280

---

were read, might, we should hope, be accounted for upon
principles of mere curiosity (as we read the *Newgate Calendar*,
and the history of the *Buccaneers*), not from any interest in
favour of a set of wretches infinitely more detestable than all
the robbers and pirates that ever existed.

   * Every lover of modern French literature, and admirer of
modern French characters, must remember the rout which was
made about LOUVET's death and LODOISKA's poison. The attempt at self-slaughter, and the process of the recovery, the
arsenic and the castor oil, were served up in daily messes from
the French papers, till the public absolutely sickened.

Yet hapless LOUVET ! where thy bones are laid,
The easy nymphs shall consecrate the shade.*
There in the laughing morn of genial spring,
Unwedded pairs shall tender couplets sing ;
Eringoes o'er the hallow'd spot shall bloom,
And flies of Spain buzz softly round the tomb.†

But hold, severer virtue claims the Muse—
ROLAND the just, with ribands in his shoes— ‡
And ROLAND's spouse, who paints with chaste delight
The doubtful conflict of her nuptial night ;—          290
Her virgin charms what fierce attacks assail'd,
And how the rigid Minister § prevail'd.

And ah ! what verse can grace thy stately mien,
Guide of the world, preferment's golden queen,
NECKAR's fair daughter, —STAEL the Epicene !
Bright o'er whose flaming cheek and pumple ‖ nose
The bloom of young desire unceasing glows !
Fain would the Muse—but ah ! she dares no more,
A mournful voice from lone *Guyana's* shore,¶

---

* *Faciles Napeœ.*          † See Anthologia, *passim.*

‡ Such was the strictness of this minister's principles, that he positively refused to go to Court in shoe-buckles. See Dumouriez's *Memoirs.*

§ See MADAME ROLAND'S *Memoirs.*—" *Rigide Ministre,*" *Brissot à ses Commettans.*

‖ The "pumple" nosed attorney of Furnival's Inn.—Congreve's *Way of the World.*" [. . . When you liv'd with honest *Pumple Nose,* the attorney of Furnival's Inn. Act 3, sc. 1.]—ED.

¶ These lines contain the Secret History of QUATREMER'S deportation. He presumed in the Council of Five Hundred to arraign MADAME DE STAEL's conduct, and even to hint a doubt of her sex. He was sent to *Guyana.* The transaction naturally brings to one's mind the dialogue between Falstaff and Hostess Quickly in Shakespeare's Henry IV.

Sad QUATREMER—the bold presumption checks,    300
Forbid to question thy ambiguous sex.

To thee, proud BARRAS bows;—thy charms control
REWBELL's brute rage, and MERLIN's subtle soul ;
Rais'd by thy hands, and fashion'd to thy will,
Thy power, thy guiding influence, governs still,
Where at the blood-stain'd board expert he plies,
The lame artificer of fraud and lies ;
He with the mitred head and cloven heel ;—
Doom'd the coarse edge of REWBELL's jests to feel ; *
To stand the playful buffet, and to hear    310
The frequent ink-stand whizzing past his ear ;
While all the five Directors laugh to see
" The limping priest so deft at his new ministry ".†

Last of th' ANOINTED FIVE behold, and least,
The Directorial LAMA, Sovereign Priest,—
LEPAUX ;—whom atheists worship ;—at whose nod
Bow their meek heads *the Men without a God.*‡

---

*Fal.* Thou art neither fish nor flesh—a man cannot tell where
to have thee.

*Quick.* Thou art an unjust man for saying so—thou or any
man knows where to have me.

\* For instance, in the course of a political discussion REW-
BELL observed to the EX-BISHOP [TALLEYRAND], " *that his understanding was as crooked as his legs* "—" Vil Emigré, tu n'as pas le
sens plus droit que les pieds "—and therewith threw an ink-
stand at him. It whizzed along, as we have been informed,
like the fragment of a rock from the hand of one of Ossian's
heroes ; but the wily apostate shrunk beneath the table, and
the weapon passed over him innocuous, and guiltless of his
blood or brains.

† See Homer's description of Vulcan. First Iliad.
   Inextinguibilis vero exoriebatur risus beatis numinibus
   Ut viderunt Vulcanum per domos *ministrantem.*

‡ *The Men without a God*—one of the new sects. Their religion is intended to consist in the adoration of a Great Book,

Ere long, perhaps, to this astonish'd isle,
Fresh from the shores of subjugated *Nile*,
Shall BUONAPARTE's victor fleet protect          320
The genuine Theo-Philanthropic sect,—
The sect of MARAT, MIRABEAU, VOLTAIRE,—
Led by their Pontiff, good LA RÉVEILLÈRE.
Rejoiced our CLUBS shall greet him, and install
The holy Hunchback in thy dome, *St. Paul!*
While countless votaries, thronging in his train,
Wave their red caps, and hymn this jocund strain:—

" *Couriers* and *Stars*, Sedition's evening host,
Thou *Morning Chronicle* and *Morning Post*,
Whether ye make the Rights of Man your theme,          330
Your country libel, and your God blaspheme,
Or dirt on private worth and virtue throw,
Still, blasphemous or blackguard, praise LEPAUX!

"And ye five other wandering bards, that move
In sweet accord of harmony and love,
COLERIDGE and SOUTHEY, LLOYD, and LAMB & Co.
Tune all your mystic harps to praise LEPAUX!

" PRIESTLEY and WAKEFIELD, humble, holy men,
Give praises to his name with tongue and pen!

" THELWALL, and ye that lecture as ye go,          340
And for your pains get pelted, praise LEPAUX!

" Praise him each Jacobin, or Fool, or Knave,
And your cropp'd heads in sign of worship wave!

in which all the virtuous actions of the society are to be entered
and registered. " In times of civil commotion they are to come
forward to exhort the citizens to unanimity, and to read them a
chapter out of the Great Book. When oppressed or proscribed,
they are to retire to a burying-ground, to wrap themselves up in
their great-coats, and wait the approach of death," &c.

*N<u>o</u> 2.* The Republican Rattle-Snake fascinating the Bedford Squirrel.

*Pub:<u>d</u> Nov<u>r</u> 16<u>th</u> 1795. by H. Humphrey New Bond S<u>t</u>*

The Rattle-Snake is a Creature of the greatest subtilty: when it is desirous of preying upon any Animal which is in a situation above itself it fixes its Eye upon the unsuspecting object, & by the noise of its Rattle fascinates & confounds the unfortunate Victim, till loosing all Sense & discernment, it falls, a prey, into the Mouth of the horrid Monster. *Plinys Nat. Hist<u>r</u> vol 368 —*

" All creeping creatures, venomous and low,
PAINE, WILLIAMS, GODWIN, HOLCROFT, praise LEPAUX !

" —— and —— with —— join'd,*
And every other beast after his kind.

" And thou, *Leviathan !* on ocean's brim
Hugest of living things that sleep and swim ;
Thou, in whose nose, by BURKE's gigantic hand    350
The hook was fixed to drag thee to the land,
With ——, ——, and ——, in thy train,
And —— wallowing in the yeasty main,— †
Still as ye snort, and puff, and spout, and blow,
In puffing, and in spouting, praise LEPAUX !

———

BRITAIN, beware ; nor let th' insidious foe,
Of force despairing, aim a deadlier blow ;
Thy Peace, thy Strength, with devilish wiles assail,
And when her Arms are vain, by Arts prevail.
True, thou art rich, art powerful !—thro' thine Isle    360
industrious skill, contented labour, smile ;
'ar Seas are studded with thy countless sails ;
Vhat wind but wafts them, and what shore but hails !
'rue, thou art brave !—o'er all the busy land
in patriot ranks embattled myriads stand ;

---

* The Reader is at liberty to fill up the blanks according to
his own opinion, and after the chances and changes of the times.
It would be highly unfair to hand down to posterity as followers
of *Leviathan,* the names of men who may, and probably will
soon, grow ashamed of their leader.
    † Though the *yeasty* sea
    Consume and swallow navigation up. *Macbeth.*
[Applied to S. Whitbread, M.P., *the Brewer.*—ED.]

Thy foes behold with impotent amaze
And drop the lifted weapon as they gaze

But what avails to guard each outward part,
If subtlest poison, circling at thy heart,
Spite of thy courage, of thy pow'r, and wealth,    370
Mine the sound fabric of thy vital health ?

So thine own Oak, by some fair streamlet's side,
Waves its broad arms, and spreads its leafy pride,
Tow'rs from the earth, and rearing to the skies
Its conscious strength, the tempest's wrath defies.
Its ample branches shield the fowls of air,
To its cool shade the panting herds repair.
The treacherous current works its noiseless way,
The fibres loosen, and the roots decay;
Prostrate the beauteous ruin lies; and all    380
That shared its shelter, perish in its fall.

O thou ! lamented SAGE ! whose prescient scan
Pierc'd through foul Anarchy's gigantic plan,
Prompt to incredulous hearers to disclose
The guilt of *France*, and Europe's world of woes;—
Thou, on whose name each distant age shall gaze,
The mighty sea-mark of these troubled days !
O large of soul, of genius unconfin'd,
Born to delight, instruct, and mend mankind !
BURKE ! in whose breast a Roman ardour glow'd ;    390
Whose copious tongue with Grecian richness flow'd;
Well hast thou found (if such thy country's doom),
A timely refuge in the sheltering tomb !

As, in far realms, where eastern kings are laid,
In pomp of death, beneath the cypress shade,

The perfum'd lamp with unextinguish'd light
Flames through the vault, and cheers the gloom of
   night :
So, mighty BURKE ! in thy sepulchral urn,
To Fancy's view, the lamp of Truth shall burn.
Thither late times shall turn their reverent eyes,    400
Led by thy light, and by thy wisdom wise.

There *are*, to whom (*their* taste such pleasures cloy)
No light thy wisdom yields, thy wit no joy.
Peace to their heavy heads, and callous hearts,
Peace—such as sloth, as ignorance imparts !
Pleas'd may they live to plan their country's good,
And crop with calm content their flow'ry food !

What though thy venturous spirit loved to urge
The labouring theme to Reason's utmost verge,
Kindling and mounting from th' enraptur'd sight ;    410
Still anxious wonder watch'd thy daring flight !
While vulgar minds, with mean malignant stare,
Gazed up, the triumph of thy fall to share !
Poor triumph ! price of that extorted praise,
Which still to daring Genius Envy pays.

Oh ! for thy playful smile, thy potent frown,
To abash bold Vice, and laugh pert Folly down !
So should the Muse, in Humour's happiest vein,
With verse that flowed in metaphoric strain,
And apt allusions to the rural trade,    420
Tell of *what wood young* JACOBINS *are made ;*
How the skill'd gardener grafts with nicest rule
The *slip* of coxcomb on the *stock* of fool ;

Forth in bright blossom bursts the tender sprig,
A thing to wonder at—* perhaps a *Whig :*
Should tell, how wise each half-fledged pedant prates
Of weightiest matters, grave distinctions states,
That rules of policy, and public good,
In Saxon times were rightly understood ;
That kings are proper, *may be* useful things,            430
But then, some gentlemen object to kings ;
That in all times the minister's to blame ;
That British liberty's an empty name,
Till each fair burgh, numerically free,
Shall choose its members by *the Rule of Three.*

So should the Muse, with verse in thunder clothed,
Proclaim the crimes by God and Nature loathed.
Which—when fell poison revels in the veins—
(That poison fell, which frantic *Gallia* drains
From the crude fruit of Freedom's blasted tree)            440
Blot the fair records of Humanity.

To feebler nations let proud *France* afford
Her damning choice,—the chalice or the sword,
To drink or die ;—O fraud ! O specious lie !
Delusive choice ! for *if* they drink, they die.

---

* *i.e.* Perhaps *a member of the* WHIG CLUB—a society that has presumed to monopolize to itself a title to which it never had any claim, but from the character of those who have now with-drawn themselves from it. "*Perhaps*" signifies that *even* the WHIG CLUB *sometimes* rejects a candidate whose PRINCIPLES (*risum teneatis*) it affects to disapprove. [Referring to the secession of the DUKE OF PORTLAND and others from the Whig Club in consequence of their not approving of all the pro-ceedings of Fox and his more violent adherents. SHERIDAN met with so much opposition to his entrance into the Whig Club, that he succeeded in getting admitted only by stratagem.—ED.]

The Sword we dread not :—of ourselves secure,
Firm were our strength, our peace and freedom sure.
Let all the world confederate all its powers,
" Be they not backed by those that should be ours,"
High on his rock shall BRITAIN'S GENIUS stand, 450
Scatter the crowded hosts, and vindicate the land.

Guard we but our own Hearts : with constant view
To ancient morals, ancient manners true ;
True to the manlier virtues, such as nerv'd
Our fathers' breasts, and this proud Isle preserv'd
For many a rugged age : and scorn the while
Each philosophic atheist's specious guile ;
The soft seductions, the refinements nice,
Of gay Morality, and easy Vice ;
So shall we brave the storm ; our 'stablish'd pow'r
Thy refuge, EUROPE, in some happier hour. 461
But, FRENCH *in heart*, though Victory crown our brow,
Low at our feet though prostrate Nations bow,
Wealth gild our Cities, Commerce crowd our shore,
LONDON MAY SHINE, but ENGLAND is NO MORE !

---

FOREIGN INTELLIGENCE.

IN the last Address which We shall have to make to
the Public, We would willingly review the whole of
what has been advanced by Us under the different Heads
of our Paper, and leave behind us a Summary of our
Opinions upon the state of each subject as We found it,
and as We conceive it to stand at the moment when our
la'ours are concluded.

Upon no point, if We are to speak our sincere opinion,

is the task more easily to be executed, or in a less com-
pass, than in what relates to Foreign Politics.

In other times, the relations of States to each other
have been matter of great study, and difficulty; have
been embarrassed with a diversity of views, and a com-
plication of interests, which it might require much experience to calculate, and much political sagacity to
reconcile.

At present, there is but one relation among all the
States of Europe :—one, at least, there is so paramount,
as to confound and swallow up all inferior considerations.
FRANCE IS BENT ON THE CONQUEST AND RUIN OF THEM
ALL. To repel this Conquest, to ward off this ruin, various
means are tried, according to the power or the prudence
of the different Nations. War, Treaty, Supplication,
Bribery, timid Neutrality, implicit Submission, and,
finally, an Incorporation into the Map of the *Great Republic*, are all at this moment exemplified in the conduct of the Countries which surround us.

Our lot, a lot imposed upon us by necessity, but which
if it were not so imposed upon us, whoever is not blind,
judicially blind to the conduct of *France* towards us, and
every other Country, would claim by choice, is WAR.

The relation in which we may stand to the other States
of Europe, or they to each other, is comparatively of
little moment. They may reciprocate Missions, and
propose Treaties,—the *Ligurian Republic* may make Peace
or War with the *Cisalpine;* the *Cisalpine* with the *Roman;*
—either of them with the KING of SARDINIA, with *Tuscany*,
or with *Naples;* and the greater Powers may mediate, or
embroil the quarrel, may offer their protection, and talk
of their Dignity:—But the question does not lie there.—

*France* has the power and the will to controul, to oppress them altogether; to limit or extend their Boundaries, as she sees good; to approve or annul their Internal Regulations, as well as their stipulations with each other : And while she has that power, whether it be by strength in herself, or by the sufferance of others; whether she may choose to vex and harass them in mass, or detail ; to keep peace between them, or to set them at variance ; to work their revolutions by her own arms, or to dele- gate that sacred office to their neighbours ; or, finally, to insist upon their performing it each for themselves ;—the result to us is the same. The People of Europe are equally enslaved ;—it matters not whether they are manacled separately, or bolted to the links of a long chain which connects and coerces them in a fellowship of misery.

*Mortalia corda*
*Per gentes humilis stravit pavor.*

To Us, the relation of these unhappy Powers, is either that of Friends forced into a Foreign Army to fight against us, or placed, hand-cuffed, on the Deck of a Line of Battle Ship to receive our fire—or it is that of a Captive languishing in a Dungeon against which We are making an attack, and who does not dare to acknow- ledge his Friend, till he can hail him as his Deliverer.

The Contest between *Great Britain* and *France*, then, is not for the existence of the former only, but for the Freedom of the World. To look to partial Interests, to talk of partial Successes, as bearing upon the main object and general issue of the War, is to take a narrow and pitiful view of the most momentous and most tremendous subject that ever was brought under the consideration of mankind.

If *Great Britain*, insensible of what she owes to herself and to the World, flinches (for she *cannot fall*), in the Contest;—she throws away not herself alone, but the peace and happiness of Nations. If she maintain herself stoutly;—to speculate on the mode, the time, the means by which success adequate to the immensity of the object at stake is to be attained, were, indeed, presumptuous;—but We risk, without apprehension of being thought sanguine in our hopes and expectations, or of being contradicted by the event, the sentiment of the greatest Orator of ancient times—" It is not, it cannot be possible, that an Empire founded on injustice, on rapacity, on perfidy, on the contempt and disregard of everything sacred towards God, or among Men;—it is not possible that such an Empire should endure."

# NOTES TO "NEW MORALITY".

## JOSEPH PRIESTLEY, LL.D. (page 278).

"I have read a communication from GEORGE III. to one of his ministers, on the subject of the riots in which PRIESTLEY'S house was burned. HIS MAJESTY says, in his short emphatic way, that the riots must be stopped *immediately*; that no man's house must be left in peril; and then he orders the march of certain troops, &c., to restore peace; and concludes with saying that, as the mischief did occur, it was impossible not to be pleased at its having fallen on PRIESTLEY rather than another, that he might *feel* the wickedness of the doctrines of democracy which he was propagating."—*J. W. Croker (MS.).*—[ED.]

---

## MADAME DE STAEL (page 282).

"MADAME DE STAEL was at Mickleham, in Surrey, in 1793, with Talleyrand, Narbonne, Jaucourt, Guibert (who proposed to her), and others. There was not a little scandal about her relations with Narbonne (see Fanny Burney's Letters). Narbonne's place was supplied by Benjamin Constant, who had a very great influence over her, as in return she had over him. At Coppet, she found consolation in a young officer of Swiss origin, named Rocca, twenty-three years her junior, whom she married privately in 1811. She had married Baron de Stael in 1786, and in 1797 they separated. He died in 1802; and she in 1817."—*Life of Mad. de Stael, by A. Stevens*, 1880.

"On the 28th of January" (says Crabb Robinson in his *Diary*, 1804), "I first waited on MADAME DE STAEL. I was shown into her bedroom, for which, not knowing Parisian customs, I was unprepared. She was sitting, most decorously, in her bed, and writing. She had her night-cap on, and her face was not made up for the day. It was by no means a captivating spectacle, but I had a very cordial reception, and two bright black eyes smiled benignantly on me. After a warm expression of her pleasure at making my acquaintance, she dismissed me till three o'clock. On my return then I found a very different person —— the accomplished Frenchwoman surrounded by admirers, some of whom were themselves distinguished. Among them was the aged WIELAND. There was on this, and, I believe, on almost every other, occasion, but one lady among the guests: in this instance FRAU VON KALB. MADAME DE STAEL did not affect to conceal her preference for the society of men to that of her own sex."

COUNT D'ORSAY related of MADAME DE STAEL, whose character was discussed, that one day, being on a sofa with MADAME DE RÉCAMIER, one who placed himself between them exclaimed: "Me voilà entre la beauté et l'esprit!" She replied: "That is the first time I was ever complimented for beauty!" MADAME DE RÉCAMIER was thought the handsomest woman in Paris, but was by no means famed for *esprit.—Crabb Robinson's Diary.*

"MADAME DE STAEL was a perfect aristocrat, and her sympathies were wholly with the great and prosperous. She saw nothing in England but the luxury, stupidity, and pride of the Tory aristocracy, and the intelligence and magnificence of the Whig aristocracy. The latter talked about truth and liberty and herself, and she supposed it was all as it should be. As to the millions, the people, she never enquired into their situation. She had a horror of the *canaille*, but anything of *sangre azul* had a charm for her. When she was dying she said; 'Let me die in peace; let my last moments be undisturbed'. Yet she ordered the cards of every visitor to be brought to her. Among them was one from the DUC DE RICHELIEU. 'What!' exclaimed she, indignantly; 'what! have you sent away the DUKE? Hurry. Fly after him. Bring him back. Tell him that though I die for all the world, I live for *him*.' "— *Bowring's Autobr. Recollections*, pp. 375-6.

MADAME DE STAEL prepared her *bons-mots* with elaborate care, some being borrowed. . . . She was ugly, and not of an intellectual ugliness. Her features were coarse, and the ordinary expression rather vulgar. She had an ugly mouth, and one or two irregularly prominent teeth, which perhaps gave her countenance an habitual gaiety. Her eye was full, dark, and expressive; and when she declaimed, which was almost whenever she spoke, she looked eloquent, and one forgot that she was plain. On the whole, she was singularly unfeminine; and if, in conversation, one forgot she was ugly, one forgot also that she was a woman.—*J. W. Croker's Note-Books.*—[ED.]

---

THE REV. GILBERT WAKEFIELD (page 284).

"It is well known that the French Revolution turned the brains of many of the noblest youths in England. Indeed when such men as COLERIDGE, WORDSWORTH, SOUTHEY, caught the infection, no wonder that those who partook of their sensibility, but had a very small portion of their intellect, were carried away. Many were ruined by the errors into which they were betrayed; many also lived to smile at the follies of their youth. 'I am no more ashamed of having been a Republican,' said SOUTHEY, 'than I am of having been a child.' The opinions held led to many political prosecutions, and I naturally had much sympathy with the sufferers. I find in my journal, Feb. 21, 1799 (says Crabb Robinson): 'An interesting and memorable day. It was the day on which GILBERT WAKEFIELD was convicted of a seditious libel, and sentenced to two years' imprisonment. This he suffered in Dorchester Gaol, which he left only to die. Originally of the Established Church, he became a Unitarian, and Professor at the Hackney College. By profession he was a scholar. His best known work was an edition of Lucretius. He had written against PORSON'S edition of the *Hecuba* of Euripides.' It is said that PORSON was at a dinner-party at which toasts were going round, and a name, accompanied by an appropriate sentence from Shakespeare, was required from each of the guests in succession. Before PORSON'S turn came, he had disappeared beneath the table, and was supposed to be insensible to what was going on. This, however, was not the case, for when a toast was required of him, he staggered up and gave: 'Gilbert Wakefield—what's *Hecuba* to him, or he to *Hecuba?*' WAKEFIELD was a political fanatic. He had the pale complexion and mild features of a Saint, was a most gentle creature in domestic life, and a very amiable man; but when he took part in any religious or political controversy, his pen was dipped in gall. The occasion of the imprisonment before alluded to was a letter in reply to WATSON, Bishop of Llandaff, who had written a pamphlet exhorting the people to loyalty. WAKEFIELD asserted that the poor, the labouring classes, could lose nothing by French conquest. Referring to the fable of the Ass and the Trumpeter, he said: 'Will the enemy make me carry two panniers?' and declared that, if the French came, they would find him at his post with the illustrious dead."—[ED.]

---

JOHN THELWALL (page 284).

"COLERIDGE and SOUTHEY spoke of THELWALL, calling him merely 'John '. SOUTHEY said: 'He is a good-hearted man; besides we ought never to forget that he was once as near as possible being hanged, as there is some merit in that '."—*Crabb Robinson's Diary.*—[ED.]

JEAN PAUL MARAT (page 284).

The following remarkable account of this scientific monster is given in an
"Historical Account of the Warrington Academy, an institution in Lancashire,"
published in the *Monthly Repository*, by the Rev. W. Turner, of Wakefield.
"After the departure of DR. REINHOLD FORSTER, various unsuccessful
attempts were made to engage a foreigner in the capacity of teacher of the
modern languages—a M. FANTIN LA TOUR, a M. LE MAITRE, *alias* MARA, and a
MR. LEWIS GUERY ; but none of them continued for any length of time. . . .
There is great reason to believe that LE MAITRE, *alias* MARA, was the infamous
MARAT. . . . It is known that he was in England about this time [1774], and
published in London "A Philosophical Essay on the connection between the
Body and the Soul of Man," and, somewhere in the country, had a principal
hand in printing, in quarto, a work of considerable ability, but of a seditious
tendency, entitled—' *The Chains of Slavery: a work wherein the clandestine and
villainous Attempts of Princes to ruin Liberty are pointed out, and the dreadful
Scenes of Despotism disclosed, etc. ; London, sold by J. Almon. . . . T. Payne,
and Richardson and Urquhart, 1774.'* MARA, as his name is spelt in the
Minutes of the Academy, very soon left Warrington, whence he went to Oxford,
robbed the Ashmolean Museum, escaped to Ireland, was apprehended in
Dublin, tried and convicted in Oxford, under the name of LE MAITRE, and
sentenced to the hulks at Woolwich. Here one of his old pupils at Warrington,
a native of Bristol, saw him. He was afterwards a Bookseller in Bristol, and
failed ; was confined in the gaol of that city, but released by the Society there
for the relief of prisoners confined for small sums. One of that society, who
had previously relieved him in Bristol Gaol, afterwards saw him in the National
Assembly in Paris in 1792."

Grave doubts have, however, been thrown upon the accuracy of the above
statement by HENRY A. BRIGHT, B.A., in a paper published in the *Transactions
of the Historic Society of Lancashire and Cheshire*, 8vo, vol. xi., session 1858-9. Yet
it was an establishment that might have attracted such a mind as Marat's.
"At WARRINGTON ACADEMY (says Mr. Bright), were collected some of the
noblest *literati* of their day. Here the free thought of the English Presby-
terians first began to crystallize into the Unitarian theology which they have
since maintained. Here, for a time, was the centre of the liberal politics and
the literary taste of the entire county. . . . The Academy was founded in
1757, and was closed in 1786. It was visited by John Howard, W. Roscoe, T.
Pennant, Currie, the biographer of Burns, &c. The first Tutors appointed
were DR. JOHN TAYLOR of Norwich, Tutor in Divinity, MR. HOLT of Kirkdale,
Tutor in Natural Philosophy, MR. DYER of London, Tutor in Languages and
Polite Literature, whose duties, however, were taken by MR. (afterwards the
REV. DR.) AIKIN, father of the celebrated Physician and Mrs. Barbauld. DR.
PRIESTLEY succeeded DR. AIKIN."

DR. PRIESTLEY, who is addressed by COLERIDGE as "Patriot, and Saint, and
Sage," was succeeded by JOHN REINHOLD FORSTER, a German Scholar and
Naturalist, who accompanied Captain Cook in his second voyage, DR. ENFIELD,
author of *The Speaker*, and the REV. GILBERT WAKEFIELD, were Tutors. Among
the students were MR. SERJEANT HEYWOOD ; ARCHIBALD HAMILTON ROWAN,
the Irish rebel ; the REV. H. MALTHUS ; LORD ENNISMORE ; SIR JAMES
CARNEGIE of Southesk ; MR. HENRY BEAUFOY, etc., all strong Whigs. The
name of neither MARA nor LE MAITRE appears on the Minutes of the Academy.

For the latest contribution to the history of MARAT's sojourn in England we
are indebted to the researches of MR. H. MORSE STEPHENS, of Balliol College,
Oxford, who, in his elaborate and painstaking *History of the French Revolution*
(1886), which includes facts unknown to Carlyle and earlier historians, gives the
following account of that "arch-destroyer"; but, as he calls him, "a much
maligned individual":—

"JEAN PAUL MARAT," says he, "was born at Boudry, near Neufchatel, in
Switzerland, on April 13, 1742. His father, who spelt his name ' MARA,' was a
physician of some ability, and on being exiled from his native island of Sardinia
for abandoning the Roman Catholic religion, had taken up his residence in
Switzerland, and married a Swiss Protestant. JEAN PAUL was the eldest of

three sons; his next brother settled down as a watchmaker at Geneva, and his youngest brother entered the service of the Empress Catherine, and distinguished himself in the Russian army under the title of the Chevalier de Boudry. JEAN PAUL was from his childhood of an intensely sensitive and excitable disposition, and also so quick at his books that he became a good classical scholar, and acquainted with most modern languages. As his chief taste, however, seemed to be for natural science, he was intended to follow his father's profession, and was, at the age of eighteen, sent to study medicine at the University of Bordeaux. He there obtained a thorough knowledge of his profession, but devoted himself particularly to the sciences of optics and electricity. From Bordeaux he went to Paris, where he effected a remarkable cure of a disease of the eyes, which had been abandoned as hopeless both by physicians and quacks, by means of electricity. From Paris he went to Amsterdam, and, finally, to LONDON, where he set up in practice in *Church Street, Soho*, then one of the most fashionable districts in London. He must soon have formed a good practice, for he stopped in London, with occasional visits to Dublin and Edinburgh, for ten years, and only left it to take up an appointment at the French court. While in London he wrote his first book, and in 1772 and 1773, he published the first two volumes of a philosophical and physiological *Essay on Man*. The point he discussed was the old problem of the relation between body and mind, and he treated it in a very interesting manner from the physiological point of view. He held some extraordinary theory about the existence of some fluid in the veins which acted on the mind; which, however, does not impair the interest of his inquiries into the cause of dreams, or diminish the respect felt for his wide reading and extensive knowledge both of ancient and modern philosophical and medical authors. He shows a wide knowledge of Latin and Greek literature, and while writing in good English freely quotes French, German, Italian, and Spanish writers. In one part of his book he declared that it was ridiculous for any one to make psychical researches without having some knowledge of anatomy and physiology, and openly attacked HELVÉTIUS for despising scientific knowledge in his famous *De l'Esprit*. VOLTAIRE naturally took the side of HELVÉTIUS, and did the young author the honour of noticing, and very severely criticising, his book. MARAT himself translated it into French, and published it at Amsterdam in 1775. His next work was of a political character. He had got mixed up with some of the popular societies in England, which were striving to obtain a thorough reform of the representation of the people in the House of Commons, and, in 1774, published a work, which he entitled *The Chains of Slavery*. In this book, which is partly historical and partly political, he begs the electors to take more care in the choice of their representatives. It is written in a very declamatory style, and strikes the note of the responsibility of representatives to their constituents, which is the key-note of all his political ideas. The book is published in quarto, and is printed on fine paper, so that it can hardly have been meant to appeal to the populace, but it, nevertheless, procured him the honorary membership of the popular societies of *Newcastle* and other great northern cities. Subsequently he again returned to his profession, and after publishing a medical tract in 1775, of which no copy is known to exist, he published *An Inquiry into the Nature, Cause, and Cure of a singular Disease of the Eyes*, in 1776. [See *Academy* of September 23, 1882.] In this little pamphlet there is no violent language; it describes the disease and the cases he had cured in perfectly simple language, and shows, at least, that he was no mere quack, but a scientific physician. On June 30, 1775, he had, while on a visit to *Scotland*, received the honorary degree of M.D. from the *University of St. Andrews* for his eminence as a doctor, and had probably received similar compliments from other Universities, because, on June 24, 1777, JEAN PAUL MARAT, ' médecin de plusieurs facultés d'Angleterre,' was appointed, for his good character and high reputation as a doctor, physician to the body-guard of the Comte d'Artois, with a salary of a thousand livres a year and allowances. To take up this court appointment he moved to Paris, and soon acquired a large practice there, and the name of 'physician of the incurables,' from the number of hopeless cases he was successful in treating. He also moved in the best society about the court, and won the affections of the *Marquise de l'Aubespine* for saving her life. For some reason or other, most probably because he had obtained a competent fortune, and desired to satisfy his ambition, he resigned his court appointment in 1783, and devoted himself to science. He had long observed the phenomena of Heat, Light, and Electricity, and in the course of the next five years published the result of his experiments, and presented them to the *Academy of Sciences*. His hard work won him the friendship of BENJAMIN FRANKLIN, but the violence with which he attacked his adversaries, and his audacity in doubting the conclusions of NEWTON, prevented him from obtaining a seat in the Academy of Sciences. When he recognised that this hostility to himself prevented due recognition of his work, he determined to win the approbation of the Academy by concealing his name; and his translation of the *Optics* of NEWTON, which was covered by the name of *M. de Beauzée*, and published in 1788, was at once crowned by the very Academy which had rejected him.

"His political work during these years was confined to a treatise, in imitation of BECCARIA, on the subject of Punishments. The approach of the States-General, however, revived his political enthusiasm, and in the March of 1789, when he believed himself to be dying, he published his *Offrande à la Patrie*, which was followed in quick succession by a supplement and other pamphlets. Of these, distinctly the most able is the *Tableau des Vices de la Constitution Anglaise*, which he presented to the Assembly in September, 1789. In it he points out what he had learnt in the popular societies of England, that the English people was by no means so well governed as it was supposed to be; that the influence of the king and the ministry was overwhelming through the extent of patronage, and that the rich there bought seats in the House of Commons as they bought estates.

"MARAT then felt that he could not express himself frequently enough in pamphlets, and on September 12 appeared the first number of a journal written entirely by himself, called the *Journal du Peuple*, which title was changed to that of *Ami du Peuple*, or *The People's Friend*, with the fourth number.

"To understand the man, it is necessary to get rid of preconceived ideas. Suspicious and irritable, excitable and sensitive to an extreme, he attacked everybody, and attacked them all with unaccustomed violence; but with all this, he was in private life a highly educated gentleman. The extent of his attainments appears from his numerous works, and it must be remembered that he could not for years have been a fashionable physician and held a court appointment without being perfectly polite and well-bred. His faults arose from his irritable and suspicious nature, and years of persecution made him half-insane towards the end of his life; but in September, 1789, he was in perfect possession of his senses, and the very popularity of his journal showed how congenial his gospel of suspicion was to the Parisians."—[ED.]

---

### JEAN PAUL MARAT'S SISTER.

The Right Hon. J. W. Croker, in a letter to John Winter Jones, dated 23rd October, 1854, says that COLIN, who had been Marat's printer or publisher, "introduced him to Marat's sister, who was as like her brother, he said— and as from all pictures and busts I readily believed—as '*deux gouttes d'eau*'. She was very small, very ugly, very sharp, and a great politician. Her ostensible livelihood was making watch-springs, but she told me she was pretty easy in her circumstances, and I either gathered from her, or saw cause to suspect, that she had some secret charitable help."—[ED.]

---

### LARÉVEILLÈRE-LEPAUX (page 283).

LARÉVEILLÈRE-LEPAUX left orders in his will that his *Memoirs* were to be printed and published. His heirs were not proud of the part the DIRECTOR had played, so, after complying with the terms of his will and *printing* the *Memoirs*, they *destroyed the whole issue at once;* and the only copy extant is the one which, in accordance with the law of France, was sent to the *Bibliothèque Nationale* at Paris.

# THE THEOPHILANTHROPISTS.

*

THESE (*Gr.* " Lovers of Gods and Men ") were a sect of *Deists* which appeared in France amid the confusion and disorder of the first Revolution. While the State was indifferent to all forms of Religion, and the Republican Directory was afraid of the Christianity which prevailed in the Church, a felt consciousness of the necessity of some religion led many to adopt a form of worship adapted to Natural Religion.

" This Sect " (says SOUTHEY, in the *Quarterly Review,* vol. xxviii.) " began with more circumstances in their favour than ever occurred to facilitate the establishment of a religion or of a sect. Many persons of considerable influence and reputation engaged in the project with zeal, and it was patronised by LA RÉVEILLÈRE LÉPAUX, one of the Directory. . . . His motives for putting himself at the head of the Theophilanthropists are said to have been twofold; if the scheme succeeded, he intended to become their High Priest ; and he hated Christianity. Through his means the Theophilanthropists obtained a decree from the Government giving them a right of holding their meetings in the Churches, as national buildings, which were open to any religion, but belonged to none.

" Nearly twenty Churches in Paris were taken possession of ; but by occupying so many, they injured themselves. . . . They took up too extended a position, and had neither numbers nor means answerable to the scale upon which they set out. . . . Their *Service* began at noon, and lasted about an hour and a half. It was, they said, a worship for those who had no other, and a moral society for those who had. The *Ritual* consisted of Prayers, Hymns original or selected from the best French Poets, readings from their Manual, and Discourses. The *Hymns* were, in general, judicious, and set to good music, and the *Prayers* well composed ; but had their books been stript of all that they had borrowed from the Gospel, and from the works of Christian writers, they would have been meagre indeed. In one part of the Service there was a short pause, during which the congregation were expected to consider each in silence what his own conduct had been since the last of these meetings. A basket of fruit or flowers, according to the season, was placed upon the altar, as a mark of acknowledgment for the bounties of the Creator ; and over the altar was the inscription, *Nous croyons à l'existence de Dieu, et à l'immortalité de l'âme.* . . . LA RÉVEILLÈRE, in a speech at the Institute, declaiming against Christianity, as being opposed to the liberty of mankind, expressed his wish that a form of religion were adopted, which should have only *a couple of articles.* He wished also for a religion without priests ; and this, it was pleasantly observed, would be like a Directory without a Director.

" This was the *Creed of the Theophilanthropists.* And on each side of it, the following sentences were inscribed in their temples, to take place of the Decalogue :—

" ' Adore God, cherish your fellow-creatures ; render yourselves useful to your country.
Good is whatever tends to preserve man, or to perfectionate him.
Evil is whatever tends to destroy him, or to deteriorate him.
Children, honour your fathers and mothers ; obey them with affection, solace their old age. Fathers and mothers, instruct your children.
Wives, behold in your husbands the heads of your houses. Husbands, love your wives, and render yourselves mutually happy.'

" At *Marriage* the bride and bridegroom were to be coupled with ribands, or garlands of flowers, the ends of which were to be held on each side by the elders of their respective families. The Bride received a ring from her husband, and a medal of union from the head of the family. There was a rite also for infants. . . . When a member *died,* the other members of the Society were invited to place a flower upon the urn, and pray the Creator to receive the deceased into his bosom. The Decades and National Holidays were observed by these Anti-Christians, and they had four Holidays of their own, for Socrates, St. Vincent de Paule, Jean Jacques Rousseau, and Washington,—oddly assorted names ! Two of them, however, stand well together in this kalendar, for the one, who was a Christian, established the Foundling Hospital at Paris ; and the other, who was a sentimentalist, a philosopher, and a Theophilanthropist, sent his own children to it. . . .

"LA RÉVEILLÈRE used to take praise to himself for having, in his Directorial character, humbled the Pope and the great Turk. The Anti-Christian language of the Directory, and its persecution of the Clergy, are imputed to him ; so far his colleagues were willing to go with him ; but his zeal for Deism they regarded as ridiculous. . . . In the way of pecuniary aid, he could obtain little :—*beaucoup d'argent* was what the Directory were accustomed to demand, not to give. . . .

" Their *Service* at Paris was numerously attended while it was a new spectacle, and the subject of conversation ; but more than two-thirds of the persons thus assembled were idlers. But this concourse soon abated ; there was nothing attractive in the ceremonies, nothing to impose upon the imagination or the senses. A propagandist reported from Montreuil that the readings and orations had been heard by an audience *avide de morale*, but he had observed with pain that the *matériel* of the worship was not what it should have been. . . . It was got up at Bourges in better style ; the orator there officiated in a white sash ornamented with blue flowers, before an altar upon which an orange tree was placed : and at the *fête des époux*, the Theophilanthropists carried *two pigeons* in procession, as an emblem of conjugal tenderness, and placed them upon the altar of the country ! "

---

[The literary association of LAMB with COLERIDGE and SOUTHEY [says SIR T. N. TALFOURD, in his life of LAMB,] drew upon him the hostility of the young scorners of *The Anti-Jacobin*, who, luxuriating in boyish pride and aristocratic patronage, tossed the arrows of their wit against all charged with innovation, whether in politics or poetry, and cared little whom they wounded. No one could be more innocent than LAMB of political heresy ; no one more strongly opposed to new theories in morality—which he always regarded with disgust. The very first number of *The Anti-Jacobin Review and Magazine* [this was, however, a new work, by different hands, but imbued with the same spirit as *The Anti-Jacobin*] was adorned by a caricature of GILLRAY'S, in which COLERIDGE and SOUTHEY were introduced with asses' heads, and LLOYD and LAMB as toad and frog. In the number of July, 1798 [of the original *Anti-Jacobin*] appeared the well-known poem of *New Morality*, in which all the prominent objects of the hatred of these champions of religion and order were introduced as offering homage to LEPAUX, a French charlatan,—of whose existence LAMB had never even heard. Not content with thus confounding persons of the most opposite opinions and the most various characters in one common libel, the party returned to the charge in their number for September [of *The Anti-Jacobin Review*], and denounced poets in a parody on the *Ode to the Passions*, under the title of *The Anarchists*. They are reprinted in the present volume.—ED.]

[The cause of Coleridge, Southey, Lloyd, and Lamb, being thus satirized as persons of the same politics, was the conjoint publication of their works. In the spring of 1796, COLERIDGE published vol. i. of his *Juvenile Poems*, including three Sonnets by LAMB ; in May, 1797, there appeared a new edition, with many poems by LLOYD and LAMB. *The Fall of Robespierre*, an historic drama, was published Sept. 22, 1794 : the first act written by COLERIDGE, the second and third by SOUTHEY. It is not difficult to understand why COLERIDGE was so severely attacked by the Government writers. In 1795, at the early age of 23, he delivered, at Bristol, some public lectures, reflecting in warm terms on the measures of PITT. Three of them were published at Bristol at the end of 1795 —the first two together, with the title of *Conciones ad Populum* ; the third as *The Plot Discovered*. The eloquent passage in conclusion of the first of these addresses was written by SOUTHEY. That he was considered by ministers a dangerous character is proved by his having been for some months watched by a Government spy while residing at Stowey, providing for his scanty maintenance by writing verses for *The Morning Post*. It was his fortune also to excite

# 300 POETRY OF

the ire of BUONAPARTE, by his anti-gallican writings in the same paper ; and a benevolent intimation of his danger by Baron von Humboldt and Cardinal Fesch alone prevented his being arrested while in Italy. (See p. 284.) SOUTHEY thus alludes to the attack upon him (by GILLRAY, in his famous caricature), in a letter addressed to C. W. W. WYNN, dated Hereford, August 15, 1798 :—"I have seen myself *Bedfordized*, and it has been a subject of much amusement. HOLCROFT'S likeness is admirably preserved. I know not what poor LAMB has done to be croaking there. What I think the worst part of *The Anti-Jacobin* abuse is the lumping together men of such opposite principles ; this was stupid. We should have all been welcoming the *Director*, not the *Theophilanthrope.* The conductors of *The Anti-Jacobin* will have much to answer for in thus inflaming the animosities of this country. They are labouring to produce the deadly hatred of Irish faction ; perhaps to produce the same end. Such an address as you mention might probably be of great use ; that I could assist you in it is less certain. I do not feel myself at all calculated for anything that requires methodical reasoning ; and though you and I should agree in the main object of the pamphlet, our opinions are at root different. The old systems of government, I think, must fall ; but in this country the immediate danger is on the other hand,—from an unconstitutional and unlimited power. BURLEIGH saw how a Parliament might be employed against the people, and MONTESQUIEU prophesied the fall of English liberty when the Legislature should become corrupt. You will not agree with me in thinking his prophecy fulfilled. Violent men there undoubtedly are among the democrats, as they are always called ; but is there any one among them whom the ministerialists will allow to be moderate ? *The Anti-Jacobin* certainly speaks the sentiments of Government.' —ED.]

---

## WORDSWORTH, COLERIDGE, SOUTHEY (page 284).

["The passionate verdicts given, both *pro* and *con*, in reference to WORDS-WORTH, COLERIDGE, and SOUTHEY, may now be looked back upon with some wonder, but all three had made themselves obnoxious to the charge of renegadism. WORDSWORTH had accepted the office of stamp-distributor from Lord Lonsdale; SOUTHEY, after attempting to suppress his demagogical drama of *Wat Tyler*, became a violent Tory, bringing a hot partisanship into the ranks to which he fled ; and COLERIDGE, a Tom-Paineite in politics and a preaching Unitarian, ended by adopting all the doctrines of orthodoxy."—*Sir John Bowring.* —ED.]

---

## EDMUND BURKE (page 286).

"ADAIR told me a great many things about BURKE, and FOX, and FITZPAT-RICK, and all the eminent men of that time with whom he lived when he was young. He said . . . that FITZPATRICK was the most agreeable of them all, but HARE the most brilliant. BURKE'S conversation was delightful, so luminous and instructive. He was very passionate ; and ADAIR said that the first time he ever saw him he unluckily asked him some question about the wild parts of Ireland, when BURKE broke out : ' You are a fool and a blockhead. There are no wild parts in Ireland.' . . . There was an attempt to bring about a reconciliation between him and FOX, and a meeting for that purpose took place of all the leading men, at Burlington House. BURKE was on the point of yielding when his son suddenly made his appearance unbidden, and, on being told what was going on, he said : ' My father shall be no party to such a compromise,' took BURKE aside, and persuaded him to reject the overtures. That son ADAIR described as the most disagreeable, violent, and wrong-headed of men, but the idol of his father, who used to say that he united all his own talents and acquirements with those of FOX and everybody else, &c."—See *The Greville Memoirs*, i. 136-7.—[ED.]

[The following remarkable passage occurs in a pamphlet written by TOM PAINE, entitled : *Thomas Paine to the People of England, on the Invasion of England : Philadelphia, printed at the Temple of Reason Press, Arch Street,* 1804. " The original plan, formed in the time of the Directory (but now much more extensive) was to build one thousand boats, each sixty feet long, sixteen feet broad, to draw about two feet water, to carry a twenty-four or thirty-six pounder in the head and a field-piece in the stern, to be run out as soon as they touched ground. Each boat was to carry a hundred men, making in the whole one hundred thousand, and to row with twenty or twenty-five oars on a side. Bonaparte was appointed to the command, and by an agreement between him and me, I was to accompany him, as the intention of the expedition was to give the people of England an opportunity of forming a government for themselves, and thereby bring about peace."—ED.]

## THE COURIER.

THE COURIER, in the time of the war, was the great paper; it obtained a large circulation, and consequently exercised considerable influence. It was started by JOHN PARRY in 1792, and he carried it on for some years with tolerable success, till he was ruined in 1799 by a government prosecution for a libel on the Emperor of Russia. It was bought by DANIEL STUART, who left *The Morning Post* for *The Courier* in 1803. During three years, says he, at the time of the overthrow of BUONAPARTE, *The Courier*, by the able management of PETER STREET, who was editor and half-proprietor, sold steadily upwards of 8000 per day ; during one fortnight it sold upwards of 10,000 daily. At the end of 1809, S. T. COLERIDGE contributed to it some Essays on the Spaniards ; and in 1811 he wrote for it on a salary. At this time the paper was much under ministerial direction. From about the year 1818 till 1829 *The Courier* was conducted by W. MUDFORD, with whom WILLIAM STEWART was a proprietor. After 1819 D. STUART took no interest in it, and parted with his last share in it in 1822. After the year 1825, JAMES STUART, a Scotch gentleman of great talent and respectability—the same that unfortunately killed SIR ALEXANDER BOSWELL in a duel, and was author of *Travels in the United States*—became editor. True to his principles, he gave in this capacity every support in his power to the Whig or Liberal party. He was appointed by LORD MELBOURNE to the situation of Factory Inspector, which he held till his death, at the age of 74, in 1849. When JAS. STUART obtained his factory appointment, SAM. LAMAN BLANCHARD became editor. The paper having become, like other evening papers, less profitable than of old, the proprietors sold it to the party they had so long opposed. It took Tory politics ; LAMAN BLANCHARD, of course, resigned ; and a few short years were sufficient to destroy a journal which had once been the most valuable newspaper property in England. Its last number appeared 6th July, 1842.

It is a curious, but not creditable, circumstance that *The Courier* was in the habit of re-printing, from year to year, without acknowledgment, the able leading articles from *The Liverpool Courier*, written by the Rev. Richard Watson, secretary to the Wesleyan Missionary Society, by whom, in conjunction with his friend, Mr. Kaye, this newspaper was established upon loyal and constitutional principles.

" *The Courier*, in 1814, was supplied by R. Peel, Lord Palmerston, and J. W. Croker, with political squibs and lyrics, resembling in general features *The Anti-Jacobin* and *The Rolliad*. The verses are chiefly parodies of Moore's *Irish Melodies*, or of Byron's songs, and are far above the ordinary level of such compositions. . . . The various pieces were collected and published in 1815, under the title of *The New Whig Guide.*"—*Croker Papers*, vol. i., p. 58.

This statement contains several inaccuracies. The pieces forming *The New Whig Guide* were first collected and published in 1819, and not in 1815, for BYRON'S *Fare thee well* was not written till April, 1816. The parody on it was entitled *The Leader's Lament. By the Right Hon. George Ponsonby.* A. Hayward says in his review of *The Poetry of the Anti-Jacobin*, in *The Edinburgh Review*, 1858—that " CANNING has been traditionally credited with the parody of Moore's

*Believe me, if all those endearing young charms,* the gentleman addressed being a distinguished commoner afterwards ennobled (the first LORD METHUEN), who was far from meriting the character [of a foolish fop] thereby fastened on him ". The other parodies were by JOHN CALCRAFT, the Hon. W. H. LYTTELTON, DUDLEY NORTH, M.P., KIRKMAN FINLAY, M.P. for Glasgow, &c. MR. METHUEN, in return, wrote many clever squibs and parodies against the Tories, which were collected, under the title of *The New Tory Guide,* and reproduced, like its rivals in 1819. "Talking of *The Morning Chronicle,*" says T. MOORE (*Diary,* 19th March, 1831), " PAUL METHUEN told us he was the author of almost all those about *The Rat Club;* which are certainly some of the best."

## THE STAR.

THE STAR, the first London daily Evening Newspaper, was started in 1788 by PETER STUART, brother to DANIEL STUART, of *The Morning Post.* Its first editor was ANDREW MACDONALD, author of *Vimonda,* a tragedy, and other works : and after him another Scottish poet, John Mayne, author of *The Siller Gun,* was editor. ROBERT BURNS was offered an engagement to write poetry for it, at the rate of one guinea an article per week. The arrangement was not completed. It was to PETER STUART that BURNS addressed his "Poem, written to a gentleman who had sent him a Newspaper, and offered to continue it free of expense". The facetious Bob Allen, of whom Charles Lamb has such pleasant reminiscences, was for many years a contributor to this paper. Subsequently, DR. A. TILLOCH, editor of *The Philosophical Magazine,* was for many years editor of *The Star.* After Oct. 15, 1831, *The Star* became incorporated with *The Albion* newspaper, under the title of *The Albion and Evening Star.*

The *Star* was during many years the leading newspaper on the Whig side, CAMPBELL the poet being one of its writers after 1804, when he was engaged at a salary of four guineas a week. The clear profits of this paper in 1820 were said, on apparently good authority, to amount to £6000.

## THE MORNING CHRONICLE.

THE MORNING CHRONICLE was, with one exception (*The Public Ledger,* which started in 1760), the oldest of the daily papers up to the period of its discontinuance March 19, 1862. The latest number in the British Museum is dated Dec. 31, 1861.

It was established on Whig principles, 28th June, 1769, by WILLIAM WOODFALL, who carried it on with great success till 1789.

Woodfall, in addition to other talents requisite to the success of a newspaper, possessed two, which were of essential service to it, namely, his prodigious memory, which enabled him to report Parliamentary Debates without the aid of notes, and the excellence of his Theatrical Criticisms, which, as MR. FOX BOURNE, in his copious and valuable work on *English Newspapers,* 2 vols., 8vo., 1887 —one to which the editor of the present publication has been under frequent obligations—says, "are a neglected mine of wealth for students of Theatrical History".

On WOODFALL'S death, in 1803, it was sold to JAMES PERRY, who borrowed £500 from RANSOME & CO., the bankers, and some more from BELLAMY, the wine merchant—who was also caterer and doorkeeper to the House of Commons—and entered into partnership with a Charterhouse schoolmaster named GRAY, who had just received a legacy of £500. With that joint capital, the two bought *The Chronicle,* the DUKE OF NORFOLK making PERRY a present of a house in the Strand, which he converted into a new publishing office. A few other influential Whigs, also, contributed a further sum, which, as the late SIR ROBERT ADAIR, who is so often satirized in *The Anti-Jacobin,* and who was a subscriber to the fund, informed the editor of the present work, was £300.

PERRY was on good terms with his contributors, and made *The Morning Chronicle* a more prosperous and influential journal than had ever before been known in England. GRAY provided the heavy articles, PERRY those of lighter sort ; and after GRAY'S death, which happened when he had been part proprietor for only a few years, other writers were employed, among them JAS. MACKIN-

TOSH and SHERIDAN, and in later times T. CAMPBELL and T. MOORE, who contributed verse, and JOHN CAMPBELL, then a young barrister, who was the Theatrical Critic, and was still so in 1810. T. CAMPBELL, on coming to London in 1802, was engaged as a political writer, but this not being his forte, he, with great judgment, confined himself to poetical pieces, among which were *Ye Mariners of England*, and *The Exile of Erin*. PERRY had another and equally famous contributor. In Sept., 1793, S. T. COLERIDGE, then aged nineteen, "sent a poem of a few lines to PERRY, soliciting a loan of a guinea for a distressed author," which prayer was immediately granted. In 1796, he accepted an offer of Perry's to write in it, but the arrangement was never carried out. In later years, COLERIDGE wrote some other poems for *The Morning Chronicle*, and his friend CHARLES LAMB was an occasional writer of prose for it.

PERRY continued as the general manager of the paper till his death on 6th Dec., 1821; but before this he had left much of the editing to others, his first assistant after GRAY's death being ROBERT SPANKIE, ultimately attorney-general of Bengal. The next was JOHN BLACK, who had joined him in 1810; and upon him, when PERRY died, the entire management devolved.

After PERRY's death the paper was purchased for £42,000, by WILLIAM CLEMENT, by whom it was held till 1834, when it was sold to SIR JOHN EAST-HOPE for £16,500.

In 1843, JOHN BLACK was dismissed to make way for ANDREW DOYLE, who had been Foreign Editor, and had married Sir John's daughter. Black died in 1855.

On 26th July, 1847, SIR JOHN EASTHOPE, who had been carrying on the paper at a loss for some time, sold it to the Duke of Newcastle, W. E. Gladstone, Sidney Herbert, and other influential Peelites. Its new Editor was JOHN DOUGLAS COOK, who had for some time been one of the reporters of *The Times*, and who gathered round him a brilliant staff of contributors, including George Sydney Smythe, afterwards Lord Strangford, Gilbert Venables, Abraham Hayward, William Vernon Harcourt, and Thackeray. Its business manager was WILLIAM DELANE, the father of the clever young editor of *The Times*, JOHN THADDEUS DELANE.

*The Chronicle* lingered on as a would-be Peelite organ till the autumn of 1854, when by a curious arrangement, the paper, with all its plant, was sold to Serjeant GLOVER, for £7500, on the understanding that, if he continued to support in it the Peelite policy, he should have the money back with interest, being paid £3000 a year for three years. That contract soon fell through, as GLOVER preferred to draw a subsidy from LOUIS NAPOLEON, and to make other experiments. At the close of 1854, the circulation of *The Morning Chronicle* averaged only about 2500, while that of *The Morning Post* was about 3000, that of *The Morning Herald* about 3500, that of *The Daily News* about 5300, that of *The Morning Advertiser* about 6600, and that of *The Times* about 55,000.

The last number of *The Morning Chronicle* appeared March 19, 1862, when what at one time had been the most influential journal in the country altogether ceased to exist

Of this paper SHERIDAN speaks in *The Critic*, and to it BYRON addressed a *Familiar Epistle*. For its columns W. HAZLITT wrote some of the finest criticisms in our own or any other language. Some of the early *Sketches by Boz* appeared in it, but they were really commenced in the old *Monthly Magazine*. DICKENS'S father was one of the staff. HAZLITT also contributed to it Parliamentary Reports, as at a later period did C. DICKENS.

Among other distinguished writers in *The Morning Chronicle* were Lord Brougham, the Duke of Sussex, David Ricardo, Cyrus Redding, Albany Fonblanque, James and John Stuart Mill, John Payne Collier, Eyre Evans Crowe, Charles Buller, Lord Holland, Joseph Parkes, Michael Joseph Quin, George Hogarth, James Fraser, W. Hazlitt, secundus, Lord Melbourne, W. Johnson Fox, Henry Mayhew, Lord Palmerston, A. B. Reach, Alex. and Charles Mackay, Tom Taylor.

## THE MORNING POST.

THE MORNING POST, the next *daily* paper in order of date to *The Chronicle*, first appeared in 1772, and was probably projected by JOHN BELL. Three years subsequently the REV. HENRY BATE (who took in 1784 the name of Dudley, and was created a baronet in 1815) joined it, and was connected with it till the end of 1780, when he quarrelled with his colleagues, and set up *The Morning Herald*, the first number of which appeared on Nov. 1 in the same year. In June, 1781, he was sentenced to a year's imprisonment for an atrocious libel on the Duke of Richmond. He was (says Horace Walpole, in his *Journal of the Reign of George III.*), the worst of all the scandalous libellers that had appeared, both on private persons as well as public. His life was dissolute, and he had fought more than one duel. Yet Lord Sandwich had procured for him a good Crown living, and he was believed to be pensioned by the Court. He died in 1824.

After BATE, as editor, came the REV. W. JACKMAN (or JACKSON)—an equally discreditable clergyman,—and he was succeeded by JOHN TAYLOR (author of *Monsieur Tonson*), for whom PETER PINDAR (DR. JOHN WOLCOT) wrote whimsical verses.

In 1792, MR. TATTERSALL was the responsible proprietor, who, knowing more about horses and sport than about the elegancies of literature, DR. WOLCOT continued to be the chief writer ; and who, besides his clever verses, gave much information upon affairs of the prize-ring and kindred amusements. In 1795, TATTERSALL sold the entire copyright, with house and printing materials, for £600. The circulation then was only 350 daily.

The purchaser was MR. DANIEL STUART ; and MR. CHRISTIE, the auctioneer, was also a proprietor. Previous to this time, ROBERT BURNS was applied to, to supply poetry, but none was ever sent. DANIEL STUART was not twenty-nine when he bought *The Morning Post ;* and JAMES (afterwards SIR JAS.) MACKINTOSH, who was his brother-in-law, and was a regular contributor, was his senior only by a year.

After 1790, the same ANDREW MACDONALD, who had been editor of *The Star*, furnished poems, as did WORDSWORTH, SOUTHEY, C. LLOYD, and other verse writers. At the commencement of 1798, S. T. COLERIDGE—then only twenty-five—was engaged to contribute poetry. The Odes, *Fire, Famine, and Slaughter ; France ; Dejection ;* and that on *The Departing Year ;* with twenty or thirty other pieces, since included in his Poetical Works, among which was *Love*—one of the most popular poems of this age—were first published in *The Morning Post*. To these must be added the first draught of *The Devil's Thoughts*, a piece afterwards much altered. About 1800, the paper was supplied with some excellent pieces, in prose, including Fashionable Intelligence, short pungent articles, and jokes, by CHARLES LAMB.

In 1798 its sale was over 2000 ; and so well had DANIEL STUART managed his property—being exceedingly well served by his principal assistant, GEORGE LANE—that when he left *The Morning Post* for *The Courier*, in 1803, the circulation amounted to 4,500. It, therefore, stood higher in point of sale than any other morning paper, the order in respect of numbers from high to low being this : *Morning Post, Morning Herald, Morning Advertiser, Times*. The amount received for it was about £25,000. According to JOHN TAYLOR, editor of *The Sun*, in his *Records of my Life*, The Morning Post was afterwards purchased by Government to silence attacks on the PRINCE REGENT.

Much of the success of *The Morning Post* was undoubtedly owing to the writings of COLERIDGE. He afterwards declared that he had wasted the prime and manhood of his intellect in writing for *The Morning Post* and *Courier*. Among his contributions to the former (March 19, 1800) was his famous character of WILLIAM PITT. The last time he wrote in it was in August, 1802.

A very competent judge, THOMAS DE QUINCEY, thus alludes to COLERIDGE'S political writings :—" Worlds of fine thinking," he says of the daily press, " lie buried in that vast abyss, never to be disentombed, or restored to human admiration. Like the sea, it has swallowed treasures without end, that no diving-bell will bring up again. But nowhere throughout its shoreless magazines of wealth does there lie such a bed of pearls, confounded with the rubbish and '*purgamenta*' of ages, as in the political papers of COLERIDGE. No more appreciable monument could be raised to the memory of COLERIDGE, than a re-publication of his Essays in *The Morning Post*, but still more of those afterwards published in *The Courier*." These have since been reprinted under the title of *Essays on his own Times*.

# APPENDIX.

## THE ANARCHISTS.—An Ode.

[A Parody on Collins's Ode to the Passions.]

—Numero plures, virtute et honore minores,
Indocti stolidique et depugnare parati.—*Hor.*

When Anarchy, sworn foe to Kings,
O'er Gallia wav'd her crimson wings,
Ere yet she spoil'd with iron hand
Fair Europe's desolated land ;
Her offspring here, a spurious brood,
In faction nurs'd, inur'd to blood,
Elate with Hope, perplex'd with Fear,
Would often raise the listening ear ;
And all their mother's wonders tell,
And throng around her secret cell,
Ranting, bribing, whispering, trembling, .
Urging, boasting, and dissembling.
By turns they felt the Gallic mind
Enlarg'd, unprejudic'd, refin'd ;
Till once, by all the goddess fir'd,
Beyond Discretion rapt, inspir'd ;
Seditious, false, and prone to ill,
They eager snatch'd the grey-goose quill.
And as they oft had heard apart
The wonders of Sedition's art,
Each, for Madness rul'd the hour,
Would prove his own subversive power.

First PAINE his *Rights of Man* display'd,
    But could no more—for falsely cross'd
Ev'n by the friends himself had made,
        Enraged he fled to Gallia's coast.
Next PRIESTLEY tried, to whom 'twas given
    Mankind's free-agency to tell ;
Ordain'd to point the road to heaven,
    In pure free will he points—to hell !
With meagre visage THELWALL came,
    In lectures told his sufferings sore ;
Till purple tyrants blush'd with shame
    And crowds the suffering saint adore.
But thou, O GODWIN ! meek and mild ;
        Speak thy metaphysic page :
        Now it cheer'd a laggard age,

20

And bade new scenes of joy at distance hail;
When tyrant Kings shall be no more,
When human wants and wars shall fail,
And sleep and death shall quit the hallow'd shore.
'Twas thus he strove to sap the throne,
With borrow'd arts and weapons not his own,
While Gallia clapp'd her hands, and hail'd her favourite child.

And longer had he sung—but, strange to say,
WAKEFIELD, the dragon-fly, rush'd on;
Eager he sought the bold rebellious fray,
And burst with anger and disdain
The web of sophistry in twain
Which GODWIN, patient sage! had spread
To catch the fluttering insects of the land.
Treason upreared her arm to strike,
Rebellion grasped the murd'rous pike,
And though, sometimes, each maddening pause between,
Soft Discretion, joined with Fear,
Whisper'd her councils in his ear,
Still Anarchy upheld the busy scene,
And raised her shield of brass to guard her vot'ry's head.

Next HOLCROFT vowed in doleful tone
No more to fire a thankless age,
Oblivion marked his labours for her own,
Neglected from the press and damn'd upon the stage.
See! faithful to their mighty dam,
COLERIDGE, SOUTHEY, LLOYD, and LAMB,
In splay-foot madrigals of love,
Soft moaning like the widowed dove,
Pour side by side their sympathetic notes.
Of equal rights and civic feasts
And tyrant Kings and knavish Priests
Swift through the land the tuneful mischief floats.
And now to softer strains they struck the lyre,
They sung the beetle, or the mole,
The dying kid, or ass's foal,
By cruel man permitted to expire.
But O, how altered was the sprightlier hour!
When FOX, the Parthian hero, rose to view;
He o'er the rest high-towering like a steeple
Leagued with a "Corresponding" crew,
Pledged in large floods of wine "their Majesties—the People".

The royal tribe accept the proffered power.
Kings from the forge, dictators from the plough,
Peeping from forth their allies low,
Before the fallen arch-seceder bow;
LEPAUX bade Gallia hail his name,
But old St. Stephen bowed his head for shame.

See NORFOLK last, with BEDFORD roll,
He of Bacchus' favours proud,
The sovereign mob most eloquent addressed;
But soon he spied the mirth-inspiring bowl,
Whose ruby treasures charmed his soul the best;
They would have thought who heard him speak,
'Twas Falstaff, with his minions at his back,
High primed with valour, turbulence, and sack,
Aping the monarch to a wondr'ing crowd.

While BEDFORD proud his lesson to rehearse,
   With studious labours urged the bold reply :
   Shouts of applause ran rattling through the sky :
   And he, the hero of the day,
   Right glad their servile suffrage to repay,
Shook golden bounty from his swelling purse.

O, England! heav'n-defended land!
With power to "threaten and command,"
Say, is thy former spirit broke,
To crouch beneath a foreign yoke,
And listen to the idiot strains
Of slaves thy better sense disdains,
As erst, in many an ardent hour,
You awed an adverse haughty power.
Thy lofty mind, to Freedom true,
May well retain what then it knew.
Where is thy former patriot soul,
Above deceit, above controul?
Arise ! as in that happier time
United, fearless, bold, sublime.
'Tis said, and I believe the tale,
Thy efforts then could more avail,
Could more true happiness dispense,
With Order, Morals, Virtue, Sense,
Than all that fires with party rage
This boastful philosophic age.
Arise ! with manly zeal advance,
To curb the lawless power of France ;
O, bid her mad endeavours cease,
And give the willing nations PEACE !
             —*Fabricius.*

# THE PASSIONS.

## *An Ode for Music.*

### WILLIAM COLLINS.

When Music, heavenly maid, was young,
While yet in early Greece she sung,
The Passions oft, to hear her shell,
Throng'd around her magic cell,
Exulting, trembling, raging, fainting,
Possess'd beyond the Muse's painting ;
By turns they felt the glowing mind,
Disturb'd, delighted, rais'd, refin'd,
Till once, 'tis said, when all were fir'd,
Fill'd with fury, rapt, inspir'd,
From the supporting myrtles round
They snatch'd her instruments of sound,
And, as they oft had heard apart
Sweet lessons of her forceful art,
Each, for Madness ruled the hour,
Would prove his own expressive power.

First Fear, his hand, its skill to try,
Amid the chords bewilder'd laid,
And back recoil'd, he knew not why,
Even at the sound himself had made.

Next Anger rush'd his eyes on fire,
In lightnings own'd his secret stings,
In one rude clash he struck the lyre,
And swept with hurried hand the strings.

With woful measures wan Despair
Low sullen sounds his grief beguil'd,
A sullen, strange, and mingled air,
'Twas sad by fits, by starts 'twas wild.

But thou, O HOPE! with eyes so fair,
What was thy delighted measure ?
Still it whisper'd promis'd pleasure,
And bade the lovely scenes at distance hail !
Still would her touch the strain prolong,
And from the rocks, the woods, the vale,
She call'd on ECHO still through all the song ;
And where her sweetest theme she chose,
A soft responsive voice was heard at every close,
And Hope enchanted smil'd, and wav'd her golden hair.

And longer had she sung,—but, with a frown,
REVENGE impatient rose,
He threw his blood-stained sword in thunder down,
    And, with a withering look,
    The war-denouncing trumpet took,
And blew a blast so loud and dread,
Were ne'er prophetic sounds so full of woe.
    And ever and anon he beat
    The doubling drum with furious heat ;
    And though sometimes, each dreary pause between,
    Dejected PITY at his side
    Her soul-subduing voice applied ;
    Yet still he kept his wild unalter'd mien,
While each strain'd ball of sight seem'd bursting from his head,


Thy numbers, JEALOUSY, to nought were fix'd,
    Sad proof of thy distressful state !
Of differing themes the veering song was mix'd,
    And now it courted LOVE, now raving call'd on HATE.
With eyes upraised, as one inspir'd,
Pale MELANCHOLY sat retir'd,
And from her wild sequester'd seat,
In notes by distance made more sweet,
Pour'd through the mellow horn her pensive soul :
    And dashing soft from rocks around,
    Bubbling runnels join'd the sound ;
Through glades and glooms the mingled measure stole,
Or o'er some haunted streams with fond delay,
    Round a holy calm diffusing,
    Love of peace and lonely musing,
In hollow murmurs died away.


But oh ! how alter'd was its sprightlier tone !
When CHEERFULNESS, a nymph of healthiest hue,
    Her bow across her shoulders flung,
    Her buskins gemm'd with morning dew,
    Blew an inspiring air that dale and thicket rung,
    The hunter's call to Faun and Dryad known ;
The oak-crown'd Sisters, and their chaste-eyed Queen,
Satyrs and Sylvan boys were seen,
Peeping from forth their alleys green ;
Brown EXERCISE rejoic'd to hear,
And SPORT leapt up, and seized his beechen spear.


Last came JOY's ecstatic trial ;
    He with viny crown advancing,
    First to the lively pipe his hand address'd ;
    But soon he saw the brisk awakening viol,
    Whose sweet entrancing voice he lov'd the best.
    They would have thought who heard the strain,
    They saw in Tempe's vale her native maids,
    Amidst the festal sounding shades,
    To some unwearied minstrel dancing :
While, as his flying fingers kiss'd the strings,
LOVE fram'd with MIRTH a gay fantastic round,
Loose were her tresses seen, her zone unbound :
And he, amidst his frolic play,
As if he would the charming air repay,
Shook thousand odours from his dewy wings.

O MUSIC! sphere-descended maid,
Friend of PLEASURE, WISDOM'S aid,
Why, goddess, why to us denied,
Lay'st thou thy ancient lyre aside?
As in that lov'd Athenian bower,
You learn'd an all-commanding power,
Thy mimic soul, O nymph endear'd,
Can well recall what then it heard.
Where is thy native simple heart,
Devote to virtue, fancy, art?
Arise, as in that elder time,
Warm, energetic, chaste, sublime!
Thy wonders, in that god-like age,
Fill thy recording Sister's page.
'Tis said, and I believe the tale,
Thy humblest reed could more prevail,
Had more of strength, diviner rage,
Than all which charms this laggard age,
E'en all at once together found
Cecilia's mingled world of sound.
O bid our vain endeavours cease,
Revive the just designs of Greece ;
Return in all thy simple state !
Confirm the tales her sons relate.

*Art.* 1. *The Republican Judge, or the American Liberty of the Press, as exhibited, explained, and exposed, in the base and partial Prosecution of William Cobbett, for a pretended Libel against the King of Spain and his Embassador, before the Supreme Court of Pennsylvania. With an Address to the People of England. By Peter Porcupine.* 8vo., *pp.* 96. *Price* 2s. *Wright, London.*

The past writings of Mr. William Cobbett, who has assumed the appellation of Peter Porcupine, are too well known in England to require any explanation from us, either of *their* tendency, or of the author's principles. Were any doubt entertained on the subject, nothing more would be requisite to dispel it than a mere reference to the comments of all the Jacobin Reviewers, who have, without exception, in defiance alike of decency and of truth, lavished on them the most indiscriminate censure and the most scurrilous abuse. Strange as it may appear, it is indisputably true that the individual exertions of Mr. Cobbett have more essentially contributed to give a proper tone to the public spirit in America than all the efforts of the well-disposed part of the native Americans : for a considerable length of time he combated alone a host of foes, "himself a host"; stemmed the impetuous tide of democracy ; and checked the irruptions of French anarchy and atheism, which threatened to overwhelm the American States, and, with the ruins of their confliction, to crush everything for which the Americans, at the period of their revolution, professed to fight, and which they have ever since professed to cherish. The adoption of such a line of conduct was alone sufficient to draw down upon our author the vengeance of all whose treasonable designs his manly efforts were intended to defeat. Accordingly, nothing was spared by the infuriated advocates of anarchy to injure him in the public mind, and, by blasting his reputation, to deprive him of that credit which was indispensably necessary to secure the success of his works. No imputation however base, no lie however atrocious, none of those black and diabolical arts, in short, which, issuing from the bubbling cauldron of democracy, were so skilfully employed to blacken the first and fairest character in France, as a necessary prelude to the establishment of the *virtuous* republic of the Great Nation, were neglected in the *glorious* attempt to achieve the ruin of this worthy individual. When these were found to fail of producing the desired effect, recourse was had to personal threats—the coward's weapon—with the hope of inducing him, by the means of intimidation, to quit a country in which his enemies endeavoured to convince him that his life was daily exposed to most imminent danger. But neither the dread of calumny, nor the fear of assassination, could lead the object of their persecution to forego his laudable design. He manfully persevered, and has at length, though not without infinite difficulty, succeeded in opening the eyes of the Americans to their own interest, and in the infamous machinations of France, and of American traitors in the pay of France—for England is not the ONLY country in which foreign gold is employed as a stimulus to domestic treason.* In the course of his exertions to produce this desirable end, honest

---

* "It is notorious that the *French Directory have newspapers in their pay*, not only in America, but in *every* country in Europe. That there should exist such

Peter had occasion to comment on the pusillanimous conduct of the Spanish monarch, in bending the knee to, and forming an alliance with, the base plunderers and assassins of his family, and on the insidious and criminal efforts of the Spanish ambassador to strengthen the hands of the French faction in America. These comments, it seems, excited the indignation of Don Carlos Martinez de Trojo, who determined to bring the author to condign punishment ; and it was the very unwarrantable conduct which the latter experienced on the occasion that gave rise to the publication before us.

PETER begins his tract by stating the dangers to which he knew himself exposed, on account of his political principles, when he established his residence in the state of Pennsylvania, "where the government, generally speaking, was in the hands of those who had (and sometimes with great indecency) manifested an uniform partiality for the sans-culotte French, and as uniform an opposition to the ministers and measures of the federal government ". That men should ever be placed in situations of trust and importance, whose principles are avowedly adverse to the constitution whence they derive their subsistence, and which it is their bounden duty to protect, is a circumstance that would excite universal astonishment if it did not, unhappily, so often occur. Still the frequency of its occurrence does not alter its nature, nor should it be allowed to diminish that ample portion of censure which must ever attach to the authors of such appointments. It is such conduct as this that justifies one of the wisest observations that ever fell from the pen of Voltaire— " A GOVERNMENT CAN ONLY PERISH BY SUICIDE"—an observation confirmed by the fate of every country that has been recently reduced beneath the iron yoke of republican France.

Aware of his danger, our author thought the best means of averting it was, by seeking for some standard, as a safe rule for his conduct in respect to the liberty of this press. "The English press was said to be *enslaved*; but, when I came to consult the practice of this enslaved press, I found it still to be far too free for me to attempt to follow its example. Finally, it appeared to me to be the safest way, to form to myself some rule founded on the liberty exercised by the *American press*. I concluded that I might without danger go as great lengths in attacking the enemies of the country as others went in attacking its friends : that as much zeal might be shown in defending the general government and administration as in accusing and traducing them : and that as great warmth would be admissible in the cause of virtue, order, and religion, as had been tolerated in the wicked cause of villainy, insurrection, and blasphemy" (p. 21). Alas! Peter, at this time, knew but little of the "spirit and temper," as MR. BARRISTER ERSKINE would express it, of democracy and Jacobinism. He knew not that the men who profess those principles are for the most part vindictive, malignant, oppressive, and intolerant ; and that under the mask of liberty they exercise the most insupportable tyranny over their families and dependents, and that in their general conduct to their inferiors—unless when impelled by interest or urged by ambition, they irritate their passions with toasts and flattery, from a tavern-chair, or influence their minds by seditious discourses and treasonable insinuations, from a tribune or a scaffold—they are supercilious, arrogant, insolent, and overbearing. He knew not, it would seem, that those whose whole duty is to defend the laws often *sleep on their posts*, while their enemies are ever vigilant, active, and alert ; that when the former are attacked, a tardiness of zeal, amounting nearly to torpor, secures, with few exceptions, impunity to the assailant ; whereas any exposure of the latter draws forth a malignity of revenge which is the certain fore-runner of persecution.

MERCENARY TRAITORS AS TO RECEIVE THE PAY OF REGICIDES AND ASSASSINS is still less astonishing than that there should be found men in the different countries, and *men of rank*, too, so base, so degenerate, and so *foolish*, as to give encouragement to their treasonable productions " (p. 57). The author speaks truth ; there is at least *one* newspaper of this description in *London*, which is encouraged—to their shame be it spoken !—by *men of rank*, and by members of the Legislature—*Representans du Peuple Souverain!*—who even degrade themselves so far as to associate with the profligate miscreants who compose its inflammatory pages.—REVIEWER.

Indeed, the inveteracy of the discontented, of that class which includes all those who aspire to the possession of place and power, and are little scrupulous about the means of attaining them ; and all the determined revolutionists or subverters of established institutions, may be traced to a natural source. Unable to support by reason a cause which reason disavows, unable to strengthen by arguments positions which set all argument at defiance, it becomes their business to inflame by passion and to dazzle with sophistry. Hence arises an extreme facility of exposing their weakness and detecting their infamy, and not having the means of resisting such exposure, being wholly destitute of the sentiments which are necessary for a successful reply, they are reduced to the degrading alternative of abandoning the field to a triumphant adversary, or of seeking, by the adoption of violent measures, to punish the opponent whom they did not dare to encounter. This it is that renders revenge an active principle in *their* minds.

The first step taken by the Spanish ambassador was an application to the federal government to prosecute our author "for certain matters published in his Gazette against himself and that poor, unfortunate, and humbled mortal, Charles IV., King of Spain". The government consented, and Peter was accordingly bound over to appear in the federal district court before *Judge Peters*. Don Carlos, however, soon found that his prosecution would be more likely to succeed, if brought in a district where the defendant had more personal enemies, and where the people were more generally disposed to the adoption of revolutionary principles. A memorial was, accordingly, "delivered in to the federal government, requesting that the trial might come on before the Supreme Court of Pennsylvania, of which Court *McKean is Chief Justice*". Of this *republican* Judge our author gives such an account as must convey to English minds a strange idea of the administration of *republican* Justice. It is to be found in P. 22—When Britons contemplate the character here delineated, and contrast it with the characters of their own Judges to which even the licentious tongue of faction has not dared to impute the smallest stain, their bosoms must glow with satisfaction of the most exalted kind ; they must exult in the superior excellence of that form of government and of those laws which effectually secure them from the evils of a vicious, corrupt, or partial distribution of justice. After giving an historical detail of the proceedings against him, accompanied by copies of the warrant to apprehend him, the imputed libels, the bill of indictment, and the Judge's charge, Peter exclaims—"This, when it comes to be served up in Britain, will be a dish for a king. The royalists will lick their lips, and the republicans will cry, God bless us ! The emigrations *for liberty's* sake will cease, and we shall have nothing but the pure unadulterated dregs of Newgate and the Fleet, the candidates for Tyburn and Botany Bay— Blessed cargo ! All *patriots* to the backbone : true philanthropists and universal citizens : fit for any place but England in this world and heaven in the next ! "

But, notwithstanding the Judge's charge, the most partial and scandalous charge, we conceive, that ever was delivered *out of France*, the Grand Jury refused to find the bill, and the prosecution of course ceased. The Judge, not less disappointed than the prosecutor, on this occasion, took an early opportunity—to his infamy be it recorded !—of declaring from the Bench that the Grand Jury would not *do their duty*. What would the disaffected in this country say were any British Judge to use such language? The gross imputations cast upon the character of our author by this *impartial* Judge, have extorted from Peter a tribute of justice to himself which the occasion most amply justifies. As the account here given perfectly accords with all the information we have received from persons of undoubted veracity who know him well, and as it fully corroborates the opinion we ourselves have formed of him, from an attentive perusal of his publications, we shall extract it for the satisfaction of our readers :—" It hardly ever becomes a man to say much of his private character or concerns ; but on this occasion I trust I shall be indulged for a moment. I will say, and I will make that saying good, whosoever shall oppose it, that I never attacked any one, whose private character is not, in every light in which it can possibly be viewed as far beneath mine as infamy is beneath honour. Nay, I defy the city of Philadelphia, populous as it is, and respectable as are many of its inhabitants, to produce me a single man who is more sober, industrious, or honest; who is a kinder husband, a tenderer father, a better master, a fonder friend, or (though last not least) a more zealous and faithful subject.

"Most certainly it is unseemly in any one to say this much of himself unless compelled to it by some public outrage on his character; but when the accusation is made notorious so ought the defence; and I do again and again repeat, that I fear not a comparison between my character and that of any man in this city: no, not even with that of the very Judge, who held me as the worst of miscreants. His Honour is welcome, if he please, to carry this comparison into *all* the actions of our lives, public and *domestic*, and to extend it beyond ourselves to *every branch of our families.*

"As to my writing, I never did slander any one, if the promulgation of useful truths be not slander. Innocence and virtue I have often endeavoured to defend, but I never defamed either. I have, indeed, stripped the close-drawn veil of hypocrisy; I have ridiculed the follies, and lashed the vices of thousands, and have done it sometimes perhaps with a rude and violent hand. But these are not the days for gentleness and mercy. Such as is the temper of the foe, such must be that of his opponent. Seeing myself published as a rogue, *and my wife a whore;* being persecuted with such infamous, such base and hellish calumny in the *philanthropic* city of Philadelphia, merely for asserting *the truth* respecting others, was not calculated, I assure you, to sweeten my temper, and turn my ink into honey-dew.

"My attachment to order and good government, nothing but the impudence of Jacobinism can deny. The object not only of my own publications, but also of all those which I have introduced or encouraged, from the first moment that I appeared on the public scene to the present day, has been to lend some aid in stemming the torrent of anarchy and confusion. To undeceive the misguided, by tearing the mask from the artful and ferocious villains who owing to the infatuation of the poor, and the supineness of the rich, have made such fearful progress in the destruction of all that is amiable and good and sacred among men. To the government of this country in particular it has been my constant study to yield all the support in my power. When that government, or the worthy men who administer it have been traduced and vilified, I have stood forward in their defence, and that too, in times when its friends were some of them locked up in silence, and others giving way to the audacious violence of its foes. Not that I am so foolishly vain as to attribute to my illiterate voter a thousandth part of the merit my friends are inclined to allow it. As I wrote the other day to a gentleman who had paid me some compliments on this score, ' I should never look on my family with a dry eye if I did not hope to outlive my works'. They are mere transitory beings to which the revolutionary storm has given life, and which with that storm will expire. But, what I contend for and what nobody can deny, I have done all that laid in my power, all that I was able by any means to accomplish in order to counteract the nefarious effects of the enemies of the American government and nation.

"With respect to religion, altho' Mr. M'Kean was pleased to number it among the things that were in danger from the licentiousness of the press, and of course from poor *me*, I think it would puzzle the devil himself to produce from my writings, a single passage, which could, by all the powers of perversion be twisted into an attack upon it. But it would on the contrary be extremely easy to prove, that I have at all times, when an opportunity offered, repelled the attacks of its enemies, the abominable battalions of Deists and Atheists, with all my heart, with all my mind, with all my soul, and with all my strength. The bitterest drop in my pen has ever been bestowed upon them; because, of all the foes of the human race, I look upon them, after the devil, as being the greatest and most dreadful. Not a sacrilegious plunderer from Henry VIII. to Condorcet, and from Condorcet to the impious Sans-culottes of France, has escaped my censure. All those, who have attempted to degrade religion whether by open insults and cruelties to the clergy, by blasphemous publications or by the more dangerous poison of the malignant modern philosophy, I have ranked amongst the most infamous of mankind, and have treated them accordingly."

In the concluding part of his tract the author clearly convicts the Judge of the most decided and most flagrant partiality. He quotes a number of infamous libels, on religious and political subjects, which had never roused the indignation, nor even excited the censure, of those whose duty it is to preserve the public peace and to enforce a due observance of the laws. If, indeed, we were to judge, from this specimen, of the mode of administring justice in America, in matters of libel, we should conclude, that every degree of licentiousness is allowed to those who seek to debauch the minds of the people, to seduce them from their allegiance, and to dissolve every tie which religion and morality have formed for the happiness of men in a social state, while the upright supporters of virtue, whose labours are directed to the prevention of anarchy and rebellion, by detecting the views and exposing the machinations of their abettors, are the sole objects not merely of *prosecution* but of *persecution*.

The abuse bestowed on the mild and beneficent sovereigns of these realms by the Democratic factions in the American Congress, is almost equal in severity to the censures lavished by some members of opposition during the *last* parliament in the British Senate, on the Kings of Prussia and Hungary, *before* those monarchs had become allies of *France*.

The following extracts will, at once, afford a criterion of the political principles of public men, in the State of Pennsylvania, and a curious specimen of republican *morality*.

"The *Governor* (Mifflin) attended at a civic festival, when the following toasts were drunk, which were published in most of the newspapers.*

"'Those *illustrious citizens* sent to Botany Bay. May they be *speedily recalled* by their country in *the day of her regeneration.*'

"'May the spirit of parliamentary reform in Britain and Ireland *burst the bonds of corruption, and overwhelm the foes of liberty.*'

"'The *sans-culottes* of France. May the robes of *all* the *Emperors, Kings, Princes*, and *Potentates* [not excepting the *King of Spain*] now employed in suppressing the flame of liberty, be cut up to make breeches.'

"This is pretty '*decent*' in a *Governor*; but without stopping to remark on the peculiar *decency* of his toasting a gang of *convicts*, let us come to another instance of his conduct, full as '*decent*' as this.

"At the civic festival, held in this city in 1794, to celebrate the dethronement of 'our great and good ally, Louis XVI.' there were 'assembled,' according to the '*procès verbal*' which was sent to the Paris convention, 'the CHIEFS, civil and *military*'. This *procès verbal* contains a letter to the convention, in which the following honourable mention is made of the governor. 'The Governor of Pennsylvania, that *ardent friend of the French republic*, was present, and partook of *all our enthusiasm* and *all our sentiments.*'†

"'I believe they spoke truth; for the cannons of the State were fired, and military companies, with drums beating and colours flying, attended the execrable fête, one of the ceremonies of which was *burning the English flag;* and as to the sentiments contained in the oaths and *speeches* (for there were both) they abounded in insults towards almost all the princes of the earth, but particularly the King of Great Britain.

"A Judge of Pennsylvania, REDMAN, was, in November, 1795, caught thieving in the shop of MR. FOLWELL, the dry-goods merchant in Front Street. MR. FOLWELL detected him, took the money ($300) from him, and kicked him into the street. His *friends*, among the most intimate of whom was His Excellency the Governor, advised him to *retire;* and he is still living at his ease about 20 miles from the city. No justice was ever done to him; he was never censured, not even in the newspapers! Such is the cowardly, base, and worthless press of America. Such are *republican judges*, and such is republican morality!

* " See BACHE of 11 February, 1795."

† The reader will not be surprised to hear that this is the identical governor who wanted a few thousands of dollars from the French minister, FAUCHET, and who drew *secretly* 15,000 dollars out of the Bank of Pennsylvania!! This man brought a whole litter of *bastards* home to his virtuous wife. He is a shameless blackguard, a drunkard, and everything that can be named that is vile. Such is a *republican governor;* a chief magistrate of state, who has infinitely greater powers over life and property than King George has!! And this I have already pointed out on sundry occasions.

But this is not the worst. I know a Judge who *committed murder!* wilful murder, and that, too, previous to his appointment by this our republican Governor !
" I only give a sort of hint here. One day or other if it pleases God to spare
my life, I will publish such a collection of facts as will shock the universe.
"A Pennsylvania *Judge's wife* had, a little while ago, a child, by a man who
kept a livery stable. The *lady* says, the stableman is the best of the two and so
has married him, though *his Honour* is still living. I need not name the parties,
for though the cowardly newspapers have never noticed the affair it is notorious
enough.
"There are more bastards born annuallyin the single state of Pennsylvania,than
in all the British dominions: and as to cuckoldom, I will only say that every
paper teems with *advertisements of wives eloped* from the bed and board of their
husbands. I do not hence insinuate that there are *no good people* here. There
are many. As many as in most countries ; but then people will, and do allow,
that the morals of the country are approaching fast to that state, which has
never yet failed to prove the ruin of every thing held in esteem amongst men.'
   In proving the falsehood of the assertion so frequentlyrepeated, as well on this
as on the other side of the Atlantic, that " in *America* the press is *free* and truth
is *not* a libel," our author adverts to a letter of DR. PRIESTLEY'S on that subject which he promises hereafter to expose more fully (a promise which we trust
he will not forget) ; and then introduces the following curious anecdote, which
we extract for the benefit of the Doctor's political friends and admirers in
Europe. "But since the Doctor wrote that letter it seems experience has changed
his opinion. He has suffered the just punishment of his malignancy in this
country ; he has been cheated, neglected, and scorned. He is now in an obscurity
hardly penetrable ; he is reduced to poverty and bursting with vexation " (may
a restless spirit of innovation, springing from, and nourished by, a bigotted
vanity and a turbulent pride ever experience a similar fate) ! All this has had
an effect ; and I will state as a fact, which I call upon him to deny if he can,
that he has lately declared "that *Republican governments are the most abitrary in
the world*" ! This MACHIAVEL had said before, and this all unprejudiced men of
reading and observation had long since admitted ; but, we confess we little expected to hear DOCTOR PRIESTLEY subscribe to the creed of the one, or to the
acknowledgments of the other. Adversity, however, is an able advocate in the
cause of TRUTH.
   The Address to the People of England, which is prefixed to the publication,
is short, but pointed and expressive. It breathes the true spirit of a Briton.
Of the literary merit of the work, after the ample analysis which we have given
of its contents, and the extracts which we have made, little remains to be said.
We agree with the publisher, who in the Advertisement says: "The author
has been more anxious to strengthen his arguments than to polish his style, to
convince the judgment than to flatter the taste," but those critics must be more
"*delicate*" or fastidious who can reject substantial advantages for fanciful defects. Though Peter aim not at embellishments, he possesses great strength
and energy of language, and generally writes with more accuracy than most of
the American authors, who, be it observed, have a phraseology peculiar to
themselves. This tract contains much important information, and we strenuously
recommend it to the serious perusal of our countrymen ; particularly to such
of them as are disposed to question the superior advantages which they enjoy,
over ALL republican states under our own well-poised and limited MONARCHY.
The following admonitions with which the author concludes, will, we trust,
have a due effect on the minds of those to whom they are addressed. " Such,
*Britons*, is the fruit of republican government *here* ; not among the apish and
wolfish French, but among a people descended from the same ancestors as yourselves. When your monarchial government bears such fruits, let it, I say, be
hewn down and cast into the fire ; but till that disgraceful and dreadful day
comes, watch over it with care and defend it to the last drop of your blood,
preserve it as you would a golden casket, the apple of your eye, or the last dear
gift of your dying parents. With this I conclude, praying the God of our fathers
to lead you in the practice of all their virtues, to give wisdom to your minds and
strength to your arms, to keep you firm and united, honest and generous, loyal,
brave, and free ; but above all, to preserve you from the desolating and degrading curse of revolutionary madness and modern *republicanism*."

# PETER PORCUPINE'S WILL.

[By WILLIAM COBBETT. Published in *The Anti-Jacobin Review and Magazine;* or Monthly Political and Literary Censor: from July to December, 1798. Vol. i., pp. 725-8.—ED.]

IN the name of Fun, Amen. I PETER PORCUPINE, Pamphleteer and News-monger, being (as yet) sound both in body and in mind, do, this fifteenth day of *April*, in the Year of our Lord, one thousand seven hundred and ninety-seven, make, declare, and publish, this my LAST WILL AND TESTAMENT, in manner, form, and substance following; to wit:

IN PRIMIS,

I leave my body to Doctor Michael Lieb a member of the Legislature of Pennsylvania, to be by him dissected (if he knows how to do it) in presence of the Rump of the Democratic Society. In it they will find a heart that held them in abhorrence, that never palpitated at their threats, and that, to its last beat, bade them defiance. But my chief motive for making this bequest is, that my spirit may look down with contempt on their cannibal-like triumph over a breathless corpse.

*Item.* As I make no doubt that the above said Doctor Lieb (and some other Doctors that I could mention) would like very well to skin me, I request that they, or one of them may do it, and that the said Lieb's father may tan my skin ; after which I desire my Executors to have seven copies of my Works complete, bound in it, one copy to be presented to the Five Sultans of France, one to each of their Divans, one to the Governor of Pennsylvania, to Citizens Maddison, Giles, and Gallatin one each, and the remaining one to the Democratic Society of Philadelphia, to be carefully preserved among their archives.

*Item.* To the Mayor, Aldermen, and Councils of the City of Philadelphia, I bequeath all the sturdy young hucksters, who infest the market, and who to maintain their bastards, tax the honest inhabitants many thousand pounds annually. I request them to take them into their worshipful keeping ; to chasten their bodies for the good of their souls ; and moreover to keep a sharp look-out after their gallants ; and remind the latter of the old proverb : *Touch pot, touch penny.*

*Item.* To T—— J——son, Philosopher, I leave a curious Norway Spider, with a hundred legs and nine pair of eyes ; likewise the first black cut-throat general he can catch hold of, to be flead alive, in order to determine with more certainty the real cause of the dark colour of his skin ; and should the said T—— J——son survive Banneker the Almanack Maker ; I request he will get the brains of said Philomath carefully dissected, to satisfy the world in what respects they differ from those of a white man.

*Item.* To the Philosophical Society of Philadelphia, I will and bequeath a correct copy of Thornton's plan for abolishing the use of the English language, and for introducing in its stead a republican one, the representative characters of which bear a strong resemblance to pot-hooks and hangers ; and for the discovery of which plan, the said society did, in the year 1793, grant to the said language maker 500 dollars premium. It is my earnest desire, that the copy of this valuable performance, which I hereby present, may be shown to all the travelling literati, as a proof of the ingenuity of the author and of the wisdom of the society.

*Item.* To Doctor Benjamin Rush, I will and bequeath a copy of *The Censor* for January, 1797 ; but, upon the express condition, that he does not in anywise or guise, either at the time of my death, or *Six months after*, pretend to speak, write, or publish an eulogium on me, my calling or character, either literary, military, civil, or political.

*Item.* To my dear fellow labourer Noah Webster, "gentleman-citizen," Esq. and News-man, I will and bequeath a prognosticating barometer of curious construction and great utility, by which, at a single glance, the said Noah will be able to discern the exact state that the public mind will be in in the ensuing year, and will thereby be enabled to *trim by degrees* and not expose himself to detection, as he now does by his sudden lee-shore tacks. I likewise bequeath to the said "gentleman-citizen," six Spanish milled dollars, to be expended on a new plate of his portrait at the head of his spelling book, that which graces it at present being so ugly that it scares the children from their lessons; but this legacy is to be paid him only upon condition that he leave out the title of *'Squire*, at the bottom of said picture, which is extremely odious in an American school-book, and must inevitably tend to corrupt the political principles of the republican babies that behold it. And I do most earnestly desire, exhort and conjure the said 'Squire news-man, to change the title of his paper, *The Minerva*, for that of *The Political Centaur*.

*Item.* To F. A. Mughlenburg, Esq., Speaker of a late house of Representatives of the United States, I leave a most superbly finished statue of Janus.

*Item.* To Tom the Tinker, I leave a liberty-cap, a tricoloured cockade, a wheel-barrow full of oysters, and a hogshead of grog : I also leave him three blank checks on the bank of Pennsylvania, leaving to him the task of *filling them up* ; requesting him, however, to be rather more merciful than he has shown himself heretofore.

*Item.* To the Governor of Pennsylvania, and to the late President and Cashier of the Bank of the said State, as to joint Legatees, I will and bequeath that good old proverb : *Honesty is the best policy*. And this legacy I have chosen for these worthy gentlemen, as the only thing about which I am sure they will never disagree.

*Item.* To T——— Coxe, of Philadelphia, citizen, I will and bequeath a crown of hemlock, as a recompense for his attempt to throw an odium on the administration of General Washington ; and I most positively enjoin my Executors, to see that the said crown be shaped exactly like that which this spindle-shanked legatee wore before Gen. Howe, when he made his triumphal entry into Philadelphia.

*Item.* To Thomas Lord Bradford (otherwise called Goosy Tom), Book-seller, Printer, News-man, and member of the Philosophical Society of Philadelphia, I will and bequeath a copy of the peerage of Great Britain, in order that the said Lord Thomas may the more exactly ascertain what probability there is of his succeeding to the seat, which his noble relation now fills in the House of Lords.

*Item.* To all and singular the authors in the United States, whether they write verse or prose, I will and bequeath a copy of my Life and Adventures ; and I advise the said authors to study with particular care the 40th and 41st pages thereof ; more especially and above all things, I exhort and conjure them never to *publish it together*, though the bookseller should be a saint.

*Item.* To Edmund Randolph, Esq., late Secretary of State, to Mr J. A. Dallas, Secretary of the State of Pennsylvania, and to His Excellency, Thomas Miflin, Governor of the said unfortunate State, I will and bequeath, to each of them, a copy of the sixteenth paragraph of Fauchet's *intercepted letter*.

*Item.* To Citizen John Swanwick, member of Congress, by the will and consent of the sovereign people, I leave bills of Exchange on London to an enormous amount ; they are *all protested*, indeed, but if properly managed, may be turned to good account. I likewise bequeath to the said John a small treatise by an Italian author, wherein the secret of pleasing the ladies is developed, and reduced to a mere mechanical operation, without the least dependence on the precarious aid of the passions. Hoping that these instances of my liberality will produce, in the mind of the little legislature, effects quite different from those produced therein by the King of Great Britain's pension to his parents.

*Item.* To the Editors of the *Boston Chronicle*, the *New York Argus*, and the *Philadelphia Merchants' Advertiser*, I will and bequeath one ounce of modesty and love of truth, to be equally divided between them.

I should have been more liberal in this bequest, were I not well assured, that one ounce is more than they will ever make use of.

*Item.* To Franklin Bache, Editor of the *Aurora of Philadelphia*, I will and bequeath a small bundle of French assignats, which I brought with me from the country of equality. If these should be too light in value for his pressing exigencies, I desire my executors, or any one of them, to bestow on him a second part to what he has lately received in Southwark : and as a further proof of my good will and affection, I request him to accept of a gag and a brand new pair of fetters, which, if he should refuse, I will and bequeath him in lieu thereof—my malediction.

*Item.* To my beloved countrymen, the people of Old England, I will and bequeath a copy of Doctor Priestley's *Charity Sermon for the benefit of poor Emigrants;* and to the said preaching philosopher himself, I bequeath a heart full of disappointment, grief, and despair.

*Item.* To the good people of France, who remain attached to their sovereign, particularly to those among whom I was hospitably received, I bequeath each a good strong dagger : hoping most sincerely that they may yet find courage enough to carry them to the hearts of their abominable tyrants.

*Item.* To Citizen M——oe, I will and bequeath my chamber looking-glass. It is a plain but exceeding true mirror ; in it he will see the exact likeness of a traitor, who has bartered the honour and interest of his country to a perfidious and savage enemy.

*Item.* To the Republican Britons, who have fled from the hands of justice in their own country, and who are a scandal, a nuisance, and a disgrace to this, I bequeath hunger and nakedness, scorn and reproach ; and I do hereby positively enjoin on my executors to contribute five hundred dollars towards the erection of gallowses and gibbets, for the accommodation of the said imported patriots, when the legislators of this unhappy state shall have the wisdom to countenance such useful establishments.

*Item.* My friend, J. T. Callender, the runaway from Scotland, is, of course, a partaker in the last mentioned legacy ; but as a particular mark of my attention, I will and bequeath him twenty feet of pine plank, which I request my executors to see made into a pillory, to be kept for his particular use, till a gibbet can be prepared.

*Item.* To Tom Paine, the author of *Common Sense, Rights of Man, Age of Reason*, and a *Letter to General Washington*, I bequeath a strong hempen collar, as the only legacy I can think of that is worthy of him as well as best adapted to render his death in some measure as infamous as his life : and I do hereby direct and order my Executors to send it to him by the first safe conveyance with my compliments, and request that he would make use of it without delay, that the national razor may not be disgraced by the head of such a monster.

*Item.* To the gaunt outlandish orator, vulgarly called the Political Sinner, who in the just order of things follows next after the last mentioned legatee, I bequeath the honour of partaking in his catastrophe ; that in their deaths, as well as in their lives, all the world may exclaim : "*See how rogues hang together*".

*Item.* To all and singular the good people of these States, I leave peace, union, abundance, happiness, untarnished honour, and an unconquerable everlasting hatred to the French Revolutionists and their destructive abominable principles.

*Item.* To each of my Subscribers I leave *a quill*, hoping that in their hands it may become a sword against every thing that is hostile to the government and independence of their country.

*Lastly.* To my three brothers, Paul, Simon, and Dick, I leave my whole estate, as well real as personal (first paying the foregoing legacies) to be equally divided between them, share and share alike. And I do hereby make and constitute my said three brothers the Executors of this my LAST WILL ; to see the same performed, according to its true intent and meaning, as far as in their power lies.

PETER PORCUPINE.

Witnesses present,

Philo Fun, }
Jack Jockus. }

# THE VISION OF LIBERTY.

*Written in the manner of Spenser.*

[As the virulent style of political writing prevalent ninety years ago is now but little known, the present edition of *The Poetry of the Anti-Jacobin* seemed a convenient medium for giving some specimens of it which appeared in *The Anti-Jacobin Review and Magazine*, a work conducted on the same principles, but by different writers, and with the cognizance of the government. Two of them were by W. COBBETT, who, had he been less arrogant and contentious, and more consistent, would have been, in the words of Lord Dalling, "a very great man in the world ; as it was he made a great noise in it". (See pp. 311-319.)

The *Vision of Liberty* is by C. KIRKPATRICK SHARPE, an author and artist much esteemed by Scottish antiquarians, of which specimens only need be given. Of *The Anarchists*, the author is not known.]

## I.

O WRETCHED man, how long wilt thou refuse
Thy Maker's favour, and His mercy great?
How long thy worldly happiness abuse,
And growl and grumble at thy present state?
Seeking accursed change both soon and late,
And newest modes allured still to try—
England, beware God's wrath to aggravate,
For foreign magic blinds thy charmed eye,
And Liberty, sweet Liberty, is now the constant cry.

## II.

As on my couch in slumber's arms I lay,
A vision did my senses entertain ;
Of late, me thought in France I miss'd my way,
Amid a columnless deserted plain ;
No man or beast upon it did remain,
Swept off by Discord's wide destroying strife:
Ne planted fence, ne field of waving grain,
Marking the toiling farmer's busy life,
But ruined huts and castles, brent, were wondrous rife.

## III.

Yet on this plain, most goodly to behold,
Saw I a temple tow'ring to the sky,
The dome where of was made of basest gold,
Most false, but yet most lovely to the eye ;
And rotting pillars reareth it on high,
Of ghastly human heads, and clotted gore,
With dust, y'mixt the mortar doth supply,
While foulest birds still round this temple soar,
And filthy serpents hiss, and giant hyenas roar.

## IV.

Among the heads that did the mass compose,
Three royal skulls were there—one of a king—
Meek saint, who never once revil'd his foes,
His bloody foes that him to scaffold bring ;
One of a maid ; O heaven ! that I could sing
With Spenser's tongue, her spotless purity,
Her holy zeal, in courts so rare a thing,
By lawless fiends condemn'd she was to die,
And sent, untimely sent, to seek her native sky.

## V.

The third I marked with melancholy eyes,
A female head, that once a crown did wear,
Cut off in life's full bloom, now low she lies,
The loose loves weeping o'er her early bier,
Nor Virtue's self denies a tender tear ;
So young a creature, wonder not she fell,
And left the paths of chastity severe,
Debauched by a court where lust did dwell
Like treach'rous Circe, skill'd in many a witching spell.

## VI.

Ah ! where are now her gorgeous robes of state,
The glitt'ring gems that did her fairness deck ?
The cringing nobles that on her did wait,
The high-born dames that kneeled at her beck ?
Alas ! a ghastly face, a bloody neck,
A simple winding-sheet is now her share ;
Look here, ye proud ones, on this mighty wreck,
And learn what perishable stuff ye are,
From her poor mangled carcase, once so sweet and fair.

## VII.

And on the ground there lay a murder'd child,
A piteous sight it was, and full of woe,
Who, when alive, by every art defil'd,
With poison, they at last did overthrow,
Wretches, who never ruth or conscience know ;
O lovely flowret cropt by villain hands,
How will thy butchers dread th' almighty brow,
Arm'd with frowns, when each at judgment stands,
And God the meed of murder from His throne commands.

## VIII.

Then o'er the portal was this motto plac'd,
" The house of liberty," in gold y'writ,
And, vent'ring in, I stood like one amaz'd
Such sights of horror on my heart-strings smit.
There Infidelity, in moody fit,
Hugg'd Suicide—there Rage, and deadly Fears,
There Lechery, with goatish leer did sit,
And Murder, quaffing up his victim's tears,
With thousand other crimes, too foul for human ears.

## IX.

In 'mid the house an image stood in state,
Like to VOLTAIRE in visage and in shape,
Wither'd his heart with fellest rage and hate
Shrivell'd and lean his carcase like an ape

21

And num'rous crowds upon the same did gape,
As he all-naked stood to every eye ;
Above an altar covered with crape,
And formed of his books one might descry,
Profane and lewd it was, and cramm'd with many a lie.

## X.

And still from 'neath the altar roared he,
As from a bull lowing in cavern deep,
" Come worship me, *O men*, come worship me ;
Spit on the cross, of Jesus take no keep,
I promise you an everlasting sleep ;
The soul and body both shall turn to clay ;
Ye penitents, why do ye sigh and weep ?
Let not damnation's terrors you affray,
Come learn my lore that drives all foolish fears away ".

. . . . . . . . . .

## XIV.

Next came that cursed felon THOMAS PAINE,
Mounted upon a tiger fierce and fell ;
And still a shower of blood on him doth rain,
With tears that from the eyes of widows well ;
Loud in his ears the cries of orphans yell ;
The axe impending o'er his head alway
While devils wait to catch his soul to hell,
The knave is fill'd with anguish and dismay—
And anxious round he looks, even straws do him affray.

## XV.

Then saw I mounted on a braying ass
WILLIAM and MARY, sooth, a couple jolly ;
Who married, note ye how it came to pass,
Although each held that marriage was but folly.

. . . . . . . . . .

## XVIII.

Then came MARIA HELEN WILLIAMS STONE,
Sitting upon a goat with bearded chin ;
And she hath written volumes many a one ;
Better the idle jade had learned to spin.

. . . . . . . . .

## XIX.

Next mounted on a monster like a louse,
With parchments loaded, came a man of law,*
Sprung from an ancient Caledonian house,
Cunningly could he quibble out a flaw ;
And this sage man would chatter like a daw,
To prove the moon green cheese, and black, pure white,
Spitting out treason from his greedy maw ;
To breed sedition was his chief delight,
And scratch men's scabs to ulcers still with all his might.

---

[* Lord Erskine.—ED.]

## XX.

Then on an Irish bull of skin and bone,
A foul churl * rode, who still a harp would strum,
A harp Hibernian, stringless saving one,
Well tun'd to harsh sedition's growling hum ;
He hit the bull on which he had his bum
Full many a bitter pang, nor gave him rest—
Dealing his blows on Teagues that round him come,
Grieving the while for man and brute opprest,
Chaunting the Irish howl, abhorr'd of man and beast.

## XXI.

O IRELAND, spot accurs'd—tho' glorions fair,
Shines there the sun, the flowers enamell'd blow,
And scent, with fragrance sweet, the balmy air,
Rippling the gliding pools that softly flow ;
No noxious reptile there to man a foe
Abides, but black revenge with cautious plan,
Cool-blooded cruelty with torments slow,
Springs rank ; with weeds the góodly soil's o'er-ran,
And all the reptile's venom rankles in the man.

## XXII.

Then in a gorgeous car of beaten gold,
Drove on a portly man, of mighty rank,†
A person comely, of extraction old ;
But, carrion-like, his reputation stank ;
Sly was the wight, with crafty quip and crank,
To cram with glittering coin his bursting bags ;
Yet whilom taxing-men play'd him a prank,
By catching in their traps some strayed nags,
And eke some livery slaves, in miser's livery rags.

## XXIII.

Then on a turtle came proud London's Mayor,
Followed by Aldermen, a frowsy crew,
Strong smelling of Cheapside, and luscious fair,
Yet apoplexy made his followers few.
Long antlers on the head of each man grew,
So that they seem'd a host of moving horn ;
Anon as on they came they'd mump and chew,
Stuffing their guts from dawning of the morn,
Till shades of evening fell—for eating only born.

## XXIV.

On a cock sparrow fed with Spanish flies,
A swilling Captain came, with liquor mellow,
And still the crowd in hideous uproar cries,‡
"Sing us a bawdy song, thou d——d good fellow ".
Incontinent he sets himself to bellow,
And shouts with all the strength that in him lies ;
The Citizets exclaim, " He's sans pareilly O";
The Citizens in raptures roll their eyes,
And drink with leathern ears, the fool's lewd ribaldries.

---

[* T. Moore in his early college days.—ED.]
[† Francis, fifth Duke of Bedford, see *Ballad*.—ED.]
[‡ Capt. Charles Morris.—ED.]

### XXV.

On came these wights, and many more beside,
Thick as the grains of sand upon the shore,
Thick as a swarm of flies in summer tide,
That on a dunghill hive and hover o'er ;
Most had their hides all scall'd, their trousers tore ;
Many sans breeches, shameless trudg'd along,
And many a noble knave and titled w——e,
With Irish bog-trotters would crowd and throng,
Carolling catches base, and filthy French chanson.

### XXVI.

Like roaring waves they cover'd all the plain ;
And tho' equality they still requir'd,
Each cudgell'd sore his breast with might and main,
Each to get foremost ardently desir'd.
Some fell into the dirt, and foul were mir'd,
The rest rode over them and took no heed.
Their yells, with patriotic ardour fired,
So made my flesh to quake with very dread,
That Morpheus left my couch, and all the vision fled.

The insertion of the foregoing poem (which was never printed) into your entertaining and useful pnblication, will much oblige,

Your humble servant,

C. K.

# INDEX TO THE *ANTI-JACOBIN*.

*4th Edition*, 1799 ; *2 vols., 8vo.*

## A.

## B.

326 POETRY OF THE ANTI-JACOBIN.

*Blasphemy* attempted without success by the *Morning Post*, vol. i., p. 505—and
by the *Courier*—fully succeeded in by the *Morning Chronicle*, vol. i., p. 325,
&c.
*Bosville*, Mr., Banker to the Corresponding Society, vol. i., p. 409.
*Brownrigg*, Mrs. : Inscription for the Door of her Cell in Newgate, vol. i., p. 35.
*British Merchant*, his Letter on the misrepresentations of the Party, with respect
to the continuance of the War, vol. i., p. 593.
*Brissot's* Ghost, vol. ii., p. 236.
*Burdett*, Sir Something : his affectionate mention of Mr. Paine at the Shake-
speare Tavern, vol. i., p. 136.
*Burdett*, Sir Francis, runner to the Corresponding Society, vol. i., p. 408.
*Buonaparté* : his health given by Mr. Macfungus, vol. i., p. 35—his Letter to the
Commandant at Zanté, vol. ii., p. 535.

## C.

*Camille Jordan*, asserts that one of our Jacobin Newspapers is in the pay of
France, vol. i., pp. 507, 622 ; vol. ii., pp. 17, 51, 86, 488.
*Cambridge Intelligencer*, detected and exposed, vol. ii., pp. 263, 296.
*Chevy Chase ;* a Ballad to the Tune of, vol. ii., p. 21.
*Choice*, The : an Ode, vol. i., p. 263.
*Clare*, The Earl of, Character of, vol. ii., p. 544.
*Clare*, Earl of : proposes a question respecting the extent of Lord Moira's
DUPERY, vol. ii., p. 518.
*Clever :* See Mr Robert Ad—r, vol. i., p. 422.
*Coughing* and laughing : See Mr. John Nicholls, vol. i., p. 186.
*Courtney*, Mr., fully convicted of kidnapping—rhymes, vol. i., p. 376.
*Coalition*, The New : an Ode, vol. i., p. 599.
*Coalition* of Kings, vol. ii., p. 546.
*Constant* Reader : his Letter on the Designs of our foreign and domestic Enemies,
vol. i., pp. 544, 597.
*Courier*, The ; a mad—and foolish—and odious—and contemptible paper, *passim.*
Picked up by a Gentleman in the streets, for the sake of its superior infor-
mation ! ! ! vol. ii., p. 230.

## D.

*Detector :* his Letter on the pretended Treaty of Pavia, vol. i., p. 474—On the
Treaty of Pilnitz, vol. ii., p. 37—On the Coalition of Kings, vol. ii., p. 546.
*Description* of a very extraordinary Plant now growing at Paris, vol. ii., p. 573.
*Description* of Mr. Fox's Radical Reform, vol. i., p. 396.
*Description* of a Scribbler for the Jacobin Papers, vol. i., p. 613.
*Description* of the Jacobin Prints, vol. ii., p. 119.
*Decius Mus :* his account of the Secessions in the Roman Common Wealth, vol.
i., p. 261.
*Dismissal* of the Duke of Norfolk, vol. i., p. 429.
*Duncan*, Lord : Anecdotes relative to his Victory, vol. i., pp. 38, 107.
*Duke*, The, and the Taxing Man, vol. i., p. 265.
*Dupery* of Lord Moira, vol. ii., pp. 36, 518, &c., &c.

## E.

*Edwards*, Mr. Bryan : offers to pay for Mr. Nicholls's dinner at the Crown and
Anchor—finds his pockets pick'd—his exclamation thereat, vol. i., p. 410.
*Elegy* on the Death of Jean Bon Saint André, vol. ii., p. 314.
*Epigram* on the Loan upon England, vol. i., p. 267.
*Epistle*, Poetical, to the Editors of the Anti-Jacobin, vol. i., p. 371. Reply to
ditto, vol. i., p. 371.
*Epistle*, Poetical, to the Author of the Anti-Jacobin, vol. i., p. 486.

# L.

# M.

# INDEX TO VOL. I.

OF THE

## ANTI-JACOBIN REVIEW AND MAGAZINE.

[This Index and the two preceding articles (by W. Cobbett, pp. 311-319) are reprinted in order to show that the same spirit which pervaded *The Anti-Jacobin* was continued in its successor, *The Anti-Jacobin Review and Magazine*, although the Editor and Contributors were different.]

THE END.

ABERDEEN UNIVERSITY PRESS.

*A Catalogue of American and Foreign Books Published or Imported by* MESSRS. SAMPSON LOW & CO. *can be had on application.*

*St. Dunstan's House, Fetter Lane, Fleet Street, London,*
*October,* 1889.

# A Selection from the List of Books

PUBLISHED BY

## SAMPSON LOW, MARSTON, SEARLE, & RIVINGTON,

*LIMITED.*

**Low's Standard Novels,** page 17.
**Low's Standard Books for Boys,** page 18.
**Low's Standard Series,** page 19.
**Sea Stories,** by W. CLARK RUSSELL, page 26.

### ALPHABETICAL LIST.

*A*BBE*Y and Parsons, Quiet life.* From drawings; the motive by Austin Dobson, 4to.

*Abney (W. de W.) and Cunningham. Pioneers of the Alps.* With photogravure portraits of guides. Imp. 8vo, gilt top, 21s.

*Adam (G. Mercer) and Wetherald. An Algonquin Maiden.* Crown 8vo, 5s.

*Alcott. Works of the late Miss Louisa May Alcott :—*
Aunt Jo's Scrap-bag. Cloth, 2s.
Eight Cousins. Illustrated, 2s.; cloth gilt, 3s. 6d.
Jack and Jill. Illustrated, 2s.; cloth gilt, 3s. 6d.
Jo's Boys. 5s.
Jimmy's Cruise in the Pinafore, &c. Illustrated, cloth, 2s.; gilt edges, 3s. 6d.
Little Men. Double vol., 2s.; cloth, gilt edges, 3s. 6d.
Little Women. 1s. ⎫ 1 vol., cloth, 2s. ; larger ed., gilt
Little Women Wedded. 1s. ⎭ edges, 3s. 6d.
Old-fashioned Girl. 2s.; cloth, gilt edges, 3s. 6d.
Rose in Bloom. 2s.; cloth gilt, 3s. 6d.
Shawl Straps. Cloth, 2s.
Silver Pitchers. Cloth, gilt edges, 3s. 6d.
Under the Lilacs. Illustrated, 2s.; cloth gilt, 5s.
Work: a Story of Experience. 1s. ⎫ 1 vol., cloth, gilt
—— Its Sequel, " Beginning Again." 1s. ⎭ edges, 3s. 6d.
—— *Life, Letters and Journals.* By EDNAH D. CHENEY. Cr. 8vo, 6s.
—— See also "Low's Standard Series."

*Alden (W. L.) Adventures of Jimmy Brown, written by himself.* Illustrated. Small crown 8vo, cloth, 2s.

—— *Trying to find Europe.* Illus., crown 8vo, 5s.

A

*Alger (J. G.) Englishmen in the French Revolution,* cr. 8vo, 7s. 6d.
*Amateur Angler's Days in Dove Dale : Three Weeks' Holiday*
in 1884. By E. M. 1s. 6d. ; boards, 1s. ; large paper, 5s.
*Andersen. Fairy Tales.* An entirely new Translation. With
over 500 Illustrations by Scandinavian Artists. Small 4to, 6s.
*Anderson (W.) Pictorial Arts of Japan.* With 80 full-page
and other Plates, 16 of them in Colours. Large imp. 4to, £8 8s. (in
four folio parts, £2 2s. each) ; Artists' Proofs, £12 12s.
*Angling.* See Amateur, "Cutcliffe," "Fennell," "Halford,"
"Hamilton," "Martin," "Orvis," "Pennell," "Pritt," "Senior,"
"Stevens," "Theakston," "Walton," "Wells," and "Willis-Bund."
*Arnold (R.) Ammonia and Ammonium Compounds.* Translated,
illus., crown 8vo, 5s.
*Art Education.* See "Biographies," "D'Anvers," "Illustrated
Text Books," "Mollett's Dictionary."
*Artistic Japan.* Illustrated with Coloured Plates. Monthly.
Royal 4to, 2s.; vol. I., 15s.; II., roy. 4to., 15s.
*Ashe (R. P.) Two Kings of Uganda ; Six Years in E. Equa-*
torial Africa. Crown 8vo, 6s.
*Attwell (Prof.) The Italian Masters.* Crown 8vo, 3s. 6d.
*Audsley (G. A.) Handbook of the Organ.* Imperial 8vo, top
edge gilt, 31s. 6d.; large paper, 63s.
—— *Ornamental Arts of Japan.* 90 Plates, 74 in Colours
and Gold, with General and Descriptive Text. 2 vols., folio, £15 15s.;
in specially designed leather, £23 2s.
—— *The Art of Chromo-Lithography.* Coloured Plates
and Text. Folio, 63s.

*BACON (Delia) Biography, with Letters of Carlyle, Emerson,*
&c. Crown 8vo, 10s. 6d.
*Baddeley (W. St. Clair) Tchay and Chianti.* Small 8vo, 5s.
—— *Travel-tide.* Small post 8vo, 7s. 6d.
*Baldwin (James) Story of Siegfried.* 6s.
—— *Story of the Golden Age.* Illustrated by HOWARD
PYLE. Crown 8vo, 6s.
—— *Story of Roland.* Crown 8vo, 6s.
*Bamford (A. J.) Turbans and Tails.* Sketches in the Un-
romantic East. Crown 8vo, 7s. 6d.
*Barlow (Alfred) Weaving. by Hand and by Power.* With
several hundred Illustrations. Third Edition, royal 8vo, £1 5s.
*Barlow (P. W.) Kaipara, Experiences of a Settler in N. New*
Zealand. Illust., crown 8vo, 6s.
*Bassett (F. S.) Legends and Superstitions of the Sea.* 7s. 6d.

# THE BAYARD SERIES.

Edited by the late J. HAIN FRISWELL.

Comprising Pleasure Books of Literature produced in the Choicest Style.

"We can hardly imagine better books for boys to read or for men to ponder over."—*Times.*

*Price 2s. 6d. each Volume, complete in itself, flexible cloth extra, gilt edges, with silk Headbands and Registers.*

The Story of the Chevalier Bayard. Joinville's St. Louis of France.
The Essays of Abraham Cowley.
Abdallah. By Edouard Laboullaye.
Napoleon, Table-Talk and Opinions.
Words of Wellington.
Johnson's Rasselas. With Notes.
Hazlitt's Round Table.
The Religio Medici, Hydriotaphia, &c. By Sir Thomas Browne, Knt.
Coleridge's Christabel, &c. With Preface by Algernon C. Swinburne.
Ballad Poetry of the Affections. By Robert Buchanan.

Lord Chesterfield's Letters, Sentences, and Maxims. With Essay by Sainte-Beuve.
The King and the Commons. Cavalier and Puritan Songs.
Vathek. By William Beckford.
Essays in Mosaic. By Ballantyne.
My Uncle Toby ; his Story and his Friends. By P. Fitzgerald.
Reflections of Rochefoucauld.
Socrates : Memoirs for English Readers from Xenophon's Memorabilia. By Edw. Levien.
Prince Albert's Golden Precepts.

*A Case containing 12 Volumes, price 31s. 6d.; or the Case separately, price 3s. 6d.*

*Beaugrand (C.) Walks Abroad of Two Young Naturalists.* By D. SHARP. Illust., 8vo, 7s. 6d.

*Beecher (H. W.) Authentic Biography, and Diary.* Ill. 8vo, 21s.

*Behnke and Browne. Child's Voice : its Treatment with regard* to After Development. Small 8vo, 3s. 6d.

*Bell (H. H. J.) Obeah : Negro Superstition in the West Indies.* Crown 8vo, 2s. 6d.

*Beyschlag. Female Costume Figures of various Centuries.* 12 reproductions of pastel designs in portfolio, imperial. 21s.

*Bickerdyke (J.) Irish Midsummer Night's Dream.* Illus. by E. M. Cox. Crown 8vo, 1s. 6d.; boards, 1s.

*Bickersteth (Bishop E. H.) Clergyman in his Home.* 1s.

—— *Evangelical Churchmanship.* 1s.

—— *From Year to Year : Original Poetical Pieces.* Small post 8vo, 3s. 6d. ; roan, 6s. and 5s.; calf or morocco, 10s. 6d.

—— *The Master's Home-Call.* N. ed. 32mo, cloth gilt, 1s.

—— *The Master's Will.* A Funeral Sermon preached on the Death of Mrs. S. Gurney Buxton. Sewn, 6d. ; cloth gilt, 1s.

—— *The Reef, and other Parables.* Crown 8vo, 2s. 6d.

—— *Shadow of the Rock.* Select Religious Poetry. 2s. 6d.

—— *Shadowed Home and the Light Beyond.* 5s.

—— See also " Hymnal Companion."

A 2

*Biographies of the Great Artists (Illustrated).* Crown 8vo, emblematical binding, 3*s.* 6*d.* per volume, except where the price is given.

Claude le Lorrain, by Owen J. Dullea.
Correggio, by M. E. Heaton. 2*s.* 6*d.*
Della Robbia and Cellini. 2*s.* 6*d.*
Albrecht Dürer, by R. F. Heath.
Figure Painters of Holland.
FraAngelico,Masaccio,andBotticelli.
Fra Bartolommeo, Albertinelli, and Andrea del Sarto.
Gainsborough and Constable.
Ghiberti and Donatello. 2*s.* 6*d.*
Giotto, by Harry Quilter.
Hans Holbein, by Joseph Cundall.
Hogarth, by Austin Dobson.
Landseer, by F. G. Stevens.
Lawrence and Romney, by Lord Ronald Gower. 2*s.* 6*d.*
Leonardo da Vinci.
Little Masters of Germany, by W. B. Scott.

Mantegna and Francia.
Meissonier, by J. W. Mollett. 2*s.* 6*d.*
Michelangelo Buonarotti,by Clément.
Murillo, by Ellen E. Minor. 2*s.* 6*d.*
Overbeck, by J. B. Atkinson.
Raphael, by N. D'Anvers.
Rembrandt, by J. W. Mollett.
Reynolds, by F. S. Pulling.
Rubens, by C. W. Kett.
Tintoretto, by W. R. Osler.
Titian, by R. F. Heath.
Turner, by Cosmo Monkhouse.
Vandyck and Hals, by P. R. Head.
Velasquez, by E. Stowe.
Vernet and Delaroche, by J. Rees.
Watteau, by J. W. Mollett. 2*s.* 6*d.*
Wilkie, by J. W. Mollett.

IN PREPARATION.

Barbizon School, by J. W. Mollett.
Cox and De Wint, Lives and Works.
George Cruikshank, Life and Works.

Miniature Painters of Eng. School.
Mulready Memorials, by Stephens.
Van de Velde and the Dutch Painters

*Bird (F. J.) American Practical Dyer's Companion.* 8vo, 42*s.*

—— *(H. E.) Chess Practice.* 8vo, 2*s.* 6*d.*

*Black (Robert) Horse Racing in France : a History.* 8vo, 14*s.*

—— See also CICERO.

*Black (W.) Penance of John Logan, and other Tales.* Crown 8vo, 10*s.* 6*d.*

——See also " Low's Standard Library."

*Blackburn (Charles F.) Hints on Catalogue Titles and Index Entries,* with a Vocabulary of Terms and Abbreviations, chiefly from Foreign Catalogues. Royal 8vo, 14*s.*

*Blackburn (Henry) Art in the Mountains, the Oberammergau Passion Play.* New ed., corrected to date, 8vo, 5*s.*

—— *Breton Folk.* With 171 Illust. by RANDOLPH CALDECOTT Imperial 8vo, gilt edges, 21*s.*; plainer binding, 10*s.* 6*d.*

—— *Pyrenees.* Illustrated by GUSTAVE DORÉ, corrected to 1881. Crown 8vo, 7*s.* 6*d.* See also CALDECOTT.

*Blackmore (R. D.) Kit and Kitty.* A novel. 3 vols , crown 8vo, 31*s.* 6*d.*

—— *Lorna Doone. Edition de luxe.* Crown 4to, very numerous Illustrations, cloth, gilt edges, 31*s.* 6*d.*; parchment, uncut, top gilt, 35*s.* ; new issue, plainer, 21*s.*

—— *Novels.* See also " Low's Standard Novels."

*Blackmore (R. D.) Springhaven.* Illust. by PARSONS and BARNARD. Sq. 8vo, 12*s.*; new edition, 7*s.* 6*d.*

*Blaikie (William) How to get Strong and how to Stay so.* Rational, Physical, Gymnastic, &c., Exercises. Illust., sm. post 8vo, 5*s.*

—— *Sound Bodies for our Boys and Girls.* 16mo, 2*s.* 6*d.*

*Bonwick. British Colonies.* Asia, 1*s.*; Africa, 1*s.*; America, 1*s.*; Australasia, 1*s.* One vol., cloth, 5*s.*

*Bosanquet (Rev. C.) Blossoms from the King's Garden : Sermons* for Children. 2nd Edition, small post 8vo, cloth extra, 6*s.*

—— *Jehoshaphat ; or, Sunlight and Clouds.* 1*s.*

*Bowden (H. ; Miss) Witch of the Atlas : a ballooning story,* Crown 8vo, 6*s.*

*Bower (G. S.) and Spencer, Law of Electric Lighting.* New edition, crown 8vo, 12*s.* 6*d.*

*Boyesen (H. H.) Modern Vikings : Stories of Life and Sport* in Norseland. Cr. 8vo, 6*s.*

—— *Story of Norway.* Illustrated, sm. 8vo, 7*s.* 6*d.*

*Boy's Froissart. King Arthur. Knightly Legends of Wales.* . *Percy.* See LANIER.

*Bradshaw (J.) New Zealand as it is.* 8vo, 12*s.* 6*d.*

—— *New Zealand of To-day,* 1884-87. 8vo, 14*s.*

*Brannt (W. T.) Animal and Vegetable Fats and Oils.* Illust., 8vo, 35*s.*

—— *Manufacture of Soap and Candles, with many Formulas.* Illust., 8vo, 35*s.*

—— *Manufacture of Vinegar, Cider, and Fruit Wines.* Illustrated, 8vo.

—— *Metallic Alloys. Chiefly from the German of Krupp* and Wildberger. Crown 8vo, 12*s.* 6*d.*

*Bright (John) Public Letters.* Crown 8vo, 7*s.* 6*d.*

*Brisse (Baron) Ménus* (366). A *ménu,* in French and English, for every Day in the Year. 2nd Edition. Crown 8vo, 5*s.*

*Brittany.* See BLACKBURN.

*Browne (G. Lennox) Voice Use and Stimulants.* Sm. 8vo, 3*s.* 6*d.*

—— *and Behnke (Emil) Voice, Song, and Speech.* N. ed., 5*s.*

*Brumm (C.) Bismarck, his Deeds and Aims; reply to " Bismarck* Dynasty." 8vo, 1*s.*

*Bruntie's Diary. A Tour round the World.* By C. E. B., 1*s.* 6*d.*

*Bryant (W. C.) and Gay (S. H.) History of the United States.* 4 vols., royal 8vo, profusely Illustrated, 60*s.*

*Bryce (Rev. Professor) Manitoba.* Illust. *Crown 8vo, 7*s.* 6*d.*

—— *Short History of the Canadian People.* 7*s.* 6*d.*

*Bulkeley (Owen T.) Lesser Antilles.* Pref. by D. MORRIS, Illus., crown 8vo, boards, 2*s.* 6*d.*

*Burnaby (Mrs. F.) High Alps in Winter; or, Mountaineering* in Search of Health. With Illustrations, &c., 14s. See also MAIN.
*Burnley (J.) History of the Silk Trade.*
—— *History of Wool and Woolcombing.* Illust. 8vo, 21s.
*Burton (Sir R. F.) Early, Public, and Private Life.* Edited by F. HITCHMAN. 2 vols., 8vo, 36s.
*Butler (Sir W. F.) Campaign of the Cataracts.* Illust., 8vo, 18s.
—— *Invasion of England, told twenty years after.* 2s. 6d.
—— *Red Cloud; or, the Solitary Sioux.* Imperial 16mo, numerous illustrations, gilt edges, 3s. 6d.; plainer binding, 2s. 6d.
—— *The Great Lone Land; Red River Expedition.* 7s. 6d.
—— *The Wild North Land; the Story of a Winter Journey* with Dogs across Northern North America. 8vo, 18s. Cr. 8vo, 7s. 6d.
*Bynner (E. L.) Agnes Surriage.* Crown 8vo, 10s. 6d.

*CABLE (G. W.) Bonaventure: A Prose Pastoral of Acadian* Louisiana. Sm. post 8vo, 5s.
*Cadogan(Lady A.) Drawing-roomPlays.* 10s. 6d.; acting ed., 6d. each.
—— *Illustrated Games of Patience.* Twenty-four Diagrams in Colours, with Text. Fcap. 4to, 12s. 6d.
—— *New Games of Patience.* Coloured Diagrams, 4to, 12s.6d.
*Caldecott (Randolph) Memoir.* By HENRY BLACKBURN. With 170 Examples of the Artist's Work. 14s.; new edit., 7s. 6d.
—— *Sketches.* With an Introduction by H. BLACKBURN. 4to, picture boards, 2s. 6d.
*California.* See NORDHOFF.
*Callan (H.) Wanderings on Wheel and on Foot.* Cr. 8vo, 1s. 6d.
*Campbell (Lady Colin) Book of the Running Brook: and of* Still Waters. 5s.
*Canadian People: Short History.* Crown 8vo, 7s. 6d.
*Carbutt (Mrs.) Five Months' Fine Weather in Canada,* West U.S., and Mexico. Crown 8vo, 5s.
*Carleton, City Legends.* Special Edition, illus., royal 8vo, 12s. 6d.; ordinary edition, crown 8vo, 1s.
—— *City Ballads.* Illustrated, 12s. 6d. New Ed. (Rose Library), 16mo, 1s.
—— *Farm Ballads, Farm Festivals, and Farm Legends.* Paper boards, 1s. each; 1 vol., small post 8vo, 3s. 6d.
*Carnegie (A.) American Four-in-Hand in Britain.* Small 4to, Illustrated, 10s. 6d. Popular Edition, paper, 1s.
—— *Round the World.* 8vo, 10s. 6d.
—— *Triumphant Democracy.* 6s.; also 1s. 6d. and 1s.
*Chairman's Handbook.* By R. F. D. PALGRAVE. 5th Edit., 2s.

*Changed Cross, &c.* Religious Poems. 16mo, 2s. 6d.; calf, 6s.

*Chess.* See BIRD (H. E.).

*Children's Praises.* Hymns for Sunday-Schools and Services. Compiled by LOUISA H. H. TRISTRAM. 4d.

*Choice Editions of Choice Books.* 2s. 6d. each. Illustrated by C. W. COPE, R.A., T. CRESWICK, R.A., E. DUNCAN, BIRKET FOSTER, J. C. HORSLEY, A.R.A., G. HICKS, R. REDGRAVE, R.A., C. STONEHOUSE, F. TAYLER, G. THOMAS, H. J. TOWNSHEND, E. H. WEHNERT, HARRISON WEIR, &c.

| | |
|---|---|
| Bloomfield's Farmer's Boy. | Milton's L'Allegro. |
| Campbell's Pleasures of Hope. | Poetry of Nature. Harrison Weir. |
| Coleridge's Ancient Mariner. | Rogers' (Sam.) Pleasures of Memory. |
| Goldsmith's Deserted Village. | Shakespeare's Songs and Sonnets. |
| Goldsmith's Vicar of Wakefield. | Tennyson's May Queen. |
| Gray's Elegy in a Churchyard. | Elizabethan Poets. |
| Keats' Eve of St. Agnes. | Wordsworth's Pastoral Poems. |

" Such works are a glorious beatification for a poet."—*Athenæum.*

*Christ in Song.* By PHILIP SCHAFF. New Ed., gilt edges, 6s.

*Chromo-Lithography.* See AUDSLEY.

*Cicero, Tusculan Disputation, I. (Death no bane).* Translated by R. BLACK. Small crown 8vo.

*Clarke (H. P.)* See WILLS.

*Clarke (P.) Three Diggers: a Tale of the Australian Fifties.* Crown 8vo, 6s.

*Cochran (W.) Pen and Pencil in Asia Minor.* Illust., 8vo, 21s.

*Collingwood (Harry) Under the Meteor Flag.* The Log of a Midshipman. Illustrated, small post 8vo, gilt, 3s. 6d.; plainer, 2s. 6d.

——— *Voyage of the " Aurora."* Gilt, 3s. 6d.; plainer, 2s. 6d.

*Collinson (Sir R.; Adm.) H.M.S. "Enterprise" in search of Sir J. Franklin.* 8vo.

*Colonial Year-book.* Edited and compiled by A. J. R. TRENDELL. Crown 8vo, 6s.

*Cook (Dutton) Book of the Play.* New Edition. 1 vol., 3s. 6d.

——— *On the Stage: Studies.* 2 vols., 8vo, cloth, 24s.

*Cozzens (F.) American Yachts.* 27 Plates, 22 × 28 inches. Proofs, £21; Artist's Proofs, £31 10s.

*Craddock (C. E.) Despot of Broomsedge Cove.* Crown 8vo, 6s.

*Crew (B. J.) Practical Treatise on Petroleum.* Illust., 8vo, 28s.

*Crouch (A.P.) Glimpses of Feverland: a Cruise in West African Waters.* Crown 8vo, 6s.

——— *On a Surf-bound Coast.* Crown 8vo, 7s. 6d.

*Cumberland(Stuart)Thought Reader'sThoughts.* Cr. 8vo., 10s.6d.

——— *Queen's Highway from Ocean to Ocean.* Ill., 8vo, 18s.; new ed., 7s. 6d.

*Cumberland (S.) Vasty deep : a Strange Story of To-day.* New
Edition, 6s.

*Cundall (Joseph).* See " Remarkable Bindings."

*Cushing (W.) Initials and Pseudonyms.* Large 8vo, 25s.;
second series, large 8vo, 21s.

*Custer (Eliz. B.) Tenting on the Plains; Gen. Custer in Kansas
and Texas.* Royal 8vo, 18s.

*Cutcliffe (H. C.) Trout Fishing in Rapid Streams.* Cr. 8vo, 3s. 6d.

*DALY (Mrs. D.) Digging, Squatting, and Pioneering in*
Northern South Australia. 8vo, 12s.

*D'Anvers. Elementary History of Art.* New ed., 360 illus.,
2 vols., cr. 8vo. I. Architecture, &c., 5s.; II. Painting, 6s.; 1 vol.,
10s. 6d.

—— *Elementary History of Music.* Crown 8vo, 2s. 6d.

*Davis (Clement) Modern Whist.* 4s.

—— *(C. T.) Bricks, Tiles, Terra-Cotta, &c.* N. ed. 8vo, 25s.

—— *Manufacture of Leather.* With many Illustrations. 52s.6d.

—— *Manufacture of Paper.* 28s.

—— *(G. B.) Outlines of International Law.* 8vo. 10s. 6d.

*Dawidowsky. Glue, Gelatine, Isinglass, Cements, &c.* 8vo, 12s.6d.

*Day of My Life at Eton.* By an ETON BOY. New ed. 16mo, 1s.

*Day's Collacon : an Encyclopædia of Prose Quotations.* Imperial 8vo, cloth, 31s. 6d.

*De Leon (E.) Under the Stars and under the Crescent.* N. ed., 6s.

*Dethroning Shakspere. Letters to the Daily Telegraph ; and*
Editorial Papers. Crown 8vo, 2s. 6d.

*Dickinson (Charles M.) The Children, and other Verses.* Sm.
8vo, gilt edges, 5s.

*Dictionary.* See TOLHAUSEN, " Technological."

*Diggle (J. W. ; Canon) Lancashire Life of Bishop Fraser.* 8vo,
12s. 6d.

*Donnelly (Ignatius) Atlantis ; or, the Antediluvian World.*
7th Edition, crown 8vo, 12s. 6d.

—— *Ragnarok : The Age of Fire and Gravel.* Illustrated,
crown 8vo, 12s. 6d.

—— *The Great Cryptogram : Francis Bacon's Cipher in the*
so-called Shakspere Plays. With facsimiles. 2 vols., 30s.

*Donkin (J. G.) Trooper and Redskin : N.W. Mounted Police,*
Canada. Crown 8vo, 8s. 6d.

*Dougall (James Dalziel) Shooting: its Appliances, Practice,*
and Purpose. New Edition, revised with additions. Crown 8vo, 7s. 6d.
"The book is admirable in every way. . . . . We wish it every success."—*Globe.*
"A very complete treatise. . . . . Likely to take high rank as an authority on
shooting."—*Daily News.*

*Doughty (H.M.) Friesland Meres, and through the Netherlands.*
Illustrated, crown 8vo, 8s. 6d.
*Dramatic Year: Brief Criticisms of Events in the U.S.* By W.
ARCHER. Crown 8vo, 6s.
*Dunstan Standard Readers.* Ed. by A. GILL, of Cheltenham.

*EARL (H. P.) Randall Trevor.* 2 vols., crown 8vo, 21s.

*Eastwood (F.) In Satan's Bonds.* 2 vols., crown 8vo, 21s.
*Edmonds (C.) Poetry of the Anti-Jacobin. With Additional*
matter. New ed. Illust., crown 8vo, 7s. 6d. ; large paper, 21s.
*Educational List and Directory for* 1887-88. 5s.
*Educational Works* published in Great Britain. A Classi-
fied Catalogue. Third Edition, 8vo, cloth extra, 6s.
*Edwards (E.) American Steam Engineer.* Illust., 12mo, 12s. 6d.
*Eight Months on the Argentine Gran Chaco.* 8vo, 8s. 6d.
*Elliott (H. W.) An Arctic Province: Alaska and the Seal*
Islands. Illustrated from Drawings ; also with Maps. 16s.
*Emerson (Dr. P. H.) English Idylls.* Small post 8vo, 2s.
—— *Pictures of East Anglian Life.* Ordinary edit., 105s. ;
édit. de luxe, 17 × 13½, vellum, morocco back, 147s.
—— *Naturalistic Photography for Art Students.* Illustrated.
New edit. 5s.
—— *and Goodall. Life and Landscape on the Norfolk*
Broads. Plates 12 × 8 inches, 126s.; large paper, 210s.
*Emerson in Concord: A Memoir written by Edward Waldo*
EMERSON. 8vo, 7s. 6d.
*English Catalogue of Books.* Vol. III., 1872—1880. Royal
8vo, half-morocco, 42s. See also "Index."
*English Etchings.* Published Quarterly. 3s. 6d. Vol. VI., 25s.
*English Philosophers.* Edited by E. B. IVAN MÜLLER, M.A.
Crown 8vo volumes of 180 or 200 pp., price 3s. 6d. each.

Francis Bacon, by Thomas Fowler. | Shaftesbury and Hutcheson.
Hamilton, by W. H. S. Monck. | Adam Smith, by J. A. Farrer.
Hartley and James Mill. |

*Esmarch (F.) Handbook of Surgery.* Translation from the
last German Edition. With 647 new Illustrations. 8vo, leathei, 24s.
*Eton. About some Fellows.* New Edition, 1s.
*Evelyn. Life of Mrs. Godolphin.* By WILLIAM HARCOURT,
of Nuneham. Steel Portrait. Extra binding, gilt top, 7s. 6d.
*Eves (C. W.) West Indies.* (Royal Colonial Institute publication.) Crown 8vo, 7s. 6d.

*FARINI (G. A.) Through the Kalahari Desert.* 8vo, 21s.

*Farm Ballads, Festivals, and Legends.* See CARLETON.

*Fay (T.) Three Germanys ; glimpses into their History.*  2 vols., 8vo, 35*s.*

*Fenn (G. Manville) Off to the Wilds: a Story for Boys.* Profusely Illustrated. Crown 8vo, gilt edges, 3*s.* 6*d.*; plainer, 2*s.* 6*d.*

——— *Silver Cañon.* Illust., gilt ed., 3*s.* 6*d.* ; plainer, 2*s.* 6*d.*

*Fennell (Greville) Book of the Roach.* New Edition, 12mo, 2*s.*

*Ferns.* See HEATH.

*Fitzgerald (P.) Book Fancier.* Cr. 8vo. 5*s.* ; large pap. 12*s.* 6 *l.*

*Fleming (Sandford) England and Canada : a Tour.* Cr. 8vo, 6*s.*

*Florence.* See YRIARTE.

*Folkard (R., Jun.) Plant Lore, Legends, and Lyrics.* 8vo, 16*s.*

*Forbes (H. O.) Naturalist in the Eastern Archipelago.* 8vo. 21*s.*

*Foreign Countries and British Colonies.* Cr. 8vo, 3*s.* 6*d.* each.

| | |
|---|---|
| Australia, by J. F. Vesey Fitzgerald. | Japan, by S. Mossman. |
| Austria, by D. Kay, F.R.G.S. | Peru, by Clements R. Markham. |
| Denmark and Iceland, by E. C. Otté. | Russia, by W. R. Morfill, M.A. |
| Egypt, by S. Lane Poole, B.A. | Spain, by Rev. Wentworth Webster. |
| France, by Miss M. Roberts. | Sweden and Norway, by Woods. |
| Germany, by S. Baring-Gould. | West Indies, by C. H. Eden, |
| Greece, by L. Sergeant, B.A. | F.R.G.S. |

*Franc (Maud Jeanne).*  Small post 8vo, uniform, gilt edges :—

| | |
|---|---|
| Emily's Choice. 5*s.* | Vermont Vale. 5*s.* |
| Hall's Vineyard. 4*s.* | Minnie's Mission. 4*s.* |
| John's Wife : A Story of Life in South Australia. 4*s.* | Little Mercy. 4*s.* |
| | Beatrice Melton's Discipline. 4*s.* |
| Marian ; or, The Light of Some One's Home. 5*s.* | No Longer a Child. 4*s.* |
| | Golden Gifts. 4*s.* |
| Silken Cords and Iron Fetters. 4*s.* | Two Sides to Every Question. 4*s.* |
| Into the Light. 4*s.* | Master of Ralston. 4*s.* |

\*\*\* There is also a re-issue in cheaper form at 2*s.* 6*d.* per vol.

*Frank's Ranche ; or, My Holiday in the Rockies.* A Contribution to the Inquiry into What we are to Do with our Boys. 5*s.*

*Fraser (Bishop).* See DIGGLE.

*French.* See JULIEN and PORCHER.

*Fresh Woods and Pastures New.* By the Author of "An Amateur Angler's Days." 1*s.* 6*d.*; large paper, 5*s.* ; new ed., 1*s.*

*Froissart.* See LANIER.

*Fuller (Edward) Fellow Travellers.* 3*s.* 6*d.*

——— See also "Dramatic Year."

*GASPARIN (Countess A. de) Sunny Fields and Shady Woods.* 6*s.*

*Geary (Grattan) Burma after the Conquest.* 7*s.* 6*d.*

*Geffcken (F. H.) British Empire.* Translated by S. J. MACMILLAN. Crown 8vo, 7*s.* 6*d.*

*Gentle Life* (Queen Edition).   2 vols. in 1, small 4to, 6*s.*

## THE GENTLE LIFE SERIES.

Price 6*s.* each ; or in calf extra, price 10*s.* 6*d.* ; Smaller Edition, cloth
extra, 2*s.* 6*d.*, except where price is named.

*The Gentle Life.*   Essays in aid of the Formation of Character.
*About in the World.*   Essays by Author of " The Gentle Life."
*Like unto Christ.*   New Translation of Thomas à Kempis.
*Familiar Words.*   A Quotation Handbook.   6*s.*; n. ed. 3*s.*6*d.*
*Essays by Montaigne.*   Edited by the Author of " The Gentle
Life."
*The Gentle Life.*   2nd Series.
*The Silent Hour.*   *Essays, Original and Selected.*
*Half-Length Portraits.*   Short Studies of Notable Persons.
By J. HAIN FRISWELL.
*Essays on English Writers,* for Students in English Literature.
*Other People's Windows.*   By J. HAIN FRISWELL.   6*s.* ; new
ed., 3*s.* 6*d.*
*A Man's Thoughts.*   By J. HAIN FRISWELL.
*Countess of Pembroke's Arcadia.*   By Sir P. SIDNEY.   6*s.*; new
ed., 3*s.* 6*d.*

---

*Germany.*   By S. BARING-GOULD.   Crown 8vo, 3*s.* 6*d.*
*Gibbon (C.) Beyond Compare : a Story.*   3 vols., cr. 8vo, 31*s.* 6*d.*
*Giles (E.) Australia twice Traversed : five Expeditions,* 1872-76.
With Maps and Illust. 2 vols, 8vo, 30*s.*
*Gillespie (W. M.) Surveying.*   Revised and enlarged by CADEY
STALEY.   8vo, 21*s.*
*Goethe.   Faustus.*   Translated in the original rhyme and metre
by A. H. HUTH.   Crown 8vo, 5*s.*
*Goldsmith.   She Stoops to Conquer.*   Introduction by AUSTIN
DOBSON ; the designs by E. A. ABBEY.   Imperial 4to, 42*s.*
*Gordon ( J. E. H.,B.A. Cantab.) Electric Lighting.*   Ill. 8vo,18*s.*
——— *Physical Treatise on Electricity and Magnetism.*   2nd
Edition, enlarged, with coloured, full-page, &c., Illust. 2 vols.,8vo, 42*s.*
——— *Electricity for Schools.*   Illustrated.   Crown 8vo, 5*s.*
*Gouffé ( Jules) Royal Cookery Book.*   New Edition, with plates
in colours, Woodcuts, &c., 8vo, gilt edges, 42*s.*
——— Domestic Edition, half-bound, 10*s.* 6*d.*
*Grant (General, U.S.) Personal Memoirs.*   With Illustrations,
Maps, &c. 2 vols., 8vo, 28*s.*
*Great Artists.*   See "Biographies."

*Great Musicians.*    Edited by F. HUEFFER.    A Series of Biographies, crown 8vo, 3*s.* each :—

| Bach. | Handel. | Rossini. |
| Beethoven. | Haydn. | Schubert. |
| Berlioz. | Mendelssohn. | Schumann. |
| English Church Composers. By BARRETT. | Mozart. Purcell. | Richard Wagner. Weber. |

*Groves* (*J. Percy*) *Charmouth Grange.* Gilt, 5*s.*; plainer, 2*s. 6d.*

*Guizot's History of France.* Translated by R. BLACK. In 8 vols., super-royal 8vo, cloth extra, gilt, each 24*s.* In cheaper binding, 8 vols., at 10*s. 6d.* each.

"It supplies a want which has long been felt, and ought to be in the hands of all students of history."—*Times.*

―――――――――――――― *Masson's School Edition.* Abridged from the Translation by Robert Black, with Chronological Index, Historical and Genealogical Tables, &c. By Professor GUSTAVE MASSON, B.A. With Portraits, Illustrations, &c. 1 vol., 8vo, 600 pp., 5*s.*

*Guyon* (*Mde.*) *Life.* By UPHAM. 6th Edition, crown 8vo, 6*s.*

*HALFORD* (*F. M.*) *Floating Flies, and how to Dress them.* New edit., with Coloured plates. 8vo, 15*s.*

―――――― *Dry Fly-Fishing, Theory and Practice.* Col. Plates, 25*s.*

*Hall* (*W. W.*) *How to Live Long; or,* 1408 *Maxims.* 2*s.*

*Hamilton* (*E.*) *Fly-fishing for Salmon, Trout, and Grayling;* their Habits, Haunts, and History. Illust., 6*s.*; large paper, 10*s. 6d.*

*Hands* (*T.*) *Numerical Exercises in Chemistry.* Cr. 8vo, 2*s. 6d.* and 2*s.*; Answers separately, 6*d.*

*Hardy* (*A. S.*) *Passe-rose : a Romance.* Crown 8vo, 6*s.*

*Hardy* (*Thomas*). See " Low's Standard Novels."

*Hare* (*J. L. Clark*) *American Constitutional Law.* 2 vls., 8vo, 63*s.*

*Harper's Magazine.* Monthly. 160 pages, fully illustrated, 1*s.* Vols., half yearly, I.—XVIII., super-royal 8vo, 8*s. 6d.* each.

"'Harper's Magazine' is so thickly sown with excellent illustrations that to coun them would be a work of time ; not that it is a picture magazine, for the engravings illustrate the text after the manner seen in some of our choicest *éditions de luxe.*"—*St. James's Gazette.*

"It is so pretty, so big, and so cheap. . . . An extraordinary shillingsworth— 160 large octavo pages, with over a score of articles, and more than three times as many illustrations."—*Edinburgh Daily Review.*

"An amazing shillingsworth . . . combining choice literature of both nations."— *Nonconformist.*

*Harper's Young People.* Vols. I.-V., profusely Illustrated with woodcuts and coloured plates. Royal 4to, extra binding, each 7*s. 6d.* ; gilt edges, 8*s.* Published Weekly, in wrapper, 1*d.* ; Annual Subscription, post free, 6*s. 6d.* ; Monthly, in wrapper, with coloured plate, 6*d.* ; Annual Subscription, post free, 7*s. 6d.*

*Harris* (*Bishop of Michigan*) *Dignity of Man : Select Sermons.* Crown 8vo, 8*s. 6d.*

*Harris* (*W. B.*) *Land of African Sultan : Travels in Morocco.* Illust., crown 8vo, 10*s. 6d.* ; large paper, 31*s. 6d.*

*Harrison (Mary) Complete Cookery Book.* Crown 8vo.
—— *Skilful Cook.* New edition, crown 8vo, 5*s.*
*Harrison (W.) Memorable London Houses: a Guide.* Illust.
New edition, 18mo, 1*s.* 6*d.*
*Hatton (Joseph) Journalistic London: with Engravings and*
Portraits of Distinguished Writers of the Day. Fcap. 4to, 12*s.* 6*d.*
—— See also LOW'S STANDARD NOVELS.
*Haweis (Mrs.) Art of Housekeeping : a Bridal Garland.* 2*s.*6*d.*
*Hawthorne (Nathaniel) Life.* By JOHN R. LOWELL.
*Heldmann (B.) Mutiny of the Ship " Leander."* Gilt edges,
3*s.* 6*d.*; plainer, 2*s.* 6*d.*
*Henty. Winning his Spurs.* Cr. 8vo, 3*s.* 6*d.* ; plainer, 2*s.* 6*d.*
—— *Cornet of Horse.* Cr. 8vo, 3*s.* 6*d.*; plainer, 2*s.* 6*d.*
—— *Jack Archer.* Illust. 3*s.* 6*d.* ; plainer, 2*s.* 6*d.*
*Henty (Richmond) Australiana : My Early Life.* 5*s.*
*Herrick (Robert) Poetry.* Preface by AUSTIN DOBSON. With
numerous Illustrations by E. A. ABBEY. 4to, gilt edges, 42*s.*
*Hetley (Mrs. E.) Native Flowers' of New Zealand.* Chromos
from Drawings. Three Parts, 63*s.*; extra binding, 73*s.* 6*d.*
*Hicks (E. S.) Our Boys: How to Enter the Merchant Service.* 5*s.*
—— *Yachts, Boats and Canoes.* Illustrated. 8vo, 10*s.* 6*d.*
*Hinman (R.) Eclectic Physical Geography.* Crown 8vo, 5*s.*
*Hitchman. Public Life of the Earl of Beaconsfield.* 3*s.* 6*d.*
*Hoey (Mrs. Cashel)* See LOW'S STANDARD NOVELS.
*Holder (C. F.) Marvels of Animal Life.* Illustrated. 8*s.* 6*d.*
—— *Ivory King: Elephant and Allies.* Illustrated. 8*s.* 6*d.*
—— *Living Lights : Phosphorescent Animals and Vegetables.*
Illustrated. 8vo, 8*s.* 6*d.*
*Holmes (O. W.) Before the Curfew, &c. Occasional Poems.* 5*s.*
—— *Last Leaf : a Holiday Volume.* 42*s.*
—— *Mortal Antipathy,* 8*s.* 6*d.* ; also 2*s.* ; paper, 1*s.*
—— *Our Hundred Days in Europe.* 6*s.* Large Paper, 15*s.*
—— *Poetical Works.* 2 vols., 18mo, gilt tops, 10*s.* 6*d.*
—— See also " Rose Library."
*Howard (Blanche Willis) Open Door.* Crown 8vo, 6*s.*
*Howorth (H. H.) Mammoth and the Flood.* 8vo, 18*s.*
*Hugo (V.) Notre Dame.* With coloured etchings and 150
engravings. 2 vols., 8vo, vellum cloth, 30*s.*
*Hundred Greatest Men (The).* 8 portfolios, 21*s.* each, or 4 vols.,
half-morocco, gilt edges, 10 guineas. New Ed., 1 vol., royal 8vo, 21*s.*
*Hymnal Companion to the Book of Common Prayer.* By
BISHOP BICKERSTETH. In various styles and bindings from 1*d.* to
31*s.* 6*d.* *Price List and Prospectus will be forwarded on application.*

*ILLUSTRATED Text-Books of Art-Education.* Edited by
EDWARD J. POYNTER, R.A. Illustrated, and strongly bound, 5*s.*
Now ready :—

PAINTING.

Classic and Italian. By HEAD. | French and Spanish.
German, Flemish, and Dutch. | English and American.

ARCHITECTURE.

Classic and Early Christian.
Gothic and Renaissance. By T. ROGER SMITH.

SCULPTURE.

Antique : Egyptian and Greek.
Renaissance and Modern. By LEADER SCOTT.

*Inderwick (F. A. ; Q.C.) Side Lights on the Stuarts. Essays.*
Illustrated, 8vo, 18*s.*

*Index to the English Catalogue, Jan.,* 1874, *to Dec.,* 1880
Royal 8vo, half-morocco, 18*s.*

*Inglis (Hon. James; "Maori") Our New Zealand Cousins.*
Small post 8vo, 6*s.*

—— *Tent Life in Tiger Land: Twelve Years a Pioneer*
Planter. Col. plates, roy. 8vo, 18*s.*

*Irving (Washington).* Library Edition of his Works in 27 vols.,
Copyright, with the Author's Latest Revisions. "Geoffrey Crayon"
Edition, large square 8vo. 12*s.* 6*d.* per vol. *See also* "Little Britain."

*JACKSON. New Style Vertical Writing Copy-Books.*
Series 1, Nos. I.—XII., 2*d.* and 1*d.* each.

—— *New Series of Vertical Writing Copy-books.* 22 Nos.

—— *Shorthand of Arithmetic : a Companion to all Arithmetics.*
Crown 8vo, 1*s.* 6*d.*

*Japan.* See ANDERSON, ARTISTIC, AUDSLEY, also MORSE.

*Jerdon (Gertrude) Key-hole Country.* Illustrated. Crown 8vo,
cloth, 2*s.*

*Johnston (H. H.) River Congo, from its Mouth to Bolobo.*
New Edition, 8vo, 21*s.*

*Johnstone (D. Lawson) Land of the Mountain Kingdom.*
Illust., crown 8vo. 5*s.*

*Julien (F.) English Student's French Examiner.* 16mo, 2*s.*

—— *Conversational French Reader.* 16mo, cloth, 2*s.* 6*d.*

——*French at Home and at School.* Book I., Accidence. 2*s.*

—— *First Lessons in Conversational French Grammar.* 1*s.*

—— *Petites Leçons de Conversation et de Grammaire.* 3*s.*

—— *Phrases of Daily Use.* Limp cloth, 6*d.*

*KARR (H. W. Seton) Shores and Alps of Alaska.* 8vo,
16*s.*

*Keats. Endymion.* Illust. by W. ST. JOHN HARPER. Imp.
4to, gilt top, 42*s.*

*Kempis* (*Thomas à*) *Daily Text-Book.* Square 16mo, 2s. 6d.; interleaved as a Birthday Book, 3s. 6d.

*Kennedy* (*E. B.*) *Blacks and Bushrangers, adventures in North* Queensland. Illust., crown 8vo, 7s. 6d.

*Kent's Commentaries :  an Abridgment for Students of American* Law. By EDEN F. THOMPSON. 10s. 6d.

*Kerr* (*W. M.*) *Far Interior : Cape of Good Hope, across the* Zambesi, to the Lake Regions. Illustrated from Sketches, 2 vols. 8vo, 32s.

*Kershaw* (*S. W.*) *Protestants from France in their English* Home. Crown 8vo, 6s.

*King* (*Henry*) *Savage London ; Riverside Characters, &c.* Crown 8vo, 6s.

*Kingston* (*W. H. G.*) *Works.* Illustrated, 16mo, gilt edges, 3s. 6d.; plainer binding, plain edges, 2s. 6d. each.

| | |
|---|---|
| Ben Burton. | Heir of Kilfinnan. |
| Captain Mugford, or, Our Salt and Fresh Water Tutors. | Snow-Shoes and Canoes. |
| | Two Supercargoes. |
| Dick Cheveley. | With Axe and Rifle. |

*Kingsley* (*Rose*) *Children of Westminster Abbey : Studies in* English History. 5s.

*Knight* (*E. J.*) *Cruise of the "Falcon."* New Ed. Cr. 8vo, 7s. 6d.

*Knox* (*Col.*) *Boy Travellers on the Congo.* Illus. Cr. 8vo, 7s. 6d.

*Kunhardt* (*C. B.*) *Small Yachts : Design and Construction.* 35s.

—— *Steam Yachts and Launches.* Illustrated. 4to, 16s.

*L*ANGLEY (*S. P.*) *New Astronomy.* Ill. Cr. 8vo. 10s. 6d.

*Lanier's Works.* Illustrated, crown 8vo, gilt edges, 7s. 6d. each.

| | |
|---|---|
| Boy's King Arthur. | Boy's Percy: Ballads of Love and |
| Boy's Froissart. | Adventure, selected from the |
| Boy's Knightly Legends of Wales. | "Reliques." |

*Lansdell* (*H.*) *Through Siberia.* 2 vols., 8vo, 30s.; 1 vol., 10s. 6d.

—— *Russia in Central Asia.* Illustrated. 2 vols., 42s.

—— *Through Central Asia ; Russo-Afghan Frontier, &c.* 8vo, 12s.

*Larden* (*W.*) *School Course on Heat.* Third Ed., Illust. 5s.

*Laurie* (*A.*) *Conquest of the Moon : a Story of the Bayouda.* Illust., crown 8vo, 7s. 6d.

*Layard* (*Mrs. Granville*) *Through the West Indies.* Small post 8vo, 2s. 6d.

*Lea* (*H. C.*). *History of the Inquisition of the Middle Ages.* 3 vols., 8vo, 42s.

*Lemon* (*M.*) *Small House over the Water, and Stories.* Illust.
by Cruikshank, &c. Crown 8vo, 6s.

*Leo XIII. : Life.* By BERNARD O'REILLY. With Steel
Portrait from Photograph, &c. Large 8vo, 18s.; *édit. de luxe*, 63s.

*Leonardo da Vinci's Literary Works.* Edited by Dr. JEAN
PAUL RICHTER. Containing his Writings on Painting, Sculpture,
and Architecture, his Philosophical Maxims, Humorous Writings, and
Miscellaneous Notes on Personal Events, on his Contemporaries, on
Literature, &c. ; published from Manuscripts. 2 vols., imperial 8vo,
containing about 200 Drawings in Autotype Reproductions, and numerous other Illustrations. Twelve Guineas.

*Library of Religious Poetry.* Best Poems of all Ages. Edited
by SCHAFF and GILMAN. Royal 8vo, 21s.; cheaper binding, 10s. 6d.

*Lindsay* (*W. S.*) *History of Merchant Shipping.* Over 150
Illustrations, Maps, and Charts. In 4 vols., demy 8vo, cloth extra.
Vols. 1 and 2, 11s. each ; vols. 3 and 4, 14s. each. 4 vols., 50s.

*Little* (*Archibald J.*) *Through the Yang-tse Gorges : Trade and
Travel in Western China.* New Edition. 8vo, 10s. 6d.

*Little Britain, The Spectre Bridegroom,* and *Legend of Sleepy
Hollow.* By WASHINGTON IRVING. An entirely New *Édition de
luxe.* Illustrated by 120 very fine Engravings on Wood, by Mr.
J. D. COOPER. Designed by Mr. CHARLES O. MURRAY. Re-issue,
square crown 8vo, cloth, 6s.

*Lodge* (*Henry Cabot*) *George Washington.* (*American Statesmen.*)
2 vols., 12s.

*Longfellow. Maidenhood.* With Coloured Plates. Oblong
4to, 2s. 6d.; gilt edges, 3s. 6d.

—— *Courtship of Miles Standish.* Illust. by BROUGHTON,
&c. Imp. 4to, 21s.

—— *Nuremberg.* 28 Photogravures. Illum. by M. and A.
COMEGYS. 4to, 31s. 6d.

*Lowell* (*J. R.*) *Vision of Sir Launfal.* Illustrated, royal 4to, 63s.

—— *Life of Nathaniel Hawthorne.* Sm. post 8vo. [*In prep.*

*Low's Standard Library of Travel and Adventure.* Crown 8vo,
uniform in cloth extra, 7s. 6d., except where price is given.

  1.  **The Great Lone Land.** By Major W. F. BUTLER, C.B.
  2.  **The Wild North Land.** By Major W. F. BUTLER, C.B.
  3.  **How I found Livingstone.** By H. M. STANLEY.
  4.  **Through the Dark Continent.** By H. M. STANLEY.   12s. 6d.
  5.  **The Threshold of the Unknown Region.** By C. R. MARK-
     HAM. (4th Edition, with Additional Chapters, 10s. 6d.)
  6.  **Cruise of the Challenger.** By W. J. J. SPRY, R.N.
  7.  **Burnaby's On Horseback through Asia Minor.**   10s. 6d.
  8.  **Schweinfurth's Heart of Africa.** 2 vols., 15s.
  9.  **Through America.** By W. G. MARSHALL.
 10.  **Through Siberia.** Il. and unabridged, 10s.6d. By H. LANSDELL.
 11.  **From Home to Home.** By STAVELEY HILL.
 12.  **Cruise of the Falcon.** By E. J. KNIGHT.

*Low's Standard Library, &c.—continued.*
13. **Through Masai Land.** By JOSEPH THOMSON.
14. **To the Central African Lakes.** By JOSEPH THOMSON.
15. **Queen's Highway.** By STUART CUMBERLAND.

*Low's Standard Novels.* Small post 8vo, cloth extra, 6s. each, unless otherwise stated.

JAMES BAKER. **John Westacott.**
WILLIAM BLACK.
    **A Daughter of Heth.—House-Boat.—In Far Lochaber.—In Silk Attire.—Kilmeny.—Lady Silverdale's Sweetheart.— Sunrise.—Three Feathers.**
R. D. BLACKMORE.
    **Alice Lorraine.—Christowell, a Dartmoor Tale.—Clara Vaughan.—Cradock Nowell.—Cripps the Carrier.—Erema; or, My Father's Sin.—Lorna Doone.—Mary Anerley.— Tommy Upmore.**
G. W. CABLE. **Bonaventure.** 5s.
Miss COLERIDGE. **An English Squire.**
C. E. CRADDOCK. **Despot of Broomsedge Cove.**
Mrs. B. M. CROKER. **Some One Else.**
STUART CUMBERLAND. **Vasty Deep.**
E. DE LEON. **Under the Stars and Crescent.**
Miss BETHAM-EDWARDS. **Halfway.**
Rev. E. GILLIAT, M.A. **Story of the Dragonnades.**
THOMAS HARDY.
    **A Laodicean.—Far from the Madding Crowd.—Mayor of Casterbridge.—Pair of Blue Eyes.—Return of the Native.— The Hand of Ethelberta.—The Trumpet Major.—Two on a Tower.**
JOSEPH HATTON. **Old House at Sandwich.—Three Recruits.**
Mrs. CASHEL HOEY.
    **A Golden Sorrow.—A Stern Chase.—Out of Court.**
BLANCHE WILLIS HOWARD. **Open Door.**
JEAN INGELOW.
    **Don John.—John Jerome (5s.).—Sarah de Berenger.**
GEORGE MAC DONALD.
    **Adela Cathcart.—Guild Court.—Mary Marston.—Stephen Archer (New Ed. of "Gifts").—The Vicar's Daughter.—Orts. —Weighed and Wanting.**
Mrs. MACQUOID. **Diane.—Elinor Dryden.**
HELEN MATHERS. **My Lady Greensleeves.**
DUFFIELD OSBORNE. **Spell of Ashtaroth (5s.)**
Mrs. J. H. RIDDELL.
    **Alaric Spenceley.—Daisies and Buttercups.—The Senior Partner.—A Struggle for Fame.**
W. CLARK RUSSELL.
    **Frozen Pirate.—Jack's Courtship.—John Holdsworth.—A Sailor's Sweetheart.—Sea Queen.—Watch Below.—Strange Voyage.—Wreck of the Grosvenor.—The Lady Maud.— Little Loo,**

*Low's Standard Novels—continued.*

FRANK R. STOCKTON.
  Bee-man of Orn.—The Late Mrs. Null.—Hundredth Man.
MRS. HARRIET B. STOWE.
  My Wife and I.—Old Town Folk.—We and our Neighbours.—
  Poganuc People, their Loves and Lives.
JOSEPH THOMSON.   Ulu: an African Romance.
LEW. WALLACE.   Ben Hur: a Tale of the Christ.
CONSTANCE FENIMORE WOOLSON.
  Anne.—East Angels.—For the Major (5*s.*).
  French Heiress in her own Chateau.

See also SEA STORIES.

*Low's Standard Novels.*   NEW ISSUE at short intervals.   Cr.
8vo, 2*s.* 6*d.*; fancy boards, 2*s.*
BLACKMORE.
  Clara Vaughan.—Cripps the Carrier.—Lorna Doone.—Mary
  Anerley.
HARDY.
  Madding Crowd.—Mayor of Casterbridge.—Trumpet-Major.
HATTON.   Three Recruits.
HOLMES.   Guardian Angel.
MAC DONALD.   Adela Cathcart.—Guild Court.
RIDDELL.   Daisies and Buttercups.—Senior Partner.
STOCKTON.   Casting Away of Mrs. Lecks.
STOWE.   Dred.
WALFORD.   Her Great Idea.

*To be followed immediately by*

BLACKMORE.   Alice Lorraine.—Tommy Upmore.
CABLE.   Bonaventure.
CROKER.   Some One Else.
DE LEON.   Under the Stars.
EDWARDS.   Half-Way.
HARDY.
  Hand of Ethelberta.—Pair of Blue Eyes.—Two on a Tower.
HATTON.   Old House at Sandwich.
HOEY.   Golden Sorrow.—Out of Court.—Stern Chase.
INGELOW.   John Jerome.—Sarah de Berenger.
MAC DONALD.   Vicar's Daughter.—Stephen Archer.
OLIPHANT.   Innocent.
STOCKTON.   Bee-Man of Orn.
STOWE.   Old Town Folk.—Poganuc People.
THOMSON.   Ulu.

*Low's Standard Books for Boys.*   With numerous Illustrations,
  2*s.* 6*d.*; gilt edges, 3*s.* 6*d.* each.
  Dick Cheveley.   By W. H. G. KINGSTON.
  Heir of Kilfinnan.   By W. H. G. KINGSTON.
  Off to the Wilds.   By G. MANVILLE FENN.
  The Two Supercargoes.   By W. H. G. KINGSTON.
  The Silver Cañon.   By G. MANVILLE FENN.
  Under the Meteor Flag.   By HARRY COLLINGWOOD.
  Jack Archer: a Tale of the Crimea.   By G. A. HENTY.

*Low's Standard Books for Boys—continued.*

The Mutiny on Board the Ship Leander.  By B. HELDMANN.

With Axe and Rifle on the Western Prairies.  By W. H. G. KINGSTON.

Red Cloud, the Solitary Sioux : a Tale of the Great Prairie. By Col. Sir WM. BUTLER, K.C.B.

The Voyage of the Aurora.  By HARRY COLLINGWOOD.

Charmouth Grange : a Tale of the 17th Century.  By J. PERCY GROVES.

Snowshoes and Canoes.  By W. H. G. KINGSTON.

The Son of the Constable of France.  By LOUIS ROUSSELET.

Captain Mugford ; or, Our Salt and Fresh Water Tutors. Edited by W. H. G. KINGSTON.

The Cornet of Horse, a Tale of Marlborough's Wars.  By G. A. HENTY.

The Adventures of Captain Mago.  By LEON CAHUN.

Noble Words and Noble Needs.

The King of the Tigers.  By ROUSSELET.

Hans Brinker; or, The Silver Skates.  By Mrs. DODGE.

The Drummer-Boy, a Story of the time of Washington.  By ROUSSELET.

Adventures in New Guinea : The Narrative of Louis Tregance.

The Crusoes of Guiana.  By BOUSSENARD.

The Gold Seekers.  A Sequel to the Above.  By BOUSSENARD.

Winning His Spurs, a Tale of the Crusades.  By G. A. HENTY.

The Blue Banner.  By LEON CAHUN.

*New Volumes for* 1889.

Startling Exploits of the Doctor.  CÉLIÈRE.

Brothers Rantzau.  ERCKMANN-CHATRIAN.

Young Naturalist.  BIART.

Ben Burton ; or, Born and Bred at Sea.  KINGSTON.

Great Hunting Grounds of the World.  MEUNIER.

Ran Away from the Dutch.  PERELAER.

My Kalulu, Prince, King, and Slave.  STANLEY.

*Low's Standard Series of Books by Popular Writers.*  Sm. cr. 8vo, cloth gilt, 2s.; gilt edges, 2s. 6d. each.

Aunt Jo's Scrap Bag.  By Miss ALCOTT.

Shawl Straps.  By Miss ALCOTT.

Little Men.  By Miss ALCOTT.

Hitherto.  By Mrs. WHITNEY.

Forecastle to Cabin.  By SAMUELS.  Illustrated.

In My Indian Garden.  By PHIL ROBINSON.

Little Women and Little Women Wedded.  By Miss ALCOTT.

Eric and Ethel.  By FRANCIS FRANCIS.  Illust.

Keyhole Country.  By GERTRUDE JERDON.  Illust.

We Girls.  By Mrs. WHITNEY.

The Other Girls.  A Sequel to " We Girls."  By Mrs. WHITNEY.

Adventures of Jimmy Brown.  Illust.  By W. L. ALDEN.

Under the Lilacs.  By Miss ALCOTT.  Illust.

Jimmy's Cruise.  By Miss ALCOTT.

Under the Punkah.  By PHIL ROBINSON.

*Low's Standard Series of Books by Popular Writers—continued.*
   **An Old-Fashioned Girl.** By Miss ALCOTT,
   **A Rose in Bloom.** By Miss ALCOTT.
   **Eight Cousins.** Illust. By Miss ALCOTT.
   **Jack and Jill.** By Miss ALCOTT.
   **Lulu's Library.** Illust. By Miss ALCOTT.
   **Silver Pitchers.** By Miss ALCOTT.
   **Work and Beginning Again.** Illust. By Miss ALCOTT.
   **A Summer in Leslie Goldthwaite's Life.** By Mrs. WHITNEY.
   **Faith Gartney's Girlhood.** By Mrs. WHITNEY.
   **Real Folks.** By Mrs. WHITNEY.
   **Dred.** By Mrs. STOWE.
   **My Wife and I.** By Mrs. STOWE.
   **An Only Sister.** By Madame DE WITT.
   **Spinning Wheel Stories.** By Miss ALCOTT.                .
   **My Summer in a Garden.** By C. DUDLEY WARNER.

*Low's Pocket Encyclopædia: a Compendium of General Know-*
   ledge for Ready Reference. Upwards of 25,000 References, with
   Plates. New ed., imp. 32mo, cloth, marbled edges, 3s. 6d.; roan, 4s. 6d.

*Low's Handbook to London Charities.* Yearly, cloth, 1s. 6d.;
   paper, 1s.

*Lusignan (Princess A. de) Twelve years' Reign of Abdul Hamid*
   II. Crown 8vo, 7s. 6d.

$M$ *cCULLOCH (H.) Men and Measures of Half a century.*
   Sketches and Comments. 8vo, 18s.

*Macdonald (D.) Oceania. Linguistic and Anthropological.*
   Illust., and Tables. Crown 8vo, 6s.

*Mac Donald (George).* See LOW'S STANDARD NOVELS.

*Macgregor (John) "Rob' Roy" on the Baltic.* 3rd Edition,
   small post 8vo, 2s. 6d.; cloth, gilt edges, 3s. 6d.

—— *A Thousand Miles in the "Rob Roy" Canoe.* 11th
   Edition, small post 8vo, 2s. 6d.; cloth, gilt edges, 3s. 6d.

—— *Voyage Alone in the Yawl "Rob Roy."* New Edition,
   with additions, small post 8vo, 3s. 6d. and 2s. 6d.

*Mackenzie (Sir Morell) Fatal Illness of Frederick the Noble.*
   Crown 8vo, limp cloth, 2s. 6d.

*Mackenzie (Rev. John) Austral Africa : Losing it or Ruling it?*
   Illustrations and Maps. 2 vols., 8vo, 32s.

*Maclean (H. E.) Maid of the Golden Age.* Illust., cr. 8vo, 6s.

*McLellan's Own Story : The War for the Union.* Illust. 18s.

*Maginn (W.) Miscellanies. Prose and Verse. With Memoir.*
   2 vols., crown 8vo, 24s.

*Main (Mrs.; Mrs. Fred Burnaby) High Life and Towers of*
   Silence. Illustrated, square 8vo, 10s. 6d.

*Malan (C. F. de M.) Eric and Connie's Cruise in the South*
   Pacific. Crown 8vo, 5s.

*Manning (E. F.) Delightful Thames.*  Illustrated.   4to, fancy boards, 5s.

*Markham (Clements R.) The Fighting Veres, Sir F. and Sir H.* 8vo, 18s.

——— *War between Peru and Chili,* 1879-1881.   Third Ed. Crown 8vo, with Maps, 10s. 6d.

——— See also "Foreign Countries," MAURY, and VERES.

*Marston (W.) Eminent Recent Actors, Reminiscences Critical,* &c.  2 vols.  Crown 8vo, 21s.; new edit., 1 vol., 6s.

*Martin (J. W.) Float Fishing and Spinning in the Nottingham* Style.  New Edition.  Crown 8vo, 2s. 6d.

*Matthews (J. W., M.D.) Incwadi Yami : Twenty years in* South Africa.  With many Engravings, royal 8vo, 14s.

*Maury (Commander) Physical Geography of the Sea, and its* Meteorology.  New Edition, with Charts and Diagrams, cr. 8vo, 6s.

——— *Life.*  By his Daughter.  Edited by Mr. CLEMENTS R. MARKHAM.  With portrait of Maury.  8vo, 12s. 6d.

*Melio (G. L.) Manual of Swedish Drill for Teachers and* Students.  Cr. 8vo, 1s. 6d.

*Men of Mark: Portraits of the most Eminent Men of the Day.* Complete in 7 Vols., 4to, handsomely bound, gilt edges, 25s. each.

*Mendelssohn Family (The),* 1729—1847.   From Letters and Journals.  Translated.  New Edition, 2 vols., 8vo, 30s.

*Mendelssohn.*  See also "Great Musicians."

*Merrifield's Nautical Astronomy.*  Crown 8vo, 7s. 6d.

*Mills (J.) Alternative Elementary Chemistry.*  Ill., cr.8vo, 1s.6d.

*Mitford (Mary Russell) Our Village.*  With 12 full-page and 157 smaller Cuts.  Cr. 4to, cloth, gilt edges, 21s.; cheaper binding, 10s. 6d.

*Mody (Mrs.) Outlines of German Literature.*  18mo, 1s.

*Moffatt (W.) Land and Work; Depression, Agricultural and* Commercial.  Crown 8vo, 5s.

*Mohammed Benani : A Story of To-day.*  8vo, 10s. 6d.

*Mollett (J. W.) Illustrated Dictionary of Words used in Art and* Archæology.  Illustrated, small 4to, 15s.

*Moore (J. M.) New Zealand for Emigant, Invalid and Tourist.* Cr. 8vo.

*Morley (Henry) English Literature in the Reign of Victoria.* 2000th volume of the Tauchnitz Collection of Authors.  18mo, 2s. 6d.

*Mormonism.*  See STENHOUSE.

*Morse (E. S.) Japanese Homes and their Surroundings.*  With more than 300 Illustrations.  Re-issue, 10s. 6d.

*Morten (Honnor) Sketches of Hospital Life.*  Cr. 8vo, sewed, 1s.

*Morwood.  Our Gipsies in City, Tent, and Van.*  8vo, 18s.

*Moss (F. J.) Through Atolls and Islands of the great South Sea.* Illust., crown 8vo, 8s. 6d.

Morten (Walter) Pleasures Semilles. Fcap. 8vo, gilt top, 3s. 6d.
Muller (E.) Noble Words and Noble Deeds. Illustrated, gilt
edges, 3s. 6d.; plainer binding, 2s. 6d.
Musgrave (Mrs.) Miriam. Crown 8vo, 6s.
Music. See "Great Musicians."

*NETHERCOTE* (C. B.) Pytchley Hunt. New Ed., cr. 8vo,
5s. 6d.
New Zealand. See BRADSHAW and WHITE (J.).
New Zealand Rulers and Statesmen. See GISBORNE.
Nicholls (J. H. Kerry) The King Country: Explorations in
New Zealand. Many Illustrations and Map. New Edition, 8vo, 21s.
Northoff (C.) California, for Health, Pleasure, and Residence.
New Edition, 8vo, with Maps and Illustrations, 12s. 6d.
Norman (C. B.) Corsairs of France. With Portraits. 8vo, 18s.
North (W.; M.A.) Roman Fever: an Inquiry during three
years' residence. Illust., 8vo, 25s.
Northbrook Gallery. Edited by LORD RONALD GOWER. 36 Per-
manent Photographs. Imperial 4to, 63s.; large paper, 105s.
Nott (Major) Wild Animals Photographed and Described. 35s.
Nursery. Playmates (Prince of). 217 Coloured Pictures for
Children by eminent Artists. Folio, in col. bds., 6s.; new ed., 2s. 6d.
Nursing Record. Yearly, 8s.; half-yearly, 4s. 6d.; quarterly,
2s. 6d; weekly, 2d.

*O'BRIEN* (R. B.) Fifty Years of Concessions to Ireland.
With a Portrait of T. Drummond. Vol. I., 16s., II., 16s.
Orient Line Guide. New edition re-written; by W. J. LOFTIE.
Maps and Plans, 2s. 6d.
Orvis (C. F.) Fishing with the Fly. Illustrated. 8vo, 12s. 6d.
Osborne (Duffield) Spell of Ashtaroth. Crown 8vo, 5s.
Our Little Ones in Heaven. Edited by the Rev. H. ROBBINS.
With Frontispiece after Sir JOSHUA REYNOLDS. New Edition, 5s.

*PALGRAVE* (R. F. D.) Oliver Cromwell and his Protec-
torate. Crown 8vo.
Palliser (Mrs.) A History of Lace. New Edition, with additional cuts and text. 8vo, 21s.
—————— The China Collector's Pocket Companion. With upwards of 1000 Illustrations of Marks and Monograms. Small 8vo, 5s.
Panton (J. E.) Homes of Taste. Hints on Furniture and Deco-
ration. Crown 8vo, 2s. 6d.
Parsons (James; A.M.) Exposition of the Principles of Partnership. 8vo, 31s. 6d.

*Pennell (H. Cholmondeley) Sporting Fish of Great Britain.*
15*s.* ; large paper, 30*s.*
——— *Modern Improvements in Fishing-tackle.* Crown 8vo, 2*s.*
*Pereboer (M. T. H.) Run Away from the Dutch ; Burma, &c.*
Illustrated, square 8vo, 7*s.* 6*d.*; new ed., 2*s.* 6*d.*
*Perry (J. J. M.) Effingham Burglary, or Circumstantial Evidence.* Crown 8vo, 3*s.* 6*d.*
*Phelps (Elizabeth Stuart) Struggle for Immortality.* Cr. 8vo, 5*s.*
*Phillips' Dictionary of Biographical Reference.* New edition,
royal 8vo, 25*s.*
*Philpot (H. J.) Diabetes Mellitus.* Crown 8vo, 5*s.*
——— *Diet System.* Tables. I. Diabetes ; II. Gout ;
III. Dyspepsia ; IV. Corpulence. In cases, 1*s.* each.
*Plunkett (Major G. T.) Primer of Orthographic Projection.*
Elementary Solid Geometry. With Problems and Exercises. 2*s.* 6*d.*
*Poe (E. A.) The Raven.* Illustr. by DORÉ. Imperial folio, 63*s.*
*Poems of the Inner Life.* Chiefly Modern. Small 8vo, 5*s.*
*Poetry of the Anti-Jacobin.* New ed., by CHARLES EDMONDS.
Cr. 8vo, 7*s.* 6*d.*; large paper, 21*s.*
*Porcher (A.) Juvenile French Plays.* With Notes and a
Vocabulary. 18mo, 1*s.*
*Porter (Admiral David D.) Naval History of Civil War.*
Portraits, Plans, &c. 4to. 25*s.*
*Portraits of Celebrated Race-horses of the Past and Present*
Centuries, with Pedigrees and Performances. 4 vols., 4to, 126*s.*
*Powles (L. D.) Land of the Pink Pearl : Life in the Bahamas.*
8vo, 10*s.* 6*d.*
*Poynter (Edward J., R.A.).* See " Illustrated Text-books."
*Prince Maskiloff : a Romance of Modern Oxford.* By ROY
TELLET. Crown 8vo, 10*s.* 6*d.*
*Prince of Nursery Playmates.* Col. plates, new ed., 2*s.* 6*d.*
*Pritt (T. E.) North Country Flies.* Illustrated from the
Author's Drawings. 10*s.* 6*d.*
*Publishers' Circular (The), and General Record of British and*
Foreign Literature. Published on the 1st and 15th of every Month, 3*d.*
*Pyle (Howard) Otto of the Silver Hand.* Illustrated by the
Author. 8vo, 8*s.* 6*d.*

*QUEEN'S Prime Ministers.* A series. Edited by S. J. REID.
Cr. 8vo, 2*s.* 6*d.* per vol.

*RAMBAUD. History of Russia.* New Edition, Illustrated.
3 vols., 8vo, 21*s.*

*Reber. History of Mediæval Art.* Translated by CLARKE.
422 Illustrations and Glossary. 8vo, .

*Redford (G.) Ancient Sculpture.* New Ed. Crown 8vo, 10s. 6d.

*Redgrave (G. R.) Century of Painters of the English School*
Crown 8vo, 10s. 6d.

*Reed (Sir E. J., M.P.) and Simpson. Modern Ships of War.*
Illust., royal 8vo, 10s. 6d.

*Reed (Talbot B.) Sir Ludar : a Tale of the Days of good Queen*
Bess. Crown 8vo, 6s.

*Remarkable Bindings in the British Museum.* India paper,
94s. 6d. ; sewed 73s. 6d. and 63s.

*Reminiscences of a Boyhood in the early part of the Century :* a
Story. Crown 8vo, 6s.

*Ricci (J. H. de) Fisheries Dispute, and the Annexation of*
Canada. Crown 8vo, 6s.

*Richards (W.) Aluminium : its History, Occurrence, &c.*
Illustrated, crown 8vo, 12s. 6d.

*Richter (Dr. Jean Paul) Italian Art in the National Gallery.*
4to. Illustrated. Cloth gilt, £2 2s.; half-morocco, uncut, £2 12s. 6d.

—— See also LEONARDO DA VINCI.

*Riddell (Mrs. J. H.)* See LOW'S STANDARD NOVELS.

*Roberts (W.) Earlier History of English Bookselling.* Crown
8vo, 7s. 6d.

*Robertson (T. W.) Principal Dramatic Works, with Portraits*
in photogravure. 2 vols., 21s.

*Robin Hood; Merry Adventures of.* Written and illustrated
by HOWARD PYLE. Imperial 8vo, 15s.

*Robinson (Phil.) In my Indian Garden.* New Edition, 16mo,
limp cloth, 2s.

—— *Noah's Ark. Unnatural History.* Sm. post 8vo, 12s. 6d.

—— *Sinners and Saints : a Tour across the United States of*
America, and Round them. Crown 8vo, 10s. 6d.

—— *Under the Punkah.* New Ed., cr. 8vo, limp cloth, 2s.

*Rockstro (W. S.) History of Music.* New Edition. 8vo, 14s.

*Roe (E. P.) Nature's Serial Story.* Illust. New ed. 3s. 6d.

*Roland, The Story of.* Crown 8vo, illustrated, 6s.

*Rose (J.) Complete Practical Machinist.* New Ed., 12mo, 12s. 6d.

—— *Key to Engines and Engine-running.* Crown 8vo, 8s. 6d.

—— *Mechanical Drawing.* Illustrated, small 4to, 16s.

—— *Modern Steam Engines.* Illustrated. 31s. 6d.

—— *Steam Boilers. Boiler Construction and Examination.*
Illust., 8vo, 12s. 6d.

*Rose Library.* Each volume, 1*s.* Many are illustrated—
└ **Little Women.** By LOUISA M. ALCOTT.
**Little Women Wedded.** Forming a Sequel to "Little Women."
**Little Women and Little Women Wedded.** 1 vol., cloth gilt, 3*s.* 6*d.*
**Little Men.** By L. M. ALCOTT. Double vol., 2*s.*; cloth gilt, 3*s.* 6*d.*
**An Old-Fashioned Girl.** By LOUISA M. ALCOTT. 2*s.*; cloth, 3*s.* 6*d.*
**Work.** A Story of Experience. By L. M. ALCOTT. 3*s.* 6*d.*; 2 vols., 1*s.* each.
**Stowe (Mrs. H. B.) The Pearl of Orr's Island.**
—— **The Minister's Wooing.**
—— **We and our Neighbours.** 2*s.*; cloth gilt, 6*s.*
—— **My Wife and I.** 2*s.*
**Hans Brinker; or, the Silver Skates.** By Mrs. DODGE. Also 2*s.* 6*d.*
**My Study Windows.** By J. R. LOWELL.
**The Guardian Angel.** By OLIVER WENDELL HOLMES. Cloth, 2*s.*
**My Summer in a Garden.** By C. D. WARNER.
**Dred.** By Mrs. BEECHER STOWE. 2*s.*; cloth gilt, 3*s.* 6*d.*
**City Ballads.** New Ed. 16mo. By WILL CARLETON.
**Farm Ballads.** By WILL CARLETON. ⎫
**Farm Festivals.** By WILL CARLETON. ⎬ 1 vol., cl., gilt ed., 3*s.* 6*d.*
**Farm Legends.** By WILL CARLETON. ⎭
**The Rose in Bloom.** By L. M. ALCOTT. 2*s.*; cloth gilt, 3*s.* 6*d.*
**Eight Cousins.** By L. M. ALCOTT. 2*s.*; cloth gilt, 3*s.* 6*d.*
**Under the Lilacs.** By L. M. ALCOTT. 2*s.*; also 3*s.* 6*d.*
**Undiscovered Country.** By W. D. HOWELLS.
**Clients of Dr. Bernagius.** By L. BIART. 2 parts.
**Silver Pitchers.** By LOUISA M. ALCOTT. Cloth, 3*s.* 6*d.*
**Jimmy's Cruise in the "Pinafore,"** and other Tales. By LOUISA M. ALCOTT. 2*s.*; cloth gilt, 3*s.* 6*d.*
**Jack and Jill.** By LOUISA M. ALCOTT. 2*s.*; Illustrated, 5*s.*
**Hitherto.** By the Author of the "Gayworthys." 2 vols., 1*s.* each; 1 vol., cloth gilt, 3*s.* 6*d.*
**A Gentleman of Leisure.** A Novel. By EDGAR FAWCETT. 1*s.*

See also LOW'S STANDARD SERIES.

*Ross (Mars) and Stonehewer Cooper. Highlands of Cantabria ;* or, Three Days from England. Illustrations and Map, 8vo, 21*s.*

*Rothschilds, the Financial Rulers of Nations.* By JOHN REEVES. Crown 8vo, 7*s.* 6*d.*

*Rousselet (Louis) Son of the Constable of France.* Small post 8vo, numerous Illustrations, gilt edges, 3*s.* 6*d.*; plainer, 2*s.* 6*d.*

—— *King of the Tigers : a Story of Central India.* Illustrated. Small post 8vo, gilt, 3*s.* 6*d.*; plainer, 2*s.* 6*d.*

—— *Drummer Boy.* Illustrated. Small post ·8vo, gilt edges, 3*s.* 6*d.*; plainer, 2*s.* 6*d.*

*Russell (Dora) Strange Message.* 3 vols., crown 8vo, 31*s.* 6*d.*

*Russell (W. Clark) Betwixt the Forelands.* Illust., crown 8vo, 10*s.* 6*d.*

*Russell* (*W. Clark*) *English Channel Ports and the Estate* of the East and West India Dock Company. Crown 8vo, 1s.

——— *Sailor's Language.* Illustrated. Crown 8vo, 3s. 6d.

——— *Wreck of the Grosvenor.* 4to, sewed, 6d.

——— See also " Low's Standard Novels," " Sea Stories."


*SAINTS and their Symbols: A Companion in the Churches* and Picture Galleries of Europe. Illustrated. Royal 16mo, 3s. 6d.

*Samuels* (*Capt. J. S.*) *From Forecastle to Cabin : Autobiography.* Illustrated. Crown 8vo, 8s. 6d.; also with fewer Illustrations, cloth, 2s.; paper, 1s.

*Saunders* (*A.*) *Our Domestic Birds: Poultry in England and* New Zealand. Crown 8vo, 6s.

——— *Our Horses : the Best Muscles controlled by the Best* Brains. 6s.

*Scherr* (*Prof. J.*) *History of English Literature.* Cr. 8vo, 8s. 6d.

*Schuyler* (*Eugène*) *American Diplomacy and the Furtherance of* Commerce. 12s. 6d.

——— *The Life of Peter the Great.* 2 vols., 8vo, 32s.

*Schweinfurth* (*Georg*) *Heart of Africa.* 2 vols., crown 8vo, 15s.

*Scott* (*Leader*) *Renaissance of Art in Italy.* 4to, 31s. 6d.

——— *Sculpture, Renaissance and Modern.* 5s.

*Sea Stories.* By W. CLARK RUSSELL. New ed. Cr. 8vo, leather back, top edge gilt, per vol., 3s. 6d.

| | |
|---|---|
| Frozen Pirate. | Sea Queen. |
| Jack's Courtship. | Strange Voyage. |
| John Holdsworth. | The Lady Maud. |
| Little Loo. | Watch Below. |
| Ocean Free Lance. | Wreck of the *Grosvenor*. |
| Sailor's Sweetheart. | |

*Semmes* (*Adm. Raphael*) *Service Afloat : The "Sumter" and* the "Alabama." Illustrated. Royal 8vo, 16s.

*Senior* (*W.*) *Near and Far : an Angler's Sketches of Home* Sport and Colonial Life. Crown 8vo, 6s.; new edit., 2s.

——— *Waterside Sketches.* Imp. 32mo, 1s. 6d.; boards, 1s.

*Shakespeare.* Edited by R. GRANT WHITE. 3 vols., crown 8vo, gilt top, 36s.; *Édition de luxe*, 6 vols., 8vo, cloth extra, 63s.

*Shakespeare's Heroines : Studies by Living English Painters.* 105s.; artists' proofs, 630s.

——— *Macbeth.* With Etchings on Copper, by J. MOYR SMITH. 105s. and 52s. 6d.

——— *Songs and Sonnets.* Illust. by Sir JOHN GILBERT, R.A. 4to, boards, 5s.

——— See also CUNDALL, DETHRONING, DONNELLY, MACKAY, and WHITE (R. GRANT).

*Sharpe (R. Bowdler) Birds in Nature.* 39 coloured plates and text. 4to, 63*s*.

*Sheridan. Rivals.* Reproductions of Water-colour, &c. 52*s*.6*d*.; artists proofs, 105*s*. nett.

*Shields (C. W.) Philosophia ultima ; from Harmony of Science* and Religion. 2 vols. 8vo, 24*s*.

*Shields (G. O.) Cruisings in the Cascades; Hunting, Photo-* graphy, Fishing. 8vo, 10*s*. 6*d*.

*Sidney (Sir Philip) Arcadia.* New Edition, 3*s*. 6*d*.

*Siegfried, The Story of.* Illustrated, crown 8vo, cloth, 6*s*.

*Simon. China : its Social Life.* Crown 8vo, 6*s*.

*Simson (A.) Wilds of Ecuador and Exploration of the Putumayor* River. Crown 8vo, 8*s*. 6*d*.

*Sinclair (Mrs.) Indigenous Flowers of the Hawaiian Islands.* 44 Plates in Colour. Imp. folio, extra binding, gilt edges, 31*s*. 6*d*.

*Sloane (T. O.) Home Experiments in Science for Old and Young.* Crown 8vo, 6*s*.

*Smith (G.) Assyrian Explorations.* Illust. New Ed., 8vo, 18*s*.

—— *The Chaldean Account of Genesis.* With many Illustra-tions. 16*s*. New Ed. By PROFESSOR SAYCE. 8vo, 18*s*.

*Smith (G. Barnett) William I. and the German Empire.* New Ed., 8vo, 3*s*. 6*d*.

*Smith (Sydney) Life and Times.* By STUART J. REID. Illus-trated. 8vo, 21*s*.

*Spiers' French Dictionary.* 29th Edition, remodelled, 2 vols., 8vo, 18*s*.; half bound, 21*s*.

*Spry (W.J.J., R.N., F.R.G.S.) Cruise of H.M.S." Challenger."* With Illustrations. 8vo, 18*s*. Cheap Edit., crown 8vo, 7*s*. 6*d*.

*Stanley (H. M.) Congo, and Founding its Free State.* Illustrated, 2 vols., 8vo, 42*s*. ; re-issue, 2 vols. 8vo, 21*s*.

—— *How I Found Livingstone.* 8vo, 10*s*. 6*d*. ; cr. 8vo, 7*s*. 6*d*.

—— *Through the Dark Continent.* Crown 8vo, 12*s*. 6*d*.

*Start (J. W. K.) Junior Mensuration Exercises.* 8*d*.

*Stenhouse (Mrs.) Tyranny of Mormonism. An Englishwoman* in Utah. New ed., cr. 8vo, cloth elegant, 3*s*. 6*d*.

*Sterry (J. Ashby) Cucumber Chronicles.* 5*s*.

*Stevens (E. W.) Fly-Fishing in Maine Lakes.* 8*s*. 6*d*.

*Stevens (T.) Around the World on a Bicycle.* Vol. II. 8vo, 16*s*.

*Stockton (Frank R.) Rudder Grange.* 3*s*. 6*d*.

—— *Bee-Man of Orn, and other Fanciful Tales.* Cr. 8vo, 5*s*.

—— *Personally conducted.* Crown 8vo, 7*s*. 6*d*.

—— *The Casting Away of Mrs. Lecks and Mrs. Aleshine.* 1*s*.

—— *The Dusantes.* Sequel to the above. Sewed, 1*s*. ; this and the preceding book in one volume, cloth, 2*s*. 6*d*.

*Stockton* (*Frank R.*) *The Hundredth Man.* Small post 8vo, 6s.
―――― *The Late Mrs. Null.* Small post 8vo, 6s.
―――― *The Story of Viteau.* Illust. Cr. 8vo, 5s.
―――― See also LOW'S STANDARD NOVELS.
*Stowe* (*Mrs. Beecher*) *Dred.* Cloth, gilt edges, 3s. 6d.; cloth, 2s.
――――― *Flowers and Fruit from her Writings.* Sm. post 8vo,
3s. 6d.
――――― *Life, in her own Words . . . with Letters and Original*
Compositions. 10s. 6d.
――――― *Little Foxes.* Cheap Ed., 1s.; Library Edition, 4s. 6d.
――――― *My Wife and I.* Cloth, 2s.
――――― *Old Town Folk.* 6s.
―――― *We and our Neighbours.* 2s.
――――― *Poganuc People.* 6s.
――――― See also ROSE LIBRARY.
*Strachan* (*J.*) *Explorations and Adventures in New Guinea.*
Illust., crown 8vo, 12s.
*Stranahan* (*C. H.*) *History of French Painting, the Academy,*
Salons, Schools, &c. 21s.
*Stutfield* (*Hugh E. M.*) *El Maghreb*: 1200 *Miles' Ride through*
Marocco. 8s. 6d.
*Sullivan* (*A. M.*) *Nutshell History of Ireland.* Paper boards, 6d.
*Sylvanus Redivivus, Rev. J. Mitford, with a Memoir of E.*
Jesse. Crown 8vo, 10s. 6d.


*TAINE* (*H. A.*) " *Origines.*" Translated by JOHN DURAND.
I.   The Ancient Regime. Demy 8vo, cloth, 16s.
II.  The French Revolution. Vol. 1.   .do.
III.    Do.        do.      Vol. 2.    do.
IV.     Do.        do.      Vol. 3.    do.
*Tauchnitz's English Editions of German Authors.* Each
volume, cloth flexible, 2s. ; or sewed, 1s. 6d. (Catalogues post free.)
*Tauchnitz* (*B.*) *German Dictionary.* 2s.; paper, 1s. 6d.; roan,
2s. 6d.
――――― *French Dictionary.* 2s.; paper, 1s. 6d.; roan, 2s. 6d.
――――― *Italian Dictionary.* 2s. ; paper, 1s. 6d.; roan, 2s. 6d.
,――――― *Latin Dictionary.* 2s.; paper, 1s. 6d.; roan, 2s. 6d.
――――― *Spanish and English.* 2s. ; paper, 1s. 6d.; roan, 2s. 6d.
――――― *Spanish and French.* 2s.; paper, 1s. 6d. ; roan, 2s. 6d.
*Taylor* (*R. L.*) *Chemical Analysis Tables.* 1s.
――――― *Chemistry for Beginners.* Small 8vo, 1s. 6d.
*Techno-Chemical Receipt Book.* With additions by BRANNT
and WAHL. 10s. 6d.

*Technological Dictionary.* See TOLHAUSEN.

*Thausing (Prof.) Malt and the Fabrication of Beer.* 8vo, 45*s.*

*Theakston (M.) British Angling Flies.* Illustrated. Cr. 8vo, 5*s.*

*Thomson (Jos.) Central African Lakes.* New edition, 2 vols. in one, crown 8vo, 7*s.* 6*d.*

—— *Through Masai Land.* Illust. 21*s.*; new edition, 7*s.* 6*d.*

—— *and Miss Harris-Smith. Ulu: an African Romance.* crown 8vo, 6*s.*

*Thomson (W.) Algebra for Colleges and Schools.* With Answers, 5*s.*; without, 4*s.* 6*d.*; Answers separate, 1*s.* 6*d.*

*Thornton (L. D.) Story of a Poodle.* By Himself and his Mistress. Illust., crown 4to, 2*s.* 6*d.*

*Thorrodsen, Lad and Lass.* Translated from the Icelandic by A. M. REEVES. Crown 8vo.

*Tissandier (G.) Eiffel Tower.* Illust., and letter of M. Eiffel in facsimile. Fcap. 8vo, 1*s.*

*Tolhausen. Technological German, English, and French Dictionary.* Vols. I., II., with Supplement, 12*s.* 6*d.* each; III., 9*s.*; Supplement, cr. 8vo, 3*s.* 6*d.*

*Topmkins (E. S. de G.) Through David's Realm.* Illust. by the Author. 8vo, 10*s.* 6*d.*

*Tucker (W. J.) Life and Society in Eastern Europe.* 15*s.*

*Tuckerman (B.) Life of General Lafayette.* 2 vols., cr. 8vo, 12*s.*

*Tupper (Martin Farquhar) My Life as an Author.* 14*s.*; new edition, 7*s.* 6*d.*

*Tytler (Sarah) Duchess Frances: a Novel.* 2 vols., 21*s.*

*U*PTON *(H.) Manual of Practical Dairy Farming.* Cr. 8vo, 2*s.*

*V*AN DAM. *Land of Rubens; a companion for visitors to* Belgium. Crown 8vo, 3*s.* 6*d.*

*Vane (Young Sir Harry),* By Prof. JAMES K. HOSMER. 8vo, 18*s.*

*Veres. Biography of Sir Francis Vere and Lord Vere, leading* Generals in the Netherlands. By CLEMENTS R. MARKHAM. 8vo, 18*s.*

*Verne (Jules) Celebrated Travels and Travellers.* 3 vols. 8vo, 7*s.* 6*d.* each; extra gilt, 9*s.*

*Victoria (Queen) Life of.* By GRACE GREENWOOD. Illust. 6*s.*

*Vincent (Mrs. Howard) Forty Thousand Miles over Land and* Water. With Illustrations. New Edit., 3*s.* 6*d.*

*Viollet-le-Duc (E.) Lectures on Architecture.* Translated by BENJAMIN BUCKNALL, Architect. 2 vols., super-royal 8vo, £3 3*s.*

| LARGE CROWN 8vo. WORKS. | { Containing 350 to 600 pp. and from 50 to 100 full-page illustrations. In very handsome cloth binding, gilt edges. | In plainer binding, plain edges. | Containing the whe text with some illus In cloth binding, gilt edges, smaller type. | Colour( or |
|---|---|---|---|---|
| | *s. d.* | *s. d.* | *s. d.* | |
| 20,000 Leagues under the Sea. Parts I. and II. . . . . . } | 10 6 | 5 0 | 3 6 | 2 vols., |
| Hector Servadac . . . . . . | 10 6 | 5 0 | 3 6 | 2 vols., |
| The Fur Country . . . . . . | 10 6 | 5 0 | 3 6 | 2 vols., |
| The Earth to the Moon and a Trip round it . . . . . . . } | 10 6 | 5 0 | { 2 vols., } 2s. ea. } | 2 vols., |
| Michael Strogoff . . . . . . | 10 6 | 5 0 | 3 6 | 2 vols., |
| Dick Sands, the Boy Captain . . | 10 6 | 5 0 | 3 6 | 2 vols., |
| Five Weeks in a Balloon . . . | 7 6 | 3 6 | 2 0 | 1 |
| Adventures of Three Englishmen and Three Russians . . . . } | 7 6 | 3 6 | 2 0 | 1 |
| Round the World in Eighty Days | 7 6 | 3 6 | 2 0 | 1 |
| A Floating City . . . . . . } | 7 6 | 3 6 | { 2 0 | 1 |
| The Blockade Runners . . . . | | | 2 0 | 1 |
| Dr. Ox's Experiment . . . . . | — | — | 2 0 | 1 |
| A Winter amid the Ice . . . . | — | — | 2 0 | 1 |
| Survivors of the "Chancellor" . } | 7 6 | 3 6 | { 3 6 | 2 vols., |
| Martin Paz . . . . . . . . | | | 2 0 | 1. |
| The Mysterious Island, 3 vols. :— | 22 6 | 10 6 | 6 0 | 3 |
| I. Dropped from the Clouds . | 7 6 | 3 6 | 2 0 | 1 |
| II. Abandoned . . . . . . | 7 6 | 3 6 | 2 0 | 1 |
| III. Secret of the Island . . | 7 6 | 3 6 | 2 0 | 1 |
| The Child of the Cavern . . . . | 7 6 | 3 6 | 2 0 | 1 |
| The Begum's Fortune . . . . | 7 6 | 3 6 | 2 0 | 1 |
| The Tribulations of a Chinaman . | 7 6 | 3 6 | 2 0 | 1 |
| The Steam House, 2 vols. :— | | | | |
| I. Demon of Cawnpore . . . } | 7 6 | 3 6 | 2 0 | 1 |
| II. Tigers and Traitors . . . | 7 6 | 3 6 | 2 0 | 1 |
| The Giant Raft, 2 vols. :— | | | | |
| I. 800 Leagues on the Amazon | 7 6 | 3 6 | 2 0 | 1 |
| II. The Cryptogram . . . . | 7 6 | 3 6 | 2 0 | 1 |
| The Green Ray . . . . . . . | 6 0 | 5 0 | — | 1 |
| Godfrey Morgan . . . . . . | 7 6 | 3 6 | 2 0 | 1 |
| Kéraban the Inflexible:— | | | | |
| I. Captain of the "Guidara" . } | 7 6 | 3 6 | 2 0 | 1 |
| II. Scarpante the Spy. . . . | 7 6 | 3 6 | 2 0 | 1 |
| The Archipelago on Fire. . . . | 7 6 | 3 6 | 2 0 | 1 |
| The Vanished Diamond . . . . | 7 6 | 3 6 | 2 0 | 1 |
| Mathias Sandorf . . . . . . | 10 6 | 5 0 | 3 6 | 2 vols. |
| The Lottery Ticket . . . . . | 7 6 | 3 6 | | |
| The Clipper of the Clouds . . . | 7 6 | 3 6 | | |
| North against South . . . . . | 7. 6 | | | |
| Adrift in the Pacific . . . . . | 7 6 | | | |
| Flight to France . . . . . . | 7 6 | | | |

CELEBRATED TRAVELS AND TRAVELLERS. 3 vols. 8vo, 600 pp,, 100 full-page illustrati gilt edges, 14s. each :—(1) THE EXPLORATION OF THE WORLD. (2) THE GREAT NAVIGAT

*WALFORD (Mrs. L. B.) Her Great Idea, and other Stories.* Cr. 8vo, 10s. 6d.; also new ed., 6s.

*Wallace (L.) Ben Hur: A Tale of the Christ.* New Edition, crown 8vo, 6s.; cheaper edition, 2s.

*Wallack (L.) Memories of 50 Years; with many Portraits, and* Facsimiles. Small 4to, 63s. nett; ordinary edition 7s. 6d.

*Waller(Rev. C.H.) Adoption and the Covenant.* On Confirmation. 2s. 6d.

—— *Silver Sockets; and other Shadows of Redemption.* Sermons at Christ Church, Hampstead. Small post 8vo, 6s.

—— *The Names on the Gates of Pearl, and other Studies.* New Edition. Crown 8vo, cloth extra, 3s. 6d.

—— *Words in the Greek Testament.* Part I. Grammar. Small post 8vo, cloth, 2s. 6d. Part II. Vocabulary, 2s. 6d.

*Walsh(A.S.) Mary, Queen of the House of David.* 8vo, 3s. 6d.

*Walton (Iz.) Wallet Book,* CIↃIↃLXXXV. Crown 8vo, half vellum, 21s.; large paper, 42s.

—— *Compleat Angler.* Lea and Dove Edition. Ed. by R. B. MARSTON. With full-page Photogravures on India paper, and the Woodcuts on India paper from blocks. 4to, half-morocco, 105s.; large paper, royal 4to, full dark green morocco, gilt top, 210s.

*Walton (T. H.) Coal Mining.* With Illustrations. 4to, 25s.

*War Scare in Europe.* Crown 8vo, 2s. 6d.

*Warner (C. D.) My Summer in a Garden.* Boards, 1s.; leatherette, 1s. 6d.; cloth, 2s.

—— *Their Pilgrimage.* Illustrated by C. S. REINHART. 8vo, 7s. 6d.

*Warren (W. F.) Paradise Found; the North Pole the Cradle* of the Human Race. Illustrated. Crown 8vo, 12s. 6d.

*Washington Irving's Little Britain.* Square crown 8vo, 6s.

*Watson (P. B.) Swedish Revolution under Gustavus Vasa.* 8vo.

*Wells (H. P.) American Salmon Fisherman.* 6s.

—— *Fly Rods and Fly Tackle.* Illustrated. 10s. 6d.

*Wells (J. W.) Three Thousand Miles through Brazil.* Illustrated from Original Sketches. 2 vols. 8vo, 32s.

*Wenzel (O.) Directory of Chemical Products of the German* Empire. 8vo, 25s.

*Westgarth (W.) Half-century of Australasian Progress. Personal* retrospect. 8vo, 12s.

*Wheatley (H. B.) Remarkable Bindings in the British Museum.* Reproductions in Colour, 94s. 6d., 73s. 6d., and 63s.

*White (J.) Ancient History of the Maori; Mythology, &c.* Vols. I.-IV. 8vo, 10s. 6d. each.

*White (R. Grant) England Without and Within.* Crown 8vo, 10s. 6d.

—— *Every-day English.* 10s. 6d.

*White* (*R. Grant*) *Fate of Mansfield Humphreys,&c.* Cr. 8vo, 6s.
———— *Studies in Shakespeare.* 10s. 6d.
———— *Words and their Uses.* New Edit., crown 8vo, 5s.
*Whitney* (*Mrs.*) *The Other Girls.* A Sequel to "We Girls."
· New ed. 12mo, 2s.
———— *We Girls.* New Edition. 2s.
*Whittier* (*J. G.*) *The King's Missive, and later Poems.* 18mo,
choice parchment cover, 3s. 6d.
———— *St. Gregory's Guest, &c.* Recent Poems. 5s.
*William I. and the German Empire.* By G. BARNETT SMITH.
.New Edition, 3s. 6d.
*Willis-Bund* (*J.*) *Salmon Problems.* 3s. 6d.; boards, 2s. 6d.
*Wills* (*Dr. C. J.*) *Persia as it is.* Crown 8vo, 8s. 6d.
*Wills, A Few Hints on Proving, without Professional Assistance.*
By a PROBATE COURT OFFICIAL. 8th Edition, revised, with Forms
of Wills, Residuary Accounts, &c. Fcap. 8vo, cloth limp, 1s.
*Wilmot* (*A.*) *Poetry of South Africa Collected.* 8vo, 6s.
*Wilmot-Buxton* (*Ethel M.*) *Wee Folk, Good Folk : a Fantasy.*
Illust., fcap. 4to, 5s.
*Winder* (*Frederick Horatio*) *Lost in Africa : a Yarn of Adven-*
ture. Illust., cr. 8vo, 6s.
*Winsor* (*Justin*) *Narrative and Critical History of America.*
8 vols., 30s. each ; large paper, per vol., 63s.
*Woolsey. Introduction to International Law.* 5th Ed., 18s.
*Woolson* (*Constance F.*) See "Low's Standard Novels."
*Wright* (*H.*) *Friendship of God.* Portrait, &c. Crown 8vo, 6s.
*Wright* (*T.*) *Town of Cowper, Olney, &c.* 6s.
*Wrigley* (*M.*) *Algiers Illustrated.* 100 Views in Photogravure.
Royal 4to, 45s.
*Written to Order ; the Journeyings of an Irresponsible Egotist.*
By the Author of "A Day of my Life at Eton." Crown 8vo, 6s.

*Y RIARTE* (*Charles*) *Florence: its History.* Translated by
C. B. PITMAN. Illustrated with 500 Engravings. Large imperial
4to, extra binding, gilt edges, 63s.; or 12 Parts, 5s. each.

*Z ILLMAN* (*J. H. L.*) *Past and Present Australian Life.*
With Stories. Crown 8vo, 2s.

London:

SAMPSON LOW, MARSTON, SEARLE, & RIVINGTON, LD.,
St. Dunstan's House,
FETTER LANE, FLEET STREET, E.C.

Gilbert and Rivington, Ld., St. John's House, Clerkenwell Road, E.C.

www.ingramcontent.com/pod-product-compliance
Lightning Source LLC
Chambersburg PA
CBHW032318280326
41932CB00009B/854